# Confucius, Buddha, Jesus, and Muhammad

**Mark W. Muesse, Ph.D.**

THE
GREAT
COURSES

PUBLISHED BY:

THE GREAT COURSES
Corporate Headquarters
4840 Westfields Boulevard, Suite 500
Chantilly, Virginia 20151-2299
Phone: 1-800-832-2412
Fax: 703-378-3819
www.thegreatcourses.com

Copyright © The Teaching Company, 2010

Printed in the United States of America

This book is in copyright. All rights reserved.

Without limiting the rights under copyright reserved above,
no part of this publication may be reproduced, stored in
or introduced into a retrieval system, or transmitted,
in any form, or by any means
(electronic, mechanical, photocopying, recording, or otherwise),
without the prior written permission of
The Teaching Company.

# Mark W. Muesse, Ph.D.

Associate Professor of Religious Studies
and Director of the Asian Studies Program
Rhodes College

Professor Mark W. Muesse is Associate Professor of Religious Studies, the W. J. Willard Chair in Religious Studies, and Director of the Asian Studies and Life: Then and Now programs at Rhodes College. He earned his bachelor of arts degree summa cum laude in English from Baylor University and a master of theological studies, a master of arts, and a doctorate in Religion from Harvard University.

Professor Muesse has taught at Harvard College, Harvard Divinity School, and the University of Southern Maine, where he also served as Associate Dean of the College of Arts and Sciences. In 1988, he became Assistant Professor of Religious Studies at Rhodes College. In 1995, he became Associate Professor, and he served as Chair of the Department of Religious Studies from 2004 to 2008. He teaches courses in world religion and philosophy, modern theology, and spirituality.

Professor Muesse has also been Visiting Professor of Theology at the Tamilnadu Theological Seminary in Madurai, India. He has traveled extensively throughout Asia and has studied at the International Buddhist Meditation Centre in Wat Mahadhat, Bangkok, Thailand; the Himalayan Yogic Institute in Kathmandu, Nepal; and the Middle East Technical University in Ankara, Turkey.

Professor Muesse has produced two previous lecture series for The Great Courses: *Great World Religions: Hinduism* and *Religions of the Axial Age: An Approach to the World's Religions*. He is the author of many articles and reviews on comparative religion and theology and is the coeditor of a collection of essays titled *Redeeming Men: Religion and Masculinities*.

In 2007, Professor Muesse received Fortress Press's Undergraduate Teaching Award at the American Academy of Religion's annual meeting. In 2008, he received the Clarence Day Award for Outstanding Teaching, Rhodes College's highest honor for a member of its faculty. Known for his experiential teaching style, Professor Muesse was honored for his "effective use of imaginative and creative pedagogy" as well as his ability to motivate his students toward lifelong study.

Professor Muesse's wife, Dhammika, is a native of Sri Lanka and teaches in the Rhodes College Chemistry Department. They have a daughter, Ariyana, who attends St. Mary's Episcopal School. ■

# Table of Contents

# Table of Contents

## THE BUDDHA

## JESUS

# Table of Contents

# Table of Contents

# Confucius, Buddha, Jesus, and Muhammad

**Scope:**

Confucius, the Buddha, Jesus, and Muhammad are among the most important and influential persons in history. They are remembered for the examples of their lives, their insights into the human condition and the nature of ultimate reality, and the religious movements they inspired. It would be hard to name another set of four persons who have more deeply affected so many human lives.

In this course, we examine these four figures both separately and comparatively in an effort to grasp the essential features of their lives and teachings and to explore the factors that contributed to their greatness. We will attend to the similarities and differences in their messages, in the patterns of their lives, and in the ways they impacted their followers and the rest of the world.

The investigation of each of the four follows the same general outline. To introduce each individual, we first sketch out the historical and cultural framework that informed his life and worldview. In each case, the subject of study was born into an ancient culture in ferment. The beginning lecture for each figure (except Jesus, for reasons noted below) expounds the nature of this societal turbulence and provides the relevant analysis for understanding each man in greater context.

Then, the next several lectures recount the major events in the life of the subject. We will consider the nature of the source material for our biographical sketches and the problems of gaining an historically accurate picture of each. We will attend to some remarkable aspects of their early lives: the claims of their noble lineages; the unusual circumstances surrounding their conception, birth, and family life; and their marital situations. In the life of each, we shall explore the pivotal moments of transformation in which some new insight is gained or new revelation received. Our biographical sketches then close with discussions of their later years and deaths. Throughout these lectures focused on the events of their lives, we will try to gain a sense of the personal qualities and attributes that made them who they were.

Outlining the life history of each man provides the framework for examining the essential dimensions of their teachings and practices. In expounding the wisdom they offered to their followers, we will be interested in a set of common questions: How did each figure understand the nature of the world and ultimate reality? What assumptions did he make about existence and the nature of the self and society? What did each man envision as the final fulfillment of humanity and human individuals? What ethical and moral principles did he promote and why? Finally, what spiritual disciplines did he practice and teach as a means of attaining full humanity and relating to the ultimate reality?

To wrap up the study of each figure as an individual, we examine the larger reverberations of his life in his immediate context and in world history. The focus of investigation will be principally the development of the religions with which he is associated, but the talk will not be limited to this. For example, we will consider Jesus as an important figure in Islam. I intend to distinguish sharply each individual "founder" (a problematic concept, as I will explain) from the religion he ostensibly establishes.

The final three lectures in the series offer us the opportunity to reflect on these four in comparative perspective and suggest ways in which their examples and teachings can continue to nourish the human spirit. One lecture is devoted mainly to a consideration of the similarities and differences in their personal lives. We will compare their cultural settings and upbringings. The next lecture will examine their teaching and practices. I will argue *against* the common perception that these four (or the religions with which they are associated) simply teach the same thing. The points of divergence are mainly conceptual and theoretical, particularly in their understandings of the nature of ultimate reality and the world. We will also note that in each case these teachers considered the "self" as a prime ingredient in the unhappiness of human beings and taught methods for inculcating humility and compassion for others. The last lecture of the series tries to glean enduring lessons from these four and apply them to the world today. We will mention specifically the ideal of living a "noble" life, of cultivating the qualities of wisdom and compassion, of allowing the mind to settle and restore itself. We will also consider the implications of this study for addressing the "problem" of religious pluralism. ■

# A Quartet of Sages
## Lecture 1

**What brings me to this study of Confucius, the Buddha, Jesus, and Muhammad is not simply an historian's interest in their impact on humanity's development ... [but] the same concern that led me to the study of religion and philosophy in the first place: the desire to know how to live life well.**

Confucius, Buddha, Jesus, Muhammad—Whatever your spiritual beliefs, you would be hard pressed to argue against the idea that these four ancient sages were among the most influential humans who ever lived. All four were also some of history's finest teachers of the art of living—living nobly, deliberately, and courageously, with virtue and discipline. Throughout these lectures, we will address both the historical and philosophical significance of these four men and the importance of their lives and teachings for us today.

The overall course structure is twofold: First, we will study each figure separately (and chronologically) in the context of his time and place; second, we will compare their lives and teachings. The historical and cultural framework that informed each man's life and worldview will be the foundation for examining their major life events. We will also look at the available source materials and discuss the problems of obtaining historically accurate profiles of men who lived so long ago. As our discussion progresses, we will notice some remarkable similarities amid the obvious differences among their life stories.

Next we turn to the wisdom each of these sages offered and ask how each understood the nature of the world and ultimate reality—in other words, each man's **metaphysics**. Next we will look at what each had to say about the nature and purpose of humankind, which theologians and philosophers call **anthropology**. (This should not, however, be confused with the independent academic discipline of the same name.) What did each man think about the nature of the self and the fulfillment of humanity? How did he understand humankind's relationship to the world and the ultimate reality?

Following metaphysics and anthropology, we will look at each sage's take on **ethics**—his advocacy of certain moral principles, including how these principles related to the divine or the cosmos. Then we will study their positions on **spiritual discipline**, asking what activities each teacher encouraged as a means of attaining full humanity and relating to the ultimate reality. There is a tendency among theologians and philosophers to focus on their ideas at the expense of their practices; in this course, we will attempt to counterbalance that view. Finally, we will examine the reverberations of each sage's life in his immediate context and in world history.

**The lives of these four were inextricably connected to their teachings.**

Just as we will begin our examination of each sage's life with a look at his historical and cultural context, so we must be aware of our own contexts and how they affect our approach to the ideas in this course. By necessity, these lectures will be presented through the lens of my own ideas and interests. No one escapes the fact of interpretation, and mine is only one voice in a vast chorus. I encourage you, therefore, to read the interpretations of others and, more importantly, to read the words of these sages for yourself.

It is also, for the purposes of this course, important that we set aside as much as possible the view that each of these four men is regarded as the founder of a major world religion. Describing Confucius, the Buddha, Jesus, and Muhammad as religious "founders" may distort our understanding of the way they thought of their own lives; recall that some of these figures are associated with religions other than the ones they ostensibly founded. Furthermore, our purpose is not to evaluate any of them on the basis of what we think about the religion that developed in his wake. We do not deny the special claims of each group of followers about these sages, but the focus of our study will be their human lives and on their vocations as teachers of wisdom and compassion.

The final part of this course will offer us the opportunity to reflect on Confucius, the Buddha, Jesus, and Muhammad from a comparative perspective and to discern ways in which their examples and teachings can continue to nourish the human spirit. Were these sages actually saying the same thing, as many today would like to believe? If not, can we resolve their differences to help our pursuit of the ideal life? We will see the one point on which they all seem to agree: that self-centeredness thwarts the happiness and well-being of humans. In the last lecture, we will try to garner enduring lessons from these four sages' wisdom for cultivating humility and compassion for others. ∎

## Important Terms

**anthropology**: The philosophical or theological study of the universal nature of humanity, as well as the meaning and purpose (if any) of human existence.

**ethics**: The study of morality and proper human behavior.

**metaphysics**: The study of the fundamental character and qualities of reality, including the origin of the universe and the nature of the divine.

**spiritual discipline**: A set of practices designed as a part of the means of attaining full humanity and relating to the ultimate reality.

## Question to Consider

1.  What is the difference between studying the lives of these four sages from the perspective of a follower of a particular religion and the perspective we are trying to adopt for this course? What are some difficulties a believer might encounter with this approach? How can these difficulties be overcome?

# A Quartet of Sages
## Lecture 1—Transcript

In 1978, an astrophysicist named Michael H. Hart published a book in which he ranked the 100 people who most influenced world history. Hart's book, which was simply entitled *The 100*, argued that the five most influential persons who ever lived were the Prophet Muhammad, Sir Isaac Newton, Jesus of Nazareth, the Buddha, and Confucius, in that order. The book's appearance caused quite a stir, especially among folks who thought their particular hero was not given a high enough rating on the list or failed to make the list at all. Much of the controversy surrounding the book was due to the failure of many people to understand the author's intention. Hart was not trying to evaluate and rank the *best* persons who ever lived. He was merely making judgments about the *influence* of prominent individuals on human history. Certainly he had a point. While we might quibble about the order, any list of, say, a dozen persons who have most affected the course of history would surely include Muhammad, Jesus, the Buddha, and Confucius.

While the influence of these four can hardly be doubted, what brings me to this study of Confucius, the Buddha, Jesus, and Muhammad is not simply an historian's interest in their impact on humanity's development, although that fact certainly justifies a comparative study. My fascination with this spiritual quartet derives from another interest, the same concern that led me to the study of religion and philosophy in the first place: the desire to know how to live life well. After nearly 30 years of studying the world's religious and philosophical traditions, I am convinced that these four figures represent some of our finest teachers of the art of living. When I speak of the art of living and living life well, I mean living nobly and deliberately, with high-mindedness, virtue, and discipline. Among the many individuals I have studied, no one has impressed me more as exemplars of the noble life than Confucius, the Buddha, Jesus, and Muhammad. There are others whom I *might* rank with these four, but no one who excels them. By their lives, they have inspired me—and obviously countless others—with their dedication to living deeply and thoughtfully and with the courage they mustered in the face of adversity. To borrow words from Henry David Thoreau, they all "suck[ed] the marrow from the bones of life."

Because of their dual significance—as persons who decidedly shaped history and as teachers who offered compelling visions of how to live—our conversations throughout these lectures will address both historical and philosophical interests. We'll talk about who they were and what they said, but also about the import their lives and teachings may have for us today.

The approach we will take to our study of these four sages is fairly simple, but it requires a bit of explanation and some justification. The overall structure of the course is twofold. We will first study each figure separately, as an individual situated in his own time and place. Then, after considering each person independently, we will turn to a comparative study of their lives and their teachings.

The study of the four as individuals will follow a chronological order. We begin with the most ancient figure, Confucius, followed by the Buddha, then Jesus, and finally Muhammad. This sequence implies nothing other than the passage of time. I am not suggesting any kind of philosophical, moral, or religious advancement or regression; we're merely considering these persons in the order in which they lived.

To introduce each man, I will sketch out the historical and cultural framework that informed his life and worldview. In each case, we will see that he was born into an ancient culture in the midst of great changes. We will examine the nature of the cultural turbulence of his day to provide the essential details for understanding each man in greater context.

The study of his historical situation will be the background against which we will recount the major events in the life of each teacher. We will first examine the nature of the source materials for our biographical sketches and discuss some of the problems of obtaining an historically accurate picture of each of our sages. I'll explain where the most recent scholarship draws the line between fact and legend in the accounts of their lives; often, there is considerable disagreement among scholars as to where that line should be drawn. As our discussion of their lives unfolds, we will begin to notice some remarkable similarities amid the obvious differences. We will observe how all four are reported to have had a royal or aristocratic lineage and yet were unable or unwilling to take advantage of the benefits of that heritage. We will note the accounts of unusual circumstances surrounding the conception and birth of each of the four and see some atypical features in their original families. In the life of each, we will explore the pivotal moments of transformation in which some new insight is realized or new revelation received. Our biographical sketches then close with discussions of their later years and their deaths. All along the way, we will try to get a sense of the personal qualities and attributes that made these individuals who they were.

Outlining the life history of each figure will provide the framework for examining the essential components of his teachings and practices. In studying the wisdom these sages offered, we will be interested a set of common questions: First, we will ask: How did each of the four understand the nature of the world and ultimate reality? This question puts us in the realm of what western philosophy calls metaphysics. Metaphysics is that aspect of human thinking that reflects upon the fundamental character and qualities of reality in its broadest sense. Whenever we wonder about the origin of the universe or whether there is something deeper or something more to the world than the way it appears, we are entering the realm of metaphysics. Metaphysics tends to be a highly abstract way of thinking, since it tries to grasp the nature of reality in its entirety. Under this category, we will examine the way each of our subjects thought about the nature of the divine and the ultimate powers governing the world.

The next questions of our set pertain to what theologians and philosophers call anthropology. Anthropology in the philosophical sense should be distinguished from the academic discipline that also goes by that name. While the discipline of anthropology tends to focus on specific human groups, philosophical and theological anthropology is interested in understanding the nature of humanity in a more universal way. It wants to know whether or not there is such a thing as human nature and what the character of this nature might be. Philosophical anthropology investigates the distinctive qualities of being human and reflects on the meaning and purpose (if any) of our human existence. As we study our four sages, we will look carefully at what each of them said, or assumed, about the nature of humanity. We will ask: What did he think about existence and the attributes of the self and of society? How did he envision the final fulfillment of humanity and human individuals? How did he understand the relationship between human beings and the rest of the world, including the ultimate reality?

Exploring the metaphysical and anthropological aspects of the teachings of each sage will clear the ground for discussing and understanding the moral principles he advocated. Here, we enter the branch of philosophy and theology known as ethics. We will ask: How did each of the four think we should treat our fellow humans and other beings? What was the basis for his ethical views? Did he see proper human behavior as rooted in the will of a god or in the structure of the cosmos itself? Or did he think that morality was simply a social convention invented by human beings to facilitate our survival as a species but without any connection to a transcendent reality? These are the questions that will take center stage when we consider the ethical dimension of the teachings of the four.

Our final area of interest is spiritual discipline. When we move into this aspect of their teachings, the central question that will occupy our attention is: What activities did each teacher encourage as a means of attaining full humanity and relating to the ultimate reality? Under this category, we'll explore the place of such things as ceremony and pilgrimage, feasting and fasting, and prayer and meditation in cultivating the life of the spirit. Over the years, I have increasingly come to appreciate the importance of spiritual exercises in the pursuit of the noble life. Confucius, the Buddha, Jesus, and Muhammad did not become the persons they were merely because they were endowed with certain gifts of understanding and insight. They all practiced specific regimens that enabled them to refine their innate talents and to deepen their wisdom and compassion for the world. Those of us who study and write about such persons often neglect the role of spiritual practices in their teachings, preferring instead to focus attention on their beliefs and ideas. I hope to counterbalance that tendency by giving a special emphasis to the practical disciplines they observed. By stressing spiritual practice, we are being more faithful, I think, to the lives and teachings of our four subjects, each of whom made *acting* a certain way as important as—if not more important than—*believing* a certain way.

To conclude the study of each figure as an individual, we will examine the reverberations of his life in his immediate context and in world history. The principal focus of investigation will now turn to the development of the traditions with which he is associated and to the way his life and teachings were interpreted in the years subsequent to his death. Our study of each figure therefore begins in history with an examination of his cultural context and returns to history with a consideration of how his life affected that context and the world at large.

Before we move on to discuss the comparative features of this course, I want to comment briefly on how I have structured the consideration of each teacher. First, you will notice that I have separated the study of each man's life from the study of his teachings. Let me admit that I am not very happy about doing this. What troubles me about this division is the fact that in a very important sense, each man's life *was* his teaching. To modify a phrase from Marshall McLuhan, the man was the message. The Hasidic tradition of Judaism relates the story of the famous rabbi Leib Saras (1730–1796) who had just returned from a visit to *his* rabbi and was asked by family and friends what words of Torah he learned. Leib Saras replied, "I did not go to my teacher to hear his words of Torah; I went to see how he ties his shoelaces." All good teachers know they teach as much by example as by the words they utter.

This was especially true for the individuals we will study in this course. Confucius was the exemplar of the kind of person he taught others to be. His protégés gained as much from observing him act as they did from listening to him talk. The Buddha not only spoke about the path to nibbana, or nirvana, as it's more commonly known; he walked that way himself and others could see the fruits of nibbana in his very life. The apostle Paul, perhaps the most important interpreter of Jesus, never once cited Jesus' parables or sayings; Paul was almost exclusively concerned with the crucified and resurrected Jesus, as if to suggest that in those events of his life the real significance of Jesus was revealed. Aisha, one of the wives of the Prophet Muhammad, was once asked about the personal qualities of her husband, and she replied, "His character was the Qur'an."

These instances all indicate that the lives of these four were inextricably connected to their teachings, yet I have structured these lectures in such a way that we are putting their lives and teachings asunder. How do I justify this? My reason is simple: to make things clearer. Later in the course, we will compare and contrast the patterns of their lives and the content of their teachings, and it will be much easier to do that once we have teased out the points of comparison as carefully and clearly as possible. We need always to bear in mind, however, that this analytical separation is an artificial one, created for the sake of helping us to see how the lives and teachings of these four both parallel and diverge. Fortunately, the fact that we cannot ever completely and neatly divide their lives and teachings will constantly remind us of this artificiality of this division.

The way we shall study the teachings is by means of another contrivance. Confucius did not sit down with his students and say, "Today, class, I'll be discussing my metaphysical position and my understanding of ultimate reality." Jesus did not gather his disciples by the Sea of Galilee and give them a lecture on his anthropological views on the nature and destiny of human beings. It might have made things easier for 21st century scholars if they *had* taught that way, but I suspect they were not terribly concerned about packaging their ideas for the benefit of 21st century scholars. These sages taught with anecdotes and parables, aphorisms and proverbs, and of course with their very lives. They were not academic philosophers and theologians, and for that, I think we can all be grateful!

Obviously, none of our four teachers would have presented their ideas in the way we will study them here. But again, the rubrics we will use is for the sake of clarity and to facilitate our comparative interests towards the end of the course. Someone else teaching about these four—or any one of them— might use a different set of categories to present their ideas. The framework I have suggested provides the best way *I* know to keep the material clearly organized, but it is not the only way. My presentations will certainly be colored by those aspects of the lives and teachings of the four that I find important and interesting. I will choose to highlight certain things and de-emphasize others. For better or worse, there will be much of my own thinking involved in this study. Yet the same would be true of *any* presentation of their lives and thought. No one escapes this fact of interpretation. Please consider me as only one voice in vast chorus of interpretations seeking to understand the lives and teachings of these great sages. I encourage you, therefore, to read the interpretations of others and more importantly to read the words of these sages for yourself and form your own opinions about their views.

We should also note that the categories we will use—metaphysics and ultimate reality, anthropology, ethics, spiritual practices—do not all occupy the same place or play the same role in the teachings of these four. While Confucius, the Buddha, Jesus, and Muhammad all had things to say that fit under each of these rubrics, they did not all assign equal importance to each area. For instance, Confucius was far more concerned with matters of ethical matters than he was with the question of ultimate reality. Jesus did not speak as much about spiritual exercises as he did about god and appropriate human behavior. Furthermore, these categories will not always appear as discrete subjects in our conversations. In some cases, for instance, metaphysics and anthropology necessarily converge, as when the human being is regarded as a part of the ultimate reality. For some of the sages, ethics is an essential component of their spirituality. The categories are thus a kind of typology that is seems nice and neat in theory but doesn't always show up that way when we begin the actual work of analyzing their teachings.

Let me make one final comment on methodology: Often, these four are regarded as the founders of four of the major world religions. I think it is important, at least for the purposes of this course, that we try not to think of them too much in this light. None of these figures thought his mission in life was to establish a new religion; at most, some of them understood themselves as calling their contemporaries to return to ancient truths. Describing Confucius, the Buddha, Jesus, and Muhammad as religious "founders" may distort our understanding of the way they thought of their own lives and might expose them, furthermore, to judgments that are better reserved for those who call themselves their followers. I hope we will not make the mistake of evaluating any one of our four sages on the basis of what we think about the religion that developed in his wake. It is not intellectually responsible to uncritically impute to Jesus the views of Christians or to hold Muhammad accountable for all actions carried out in the name of Islam.

It is also important to remember that some of these figures are associated with religions *other* than the one they ostensibly founded. The Buddha, for instance, spent much of his life as what we today would call a Hindu, although that label would not have been available to him during his lifetime. He would not have identified himself as either a Hindu or a Buddhist. Furthermore, the Buddha is still associated with Hinduism, as many Hindus regard him as a manifestation of the god Vishnu, and he even played a small but fascinating role in Christian history, as we shall see when we study the Buddha's legacy to the world.

And although Jesus is frequently called the founder of Christianity, Jesus was not a Christian. He was born a Jew and remained a Jew all his life. Occasionally, when I mention that I teach a course on Confucius, Buddha, Jesus, and Muhammad, someone asks why I have not included a Jew in my list of sages. I reply that it might be better to ask why I have not included a Christian, since Jesus was Jewish. If this were a course on the founders of the world religions, I would probably substitute the Apostle Paul for Jesus. Paul seems to me to be the more legitimate candidate as the founder of Christianity. Christianity is the religion *about* Jesus, but it was not the religion *of* Jesus. Moreover, Jesus is a major figure in Islam. He is embraced by Islam as a *muslim*, that is, one who submits to the will of god, and as a great prophet to the world, second only to Muhammad himself.

Thus, I hope we can refrain from thinking of these four primarily as representatives or founders of four major religions. Let us first consider them as individual teachers in their historical and cultural settings before viewing them in relationship to the very complex realities that became the religions with which they are commonly associated.

The final part of this course will offer us the opportunity to reflect on Confucius, the Buddha, Jesus, and Muhammad from a comparative perspective and to discern ways in which their examples and teachings can continue to nourish the human spirit. One lecture will be devoted to comparing the patterns of their personal lives. Although they were unique individuals separated by time and place, certain features of their biographies are surprisingly similar. I have already mentioned that they each lived at a time of cultural upheaval and that each could lay claim to an aristocratic heritage. We'll also see some other unexpected commonalities, such as the fact that each survived at least one assassination attempt. The next lecture will then compare their teachings and practices. We will ask: were these sages actually saying the same thing, as many today would like to believe? While I think the answer to that question is basically no, at least on one essential point they do seem to agree, which is that self-centeredness thwarts the happiness and well-being of humans. To counteract selfishness, they all taught methods for cultivating humility and compassion for others. The last lecture of the course will try to garner enduring lessons from these four and apply them to the world today.

One might contend that trying to compare these four figures is like comparing apples and oranges. Each was a unique individual and his significance for his followers was and is equally unique. In the minds of Christians, Jesus is the savior, the second person of the Trinity, God in human form. Consequently, some Christians might think that he should not be placed on the same level as the other three—or any other human being. For Buddhists, the Buddha was indeed a human, like Jesus and the others, but by attaining Buddhahood, he transcended even the gods, raising him to a rank not only beyond the human but also beyond the divine. Muhammad, for Muslims, was one in a long line of over 100,000 prophets who presented God's will to humanity. But Muhammad was, nonetheless, different from all others; he was God's *final* messenger, the "seal of the prophets." His message was the *final* revelation, God's ultimate communication to the world. That fact sets him apart from all other humans, including the other prophets like Jesus.

On what basis, then, can we compare these four? In a sense, trying to compare the four really *is* like comparing apples and oranges (and pears and bananas, to extend the metaphor a bit to fit our discussion). But the fact is you actually *can* compare apples, oranges, pears, and bananas. After all, they are all edible fruit, and they all grow on trees. Although different in many ways, they do share some bases for comparison, and so do Confucius,

Buddha, Jesus, and Muhammad. For instance, they were all human beings—even though some of them were subject to claims of divinity or something greater—and they were all teachers of wisdom and compassion. On these points, I think everyone will agree, including those who want to press further to claim a particular uniqueness for their sage. And so it is on this basis that we will take up our study. We do not deny that Jesus was the messiah for his followers or that the Buddha excelled the common lot of humanity according to Buddhists. But the focus of our study will be their human lives and on their vocations as teachers of wisdom and compassion.

When we mention Confucius, Buddha, Jesus, and Muhammad, we are not merely speaking of historical figures like Napoleon or Marie Curie or even Isaac Newton. For billions of persons around the world, one or more of these four is a *sacred* figure, which puts him in a different category altogether. In this series, I will strive to be sensitive these sentiments. Accordingly, we will not attempt to rank these four in relation to one another. Although we will compare and contrast these individuals with each other, we will do so to gain deeper insight into their lives and teachings, not to rate them. I will do my best to treat all four with an even hand and show no favoritism to one over the others.

In our next time together, we will begin the study of Confucius, the great sage of China. Our journey has begun. Welcome to the course.

# Confucius's China
## Lecture 2

---

**When Confucius reflected on his cultural identity, he thought not only of his immediate era but the whole of its past as well. For Confucius, the past was profoundly significant and simply could not be separated from the present.**

By the time of Confucius, China was already an ancient civilization, which its inhabitants referred to by many names, including **Huáxià**— "grand florescence" or "illustrious blossoming." The ancient Chinese identified themselves not as citizens of a state but as participants in a particular—and particularly refined—way of life. They also referred to their world as **Zhōngguó**, "the central kingdom," a term both literal and metaphorical: They thought of themselves as the center of civilization, and the ruling Zhōu dynasty governed from a kingdom near the Yellow River Valley at the heart of numerous vassal states.

Ancient Chinese cultural identity embraced the whole of the past as well as its present, the ancient and the contemporary. One can observe this characteristic in ancestor reverence, a fundamental religious practice throughout Chinese history in which the dead are treated as still existent and significant in everyday life. Confucius would have regarded our modern, Western, rather cavalier attitude toward the past as both a symptom and a cause of the sorry state of the world. This attitude, incidentally, sets Confucius apart from the other three sages we will discuss in this course.

The Yellow River Valley culture into which Confucius was born dates to about the 5th millennium B.C.E. and is considered one of the cradles of civilization. By approximately 3000 B.C.E., citizens of this area were already practicing elaborate religious rituals and had social hierarchies regulated by patrilineal descent. Chinese tradition recalls this era as an age when the wise and benevolent philosopher-kings of the legendary (and perhaps mythical) Xià dynasty ruled the land. The Xià were followed by the kings of the Shang dynasty, whose rule began in the 16th or 15th century B.C.E. Most of our tangible evidence from this period comes from "dragon bones," or oracle bones: inscribed pieces of cow bone and tortoise shell used in divination. From these inscriptions, we know the Shang revered the dead; we know they valued properly performed rituals; we know they believed that the kingdom's welfare hung on the king's good relations with the spirit realm; and we know Shang armies fought frequent wars with neighboring realms and steppe nomads. These four concerns—ancestor worship, ritual behavior, the king's responsibilities toward his subjects, and the ethics of war and peace—would later figure heavily in Confucius's writings.

Around 1045 B.C.E., the Shang rulers were deposed by the Zhōu dynasty, which ruled for the next 800 years. Their first king, Wen, is credited as one of the creators of the book of divination called the *Yì Jīng*, or *Book of Changes*.

But for Confucius, the most significant figure was Wen's son Dàn, usually known as the Duke of Zhōu. The duke was never king himself but faithfully served as his nephew's regent. For this selflessness, he was regarded as a paragon of leadership and moral behavior by many Chinese, including Confucius. The duke is also credited with creating the concept of *tiānmíng*, the mandate of heaven—that is, the ruler governed with divine sanction as long as he was virtuous; therefore,

The Teaching Company Collection.

**The Duke of Zhōu is credited with creating the concept of *tiānmíng*, the mandate of heaven.**

opposing and even deposing a poor king could be morally justified. The mandate of heaven assumed a critical role throughout Chinese history up until the 20th century.

Despite the Zhōu rulers' claims of virtue, in reality the Zhōu period was a turbulent era marked by invasion, lawlessness, and civil war. Political power became invested in local hegemons, or warlords. The final stage of the Zhōu period is called the **Period of Warring States**. By now, the nature of war itself was changing: Chariot warfare conducted by aristocrats was replaced by mounted cavalry and a conscripted peasant infantry. Military leadership was allotted the skilled, not the well-born. The political chaos engendered rapid social changes as well. Increasingly, the nobility (of which Confucius was a member) were required to prove themselves by talent and hard work. Government bureaucracy increased, and the new meritocracy offered opportunities to the peasant class, including land ownership.

The Period of Warring States was also known as the Period of One Hundred Schools because it was an immensely creative period both philosophically and religiously—a logical response of the intellectual class to the turmoil. (One of the themes we will return to is how our sages all lived and taught in times of immense political or cultural ferment.) Philosophy revolved around the question of human harmony. Although the issue is practical and material, it involved deeper questions and assumptions about reality, human nature, and the purposes of human life. Confucianism was one of the many voices in this debate.

Although Confucius was addressing the specific problems of his day, I contend they were not all that different from the problems of the eras that followed his, including our own. ■

## Important Terms

**Huáxià**: Literally, "grand florescence" or "illustrious blossoming"; one of ancient Chinese culture's names for itself, implying a sense of cultural superiority.

**Period of Warring States**: The last phase of the Zhōu dynasty, during which great social and political unrest led to a flourishing of Chinese philosophy and religion.

*tiānming*: Literally, "the mandate of heaven"; the Chinese belief that the right to rule is conferred by the gods on virtuous leaders and removed by the gods from the corrupt, which implies the right of the people to rebel against and depose a leader who is not morally upright.

**Zhōngguó**: Literally, "central kingdom"; a name for the ancient Chinese kingdom that grew up in the Yellow River Valley under the Zhōu dynasty.

## Questions to Consider

1. Why do you think that social and political upheaval under the Zhōu led to more philosophical and religious debate, rather than more unity? Can you think of other times and places in human history where this has occurred?

2. Confucius's response to his troubled culture was in part to look to the past—the good old days. Have we seen this response in Western history as well? Can we detect this attitude in the philosophy and religion of the present day?

# Confucius's China
## Lecture 2—Transcript

By the time of Confucius, China was already an ancient civilization. China was also an anguished civilization in desperate need of renewal. Confucius was acutely aware of both facts. China's antiquity and its political and social problems profoundly informed Confucius' personal life and the insights that ultimately shaped his philosophical vision and spiritual practice. To understand his life and teachings thus requires that we have a good grasp of China as it was 2,500 years ago, to the degree that our historical sources will allow. In our discussion today, we'll sketch out a picture of the world as Confucius and his contemporaries would have known it. Because written documents from this time are rather scarce, the fine details of this sketch may at times recede into indistinctness, rendering an image that leaves much to the imagination, not unlike an old Chinese ink drawing. The image we construct will become the background against which we will brush in our portrait of Confucius himself.

Today we refer to the world of Confucius as "China," but this was not a word that he would have known. It's a bit ironic that the man who is renowned as perhaps the greatest Chinese of all time could not have identified himself as "Chinese." The term "China" is a word of Sanskritic and Persian origin, most likely based on the name Qin, one of the many ruling dynasties of East Asia. Since the Qin Dynasty did not come to power until the 3rd century B.C.E., long after the death of Confucius, he would not have thought of himself as living in a country called China.

Confucius and his contemporaries would have referred to their civilization by many names, including *huáxià*—a word that could be translated as the Grand Florescence or Illustrious Blossoming. As this translation implies, the term *huáxià* suggests a cultural rather than a geographical or political identity. Rather than thinking of themselves as subjects of a kingdom or inhabitants of a terrestrial location, ancient Chinese primarily identified themselves as participants in a particular way of life. Furthermore, they regarded their way of life as more refined than others. It is instructive to note that those outside of *huáxià* culture were considered "barbarian." These "barbarians" may have been ethnically indistinguishable from the "Chinese" and may have even lived within the geographical region we would call "China," but their style of life was different from that of *huáxià*. Since the difference between Chinese and barbarian was cultural and not ethnic, barbarians could become "civilized"—that is, become Chinese—simply by adopting the distinguishing marks of *huáxià* culture, such as wearing particular clothing, eating certain kinds of food, and most importantly, practicing Chinese etiquette. We know today that the *huáxià* culture of Confucius' day was itself an amalgam of many different and distinct regional cultures that gradually influenced one another to form the grand florescence that Confucius and later Chinese considered to be a single culture and the primary identifier of the "Chinese" people.

Another word that denotes this sense of cultural rather than ethnic identity is *zhōngguó*, a term meaning the "central kingdom." As the name intimates, those who belonged to the central kingdom regarded themselves at the center of civilization, not unlike the way Bostonians like to refer to their city as the "Hub of the Universe." But *zhōngguó* also had a more literal sense. By the time of Confucius, the ruling dynasty of this region, the Zhōu Dynasty, governed from a kingdom surrounded by numerous vassal states that owed allegiance to the Zhōu family. The central kingdom was indeed in the middle of things.

Throughout its long history, the geopolitical contours of *huáxià* culture have changed greatly. For much of its past, Chinese culture was centered in the Yellow River valley, located in the northeastern quadrant of the area occupied by the present-day People's Republic of China. In the last four millennia, the external boundaries of China have expanded, contracted, and assumed an array of shapes; its internal divisions, likewise, have changed in many different ways.

When Confucius reflected on his cultural identity, he thought not only of his immediate era but the whole of its past as well. For Confucius, the past was profoundly significant and simply could not be separated from the present. His view of the world embraced the ancient as well as the contemporary. In a sense that westerners might find difficult to grasp, the past was still alive for the Chinese. One can observe this characteristic in ancestor reverence, a fundamental religious practice that runs throughout Chinese history. In ancestor worship, the dead are treated as still existent and significant in everyday life. Ancestors must not be neglected by their descendents, who must attend to them with food and gifts and seek their advice on important matters. The veneration of ancestors symbolizes the way past and present interrelate in Chinese thought.

As moderns, we often take a cavalier attitude toward the past, in part because we frequently judge our own era as more advanced than that of bygone ages. As Henry Ford so bluntly put it, "History is more or less bunk." Such a judgment about the past would have appalled Confucius. In fact, he would have considered that judgment itself both a symptom and a *cause* of the sorry state of the world. For Confucius, forgetting the past did not condemn us to repeat it, as the philosopher George Santayana famously said, but rather dooms us to moral and spiritual decline. A true conservative, Confucius *longed* to repeat the past, or at least one outstanding part of it.

His orientation to the past is one of the things that seem to set Confucius apart from the Buddha, Jesus, and Muhammad. While these other three were not necessarily inattentive to the past, the focus of their attention and their teachings took different temporal directions. The Buddha, as we shall see, grounded his spirituality in the present moment, even to the extent that some of his later interpreters regarded him as denying the reality of the past and the future altogether. Jesus and Muhammad, on the other hand, placed a great emphasis on the future. Jesus proclaimed the coming of the Kingdom of God, and Muhammad regarded the Day of Requital as the final moment of reckoning for believers and unbelievers alike. Only in Confucius do we find a teacher whose fundamental spiritual practice involved taking the past as the guide to, and as the standard for, living in present. "If by keeping the old warm one can provide understanding of the new," he told his followers, "one is fit to be a teacher."

The past for which Confucius pined was rooted in the early societies of the Yellow River valley that date to at least the 5th millennium B.C.E. The Yellow River culture was old enough and sophisticated enough for it to be considered in modern times as one of "cradles of civilization." The evidence disclosed by archaeologists suggests that by the end of the Neolithic period, the citizens of this area were practicing elaborate burials and other rituals and had established social hierarchies regulated by patrilineal descent. Both ritual performance and social stratification were extremely important elements throughout later Chinese history and both figured prominently in the life and teachings of Confucius. Sometime after 2000 B.C.E., the citizens of the ancient Yellow River culture had mastered of the use of bronze and developed the rudiments of a writing system.

By tradition, the Chinese remember this ancient past in a slightly different manner than I have just described. To be sure, Chinese tradition, like modern historiography, regarded this pre-dynastic period as the time in which the basic features of civilization were established, among them agriculture, carpentry, religious rituals, government, and writing. But the traditional legends also recall this era as an age when wise and benevolent monarchs ruled the land. Stories mention numerous philosopher-kings who were pious individuals reigning with only the welfare of the people at heart. Of special note were Yáo, Shùn, and Yǔ, the last three of a group called the Five Emperors.

From the perspective of the modern discipline of history, these figures were either all together fictional or greatly exaggerated representations of actual rulers. Be that as it may, these three were often invoked as models of moral kingship, an ideal image against which lesser rulers were compared when times were bad, as they were in Confucius' day. The last of these great sage-emperors—Yŭ—is traditionally considered the founder of China's first dynasty, the Xià. But just as the historicity of these great kings is doubt, so, too, scholars debate the historicity of the Xià Dynasty. This time in China's past is obviously in that area of our sketch where the details become fuzzy and ultimately vanish.

As we enter the next era of Chinese history, matters begin slowly to come into greater clarity, although still without any great sharpness. This period is known as the Shang Dynasty, the earliest epoch that has been amply verified as historical. The Shang probably began sometime in the 16th or 15th century B.C.E. in the Yellow River valley. For many years, most scholars thought that the Shang Dynasty was part of the mythic "pre-history" of China, simply because there was no tangible evidence from the Shang period.

A little more than 100 years ago, however, the discovery of a curiosity first known as "dragon bones" changed that. These dragon bones, which actually turned out to be tortoise shells and shoulder blades of cattle, not only proved the historicity of the Shang Dynasty; they also revealed a good deal about the religious and political practices of the time. Inscribed on these shells and bones—in an archaic script—were all manner of questions inquiring about such things as the best time to plant a crop, the meaning of a dream, whether or not a particular ancestor was pleased with a sacrificial gift, and when to leave for a journey or to set out on a military expedition. After they were inscribed, the shells or bones were heated, which caused them to crack. The resulting patterns were then interpreted as providing answers to the questions they posed.

There is no doubt that these animal artifacts were used for the practice of divining, the art of consulting the spirit world to gain knowledge that could not otherwise be available to human beings. The fact that over 100,000 such fragments of bone and shell have been recovered indicates that divination was an extremely important part of this early period in China and that it was used for both religious and political purposes. The questions etched into these fragments are what provide us with the greatest insight into the Shang period. From them, we learn that the Shang was an agrarian culture whose members revered the dead and ritually offered them sacrifices of food and wine. We know that the king played an especially important role in these rituals, and his success in pleasing the ancestors and keeping harmony with the spirit-world was essential to the welfare of the kingdom. We also learn that Shang armies fought frequent wars with neighboring realms and with nomads from the inner Asian steppes. These facts are significant for our purposes because they bear greatly on our understanding of Confucius, who had much to say about respect for ancestors and family members, about the king's role in effecting the happiness of his subjects, about war and peace, and about the importance of ritual. Confucius' concern with these subjects put him in a long-standing Chinese tradition.

Scholars are not absolutely sure when the Shang dynasty began, but they do have a more precise idea of when it ended. In or around the year 1045 B.C.E., the Shang rulers were conquered and deposed by the rulers of a neighboring realm, thus initiating the next epoch in Chinese history, the Zhōu dynasty. This dynasty ruled, at least in name, some 800 years, until it was supplanted by the Qin Dynasty in 221 B.C.E.

The founder of the Zhōu Dynasty is traditionally considered to be King Wen, who was known as the "Cultured King" and who was also credited with contributing to a very important book of divination called the *Yi Jing*. Wen had been a feudal lord who was imprisoned by the last Shang king. When Wen's son Wu overthrew Shang rule, he freed his father from imprisonment and bestowed on him the honorary title "king," although Wu himself was the actual ruler. But shortly after the conquest, King Wu died, leaving the throne to his 13 year old son. Fortunately for the nascent dynasty, Wu's younger brother Dàn stepped in to act as regent for the teenage sovereign.

Although he might have attempted to gain the monarchy for himself, Dàn, who was usually known by his title, the Duke of Zhōu, chose instead to serve as the power behind the throne. These figures in the early history of the Zhōu Dynasty—especially the Duke—came to be regarded as the paragons of leadership and moral behavior by later Chinese, including Confucius. Confucius' admiration of Dàn was so deep that he reports having frequent dreams about the Duke. Surely part of Confucius' veneration of the Duke of Zhōu derived from his own aspiration to high office as an advisor to royalty.

The Duke's reputation as a moral exemplar was shaped by what cynics might regard as a P.R. campaign to legitimize the Zhōu conquest of the Shang. Most scholars believe that the Duke essentially invented the theory of *tiānming*, the Mandate of Heaven. According to this concept, the ruler governed with divine sanction *as long as* he was virtuous. If a ruler became corrupt or inept, Heaven withdrew its mandate and the ruler's reign was no longer morally legitimate. On the basis of this doctrine, opposing and even deposing the king could be morally justified—and of course wresting power from the Shang rulers was exactly what the Zhōu family did. The Zhōu people now claimed that the Shang kings had neglected their commitment to virtue—and there probably was some merit to that allegation—and that consequently Heaven's Mandate had passed to the Zhōu. From that point on, the theory of the Mandate of Heaven came to assume a critical role throughout Chinese history, all the way up until the 20th century. Those who would govern China had to invoke this doctrine to demonstrate their legitimacy as rulers.

Despite the high esteem in which later Chinese held the early Zhōu rulers, the Zhōu reign was not as culturally advanced as the Shang Dynasty it replaced. Zhōu culture lacked a writing system and skill in bronze-work, but it soon acquired these practices. The Zhōu rulers also adopted much of the Shang's religious observances. The Zhōu kings actually gave a parcel of land to the remaining Shang family members so that they could continue to worship and sacrifice to their ancestors. The Zhōu rulers themselves probably worshiped the Shang ancestors, even though they had ousted their descendants!

Despite the adoption of Shang ways and the claim to govern by virtue of moral superiority, the Zhōu period was not an all together happy time in Chinese history. Even though it lasted 800 years and was China's longest dynasty, serious rifts began to appear just a few centuries after its establishment. In the year 771 B.C.E., the Zhōu king was murdered by an invading alliance of Chinese and barbarians, and the capital had to be moved further eastward. This eastward move marked a division between what is known as the Western Zhōu and Eastern Zhōu periods. The Eastern Zhōu, which lasted about 550 years, was further divided into two eras known as the Spring and Autumn Period and the Period of Warring States.

The Spring and Autumn age obtained its designation from a book entitled *The Spring and Autumn Annals*, a chronicle that was traditionally—but probably incorrectly—attributed to Confucius. During this era, the power of the Zhōu dynasty declined significantly, destabilizing the entire region. Many smaller kingdoms that had been subject to the Zhōu rulers saw this weakening as a chance to assert their independence. As these vassal states began to vie with one another to succeed the ancient dynasty, violence and lawlessness ran rampant. Political power became more localized and invested in so-called "hegemons," who were essentially warlords powerful enough to dominant weaker rivals. Might, rather than virtue, now came to be seen as the hallmark of the ruler. This political flux engendered rapid social changes as well. The old nobility began to lose privileges based on birth, creating a new class of persons who were of noble descent yet who were increasingly required to prove themselves by talent and hard work. Confucius was born into this new social rank.

The political situation had greatly deteriorated when the Period of Warring States began. This era, which lasted from 403 to 221 B.C.E., was characterized by extensive fighting among the many principalities that had once been loyal to the Zhōu kingdom. By now, the nature of war itself had begun to change. Chariot warfare conducted by aristocrats was being replaced by a mounted cavalry and an infantry composed mainly of conscripted peasants armed the crossbow and weapons of iron. Military leadership was increasingly allotted to individuals who could prove their skill and expertise rather than automatically given to the nobles simply by virtue of their pedigree.

The pace of social and political changes continued to accelerate during this final phase of the Zhōu Dynasty. Government bureaucracy increased. New offices were created and filled by appointed administrators to regulate a population that was growing as a result of advances in agriculture and industry. As the old aristocracy gave way to a meritocracy, the peasantry began to have new opportunities—represented, for instance, by the emergence of a large class of peasants who were landowners. All of these changes were facilitated by the use of currency rather than barter as a means of exchange.

Interestingly, the Period of Warring States was also known as the Period of One Hundred Schools because it was an immensely creative time philosophically and religiously. Although it is a poetic exaggeration, this alternative name indicates that this age of political and social disruption was a stimulus to innovative thought and lively debate among rival viewpoints. Clearly, the commotion created by the many changes rocking ancient China prompted the intellectuals to address the pressing issues of the day. One of the themes of this course to which we shall return in future lectures is the fact that the central figures in our study all lived and taught in times of immense political or cultural ferment.

For the thinkers of Confucius' day, the most urgent problems were social and ethical in nature. Essentially, debate revolved around the question of human harmony. What does it take for people to get along with each other? Many thinkers weighed in on this issue with proposals of various kinds. Although the issue is of a basic practical nature, it necessarily involved deeper questions and assumptions about the fundamental character of reality, the basic qualities of human beings, and the purposes for which human life was intended.

Confucianism was one of these schools of thought contributing to this lively philosophical conversation. China's other great indigenous philosophy, Daoism, was another. How many different schools there were, we do not know for certain, but there were at least half-dozen prominent contenders. In terms of influence and longevity, Confucianism and Daoism have been the most successful, even though they provided perspectives that often seemed at odds with one another.

In futures lectures, we will explore Confucius' solution to the problems of his day, which I would contend, are not all that different from our own, thus rendering him relevant 2,500 years after his time. In our next talk, we will get better acquainted with this Confucius, beginning with a study of his early life and the formative factors that made him such an important individual in Chinese and Asian history and allowed Confucianism to flourish so long after he himself joined the ancestors.

# Becoming a Sage
## Lecture 3

---

**Sīmǎ Qiān's biography ... must therefore be regarded with a healthy dose of suspicion, since it recounts the life of an individual who lived four centuries earlier. ... Nevertheless [it helps] us understand how the example of Confucius was understood by many Chinese, even if that portrayal does not precisely correspond to the historical Confucius.**

Confucius and his way of thought have a place of privilege in the Chinese world as the fountainhead of Chinese culture and philosophy, but for most of his life, Confucius was a virtual unknown. His given name was **Kongqiū**; the name "Confucius" is a latinization of **K'ung-fu-tzu**, meaning "Mister K'ung." Throughout Chinese history, however, he has often simply been called the Sage. What we can say with confidence about the historical Confucius is limited. We have no documents about him written during his lifetime and no writing in his own hand. All of our sources come from others' memories—sometimes second- or third-hand memories—so we have to approach them with a skeptical eye.

Although a minority of scholars have suggested that Confucius is a composite of several ancient sages, most believe he was an authentic historical figure. Sīmǎ Qiān, a court historian of the Han dynasty, wrote the first biography of Confucius about 400 years after the Sage's death; its late date and political ramifications for the Confucian Han court must color our reading. The best source for glimpsing the real Confucius is the *Analects* (in Chinese, the *Lunyu*), but in terms of biography, it has little to report. It is a collection of aphorisms, conversations, and anecdotes compiled by Confucius's disciples after his death; their brief and sometimes cryptic nature has helped shape the popular Western image of Confucius as an old man uttering wisdom and riddles. There is no consensus among modern historians about how much of the *Analects* is historically reliable. Contradictions within the text suggest that many hands were involved in its composition. Only the first half of the book is generally regarded as reflecting the thought and words of Confucius himself, but others grant that status to less or even none of the text.

The time-honored (if not universally accepted) dates for Confucius's lifetime are 551 B.C.E. to 479 B.C.E. Sīmǎ Qiān claims that Confucius was descended from the royal family of the state of Song, one of the principalities of the early Zhōu dynasty. He tells us that Confucius's great-grandfather fled Song for the state of Lu, which had been established by the Duke of Zhōu. There the family fell on hard times from which they never recovered. Confucius was conceived (possibly out of wedlock) in a field, and his parents prayed for his conception at a sacred mountain. Interestingly, the name "Kong" can be translated as "gratitude for an answered prayer" and "Qiu" as "hill," so we might suspect the story is simply a clever play on his name. The important point is that an unusual conception has been accepted as part of Confucius's life story for over 2,000 years.

The Teaching Company Collection.

**Confucius's teaching style was most likely informal, allowing specific situations to provide the occasion for a particular lesson.**

The facts of his youth are as murky as those of his birth. His father likely died when he was a toddler, and his mother raised him in poverty. Tradition tells us he was born with a concavity on the crown of his head and in adulthood was uncommonly tall. Sīmǎ says as a boy he enjoyed pretending to officiate at mock rituals. The *Analects* says he was "skilled in many menial things," meaning he likely accepted many lowly jobs in his youth. But he was entitled to an education by virtue of his social standing as part of the emerging *shi*, or common gentlemen, situated between the declining nobility and the common peasantry. He was an eager and dedicated student, and we may assume he was schooled in all or most of the "six arts" of ancient China: ritual, music, archery, charioteering, calligraphy, and mathematics. Ritual and music would later figure prominently in his philosophy and teaching.

Confucius not only loved learning, but he seems to have discovered the importance of mindfulness in the process of learning. He expected his students to share his love of

> **"If I hold up one corner of a problem, and the student cannot come back to me with the other three, I will not attempt to instruct him again."**
> **— Analects 7.8**

learning and practice the discipline of paying attention: "I will not open the door for a mind that is not already striving to understand, nor will I provide words to a tongue that is not already struggling to speak."

We know Confucius was a father and husband, and there are suggestions in the early literature that his marriage ended in divorce. Familial relationships were an important aspect of Confucian ethics, so our lack of details on his family life is frustrating. As we begin to consider the similarities and differences among our four sages toward the end of the course, we will return to the question of marriage and reflect on its bearing on their lives and teachings. ■

## Important Terms

**Kongqiū**: Confucius's given name. "Kong" translates loosely to "gratitude for an answered prayer" and "qiū" translates to "hill."

**K'ung-fu-tzu**: Literally, "Mister K'ung"; the honorific that was Latinized into "Confucius."

*Lunyu*: The Chinese name of Confucius's *Analects*.

## Questions to Consider

1. Imagine you are a historian researching an ancient notable like Confucius. What sort of clues would you look for when trying to determine the authenticity of a story or text about your subject?

**2.** How important do you think mindfulness is to the learning process? What are the aids and barriers to mindfulness in modern educational environments?

# Becoming a Sage
## Lecture 3—Transcript

As we noted in the previous lecture, the name China probably derived from Qin, a dynasty that postdated the life of Confucius. Although the Qin emperors ruled for only 15 years, they unified China and established it as an imperial power. But they had no use for Confucius and his philosophy. During this dynasty, his teaching fell into disfavor because his views were at odds with the highly authoritarian philosophy of the Qin government. The Confucian school was officially and vigorously suppressed; Confucian texts were burned and hundreds of Confucian scholars were stoned to death or buried alive.

In the long history of Chinese culture, however, this episode was clearly and simply a blip, an aberration. Soon after the brief reign of the Qin rulers, Confucius and his way of thought were restored to a place of privilege in the Chinese world. Eventually, the man himself would be regarded as a demigod by many and his temples would be dedicated to his spirit and sacrifices made in his honor. After surviving the efforts of the Qin dynasty to eradicate his teachings, Confucius became the fountainhead of virtually all aspects of Chinese life. Historian Annping Chin says in her recent biography: "Until the mid-20th century, China was so inseparable from the idea of Confucius that her scheme of government and society, her concept of self and human relationships, and her construct of culture and history all seemed to have originated from his mind alone." Confucius has even been credited with inventing the popular game of Mahjongg! An even more exalted accolade was offered by Mencius (Mengzi), the brilliant philosopher who lived almost two centuries after the Sage. Mencius says, "Ever since man came into this world, there has never been one greater than Confucius." To judge solely by his humble beginnings and the course of most of his life, such high acclaim would hardly seem expected. For most of his 70-odd years, Confucius was a virtual unknown.

Beginning with this lecture, we shall investigate the life and teachings of this man to try to determine what it was that garnered him such praise from people like Mencius and what made his example and philosophy such a menace to people like the Qin emperors. Today, we start this journey by considering Confucius' ancestry and early life, focusing our attention on his love for learning, the characteristic that perhaps more than anything else made this modest man a master of wisdom.

Just as he would not have identified himself as Chinese, he would not have identified himself as *Confucius*. That was neither his given name nor the name by which the Chinese have known him, at least until rather recently. Throughout the history of China, he has been called Kongzi or simply "The Sage." Kong was his family name. His personal, or taboo, name was Qiū, and his courtesy, or social, name was Zhòngní. As is still common in many parts of Asia, it was considered impolite or disrespectful to call someone by their personal name, and so they have a social name or nickname for public use. My wife, who is Sri Lankan and a modern chemist, still observes this traditional custom and never calls me by my given name, and the members of our Sri Lankan family refer to me only by titles like *aiya*, or "elder brother," or nicknames like *mahaththeya,* "the gentleman." The name Confucius did not come into existence until the 17th century when European Jesuit missionaries to China Latinized his honorific title, K'ung-fu-tzu, which essentially means "Mister K'ung." And Confucius is the name that has stuck, even for scholars who are quite aware of its imprecision.

What we can say about the life of Confucius with historical dependability is not a lot. We will discover this to be true with lives of the Buddha and Jesus as well. In the case of Muhammad, the historical reliability of sources is also an issue, but much less so than with the other three. As we take up the life story of each of these individuals, I'll discuss the matter of their historicity as real persons and the problems scholars have in gaining a clear picture of who they were and what they actually did and said. I am going to spend some time discussing the problem of historicity as it pertains to Confucius, mainly because his case illustrates many of the issues we encounter when we try to gain access to individuals from the ancient world by modern historiographical methods.

In the instance of Confucius, we have no documents written during his lifetime on which to base our portrait of him as a person. This is also true of the Buddha, Jesus, and Muhammad. Nor do we have any writings from their own hands. None of them committed their teachings to the written word, or if they did, no evidence of it remains. All four lived in cultures in which the spoken word was supreme, and writing was mainly reserved for legal and political matters. Literacy rates were very low. At the time of Jesus, for example, only around 5% of the population of Judea could read and write. It is not clear whether or not the Buddha and Jesus were literate, but it is almost certain that Confucius was and that Muhammad was not. If Confucius were literate, the absence of his own writings might be due to his conviction that the words of the ancient sages were more important that anything *he* had to say. In any event, all of our primary sources come from followers and others who lived afterwards, who were reporting their memories or the memories of others. No doubt some of them were even inventing "memories," so to speak, consistent with their idea of who the individual was.

The first biography of Confucius probably contained both authentic and invented memories. It was written by Sīmǎ Qiān, a court historian of the Han dynasty, around the year 100 B.C.E., four hundred years after the Sage's death. Sīmǎ Qiān wrote under the new regime that arose after the Qin dynasty came to a close. Under the Han Dynasty, China became a Confucian state. Sīmǎ Qiān's biography of Confucius, which appears in a work called *Records of the Grand Historian*, must therefore be regarded with a healthy dose of suspicion, since it recounts the life of an individual who lived four centuries earlier and since it would have served the interests of the state to make Confucius seem larger than life. Nevertheless, this early biography is useful to help us understand how the example of Confucius was understood by many Chinese, even if that portrayal does not precisely correspond to the historical Confucius.

Despite the value of Sīmǎ Qiān's biography, the best source for glimpsing the man Confucius has to be the *Analects*, the text known in Chinese as the *Lunyu*, a work that most scholars believe bears the imprint of his own thinking, if not some of his very words. Yet the *Analects* is by no means a biography—or even a narrative. Rather, it is a collection of aphorisms, conversations, and anecdotes related to his life, most of which are attributed to Confucius himself. It is evident to critical scholars, though, that the text was written and compiled by his disciples after his death and that it probably took shape over the span over many generations.

The sayings and vignettes comprising the *Analects* are often very brief and sometimes quite cryptic, which has helped shape the popular image of Confucius in the west as an old man uttering jewels of wisdom, as well as offering perplexing and sometimes irrelevant opinions. Not only are many of the pieces in the *Analects* obscure in themselves, they do not seem to be compiled according to any organizing principle. One scholar of Chinese and translator of the *Analects* describes its arrangement as "slapdash." Furthermore, as a source for understanding Confucius' life, it is woefully incomplete. There is so much about Confucius that the *Analects* does not consider important to report. Where there were gaps, later biographers usually filled them in with imaginative stories congruous with the picture they had of the great sage. Despite its shortcomings, the *Analects* at least possesses the virtue of portraying Confucius as an ordinary person rather than the demigod he was later taken to be.

Compounding these interpretive difficulties is the fact that there is no consensus among modern historians about how much of the *Analects* is historically reliable. Almost everyone agrees that much of the text reflects the perspectives and words of his followers, some of whom may have been removed from him by many generations. Subtle—and sometimes glaring—contradictions within parts of the text itself suggest that many hands were involved in its composition. Of 20 relatively short chapters, only the first half of the book is generally regarded as reflecting the thought and words of Confucius himself, but even here there is no universal agreement. Some say only chapters 3-9 contains words that Confucius may have actually spoken. Two scholars have recently argued that only a single section of chapter 4 is authentic. Still another has gone so far as to claim that Confucius was not an historical figure at all but an invented character who personified the values of the Chinese elite. Since almost all scholars believe a similar thing about Laozi, the reputed founder of Daoism, the idea that Confucius was fictional is plausible, but the argument has not yet convinced most researchers.

Most Confucius scholars believe there was an authentic historical person who at least inspired the school of thought associated with his name. For the last two millennia, virtually all readers of the *Analects* have assumed that all parts of the *Analects* derive from a real person named Confucius or Kongzi. For our purposes, we will not spend more time on these matters, even though they are part of a lively conversation among academics. I suggest we take Confucius to be an historical person (as I believe he was) and rely mainly on the *Analects* as the chief source for our investigation.

But even though the *Analects* is our best source for constructing a picture of Confucius, it is hardly an ideal work for biographical purposes. Although it is marked by the mind of Confucius—or at least someone known to history by that name—and probably contains some of the sage's actual words, it is not a contemporaneous writing and it is very fragmentary. Trying to sketch a literary portrait of Confucius from the *Analects* is somewhat akin to the way paleontologists try to understand how a prehistoric animal looked and lived based on a few fossil fragments. This doesn't doom the project from the outset, but it certainly advises caution in pressing our claims with too much conviction.

So with the bits and pieces available to us, let's begin our sketch. At each point along the way, I will note when I think we are on firm historical ground and when I think we are moving into the legendary and mythical areas.

Chinese tradition suggests that Confucius was born around the year 551 B.C.E., during the Spring and Autumn Period, in the province of Lu, one of the several small principalities that began to compete with one another as the Eastern Zhōu dynasty began its slow decline. The same sources indicate that he died in 479 B.C.E. That would mean the Sage lived 72 or 73 years. Of course, as we'll also discover in the case of the Buddha, the traditional dates for Confucius are not accepted by everyone. There is good reason to be suspicious of the exactness of these traditional dates, since the sage lived during a time when the births and deaths of individuals were not recorded with great precision. Recently, some Confucius scholars have made the case that he lived closer to the end of the Zhōu dynasty, around the time of the Warring States Period. But in the absence of compelling evidence to the contrary, I suggest we simply stay with the time-honored dates.

Although the *Analects* say nothing about this, the historian Sīmǎ Qiān claims that Confucius' lineage extends back to the royal family of the state of Song, one of the principalities of the early Zhōu Dynasty. The members of this noble family were appointed to conduct rituals dedicated to the Shang ancestors. There is no real evidence that Confucius was actually the descendant of such a family, but the theme of royal figures charged with maintaining ritual observances fits the image of Confucius perfectly, as we shall later see. In fact, this ancestral claim fits him almost *too* perfectly, which is one reason this heritage seems doubtful. As I mentioned at the start of the course, our four sages were all accorded aristocratic or royal heritage by later writers, although in each and every case the sage was unable or refused to enjoy the life of worldly privilege afforded by his noble descent.

Sīmǎ goes on to flesh out the story of Confucius' ancestry. Confucius' great-grandfather had fled the state of Song, which was in political turmoil, and he moved to the state of Lu, somewhere near the present town of Qufu in southeastern Shandong province. Following the migration, however, the family fell on hard times and became impoverished, from which it never recovered. It was here that Confucius was born. Lu had been established five centuries earlier by one of the sons of Dàn, the Duke of Zhou and the great regent who, as we noted in the previous lecture, became the model of the ideal person for Confucius. Because of its connection to the Duke, Confucius took pride in claiming Lu as his home province.

The story of Confucius' birth, as reported by Sīmǎ Qiān, is interesting in terms of our comparisons with the other three figures in our study, although the tale lacks independent corroboration. Apparently, Confucius' father, Shu-liang, was a very old man and his mother a mere girl in her teens when Confucius was conceived. It is not clear if their relationship constituted a legitimate marriage; that point remains uncertain. Shu-liang already had nine daughters by his chief wife and a crippled son by a concubine. Perhaps as he approached death he wanted a healthy male heir and divorced his wife; or perhaps she had died. Sīmǎ does not say. He does say that Confucius was conceived while his parents were "making love in the field," a reference that might suggest an illicit union because it does not occur under the auspices of a formal ritual. At least one scholar thinks this reference might also suggest a divine conception. After this unconventional consummation, his parents' went to a sacred mountain to pray for a child, and when Confucius was born months later, they considered him to be the answer to their prayers. It is interesting to observe that Confucius' personal name was Qiu, the same Chinese word for "hill," and that Kong, his family name, can be used as an expression of gratitude for answered prayers. We cannot know if there is any historical validity to this story. It may in fact have been invented by Sīmă Qiān as a clever wordplay on Confucius' Chinese names. What we want to observe at this juncture is simply the elements of an unusual conception that have become part of the life-story of Confucius as it has been accepted for over 2000 years.

About his youth, we know almost nothing with historical assurance. His father probably died early in his life, around the age of three, leaving him to be raised by his young mother. She too died when he was only 23. The *Analects* reports that Confucius and his mother endured a poverty-stricken life. As a young man, he had to accept lowly jobs such as keeping accounts and caring for livestock. Later in life, he tells his disciples that he was "skilled in many menial things," not out of desire but out of necessity. Sīmă tells us that as a boy he enjoyed pretending to officiate at mock rituals, a story that I find endearing since I also liked playing rituals as a boy, such as conducting little funerals for my friends' pets. Confucius seemed to delight in arranging ritual vases on sacrificial altars, or so the story goes. Again, this anecdote fits the later Confucius almost too perfectly, but it may bear some authenticity. One final note on his early life concerns his physical appearance. Tradition says he was born with a concavity on the crown of his head and was uncommonly tall for ancient Chinese, reaching well over six feet at adulthood. He must have cut a striking figure indeed.

Despite his modest beginning—or perhaps more accurately, because of it—Confucius was an eager and dedicated student. He says in one of the famous passages from the *Analects*, "At 15, I set my heart on learning," and this love of learning stayed with him for his entire life. He later described this dedication as one of his distinctive qualities: "In a community of ten households there will certainly be someone as loyal and trustworthy as I am, but not someone so fond of learning as I am." With no wealth or prestige, Confucius was nonetheless entitled to an education, by virtue of his social standing. His ancestry placed him in the growing new class called the shi, or the common gentleman, situated between the declining nobility and the common peasantry. This emerging social rank comprised members of formerly aristocratic families whose success in life now depended on their own talents and determination rather than mere birth. We do not know exactly how Confucius was educated, but it is safe to assume that he was schooled in all or most of the so-called "Six Arts" of ancient China: ritual, music, archery, charioteering, calligraphy, and mathematics. It is almost certain that he mastered at least ritual and music, because these two skills figured so prominently in his own philosophy and teaching. As we shall see later, Confucius believed that ritual and music had important moral dimensions; performing ceremonies and listening to proper music served to make one a better person. Indeed, becoming a better person was what Confucius thought education was all about.

Confucius not only *loved* learning; he seems to have discovered a key aspect about the process of learning. The *Analects* quote him as saying, "when I study, I do not get bored; in teaching others I do not grow weary." I don't think Confucius is being merely descriptive here; he's not simply telling us about one of his in-born character traits, as if not getting bored were in his nature. I think he is talking about a skill that is an essential ingredient in learning. I recall something that the 20th century American composer John Cage once wrote that has left a lasting impression on me. Cage is probably most renowned for his controversial piece, 4'33", a composition of what many consider to be four minutes and 33 seconds of silence.

Like many American artists, writers, and musicians in the mid-20th century, Cage was influenced by Zen Buddhism, a tradition, incidentally, that essentially developed in China. This quotation has definite Zennishness to it. Cage wrote, "If something is boring after two minutes, try it for four. If still boring, try it for eight. Then 16. Then 32. Eventually one discovers that it's not boring at all." What impressed me about Cage's remark—and why I apply it now to Confucius' self-description—is the notion that boredom is not generated by anything outside oneself. The experience of boredom is really about the state of our own minds rather than about the thing we're reading or watching or listening to. "When people are bored," said philosopher Eric Hoffer, "it is primarily with their own selves that they are bored." Cage believed that with the proper frame of mind, anything could be interesting, and that without it anything could be boring. I think Confucius was aware of the importance of this quality in the art of learning. I would call this quality mindfulness—or simply paying attention. Thus, he expected his students to share his loving of learning and practice the discipline of paying attention.

> The Master said, "I will not open the door for a mind that is not already striving to understand, nor will I provide words to a tongue that is not already struggling to speak. If I hold up one corner of a problem, and the student cannot come back to me with the other three, I will not attempt to instruct him again.

Or to use the words of another august teacher in the series, Confucius refused to cast his pearls before swine.

To add some finishing touches to our sketch of young man Confucius, let me briefly mention what takes him to the threshold of maturity: his marriage. We do know that he was married, although we know next to nothing about his wife. The pair married in their late teens and had a son and a daughter together. The son predeceased Confucius. We do not know what Confucius was like as a father or a husband, but there are suggestions in the early literature that his marriage ended in divorce. It is unfortunate that we have such sparse information about his family life, because familial relationships were an important aspect of Confucian ethics. In fact, he viewed the political domain as the family writ large, and he derived many of his precepts for governance from what he understood to be appropriate for family life.

If what the early literature says about Confucius' marriage is true, then the four individuals of our course represent a gamut of marital and familial arrangements. Confucius had married and was divorced; Gotama, who became the Buddha, was married and had a son; Jesus was a lifelong bachelor; and Muhammad had many wives, children, and wards. As we begin to consider the similarities and differences among these figures towards the end of the course, we will return to the question of marriage and reflect on its bearing on their lives and teachings.

In our next lecture, we will continue to add to our picture of Confucius by examining his adult life and his personal qualities as remembered by his closest associates and as revealed through his sayings. We will meet an individual who still impresses us today with his dignity, moral integrity, and keen insight into what brings out the best of our humanity.

# A Gentleman and a Scholar
## Lecture 4

**Confucius believed that the pursuit of virtue by leaders—whether of the state or of the family—had salutary ramifications throughout the collective body. … For legends to suggest that when Confucius assumed office the world became a much better place would be quite consistent with this belief.**

The *Analects* and other sources provide us with more and better information about the last quarter of Confucius's life than we have about his first 50 years. We have noted how his love of learning distinguished him from others in his situation, and his study of the texts of Huáxià culture was to influence both his thinking and his success. By his late 20s, he was recognized as an authority on history, ritual, and music, and served as an occasional ceremonial consultant to several rulers and aristocratic families. In his 30s, he began teaching the classics to male students from all walks of life; he only required that his students be zealous learners like he was. What Confucius taught was gentlemanly conduct, how to comport oneself to best serve the state and hence one's fellow humans. But it was not until he was nearly 50 that Confucius became a state official himself.

His first appointment was as Deputy Minister of Public Works, followed shortly by his selection as Minister of Crime. His tenure was fairly unremarkable, although Xunzi, one of his early interpreters, and Sīmă Qiān both claimed his appointment triggered a new wave of morality throughout the province, driven almost solely by his reputation. While such stories are surely exaggerations, they highlight Confucius's belief that the pursuit of virtue by leaders had salutary ramifications throughout the collective body. They also correspond to the image of the Sage in the *Analects*: the paragon of wisdom, compassion, and humility.

Other sources describe Confucius as gentle, benevolent, respectful, frugal, and deferential. He did not consider himself to be the ideal person that others took him to be. To the contrary, he appeared to be more focused on correcting his deficiencies than displaying his assets. Confucius was also a person capable of great empathy for others, particularly for those who were suffering, and paid keen attention to gestures of respect and courtesy. While these early literary images of Confucius may not have been wholly accurate, they cannot have been wholly disconnected from the person he was.

**Piecing together his aphorisms and the impressions of his disciples, [the *Analects*] portrays the Sage as the paragon of wisdom, compassion, and humility.**

Confucius's achievements as police commissioner of Lu were modest but not insignificant. He is credited with negotiating the return of Lu lands from an invading neighbor when several military expeditions had already failed. Although resolution by violence is a last resort in Confucian philosophy, he was not a proponent of total nonviolence. He ordered several executions, including the death of Shaozheng Mao, a fellow teacher of virtue, on the charges of moral pretense and subversion (not unlike the accusations leveled against Socrates and Jesus). Confucius's later interpreters were at pains to reconcile his actions with his teachings on benevolence and the sacredness of human life.

Within four or five years of his ministerial appointment, Confucius resigned and left Lu to seek another master to serve. His reasons are lost to us, but there are some hints that it was a gesture of protest against the corrupting influence of outsiders on Lu's court. Along with an entourage of protégés, he became an itinerant political consultant, wandering from kingdom to kingdom for over a dozen years, never finding a court where he could settle. The travel was arduous and provided good material for later writers to highlight the finer aspects of Confucian attitudes toward suffering, adversity, and the earthly rewards of virtue (or rather, the lack thereof). In fact, Confucius's belief mirrored the Buddha's teaching that nobility does not imply avoidance of adversity but meeting it with an inner resolve and serenity, and like our other three sages, he measured his success not by popularity or acceptance but by more personal criteria—in this case, depth of self-understanding and personal refinement.

By his mid-60s, Confucius was convinced that his work in the world had been sanctioned by the highest realities. He had survived a difficult childhood, travails in the wilderness, and two assassination attempts—once again, not unlike our other three sages. Each had discovered a source of courage rooted in a truth beyond the triumphs and failures of their individual lives. The itinerant years were important in maturing Confucius's thought and the personal qualities that made him so attractive to many, but in the end, he returned to Lu around 484 B.C.E. No longer interested in active political service, he returned to teaching, though occasionally consulting with kings and counselors. In this way—learning and teaching, constantly striving for self-improvement—Confucius occupied himself until the end of his days. ■

## Questions to Consider

1. If nobility, in the Confucian sense, is to meet adversity with inner resolve and serenity, what rituals or spiritual practices did Confucius use to help his students develop this trait? How do other faiths, philosophies, and ritual systems define and foster nobility?

2. From what you have heard so far, do you think Confucius taught a particularly strict or challenging philosophy?

# A Gentleman and a Scholar
## Lecture 4—Transcript

Throughout his adult life, Confucius had a single and very lofty ambition: to restore moral vision and virtue to the world. For a young man of the *shì* class, the "common gentleman" whose worth was measured by achievement and not heredity, there was really only one avenue by which such an aspiration could have any hope of being fulfilled—to secure an office in government that would allow him to serve as an advisor to a king or duke. But Confucius was never able to obtain the influential position he sought. His highest political attainment was the Minister of Crime, the equivalent of police commissioner, in his home state of Lu. He was just over 50 when Duke Ding appointed him to this mid-level post.

Yet he was not to keep the job for long. Within a few years, he abruptly abandoned his station, left Lu, and struck out with a handful of disciples for a 14-year trek through neighboring states, seeking a way to "be of use," to cite one of his favorite phrases. After over a decade of self-imposed exile, he returned to Lu and dedicated himself to teaching until his death in 479 B.C.E. About these events in the last quarter century of his life, the *Analects* and other sources provide us with more and better information than we have about his first 50 years. In our study today, we will discuss the important episodes in this final third of the Sage's life giving special attention to the personal qualities that emerge from his aphorisms and the memories of his associates.

As we've said, Confucius lived a meager existence as a young man, taking what he considered to be menial jobs to support himself and his family. What distinguished him from others in similar circumstances was his dedication to learning. From the time of his adolescence and marriage until his appointment as the Minister of Crime, Confucius was principally occupied with the study of the classic texts and traditions of *huáxià* culture. It was on the basis of what he learned by examining the past that Confucius pondered the decline of Chinese culture and developed his vision of what it would take to return China to the glory days of the Zhōu and earlier dynasties. By his late 20s, he was recognized as an authority on history, ritual, and music, and served as an occasional ceremonial consultant to several rulers and aristocratic families in Lu and adjacent states. In his 30s, he began a private school to teach the classics to a wide range of male students, from the sons of the nobility to those brought up in humble conditions as he had been. Some of his followers had even been criminals. He only required that his students be zealous learners like he was. Confucius was one of the first in Chinese history to offer such instruction to the members of lower classes, who were now beginning to regard education as the best way to improve their lot in life. What Confucius had to give them was training in gentlemanly conduct, how to comport themselves so that they might serve the state and hence their fellow humans. Almost all of his disciples sought a career in government service, and it was to that end that they sought the services of Master Kong.

It was not until around 500 B.C.E., when he was near the age of 50, that Confucius enters the records of Chinese history as a state official. His first appointment was as Deputy Minister of Public Works, followed shortly by his selection as Minister of Crime. In this capacity, Confucius had opportunities to appear before the ruling court and confer with more powerful ministers of state. His tenure in the position was fairly unremarkable for the most part, although his later admirers go a bit over the top in describing his accomplishments. Xunzi, one his early interpreters, and Sima Qian both claimed that almost immediately after Confucius assumed office, a new wave of morality swept through the province, driven almost solely by his reputation. Shepherds stopped bloating their sheep with water before taking them to market; horse and cattle dealers no longer tried to swindle their buyers; husbands forced out their adulterous wives, and outsiders were made to feel welcome. If we are to believe reports such as these, we would have to accept that within just months of his appointment, Confucius had restored social harmony where there had been rampant discord for generations.

While such stories are surely exaggerations, they nonetheless highlight two important matters, one pertaining to Confucius' philosophy and the other to his personality. Concerning the first, Confucius believed that the pursuit of virtue by leaders—whether of the state or of the family—had salutary ramifications throughout the collective body. Virtuous leaders inspire virtuous behavior in their subordinates, thus stabilizing and harmonizing society. For legends to suggest that when Confucius assumed office the world became a much better place would be quite consistent with this belief. These accounts also say something about Confucius' personal qualities. Obviously, the stories are intended to relate that Confucius was the kind of person whose example and power of virtue could bring about such wholesome changes.

This is precisely the image of Confucius that emerges in the *Analects*. Piecing together his aphorisms and the impressions of his disciples, Sage emerges as the paragon of wisdom, compassion, and humility. One summary of his personal character describes him as "absolutely free from four things: free from conjecture [or unnecessary speculation], free from arbitrariness, free from obstinacy, free from egoism." Freedom from egoism—in other words, humility—seems to be the quality that most impressed his contemporaries. They remark upon it in a variety of ways. It was evident even in his physical carriage and demeanor: The *Analects* report that "On entering the Palace Gate he seemed to contract his body, as though there were not sufficient room to admit him." He was "was genial and yet strict, imposing and yet not intimidating, courteous and yet at ease."

According to one of his closest followers, Zǐgòng, the master was gentle, benevolent, respectful, frugal, and deferential. Other disciples described him as "rather unassuming" and as someone who "seemed as if he were an inarticulate person." Yet at court he always spoke eloquently, with caution, carefully choosing his words. There seemed to have been not a shred of pretense in him. He never claimed to be a special individual or to possess any great knowledge. "As for sageness and humaneness," he said, "how dare I claim them?" He did not consider himself to be the ideal person that others took him to be. To the contrary, he appeared to be more focused on correcting his deficiencies than displaying his assets. The *Analects* quote him as saying, "Virtue uncultivated, learning undiscussed, the inability to move toward righteousness after hearing it, and the inability to correct my imperfections—these are my anxieties." He advised his followers: "When you come across an inferior person, turn inwards and examine yourself." They confirmed that "When he made a mistake, he was not afraid to correct it."

Confucius was also a person capable of great empathy for others, particularly for those who were suffering. "On seeing a man in mourning, even an intimate friend, he always changed his countenance." If he "dined beside a bereaved person, he never ate his fill" His empathy for others evoked in him a keen attention to the gestures of respect and courtesy: "When the Master saw a man in mourning, or one wearing an official hat and suit, or a blind man—when he saw one, even a younger person, he always rose; when he passed one, he always quickened his pace" which was regarded a sign of respect. When there were state ceremonies honoring the elderly, he would not leave until all the senior honorands had left. Yet despite his concern with personal decorum and conduct, Confucius was never stiff or pompous.

These images and memories signify the way Confucius appeared to his close followers and to others. I believe these images and personal attributes probably have some basis in the historical Confucius, although I cannot prove it. The details may be debatable and perhaps occasionally altogether wrong; but the early literary images of Confucius cannot have been wholly disconnected from the person he was. Confucius appears in the *Analects* as wise, compassionate, and modest because he was in fact that kind of person.

That is what led his biographers to make such high claims about his term as a government official. In all likelihood, Confucius' achievements as police commissioner of Lu were much more modest than his later biographers thought, but they were not insignificant. He is credited with negotiating an important agreement with the neighboring state of Qi that resulted in the return of previously stolen lands to the kingdom of Lu. This diplomatic victory was impressive because Confucius was able to succeed, using his powers of moral persuasion, where several military expeditions had failed. The appeal to virtue and rehabilitation was always a first resort for Confucius, and the use of violence and punishment was always an inferior final solution.

That preference, however, did not mean that Confucius was a pacifist or a proponent of absolute nonviolence. Although there are clear similarities in their teachings on virtue and expediency, Confucius was no Gandhi. In his role as Minister of Crime, Master Kong was directly responsible for the deaths of several individuals. One incident occurred at the very negotiation celebration at Qi I just mentioned, where Confucius ordered the execution of a troupe of singers and dancers who had been sent to entertain the Duke of Lu. Confucius justifies the order by saying the entertainers had "made a mockery" of the dignity of their ruler. Presumably, Confucius found their spectacle "lewd" and "vulgar," and hence contrary to the rites of propriety. This was by no means the only occasion on which Confucius voiced his objections to what he considered rude entertainments.

Nor was it the only time he sent someone to his death. During his appointment as Minister of Crime, he ordered the execution of one Shaozheng Mao, a man well-known in Lu and respected by many as a teacher of virtue. Shaozheng had violated no laws of the state, yet Confucius condemned him for what amounted to moral pretense and subversion, believing he constituted a threat to the social fabric by stealthily teaching dangerous ideas under the guise of integrity. The charges were not unlike those leveled against Socrates and Jesus, which of course resulted in their executions.

The condemnation of Shaozheng scandalized many of Confucius' own disciples, some of whom thought he was trying to eliminate a rival teacher. Yet, Confucius never regretted his decision. His later interpreters were at pains to reconcile his action with his teachings on benevolence and the sacredness of human life. In Xunzi's spin centuries later, the episode portrays Confucius as a man of "keen discernment," to use one of the Sage's own terms, capable of extraordinary penetration of the depths of personal character. No one else could see it, but Confucius recognized Shaozheng as a wolf in sheep's clothing, and hence deserving the ultimate penalty.

I must confess, these executions trouble me and don't fit the image I have of Confucius, or perhaps the image I want to have of him. I prefer to think of Confucius as a believer in the redeemability of everyone, regardless of the depth of their depravity. Even if Shaozheng was as wicked as Confucius thought, I would like to think that somehow a sage like Confucius could have put him on the straight path. But perhaps this is too much to ask for even from Confucius, who never professed to be perfect—or even to be a sage. He lived in desperate times, and his actions need to be viewed in that context. Capital executions and brutal military violence were standard practices of the day. Perhaps there is some comfort in knowing that Confucius exercised this power sparingly and with considerable forethought and conviction. But to me it offers little consolation.

Confucius' career as Minister of Crime was not long-lived. Within four or five years of his appointment, he unexpectedly left the position—and the province of Lu—to seek another ruler to serve in another state. The reasons for his departure are not clear and have long been the subject of scholarly speculation. Characteristically, the *Analects* are obscure on the matter, offering only a very terse statement. "When the Duke of Qi presented a group of singing girls, Jihuánzĭ, the prime minister of Lu, accepted them and there was no court for the next three days. Confucius left."

His interpreters, of course, felt compelled to elaborate on this incident to help explain an otherwise baffling event. Most regarded the exodus as a form of protest: Confucius refused to work for a government that was vulnerable to morally corrupting influences from outside officials. And then there are those entertainers again! We're not sure if Confucius objected to their music or sexually provocative behavior or both. In any event, it was the prime minister's fascination with the singing girls that left Confucius disconcerted. Mencius adds another element to the story, indicating that in spite of the prime minister's impropriety, Confucius decided to give the ruler another chance. When Confucius was not offered a sliver of the sacrificial meat at a state ritual a short time later, he quietly stood up and left. Some commentators suggested that the ceremonial blunder was part of a conspiracy cooked up by those in the kingdom intent on halting Confucius' campaign to restore virtue to the government. Mencius wants us to understand that Confucius was not *personally* offended by the slight, but that the omission confirmed that the Lu rulers were not serious about observing traditional ritual and hence not serious about promoting moral reform. Confucius had no choice but to leave. To stay would be to squander his talents, which could be of genuine use elsewhere.

So Confucius upped and left. Along with an entourage of protégés, he became an itinerant political consultant. He wandered from kingdom to kingdom for over a dozen years, seeking opportunities to put his ideas into practice as well as to continue to learn. But he could never find a job that suited him, and in many cases he consented to serve rulers who were far less worthy than those he left in Lu. Some of them, like Duke Ling of Wei, frankly admitted that they were more interested in military conquest and sexual exploits than in taking seriously what Confucius had to offer. Apparently, the rulers of these kingdoms were simply not prepared to receive Confucius' advice on how to govern on the basis of virtue and ritual observance. After a while in one location, he and his followers would pack up and move along on foot to seek better horizons. He must have covered over a thousand miles in his years abroad and sought residence in at least four other kingdoms.

The journeys between states were arduous. On one occasion, Confucius and his company almost starved to death after their provisions were depleted in the wilderness. We are not certain how they were able to survive the ordeal, but they did, and the experience provided some good material for later writers to highlight the finer aspects of Confucian thought. The *Analects* report that after they ran out of food, Confucius' disciple Zìlǔ approached the master with considerable resentment and asked sarcastically, "So the superior person is also susceptible to adversity?" To which Confucius responded: "The noble one rests at ease in adversity; the petty person when faced with adversity is reduced to recklessness." Confucius' retort sounds remarkably similar to his near-contemporary, the Buddha, who also had much to say about the characteristics of the noble one and his or her capacity to face the sufferings of life with equanimity. Both the Buddha and Confucius indicate that nobility does not imply avoidance of adversity but meeting it with an inner resolve and serenity. Furthermore, Confucius goes on to challenge his disciples' assumption that the pursuit of virtue necessarily results in some tangible or worldly reward. Shortly after Zìlǔ left, according to Sima Qian, Zǐgòng arrives and tells Confucius: "Your way is too demanding. The world is unable to attain it. Why don't you make it a bit easier?" To which Confucius responded:

A good farmer can work as hard as he can but does not always reap a harvest. A fine artisan can produce wonderful craftsmanship but is not always appreciated. A gentleman can be cultivating a [superior] way for himself; he can outline and summarize what he has learned, and gather all the strands and sort them into [interlocking] principles. Yet people will not always accept what he can teach them. Now it seems you are not pursuing [learning and] self-understanding. Rather, you seek to have your ideas gain acceptance. Your goal is not far enough!

Confucius, the Buddha, Jesus, and Muhammad all had to deal with someone trying to persuade them to modify their teachings to make them more palatable and popular. All had to contend with rejection by others and a sense of failing to accomplish their goals. The response of each teacher was to locate the criterion for success in something other than popular acceptance and applause. For Confucius, success was to be measured by the depth of self-understanding and personal refinement, qualities that could be attained regardless of circumstance or popular response.

During his journeys, Confucius not only faced death by starvation but was twice the object of attempted murder. In one case, the would-be assassins mistook him for someone else; in the second, the Minister of the Army of the state of Song, Huan Tui, chopped down a tree in an effort to crush Confucius while he was performing a ritual. This was no case of mistaken identity, but we are not told of the army minister's motivations. In both instances, Confucius responded by recalling his sense of divine mission: "Heaven has given me this power—this virtue. What can Huan Tui do to me!" By now— in his mid-60s—Confucius had been convinced that his work in the world had been sanctioned by the highest realities and that imprimatur secured the worth of his vision and the significance of his mission. Like Confucius, the Buddha, Jesus, and Muhammad also survived assassination attempts, and all remained undeterred by them. Each had discovered a source of courage rooted in a truth beyond the triumphs and failures of their individual lives.

Fourteen years on the road seemed to have nourished Confucius' courage and confidence. Certainly, it took a good measure of fortitude for him to leave Lu in the first place and strike out on his own after finally landing a job he had long sought; but it is also fair to say that these years of itinerancy were important in maturing Confucius' thought and the personal qualities that made him so attractive to many. Opening to the unfamiliar and the unexpected has a way of stripping away the inessential and revealing ourselves to ourselves. Whatever agents of transformation were in play during his wanderings, at the end of his exile Confucius was sufficiently at home in his own skin to return to Lu.

His homecoming was probably prompted by an invitation from the government of Lu. He arrived home in 484 B.C.E., enjoying an even greater reputation than he had when he left. There was no lack of young men interested in apprenticing themselves to him. In part, his new status was due to the professional success of some of his older protégés who had left years earlier and proven themselves in the government bureaucracies. By now, Confucius was in his mid-60s and no longer so keen to be intimately and actively involved in politics. Nor were the rulers of Lu really so keen to accept his advice, despite the enticements to bring him home. In his later years, he occasionally consulted with kings and counselors but increasingly turned his energies towards educating his young followers. Tradition tells us that in these years he also devoted himself to editing the texts that became classics in later Confucianism, including the *Book of Songs*, the *Spring and Autumn Annals*, and the *Yi Jing,* the much revered book of divination we talked about in lecture two. These claims are doubtful, though, and may only reflect the later tradition's image of the man as a dedicated scholar doing what scholars do. Be that as it may, it is clear that during this period, his zeal for learning and teaching had not diminished in the least. The *Analects* record his incisive mind still at work, prodding his disciples to think for themselves and practice the hard, straight way that had become his hallmark.

In this way—learning and teaching, constantly striving for self-improvement—Confucius occupied himself until the end of his days. Although less absorbed with the realm of politics, he never withdrew completely from society to become a recluse, like other notable sages of his day. A man of the world throughout his life, he remained so up until his death. He died in 479 and was buried in the time-honored manner by his followers, who then entered a three-year mourning period, the traditional ritual observed following the death of a parent.

I mentioned at the beginning of our study of Confucius that some recent scholars have argued that Confucius was only a fictional character thought up by later Confucians just as Laozi was an invention of Daoist philosophers. I have often thought that if that were true, the fact hardly matters. "Confucius"—whether that name applies to a fictional character or an actual individual—was a superb embodiment of the Confucian worldview. In the final analysis, it was the *image* of Confucius—as portrayed in the *Analects* and the other sources—that succeeding generations of Chinese held up as their model of ideal humanity and not the historical Confucius, who may have been more or less consistent with the literary portrait of him. Upon our return, we will turn our attention to the teachings of Confucius, but we will never be far removed from the life of the one who, according to Chinese tradition, embodied virtue more than any other.

# Heaven and Earth
## Lecture 5

> Among our four figures, Confucius is the one who seems to have said the least about metaphysics; he was far more loquacious about human behavior than he was about the basic structure of reality. ... Confucius never denied the existence of spiritual beings, but neither did he make belief in them central to his view.

As with the study of Confucius's life, our investigation into his philosophy and spirituality relies principally on the *Analects*. For all of its brevity, the book is not easy to comprehend. It appears to be little more than a disjointed collection of proverbs and pieces of conversation. To make it accessible, we will look at the text in terms of its various themes. We begin by discussing the basic features and assumptions of Confucian thought, the metaphysics of his worldview.

Among our four figures, Confucius is the one who seems to have said the least about metaphysics. Confucius never denied the existence of spiritual beings, but neither did he make belief in them central to his view. Scattered throughout the *Analects* are references to the principal metaphysical concepts of ancient China. Confucius clearly thought that acknowledging the divine was essential to human welfare.

Like all Chinese of his day, Confucius accepted the ancient belief that reality comprised two worlds, the realm of heaven—*tiān*, the domain of gods, spirits, and ancestors—and the realm of earth—*di*, the sphere of humans and nature. The many gods and spirits of the universe were thought to be immediately available to human beings, and hence they could be consulted by means of divination and could even enter and possess individuals. Due to this interdependence, the well-being of everyone and everything in them rested on the harmonious relationship between the gods and humans, and preserving this harmony through rituals and sacrifices was one of the king's principal functions.

The Shang imagined *tiān* as a heavenly court that paralleled the royal court on earth. They called the high god **Shang Di**, the Supreme Emperor or the Supreme Ancestor, presiding over a court of lesser divinities, or *shen*, whom the Chinese turned to for help in matters of agriculture, hunting, military campaigns, health, and longevity. The relationships between the ancient Chinese and their gods were formal and rather businesslike. We find no evidence that individuals sought close, personal relationships with the gods, which would have encroached on the dignity of the divine.

The image of *tiān* as a polytheistic heavenly court persisted throughout the Zhōu era, but the idea of heaven became more ambiguous and acquired richer meanings. The Zhōu people initially used the names Shang Di and *tiān* interchangeably. By the time of Confucius, however, *tiān* had assumed the character of an overarching principle or force, somewhat akin to the Western idea of fate. *Tiān* also acquired a moral dimension—at first, mainly an interest in who the ruler was and how he treated his subjects, but by the Spring and Autumn Period, the Chinese believed the will of heaven concerned everyone. Interestingly, this attribution of moral preferences to the divine world was part of a larger process occurring in most of the major centers of civilization during the 1st millennium B.C.E., a period known as the **Axial Age**.

The Teaching Company Collection.

**Confucius was an eager and dedicated student. He says in one of the famous passages from the *Analects*, "At fifteen, I set my heart on learning."**

During the period called the Enlightenment, many intellectuals in Europe saw Confucius as a fellow rationalist who had articulated a sophisticated, agnostic ethical system. But this reading of the *Analects* neglects the formal, reserved way the Chinese have historically related to their gods and spirits. To advocate maintaining one's distance from the gods is nowhere near the same as professing agnosticism. Yet there is no denying that the role the gods played in his worldview was tangential. We will see that when he promoted ritual veneration of the deities, he did so not to benefit the gods but to evoke specific qualities in human beings. The conception of heaven was more central; he seemed to think of *tiān* as the cosmological reality to which humanity and the gods and spirits are all subject.

Confucius understood heaven as a dynamic, creative reality that gave and supported life on earth, the source of all things and of the processes of change. Although he sometimes described heaven as a kind of fate, it would be a mistake to think that Confucius was fatalistic. He certainly thought it was possible for human beings to resist the will of heaven. Heaven had certain powers but not absolute power. Confucius was unambiguous, though, in his belief that heaven was moral and wanted human beings to be good and that heaven's will for human beings was disclosed not by revealed commandments but in the lives and teachings of the virtuous sages of old. ∎

## Important Terms

**Axial Age**: The era of exceptional religious and philosophical creativity during the 1ˢᵗ millennium B.C.E. that gave rise to the world's major religions.

*di*: In Chinese religion, earth; the material realm.

**Shang Di**: The supreme god of the ancient Chinese.

*shen*: The minor deities of ancient Chinese religion.

*tiān*: In Chinese religion, heaven; the spiritual realm. It was sometimes conceived of as a force and sometimes as a being.

1. What do you think of the claim that Confucianism is a philosophy, not a religion? What makes a religion a religion?

# Heaven and Earth
## Lecture 5—Transcript

Confucius would probably be surprised to find us engaged in a study of his thought, since he did not consider himself a great thinker. He was far more comfortable calling himself a "learner." He once told his followers: "I used to go without food all day, without sleep all night, [in order] to think. No use, better to learn." He refused to claim originality for his ideas. "The Master said: I transmit rather than innovate. I trust in and love the ancient ways." Like many others through history, Confucius believed in a bygone golden age. He shared with other Chinese the belief that this brilliant period extended from the earliest dynasties down to founding of the Zhōu, some 500 years before his time. They regarded these golden days as a time in which virtuous rulers governed virtuous subjects, and high culture flourished.

Much of the lore about this age, as we have already discussed, was mythical. Yet Confucius took this belief seriously. His study of the past had convinced him that the China of his day was in turmoil precisely because its leaders had neglected the traditions and values of these earlier eras. What was desperately needed was to return China to its foundations, to the pristine practices and values on which it had been established. Discerning lessons from the past and implementing them in the present was necessary, he thought, to restore social harmony and well-being. Confucius would certainly have applauded our efforts to learn from our wise forebears, but he may have urged us to look past him to the sages of an even earlier era.

Needless to say, we shall disregard that suggestion. Notwithstanding his self-assessment, Confucius' interpretation of the past and his particular way of applying the received tradition to his own time attest to a keen intellect matched with a compassionate heart. One of his 20th century interpreters writes: "When I began to read Confucius I found him to be a prosaic and parochial moralizer. ... Later, I found him a thinker with profound insight and with an imaginative vision of [hu]man[ity] equal in its grandeur to any I know. He tells us things not being said elsewhere. ... He has a new lesson to teach." That's high praise to give to someone who considered himself only a conduit of tradition.

As with the study of Confucius, our investigation into his philosophy and spirituality relies principally on the *Analects*. It is hard to overestimate the importance of this small text for understanding not only Confucius but the last 2500 years of Chinese history as well. As one recent translator put it, "if a single book can be upheld as the common code of a whole people, it is perhaps ... *The Analects of Confucius*."

With little more than this single, brief text to comprehend, grasping the Confucian worldview might seem fairly easy, but that would be wrong. Understanding Confucian philosophy through the *Analects* is not a simple thing at all. As I've mentioned before, the book is not easy to read. It appears to be little more than a disjointed collection of proverbs and pieces of conversation. To present Confucius' ideas and practices in a more accessible way, we'll use a structure by which we can discuss the salient themes in his sayings. Of course, it is highly unlikely that Confucius himself would have presented his thought in this way. His style of teaching was much more informal, allowing specific situations to provide the occasion for a particular lesson, which was usually imparted in an exchange with his students. Since we don't have the opportunity for such casual conversations here, we will just have to settle for this rather un-Confucian approach to Confucius.

The framework that we will use is the one I outlined in the introductory talk for the course. We begin by discussing the basic features and assumptions of Confucian thought, the metaphysics of his worldview. Under this rubric, we explore what Confucius thought about the nature of reality, particularly the divine and its relationship to the human. Then, in the following two lectures, we examine the anthropological and ethical dimensions of the Sage's philosophy, his ideas about how we should act as individuals and as a society, and then conclude with a discussion of the disciplines of Confucian spirituality.

Among our four figures, Confucius is the one who seems to have said the least about metaphysics; he was far more loquacious about human behavior than he was about the basic structure of reality. He shared with the Buddha a reticence about the world of gods and spirits, but even the Buddha was more forthcoming about his understanding of the nature and character of reality. Like the Buddha, Confucius never denied the existence of spiritual beings, but neither did he make belief in them central to his view. In the *Analects*, a student recalled—with only slight exaggeration—that the Master did not speak of "mysteries, violence, rebellions, and gods."

The marginal role of god and the gods in the thought of Confucius and the Buddha has led many western observers to argue that their worldviews are better characterized as philosophies than religions. I have some sympathies with that argument, but ultimately I think it is based on unnecessarily narrow definitions of religion. As we shall see, both Confucius and the Buddha practiced and taught specific spiritual disciplines and held particular realities as sacred, both of which are elements that characterize religious worldviews. Although divine beings do not figure prominently in the thought of Confucius and the Buddha, we are justified in describing their thinking and practice as *both* philosophical *and* religious. When we reach the comparative portion of our course, we will have occasion to discuss these issues in further detail. For now, we need only observe the reluctance of Confucius to speak of the gods and spirits and note his general hesitancy to make metaphysical assertions.

But hesitancy does not mean silence in this case. Scattered throughout the *Analects* are references to the principal metaphysical concepts of ancient China. We will discuss these foundational ideas and then examine how they functioned in Confucius' thought. Although Confucius did not speculate or speak much about the world of gods and spirits, he clearly thought that acknowledging the divine in certain ways was essential to human welfare.

Like all Chinese of his day, Confucius accepted the ancient belief that reality comprised two worlds, the realm of Heaven and the realm of Earth. Heaven, or *tiān*, was the domain of gods, spirits, and ancestors; Earth, or *di*, was the sphere of humans and nature. One of the Chinese terms for the universe or cosmos was *tiāndi*, a simple compound of both words. As this compound suggests, Heaven and Earth could not be thought of apart from one another. They formed a holistic and symbiotic unity. Each one depended on the other. The western conception of the absolute transcendence of god, as exemplified in Søren Kierkegaard's famous claim that there is an "infinite qualitative difference" between god and humanity, was utterly foreign to the Chinese way of thinking. Heaven and Earth were permeable realms, and there was an intimate connection between them. The many gods and spirits of the universe were thought to be immediately available to human beings, and hence they could be consulted by means of divination and could even enter and possess individuals.

Due to the interdependence of Heaven and Earth, the well-being of everyone and everything in them rested on their harmonious relationship. Preserving this harmony was one of the king's principal functions. One of the earliest narratives of Chinese history states that the ruler's primary responsibility was "pacifying the multitude of spirits and putting in harmony the myriad of people," and if this was not done, "the spirits will be incensed against him and the people will revolt." Accordingly, the king was charged with performing the appropriate rituals and sacrifices to curry the favor of the divine figures whose good graces were essential to the well-being of the state and its citizens.

The idea of Heaven in Chinese philosophy and religion meant more than just the dwelling place of the divine beings, although it certainly included that. Originally, *tiān* simply meant the "sky," but over the centuries from the Shang dynasty down to Confucius' time, the idea of Heaven came to accumulate a rich variety of meanings. During the Shang, *tiān* appears to have been a generic term for the heavenly realm. The people of the Shang imagined this divine world as a heavenly court that paralleled the royal court on earth.

As the earthly king governed through a bureaucracy of nobles, counselors, and various other ministers of state, so the high god ruled heaven with his spiritual minions and assistants. The Shang people called the high god Shang Di, the Supreme Emperor or the Supreme Ancestor. Although he was never depicted by physical representations, Shang Di was imagined to preside over a court that included many lesser divinities, or *shen*, that controlled, or at least influenced, the powers of the natural and human worlds. These were the gods and spirits the Chinese turned to for help in matters of agriculture, hunting, military campaigns, health, and longevity. The high god would not be bothered for these trivial, mundane concerns. Unlike Shang Di, the lower gods were not universal and did not have broad powers; most were decidedly local, such as the town or village gods whose power extended only as far as the city limits, like the jurisdiction of a municipal magistrate.

In addition to the divine hierarchy, Heaven was also home to ancestors and ghosts. The ancestors—who were not sharply distinguished from the gods—were the deceased individuals who now existed in the spirit world. Ghosts were the spirits of the dead who had suffered an unfortunate or tragic death. They often caused misfortune to the living, particularly those who were involved in their deaths. The ancestors, on the other hand, were generally benevolent. Throughout Chinese history, the ancestors have been seen as having a continuing interest in the welfare of their earthly families. They were to be consulted on matters of family, and they needed to be honored with sacrifices and gifts. They were also believed to mediate with the higher gods, especially if they were ancestors of a powerful family such as that of the king. Confucius did not say much about the ancestors, although he thought it was necessary to revere them in ritual. He did, however, have a great deal to say about venerating the members of one's family who were still alive, especially one's parents. The virtue of filial piety, as we will see in our next discussion, was a cornerstone of his entire ethical outlook.

The relationships between the ancient Chinese and their gods were formal and rather business-like. The human interest in gods was delimited by what the god could do. We find no evidence to suggest that individuals sought friendships or close, personal relationships with the gods of the sort we shall see in the life of Jesus. A collection entitled the *Sayings of the State* reflects on China's golden age and comments on the relationship between divine beings and humans: In those days, according to this commentary, "the people, having their duties differentiated from those of the spirits, were *respectful and not unduly familiar*. Therefore the spirits conferred prosperous harvest upon them and the people offered things up out of gratitude. Natural calamities did not arrive, and there was an inexhaustible supply of what would be useful." An intimate relationship between an individual and a god would have been regarded as encroaching upon the dignity of the divine and a threat to the proper order of things. A human being would no more try to buddy up to a god than a peasant would try to strike up a friendship with the emperor.

For their part, the gods were also reserved in their involvements with humans. In the earliest part of Chinese history, the gods were not even concerned with the moral behavior of human beings. These gods did not give commandments or grant favors on the basis of how well humans treated each other, and the ancient Chinese did not interpret disasters or other misfortunes as the gods' retribution for immoral behavior. The divine-human relationship was simply a *quid pro quo* arrangement. In exchange for agreeable sacrifices and tribute, the gods would assist humans with commonplace things such as producing an abundant crop, gaining victory over one's enemies, healing illness, and living a long life with many descendants. This sacred economy bound together the divine and human worlds.

The image of a polytheistic heavenly court that prevailed during the Shang dynasty persisted into and throughout the Zhōu era even as other theological developments were taking place. During the Zhōu dynasty, the idea of Heaven became more ambiguous and acquired richer meanings than it had in previous periods. Unlike the Shang, the Zhōu people considered *tiān* a *personal* deity, that is, a divine being conceptualized in anthropomorphic terms, as Shang Di had been. In fact, the people of Zhōu initially used the names Shang Di and *tiān* interchangeably to refer to the highest god. Over time, however, the name *tiān* came to be used with much greater frequency and was viewed as less anthropomorphic and more impersonal than Shang Di. By impersonal, I mean that *tiān* assumed the character of an overarching principle or force, somewhat akin to the way westerners might think of fate. By the time of Confucius, *tiān* could mean both a supreme being conceived in personal terms and an impersonal, ultimate principle or power, although the latter meaning predominated.

The crucial difference between the Zhōu and the Shang concepts of the divine powers was not the question of personality, but of morality. As we have just observed, the Shang gods had little interest in how human beings behaved towards each other and did not make moral character a condition for granting favors. As long as the sacrifices were pleasing, the gods really couldn't care less if you were a nice person.

During the Zhōu era, however, *tiān* acquired a moral dimension. It is not completely clear just how far *tiān*'s moral interests initially extended, but it was evident that Heaven had an interest in who the ruler was and how he treated his subjects. At the very beginning of the Zhōu dynasty, you will recall, the concept of the Mandate of Heaven entered the Chinese lexicon, specifying that the ruler must govern morally for his reign to be legitimate. By the Spring and Autumn Period, the Chinese believed the will of Heaven concerned not only the ruler but everyone.

Interestingly, this attribution of moral preferences to the divine world was part of larger process occurring in most of the major centers of civilization during the first century B.C.E. During this period, which is known as the Axial Age, metaphysical conceptions such as god, rebirth, and the afterlife came to be closely associated with moral human behavior, a process known as ethicization. In ancient Iran, for example, the prophet Zoroaster taught that the individual's personal destiny in the life-to-come was predicated on whether or not one identified with the supreme god whose fundamental quality was absolute goodness. In ancient India, the belief in rebirth was connected to the principle of karma, which meant that one's status in the next life was determined by his or her moral actions in present existence.

Today, because we live on this side of the Axial Age, we usually take the moral character of ultimate reality for granted. Yet the moral quality now usually assumed in concepts of the gods has not always been a part of the way humans have thought about the divine. Morality and divinity were joined during a specific period of human history—the Axial Age.

Our overview of the evolving idea of Heaven has revealed a rich variety of theological conceptions circulating in ancient China at the time of Confucius. The ultimate reality could have been understood as a kind of polytheism, with a supreme being in charge of a retinue of lesser gods and spirits. It could have been thought of as a virtual monotheism, if one focused exclusively on *tiān* as an anthropomorphized entity. Or the ultimate reality might have been regarded as a rather abstract, impersonal force or cosmic principle, to which the gods, humanity, and nature were subject. Further complicating these conceptions was the issue of morality—whether the ultimate reality was considered basically moral or amoral. Now, let us turn to see how Confucius appropriated this rich tradition in his philosophy.

During the Enlightenment, when the teachings of Confucius became more widely known among scholars in the west, many intellectuals saw Confucius as a fellow rationalist who had articulated a sophisticated ethical system without the burden of belief in god. Weary of the animosity generated by centuries of religious sectarianism, these western thinkers wanted to develop a wholly secular, rational ethic, devoid of reference to god. They were able to point to certain passages in the *Analects* that suggested an agnosticism or theological skepticism on the part of Confucius. The most prominent of these passages was one in which a disciple asked the Sage about wisdom. The Master replied, "To apply oneself to the duties of humanity and, while revering the spirits and gods, *to keep away from them*—this may be called wisdom."

Many interpreters of Confucius, from the Enlightenment into the 21th century, construed this statement as evidence that he was at least agnostic, if not an outright atheist. Why else would Confucius counsel the wise to stay away from the gods? But this reading of the *Analects* neglects the formal, reserved way the Chinese have historically related to their gods and spirits. Confucius was merely encouraging the ancient practice of respecting the dignity of the divine. To advocate maintaining one's distance from the gods is nowhere near the same as professing agnosticism. Yet, there is no denying that Confucius said very little about the gods and spirits, and the role that they played in his worldview was only tangential. What we shall soon discover in our study is that Confucius considered the formal rituals associated with revering the gods to be intrinsically beneficial to human flourishing. When he promoted ritual veneration of the deities, he did so not to benefit the gods, but to evoke specific qualities in human beings.

While understanding the gods and spirits had this very peripheral function in his thinking, the conception of Heaven was more central, although it was still fairly reserved on that topic. When Confucius spoke of Heaven, he occasionally seemed close to thinking of Heaven as a supreme anthropomorphic being, as when he claimed that Heaven ordained his teachings or when he exclaimed, "The only one who understands me is perhaps Heaven!" Still, the impersonal sense of tiān overwhelmingly dominated Confucius' sayings. One of his students remembered that Confucius had said, "Life and death are the decree of Heaven; riches and reputation depend on Heaven." In this aphorism, Confucius seemed to understand Heaven as a kind of impersonal fate, as the source of events over which humans have no control.

Confucius seemed to think of *tiān* as the cosmological reality to which humanity and the gods and spirits are all subject. The gods, therefore, were not the ultimate or highest reality. In this sense, the Enlightenment interpreters of Confucius were correct, for he did not base his worldview on a god or the gods—at least not as divine beings are ordinarily understood in the west. Yet to regard Confucius' philosophy as completely devoid of a transcendent dimension is simply not true to Confucius.

Confucius understood Heaven as a dynamic, creative reality that gave and supported life on Earth. It was the source of all things and of the processes of change. Although he sometimes thought of Heaven as a kind of fate, it would be a mistake to think that Confucius was fatalistic, believing that *everything* that happens is inevitable or predestined. Confucius certainly thought, for example, that it was possible for human beings to resist the Will of Heaven. Heaven had certain powers, such as determining the span of one's existence, yet it did not have *absolute* power, in his view.

Confucius was unambiguous, though, in his belief that Heaven was moral and wanted human beings to be good. On this point, Confucius stood firmly with the view of *tiān* that was emergent in the Zhōu dynasty. Heaven's will for human beings was disclosed not by revealed commandments but in the lives and teachings of the virtuous sages of old, and now—he believed—in his own teaching. Furthermore, Confucius thought that Heaven not only *wanted* human goodness but had also endowed human beings with a nature that makes it possible for us to cultivate this goodness in ourselves. In this sense, Confucius believed humans could work as collaborators with Heaven, in a creative process of realizing our potential goodness and thereby fulfilling our purpose as human beings. When we turn to the anthropology and ethics of Confucius in our next talk, we will explore the nature of human goodness and the way in which it could be fully realized in life.

# Doing unto Others
## Lecture 6

> Confucius believed that attending to the concerns of this world took precedence over understanding the world beyond. But [this] does not suggest that Confucius was only concerned with this world. What it indicates is that attending to the concerns of earth is a prerequisite for comprehending heaven.

Confucius's preference to speak infrequently of heaven is remarkable, and it warrants closer scrutiny. In the *Analects*, a student asks Confucius how to serve the gods and the ancestors. He responds: "You are not able even to serve your fellow humans. How can you ask about the gods and spirits?" When the student asks about death, the Sage says, "You do not understand even life. How can you understand death?" In other words, we must begin with the things nearest to hand before we approach the things farther away. The ultimate reality is manifested through ordinary things; the higher is revealed through the lower.

Accordingly, Confucius recognized the sacred through humanity and saw humanity as sacred. As with his metaphysical views, Confucius was less than explicit about what he thought of human nature, but he indicated that he believed all persons shared a common nature: "By nature, people are close to one another; through practice, they drift far apart." Even barbarians could become civilized by the adoption of Chinese mores. Confucius did not say whether he considered human nature good or evil, but he clearly thought that it could be fashioned in good or evil ways. We could say that Confucius viewed humans as unfinished beings, whose life's work is to bring ourselves to completion.

Confucius thought that not only was perfect goodness a human possibility; it was also the will of heaven that we pursue it. Because perfection was the ideal, he helped his followers envision this objective and prescribed specific methods to achieve it—in particular, looking to China's legendary sages as their models.

All told, Confucius mentioned nearly two dozen traits of the morally perfect individual, including respectfulness, refinement, deference, simplicity, and sincerity. The most important among all of them was **ren**, or humaneness. The *Analects* never fully explains the concept of *ren*, but the word is written in Chinese by adding the number 2 to the basic character for "person"— implying that *ren* manifests in interpersonal relationships. Some alternative English translations for *ren* are kindness, benevolence, goodness, compassion, and nobility.

One of the clearest expressions of *ren* is Confucius's version of the Golden Rule: "What you do not wish for yourself, do not impose on others." By using our own likes and dislikes as clues, we may imagine what others desire or seek to avoid. Once we develop a basic sense of what others want and do not want, we must train ourselves to act on that knowledge in a compassionate way. Confucius recognized the barrier to this as what we might call schadenfreude— delight in others' failures—

Confucius's fundamental spiritual practice involved taking the past as the guide to, and the standard for, living in the present.

and thought it a major obstacle to realizing our full humanity. The full expression of *ren* is accomplished only through great discipline.

Confucius also used the language of love to help his followers understand *ren*, but to connect *ren* and the English word "love" might be misleading. *Ren* did not mean to love everyone equally. Since our parents have given us the priceless gift of life, he said we are obligated to love and care for them most of all—consistent with the Chinese traditions of **filial piety** and ancestor worship. In fact, Confucius thought that filiality was not only the most natural form of love but the very basis of all forms of loving. The person of noble humanity next extends love to the members of his or her immediate family, then to the extended family and to friends, to the village, the province, and on to the whole world, all with decreasing intensity.

> **In spite of the deeply troubled times in which he lived, Confucius had the audacity to believe that human beings were perfectible.**

Confucius discussed other characteristics of the perfected person throughout his teachings, often as character types, such as the sage, the good man, and the complete man, which were each associated with particular stations in society. The ideal type he stressed above all others was the *jūnzi*, the "gentleman" or "superior man." The *jūnzi* was not the highest ideal (that was the sage), but it was the ideal for those destined for a political career. The *jūnzi* had attained a noble character and superior status by hard work and self-cultivation. His hallmarks were humaneness, generosity, reciprocity, filiality, and wisdom—that is, being a good judge of character, possessing self-knowledge, and thinking for oneself. Finally, just as the *jūnzi* displays impartiality in his dealings with others, he practices equanimity with respect to all circumstances of his life.

As we noted before, some of Confucius's followers found this path a hard one to walk. Striving for goodness is a lifelong process, and in the end it may not be attained. Those who take the path of cultivating goodness must do so for its own sake and not for any other reason. ■

## Important Terms

**filial piety**: The practice of revering and honoring one's parents both during their lives and after their deaths. To Confucius, filiality was the root of all forms of love.

**jūnzi**: The gentleman; in Confucian thought, this character type is the ideal for a life of political service.

*ren*: Humaneness; in Conficianism, the chief virtue of the morally perfect individual.

1. How does Confucius's view of human beings as incomplete but perfectible compare with Western ideas of human nature, both modern and ancient?

2. Do you agree with Confucius that filial love is the root of all love? Why or why not?

# Doing unto Others
## Lecture 6—Transcript

Heaven was an important part of Confucius' understanding of the world, yet he had relatively little to say about it, a detail that helped support the modern west's early opinion that Confucius was unconcerned with a transcendent reality. That interpretation, however, ignored China's traditionally reserved way of relating to the divine world, as well as Confucius' own conviction that his teachings were sanctioned by divine authority. Nevertheless, Confucius' preference to speak infrequently of Heaven *is* remarkable, and it warrants closer scrutiny, especially as we move to discuss his anthropological and ethical viewpoints. As we'll see, Confucius' understanding of human beings helps illuminate why he did not feel compelled to make Heaven the subject of lengthy discourse.

A clue lies in an anecdote from the *Analects*. As the story goes, a student approached Confucius to ask how to serve the gods and the ancestors. The Master responded: "You are not able even to serve your fellow humans. How can you ask about the gods and spirits?" When the student went on to ask about death, the Master said, "You do not understand even life. How can you understand death?" As this exchange confirms, Confucius believed that attending to the concerns of *this* world took precedence over understanding the world beyond. But the story does not suggest that Confucius was *only* concerned with this world. What it indicates is that attending to the concerns of Earth is a *prerequisite* for comprehending Heaven. We must begin with the things nearest to hand before we approach the things farther away. He told his protégés, "I learned lower things and perceive higher things." Another translator renders the passage this way: "In my studies, I start from below and get through to what is up above." By devoting himself to understanding human affairs, Confucius came to know Heaven and believed others would as well.

Many early western interpreters failed to grasp this important aspect of Confucius' philosophy, and consequently they were unable to appreciate the sacred dimension in his thought. For Confucius, the ultimate reality is manifested through the most ordinary things; the higher is revealed through the lower; what is above comes through what is below; the transcendent saturates the immanent. Accordingly, Confucius recognized the sacred through humanity and saw humanity as sacred. To better appreciate the connection between the sacred and the human, we will devote today's discussion to exploring Confucius' rather complex views about human character and relationships.

In spite of the deeply troubled times in which he lived, Confucius had the audacity to believe that human beings were perfectible. Every person, he thought, has the capacity to become a sage, an individual of great compassion and wisdom. That was an astounding conviction when one considers that not much in Confucius' world could be invoked as evidence to support that belief. During the Spring and Autumn Period, one might have been more inclined to conclude that people were just no damn good and utterly unable to reform themselves. Confucius' faith in human possibility, however, was based not on what he *saw* in the China of his day, but on the *study* of great sages of the past and on his own self-awareness.

The focus of Confucius' understanding of human character was less on the way human beings *are* and more on the way he believed we *could be*. As with his metaphysical views, Confucius was less than explicit about what he thought of human nature. His disciple Zigong once complained, "The Master's cultural accomplishments—we get to hear about them, but the Master's ideas on human nature and the way of Heaven—we hardly get to hear them." But the Sage did say enough to indicate that he believed that all persons shared a common nature. "By nature," he said, "people are close to one another; through practice, they drift far apart." This maxim, by the way, was quoted and affirmed by UNESCO, the United Nations Educational, Scientific, and Cultural Organization, in its 1950 statement entitled "The Race Question." That document, which was drawn up largely in response to Nazi racial ideology, maintained that all human beings are fundamentally united as members of the same species and that putative racial differences are social fictions, not biological realities.

Confucius would agree. Even the people known to the Chinese as barbarians were not considered different by nature; they could always become civilized by the adoption of Chinese mores. Confucius thought human beings come into the world with the same raw material, but the ways we are socialized and conditioned, and the choices we make as individuals, shape that basic substance into divergent forms. Confucius did not offer an assessment or an analysis of our basic stuff. He did not say whether he considered human nature good or evil, but he clearly thought that it could be fashioned in good or evil ways. Humans are malleable creatures; our natures are such that we can become good, evil, and anything in between. We could say that Confucius viewed humans as unfinished beings, whose life-work was to bring ourselves to completion.

Although human character can be molded in any number of ways, for Confucius there was only one way worthy of pursuit: perfect goodness. The Master thought that not only was perfect goodness within the realm of human possibility; it was also the will of Heaven that we pursue it. The aspiration for moral excellence is, therefore, embedded in the fabric of the universe; moral goodness lies latent in our human nature and in the urging of Heaven itself. For Confucius, to become morally perfect was to attain human fulfillment. Perfect goodness functioned in Confucius' philosophy the way nibbana—or nirvana—functioned in the Buddha's teaching—as the person's ultimate completion. We become fully human when we live the most moral life we are capable of achieving.

Because perfection was the ideal, the Master helped his followers envision this objective and prescribed specific methods to achieve it. Since humans have a great responsibility in cultivating their moral character, we must be very careful about how we shape it. It is not surprising that for this reason Confucius directed his contemporaries to look to China's legendary sages as worthy models. In the ancient sages, persons aspiring to moral perfection have both a vision of the destination and a map for the journey.

Throughout the *Analects*, Confucius referred to a wide array of characteristics that he thought were part of the make-up of the morally perfect individual. All told, he must have mentioned nearly two dozen such traits, including respectfulness, refinement, deference, simplicity, and sincerity.

The most important among all of them was *ren*, or humaneness or humanity. Yet despite its centrality in Confucian thought, the *Analects* never fully explains the concept of *ren*. Confucius apparently regarded this quality as rather mysterious—perhaps even magical. Fortunately, Confucius did say enough for us to form an impressionistic sense of *ren*. A good place to begin is with the way the word is written in Chinese. In its ordinary sense, *ren* simply means person, and the Chinese character is two strokes that suggest the image of a human being: 人. As a technical term in Confucius' philosophy, ren is written by adding the number two to the basic character for person: 人二. This addition turns "human" into "humaneness" and implies that ren is a trait manifested in interpersonal relationships. Some of the alternative English translations such as kindness, benevolence, goodness, and compassion help highlight the relational dimension of this concept. The word "noble" is also apt because ren suggests the quality of an exalted character. Perhaps "noble humaneness" or "uncommon kindness" helps get us closer to Confucius' meaning.

Although the concept did not originate with him, Confucius was the first to make *ren* central to his philosophy. He understood *ren* to be the wellspring of all the virtues of the perfect person. To embody this quality in full measure was to attain perfect goodness. Rather than offer a clear and systematic description, Confucius referred to it obliquely by offering examples of persons who manifested it in their lives. Because he taught about it this way, it is not clear whether Confucius thought that *ren* was innate to human nature or an acquired characteristic. Either way, *ren* was a virtue to which one had to aspire, and human beings were endowed by Heaven with the capacity to cultivate and nurture it to full expression.

One of the clearest expressions of his understanding of humaneness came in a version of the Golden Rule: "What you do not wish for yourself, do not impose on others." For Confucius, this principle was based on *shu*, or reciprocity. Reciprocity is a way of judging what others may want or not want. The Master said: "The humane person, wanting to establish himself, helps others establish themselves, and wanting to be successful, helps others to be successful. Taking one's own feelings as a guide may be called the method of humaneness."

Simply by using our own likes and dislikes as clues, we may imagine what others desire or seek to avoid. We might call this practice empathy; the Buddha called it "seeing others as being like yourself."

The principle of reciprocity, of course, is only the first step on the way to full humaneness. Not only must we develop a basic sense of what others want and do not want, we must train ourselves to act on that knowledge in a compassionate way. Confucius thought the truly noble person actively promotes the success of others and celebrates their accomplishments. Those of us who have not yet fully realized the virtue of humaneness may recognize, if we are truthful with ourselves, that we often fall short of that standard. Not only do we find it difficult to wish for the success of others, we often take positive delight in their failures. Confucius believed that this *schadenfreude* was a major obstacle to realizing our full humanity and surmounting it required great effort. Indeed, the very difficulty of such an accomplishment is part of the reason the word noble is so pertinent in discussing the virtue of humaneness. The full expression of ren is accomplished only through great discipline.

Confucius also used the language of love to help his followers understand humaneness. For one student, he summarized this virtue by saying "It is to love others." But simply translating *ren* as love has many problems, not the least of which is the way love is so closely associated with romance in the western world. To connect *ren* and the English word love might be misleading if we do not understand the full context of Confucian teachings. The Sage did not believe that the humane person would—or even *should*—

love everyone equally. He thought that we should love those closest to us more than those farther away. Those who have assisted us the most are the ones most deserving of our love. Since our parents have given us the priceless gift of life, we are obligated to love and care for them most. The debt we owe them, in fact, is beyond measure and can never really be repaid. The only proper response is reverential love.

By affirming the priority of love of one's parents and family, Confucius stayed faithful to Chinese tradition. An old proverb declared that filial piety, the love and veneration of parents, is the first of virtues. In conversations with his protégés, Confucius offered examples of filial behavior. To the traditional duties of the filial child—to feed parents when they are alive, mourn them when they die, and sacrifice to them when the mourning period ends—Confucius added other precepts that went beyond conventional expectations and encouraged the cultivation of noble humaneness. For example, he urged his students to be gentle if they ever found it necessary to correct their parents. If parents resist respectful remonstration, the child must continue to be reverential and express no disobedience or resentment. One must always be patient with one's parents, no matter what.

Confucius thought that filiality was not only the most natural form of love; he also believed it was the very basis of *all* forms of loving. He said, "The noble person is concerned with the root; and if the root is firmly planted the Way grows. Filial piety and fraternal duty—surely these are the roots of humaneness." Family life, Confucius might say, is the classroom where we learn to love. Being a good son or daughter is the foundation for being a good person. If we cannot learn to love our parents, who have given us so much, how can we even hope to love others?

Although love for others begins in the family, it does not stop there. Love of family is the root, not the whole tree. From parents, the person of noble humanity next extends love to the members of his or her immediate family, then to the extended family and to friends, to the village, the province, and on to the whole world, all with decreasing intensity. Confucius did not suggest that we love *only* those near to us; but we should love those far away less than those close by. Confucius' form of "graded love," stands in tension with the more universal forms of compassion and love espoused by the Buddha and Jesus. It was also at odds with a school of thought known as Mohism, established by Chinese philosopher Mozi. When we come to the comparative portion of our course, we will return to this topic to examine these differences in more detail.

Noble humaneness, based on the principle of reciprocity and nourished by filial piety, was the essential ingredient of the virtuous life, the life well-lived. But it was not the only component of a life of superior character. As I mentioned earlier, Confucius discussed more than a few virtues throughout his teachings. Often he spoke of these other characteristics and aspirations in the context of explaining a particular ideal type. Although they were abstractions rather than historical individuals, these ideal persons functioned as saints do in other traditions, providing worthy models for imitation. Indeed, education in ancient China was largely a matter of training in emulation as much as acquiring knowledge from books.

For Confucius, there were several such ideal models. The highest ideal was the "sage." The sage represented the complete fulfillment of human potential, the person in whom humaneness has been perfected. Although, he believed that anyone was capable of becoming one, Confucius also admitted that he had never actually met a sage and had given up hope of ever doing so. He even disavowed the title of sage for himself. Confucius also mentioned the ideals of the "good man" and the "complete man," and often these were associated with particular stations in society.

By casting these terms in the male gender, I'm simply repeating the way Confucius thought about them; clearly, he prized patriarchical values in the family and the society, and when he discussed these ideals he plainly had men in mind. But in terms of the virtues that constitute these saintly persons, there is nothing intrinsically male or female about them.

We should bear this point in mind as we examine the ideal type he stressed above all others: the *jūnzi*, usually translated as the "gentleman" or "superior man." The *jūnzi* was not the highest ideal, but it was the ideal for those destined for a political career. Sometimes, *jūnzi* is translated as "scholar-official" in recognition of its association with government work. Gentleman is probably a better rendering if we bear in mind that is not to be taken as a generic term for all men, as when the word is written on public restroom doors. For Confucius, a gentleman was a specific kind of person, someone who, among other things, was courteous and honorable, as in the expression "a gentleman's agreement." A *jūnzi* was someone who had attained a noble character and superior status by hard work and self-cultivation. Confucius distinguished the *jūnzi* from the "small" or "petty man." The small person, in contrast to the gentleman, was self-centered, narrow-thinking, materialistic, and undisciplined.

Based on his study of earlier Chinese culture, Confucius maintained that there were certain qualities or traits that were hallmarks of the gentleman. Humaneness, generosity, reciprocity, and filiality were fundamental, of course. But there were others. The gentleman was not only compassionate, but wise. By wisdom, Confucius meant that one knew what was right and what was wrong; one was a good judge of character and possessed self-knowledge. He told his followers: "When you understand something, to recognize that you understand it; but when you do not understand something, to recognize that you do not understand it—that is wisdom."

The quality of wisdom also meant that one thought for oneself and made independent judgments. A gentleman did not blindly follow others or show partiality: "The Master said: The gentleman, in his attitude toward all under heaven, neither favors anyone nor disfavors anyone. He keeps close to whoever is righteous."

Just as the gentleman displayed impartiality in his dealings with others, he practiced equanimity with respect to all circumstances of his life. Confucius greatly admired one of his protégés for the way he was able to live in near-poverty without ever complaining or allowing his situation to dictate his disposition. The disciple lived in small hut and had only a bowl of rice to eat and a ladle of water to drink each day. Yet such wretched conditions never ruined his happiness.

For Confucius, matters such as living circumstances, wealth, and fame were determined by Heaven, not by the individual. We don't have control over these situations, but we can choose to respond to those circumstances with dignity and nobility.

The quality of equanimity pertained also to the opinions of others. In the very first passage of the *Analects*, Confucius defined this quality according to his usual high standards: "not to be resentful at others' failure to appreciate one—surely that is to be a true gentleman." In the same section he took this trait to near the saintly level: "it is not the failure of others to appreciate your abilities that should trouble you, but rather your failure to appreciate theirs." To develop such an attitude obviously entails a radical reorientation of the way most of us, I dare say, experience life. Yet, if we can imagine such a possibility, consider the sense of freedom one would have without having to be so self-absorbed. No wonder Confucius characterized the gentleman as "self-assured and relaxed."

As we noted before, some his followers found this path a hard one to walk. Discussing the Confucian way with another disciple,

> Master Zeng said, "A Gentleman must be strong and resolute, for his burden is heavy and the road is long. He takes benevolence as his burden. Is that not heavy? Only with death does the road come to an end. Is that not long?

The discipline of striving for goodness is a life-long process, and in the end it may not be attained. A gatekeeper who had heard of the reputation of Confucius asked one his disciples: "Is that the [Kong] who keeps working towards a goal the realization of which he knows to be hopeless?" With no assurance of reward or success, Confucius did ensure that those who took the path of cultivating goodness did so for its own sake and not for any other reason. Confucius said, "The man of humanity first of all considers what is difficult in the task and then thinks of success. Such a man may be called humane."

Today, we have focused on the fundamental aspects of the teachings of Confucius. We have observed how his philosophy is centrally concerned with human character and the importance of shaping it in particular ways that express humaneness, a quality that he believed fulfilled our potential as individual human beings. The responsibility for this development lay, of course, with the individual him- or herself. The road was long and difficult, but worth the effort. Taking the hard way was beneficial to oneself and to society at large. In our next lecture, we'll examine how the individual's self-refinement and virtue helped bring harmony and security to the world.

# How to Rule a Kingdom
## Lecture 7

Confucian political philosophy shared some things with Legalism and Daoism but differed from them in several important ways. Like the Daoists, Confucius believed the solution to China's problems lay in the rulers' pursuit of the virtuous life. But Confucius had a different idea about how virtue was to be cultivated.

Among our four sages, Confucius had perhaps the greatest conviction about the importance of the political dimension of human existence. Despite his own meager achievements in the political realm, from his early adulthood until the end of his life, Confucius thought about, taught about, and trained his protégés in the art of governing.

Confucianism was only one of many Chinese philosophies in the latter half of the 1st millennium B.C.E. to offer opinions on governance. **Legalism** sought to make the ruler's authority more absolute. It was the ancient Chinese version of a political philosophy manifested throughout history in a variety of forms and championed by the likes of Machiavelli and Mao Zedong. It regards the interests of the state as paramount and protects those interests through terror and violence. On the opposite end of the spectrum, **Daoism** contended that overregulation and governmental heavy-handedness, along with the self-centeredness of the ruling class, were the real sources of China's malaise. Daoist philosophers contended that those at the top of the social hierarchy were obliged to curtail their extravagance and live simply. The early Daoists believed that the world would be an infinitely better place if the rulers would simply stay out of other people's lives.

Like the Daoists, Confucius believed the solution to China's problems lay in the rulers' pursuit of the virtuous life. But the Daoists thought virtue came naturally by following the way of nature, whereas Confucius believed it had to be nurtured with ritual and decorum. Confucius shared Legalism's appreciation for order and hierarchy, but he disdained legislation and the use of fear as a tactic to enforce social harmony. In contrast to both schools, Confucius believed governments should exist to promote the moral well-being of all citizens and facilitate each person's pursuit of completeness. Confucius's sage-kings and gentleman-officials would rule their subjects primarily through instruction and example rather than legislation and enforcement.

The ancient Chinese always saw laws as human products, subject to human flaws, and Confucius was particularly sensitive to the potential deficiency of human legal systems. He preferred to allow morally qualified persons to judge what is right or wrong in particular cases while longing for the day when litigation would not be necessary. But most importantly, Confucius resisted rule by laws that appeal to fear, not to the better part of our natures. Virtue, rather than law, was the Confucian ideal.

**Virtue, rather than law, was the Confucian ideal.**

The word virtue is the usual English translation for the Chinese term *de*. Not only was *de* thought to be virtue; it was also regarded as a force or power through which the virtuous could transform others. Witnessing *de* evoked *bao*, the natural wish to respond to a kindness with kindness. Thus virtue in a ruler could transform the whole state.

The Confucian view of society did suggest a rather passive role for the masses. Confucius believed in a government for the people but not by the people. Commoners were also expected to participate in the well-being of society by living virtuous lives. Appropriate behavior in society followed the same patterns and values as life in the family. Practicing filiality was well within everyone's ability and strengthened not only the family but the world at large. Thus moral charisma could flow upward as well as down.

If the most important component for ruling a kingdom was the ruler's personal moral character, then the next ingredient was the practice of ritual, or *li*. In the Shang and early Zhōu dynasties, ritual was understood primarily as the performance of sacrifice and divination; simply going through the motions was sufficient. Later, *li* came to include the sense of reverence and sincerity on the part of the ritual's participants. Confucius took this a step further by connecting it with the quality of humaneness: Ritual was an act performed not primarily to please divine beings but to shape the moral character of the participants and observers. Furthermore, Confucius expanded *li* to include manners and etiquette.

Proper performance of ritual evoked humaneness through requiring the performer's knowledge, discipline, and self-restraint as well as by inducing his reverence, gratitude, and humility. Rituals also created a sense of the interconnectedness of humanity and divinity, providing a reminder that one was part of a vast web of interdependent relationships involving heaven, earth, and humanity. Confucius was confident that returning to the serious practice of the ancient rites would restore harmony among the people more surely than the enactment and enforcement of laws. ■

## Important Terms

*bao*: The impulse to respond to kindness with kindness.

**Daoism**: An ancient Chinese school of thought that stressed the naturalness of virtue and the value of living simply.

*de*: Virtue; also, moral charisma.

**Legalism**: An ancient Chinese school of thought that favored absolutism and the welfare of the state above the welfare of the people.

*li*: The practice of ritual; according to Confucius, this also encompasses etiquette.

## Questions to Consider

1. How do you measure virtue in your leaders? Which foibles or flaws are forgivable, and which are beyond the pale? How do these character traits relate to good (or bad) governance?

2. In your own faith tradition or philosophical practice, how important is your state of mind or heart when approaching a ritual? Must one always be fully invested, or is there a perceived value in "going through the motions"?

# How to Rule a Kingdom
## Lecture 7—Transcript

Confucius, the Buddha, Jesus, and Muhammad all had different relationships with the political dimension of human experience, and each had a different outlook on its importance in the grand of scheme of things. Of the four, only the Buddha was born into the ruling class. He was groomed to become head of state, but an epiphany as young man suddenly convinced him to renounce his right to rule and pursue a life of greater significance than what he thought politics could offer.

In his teachings, the Buddha had relatively little to say about political affairs, because the pursuit of human fulfillment was an individual quest that could be achieved irrespective of the political situation. Like the Buddha, Jesus seemed to attach little significance to matters of human governance; he preached about a new order centered in god that would overcome and supplant human rule, and he made a point of breaking conventional social regulations to dramatize his message. Ultimately, that proclamation led to his being charged with sedition, for which he was tried and executed.

In the Prophet Muhammad's early life, he apparently cared little about government, for there was little government to speak of in Arabia 1400 years ago, but he had a keen interest in the principles of fairness and justice, as did Jesus. As the Muslim community grew, Muhammad necessarily had to attend to political concerns, and he eventually assumed the civic and military leadership of the Arabian city of Madinah. Many of the revelations he received were centrally concerned with matters of politics, law, and governance. Confucius' thought was not based on revelation and he never had same the leadership responsibilities as the Prophet, but his conviction about the importance of the political dimension may have exceeded even that of Muhammad.

Politics probably mattered more to Confucius than to any of the other three. From his early adulthood until the end of his life, Confucius thought about, taught about, and trained his protégés in the art of governing. Confucius aspired to hold a major office to be in a position to implement his ideas on governance, but he was unable to hold such a position. Yet despite what he considered the failure of his political career, almost all of his students sought him as a teacher to help them secure positions as government officials.

There is no wonder why Confucius devoted so much attention to political matters. In the late Zhōu period, governance was the main issue of the day. The dynasty's early political and social stability had dissolved as the smaller kingdoms that had once been loyal to the Zhōu commenced fighting among themselves for supreme power. The escalating warfare took its toll domestically as rulers increasingly became more interested in self-aggrandizement than in tending to the needs of their subjects. The suffering was massive.

Confucius was only one of many Chinese philosophers in the latter half of the first millennium B.C.E. to offer opinions on how to address this dire situation. One school of thought, which came to prominence in the Qin dynasty, sought to make the ruler's authority more absolute. The School of Law, or Legalism as it came to be called, argued that the head of state must maintain an aura of authority and mystery to command the obedience of the people. The ruler was charged with keeping order within the kingdom to further the interests of the state. He was to maintain stability by promulgating clear and explicit laws that were to be enforced swiftly and surely. Punishments had to be severe to serve as deterrents to further misconduct. Legalism was the ancient Chinese version of a political philosophy manifested throughout history in a variety of forms and championed by the likes of Machiavelli and Mao Zedong. In essence, this approach regards the interests of the state as paramount and protects those interests by instilling fear in the hearts of those who are perceived to threaten them. It relies on violence and the threat of violence to motivate people to obey the law.

Another contemporary school encouraged a political tack the opposite of Legalism. Daoism contended that over-regulation and governmental heavy-handedness, along with the self-centeredness of the ruling class, was the real source of China's malaise.

According to the *Daodejing,* the classic text of this tradition,

> When rulers take grain so that they may feast,
> Their people become hungry;
> When rulers take action to serve their own interests,
> Their people become rebellious;
> When rulers take lives so that their own lives are maintained,
> Their people no longer fear death.
> When people act without regard for their own lives
> They overcome those who value only their own lives.

Since the suffering of the masses was rooted in the rulers' greed and callous disregard for others, the Daoist philosophers contended that those at the top of the social hierarchy were obliged to curtail their extravagance and live simply. "When it comes to serving Heaven or ruling the people," said the *Daodejing*, "there is no virtue as good as frugality." The early Daoists believed that the world would be an infinitely better place, if the rulers would simply stay out of other people's lives.

Confucian political philosophy shared some things with Legalism and Daoism but differed from them in several important ways. Like the Daoists, Confucius believed the solution to China's problems lay in the rulers' pursuit of the virtuous life. But Confucius had a different idea about how virtue was to be cultivated. The Daoists thought virtue came naturally by following the way of nature; Confucius believed it had to be nurtured with ritual and decorum. Confucius shared Legalism's appreciation for order and hierarchy, especially when compared to Daoism's more anarchistic predilections. But he greatly disdained legislation and the use of fear as a tactic to enforce social harmony. Confucius also had a different understanding of the purpose of government from both Legalism and Daoism. The Legalists subordinated the interests of persons to that of the state; individuals were expected to serve the state. The Daoists regarded government as a necessary evil and looked forward to the day when governments as such could be eliminated all together, because everyone lived in accord with the way of nature.

In distinction to both schools, Confucius believed governments should exist to promote the moral well-being of all citizens. That view of politics derived directly from his anthropological perspective. Since the purpose of human existence is to manifest our humaneness to the fullest, governments ought to facilitate progress toward that end. Confucius had no desire to abolish government or to intensify its power by making the state an end in itself. He never advocated changing the basic structure of the way China was ruled. The idea of a democracy or a republic was completely alien to his mind. He fully accepted the notion that countries had to be administered by trained and qualified specialists—trained and qualified not in economics or jurisprudence or military science but in humaneness and the rituals that nurture it. He imagined a kingdom governed by a sovereign who was a sage and officials who were gentlemen.

Confucius once said: "Good government consists in the ruler being a ruler, the minister being a minister, the father being a father, and the son being a son." Not only does this statement underscore Confucius' belief in the necessity of clearly established hierarchies; it also highlights his conviction that each individual had to live up to the role to which he or she has been assigned by Heaven. A prince had to be a prince: that is to say, a prince had to take his responsibility seriously and discharge it to the best of his ability. Perhaps that sounds trite. But remember, Confucius lived at time when these responsibilities were *not* being accepted by those who were charged with them. To take these responsibilities seriously, for Confucius, meant to keep paramount the welfare of the people and to suppress the temptation to seek personal gain through one's office. What a revolutionary idea!

These sage-kings and gentleman-officials would rule their subjects primarily through instruction and example rather than legislation and enforcement. In general, Confucius was suspicious of laws. The Chinese never believed that laws were handed down by a god, like Yahweh giving the Ten Commandments to Moses or Muhammad receiving revelations from the angel Gabriel. The ancient Chinese always saw the regulations governing society as human products, subject to human flaws. Confucius was particularly sensitive to the potential deficiency of human legal systems. He did not think laws could be written to cover every conceivable situation. He preferred to allow morally qualified persons judge what is right or wrong in particular cases. He was also fearful that the production of laws would increase litigation, and he longed for the day when litigation would not be necessary. But most importantly, Confucius resisted rule by law because it did not appeal to the better part of our natures. If laws work to maintain order in society, he thought, it is because people fear the repercussions of breaking them. And fear is not a good basis for establishing social harmony or personal well-being. *Angst isst die Seele auf*, the Germans say. Fear eats up the soul.

The Master said: "If you govern them with decrees and regulate them with punishments, the people will evade them but will have no sense of conscience. If you govern them with virtue and regulate them with rituals, they will have a sense of conscience and will flock to you." Virtue rather than law was the Confucian ideal. Only virtue can evoke what is best in persons and allow society to flourish.

But what did Confucius mean by ruling with virtue? In part, it meant for the ruler and the ruling class to be moral examples for their subjects. It meant that the rulers would instruct their citizens on moral conduct through schools and the promotion of study. But most of all, rule by virtue consisted in a force generated by a virtuous superior that would arouse virtuous conduct in subordinates. To grasp this fascinating idea, we need to understand the Chinese concept of virtue.

**The Power of Virtue**

The word virtue is the usual English translation for the Chinese term *de*. The Daoist classic I mentioned a few moments ago has the word in its title, the *Daodejing*, which is often rendered as the "Classic of the Way and the Power." That translation gets us a little closer to the ancient Chinese understanding of *de*. Not only was *de* thought to be a quality or an aspiration, as suggested by the word virtue; it was also regarded as a force or power, as suggested by the title of the Daoist classic. Those who sought to live virtuous lives, and who consistently performed acts of kindness and generosity accumulated within themselves a powerful moral presence or charisma. Virtuous power was generated by an individual's inner disposition or attitude. That moral energy dwelling within the person of high virtue could mysteriously—and I want to say almost magically and effortlessly—transform others in wholesome ways. Those who benefited from or witnessed the acts of virtuous persons were believed to feel a deep indebtedness and would want to respond in like manner. The Chinese called this desire *bao*, the natural wish to respond to a kindness with kindness. Thus, virtuous acts encourage virtue in others. You will remember some of the legends about Confucius' appointment to the office of Minister of Crime and how almost immediately there was a sudden outbreak of morality throughout the state of Lu. Those stories illustrated the charismatic force of virtue as understood by the ancient Chinese.

This conception helps us to see why moral self-cultivation was essential to the ruler and his ministers. The mysterious power of virtuous rulers could do what laws and police could not: to make others *want* to do what was right. Confucius knew very well that it was impractical and ultimately counterproductive to have the police stationed at every street corner to make sure the populace behaved. The power of virtue, on the other hand, is less obvious but far more effective. "The gentleman's moral character is wind," Confucius said in a metaphor that became famous in Chinese literature, "and the small man's moral character is grass. When the wind blows, the grass must surely bend." The power of transformative virtue was so great, that the use of physical force would become unnecessary. In advising a magistrate, the Master said: "If one's character is rectified, then things will get done without orders being issued; but if one's character is not rectified, then although orders are issued they are not followed." A hundred years of moral rule, he predicted, could completely eliminate killing within a realm.

### The Role of the People

The Confucian view of society did suggest a rather passive role for the masses. The ordinary people were to be influenced and guided but not consulted about matters of state. Confucius believed in a government "for the people" but not "by the people." Yet, it was essential that rulers enjoy the confidence of their subjects. The Master said: "If the people do not trust you, you have nothing to stand on." In the early Zhōu, rulers could count on the trust of the governed by invoking the Mandate of Heaven. But in the days of Confucius, such a claim would hold little water if not supported by the ruler's moral character; the governor had to earn the confidence of the governed. Without that basic faith, the ruler could not exert the moral suasion vital to good governance.

But the role of the ordinary folk was more than simply being the passive recipients of the power of virtue, streaming down from on high. Commoners were also expected to participate in the well-being of society by living virtuous lives. When someone asked Confucius why he was not involved in government, he indicated that one could serve the purpose of government without holding an office. He said, "Just by being a dutiful son and an honorable brother, a man can influence government. By following virtue a man is, in fact, taking part in government."

The Chinese have long regarded society as a great extended family, with the ruler as *paterfamilias* and the people as his children. Appropriate behavior in society followed the same patterns and values of life in the family. I doubt that Confucius believed that everyone could to follow his path to perfect goodness. Even his highly motivated protégés found it hard going at times. But practicing filiality—the love and respect for one's parents—was well within everyone's ability and strengthened not only the family but the world at large.

Thus, the direction of moral charisma was not only from the top down. Confucius believed that social superiors could be influenced by their subordinates, just as children could positively influence their parents. This is one reason why he encouraged his followers to take government positions, where they would be situated both to influence the lower classes as well as the ruler and his court. For Confucius, the personal moral character of all citizens reverberates throughout a society. The goodness of the individual makes a difference in the world.

*Li*

If the most important component for ruling a kingdom was the ruler's personal moral character, then the next ingredient was the practice of ritual.

Proper observance of ritual, Confucius thought, was absolutely essential to the welfare of the State. He said: "If a ruler understands the rites at the altars of Heaven and Earth and comprehends the meaning of the ancestral sacrifices, then ruling his kingdom would be easy as looking at the palm of his hand"

I suspect the importance placed on ritual in government will strike many modern persons as a bit odd. The secularized modern world has a hard time appreciating the role of ceremony in traditional cultures and might especially find it difficult to grasp its function in matters of state. But as moderns, we have not completely lost touch with the value of state rituals. We still inaugurate our leaders and conduct state funerals when they die. Visiting dignitaries are welcomed by ceremonies and honored with formal state dinners. The signings of treaties are conducted under ceremonial auspices. But these occasions are mere vestiges of times when ritual was far more central to the lives of individuals and societies. In the Han Dynasty, the Chinese government even had a Board of Rites, which functioned alongside the Boards of Revenue, War, and Public Works. Imagine a Secretary of Ceremony in the cabinet of the President of the United States!

Ritual, or *li* to use the indigenous term, had always been important in Chinese government, but Confucius gave it new significance. In the Shang and early Zhōu dynasties, emperors sacrificed to the gods and ancestors and employed divination to maintain harmony between Heaven and Earth. Ritual was understood primarily as the performance of these acts. Simply going through the prescribed motions was sufficient to make the ritual do what it was intended to do. Nearer to the time of Confucius, however, the idea of *li* came to include the sense of reverence and sincerity on the part of the ritual's participants. The sacrifice had to be enacted in the proper spirit lest it be ineffective and displeasing to the gods and ancestors it intended to honor. Confucius took this concern with the interior dimension of ceremony a step further by connecting it with the quality of humaneness. As we learned earlier, for Confucius, ritual was an act performed not primarily to please divine beings but to shape the moral character of the participants and observers. I suspect that even if Confucius did not truly believe in gods and spirits, he would have still thought that sacrifices and rituals were immensely beneficial activities.

Furthermore, Confucius expanded the meaning of *li* to include not only what we ordinarily think of as ceremony, such as sacrifices and state funerals, but also the ritualized forms of everyday behavior, what we would call manners and etiquette. When we study the spiritual disciplines of Confucianism in our next talk, we will have an opportunity to discuss li in this sense. But to prepare for that discussion, let's explore for a few moments how Confucius understood li as public ritual rather than private conduct.

The ceremonies performed on state occasions were elaborate events. They required extensive study before they could be performed. These rituals often required many persons to be directly involved with the ceremony. There were not only the specialists who conducted the rites but also musicians, dancers, and actors who performed for the pleasure of the audience, which consisted of both human and divine beings. If you were fortunate enough to observe the opening and closing ceremonies of the 2008 Summer Olympics in Beijing, you had a taste of the traditional Chinese love of pageantry as well as the colossal forethought and coordination required for such grand occasions. Of course, the state rituals of ancient China were nowhere near the magnitude of the Olympic ceremonies; but both the ancient state rituals and this modern instance were informed by the same seriousness and attention to detail.

Unlike the rituals at the Beijing Olympics—but very much like the Games in ancient Greece—the gods were invited to attend the state functions of ancient China. They were offered food, but humans were also allowed to partake. The offerings were usually animals publicly sacrificed for the occasion and cooked or burnt whole. The most common victims were oxen, pigs, and sheep. A ritual that included one of each species was especially pleasing to the gods. Sometimes the spirits were offered gifts of silk and jade or rice and millet. But more important than the gifts themselves was the reverential and gracious attitude with which they were offered. According to the *Book of Songs*, the spirits rewarded with a long life those who sacrificed with the correct frame of mind.

There were many aspects to the rituals that Confucius saw as evoking and refining the sense of humaneness. The study to perform these rituals served as a kind of discipline and self-restraint and provided knowledge about the meaning of the ritual itself, which Confucius believed embodied the mysteries of Heaven. Beyond this mystical dimension, the rituals had more mundane elements that contributed to moral development. They induced certain emotions and moods, such reverence, gratitude, and humility. They promoted a spirit of cooperation among people and instilled a sense of the importance of subordinating personal needs and desires to the social endeavor. Rituals required concentration and attention to detail. They created a sense of the interconnectedness of humanity and divinity, providing a reminder that one was part of a vast web of interdependent relationships involving Heaven, Earth, and Humanity.

Confucius was confident that returning to the serious practice of the ancient rites would restore harmony among the people more surely than the enactment and enforcement of laws. By simply attending to their ancient charge to perform state rituals, and conducting them with sincerity and the proper frame of mind, the rulers would effect a great change among the people. The past would be honored and the spirits of all persons would be lifted. Life would be good.

# What a Sage Does
## Lecture 8

**Confucius thought that becoming a sage was within the grasp of everyone. But he never said it would be easy. ... At most, those on the way—or the rare individual who reached the destination—could enjoy the satisfaction of knowing that they had lifted themselves above the common lot and pursued the purpose for which humanity had been intended.**

We have been looking at the conceptual dimensions of Confucius's philosophy, but in fact the Sage intended his teachings to be implemented and practiced, not merely pondered and evaluated. We turn now to Confucian spiritual discipline, the exercises and activities he promoted as steps along the path toward human fulfillment, however that might be understood.

We should not think of "discipline" in the sense of "punishment," although some spiritual disciplines can be hard to bear, and some can serve a corrective function. Spiritual disciplines are not imposed but voluntary. Motivation must come from within. The nature of the spiritual path (or *dao* in Confucian terms), furthermore, is such that one is destined to fail before one succeeds. Failure, in fact, is essential to following any spiritual path. Failure is required because the real strength of spirit is achieved when one has to find the gumption to get on the straight path yet again. In other words, it is the practice that makes perfect.

Confucian spiritual discipline is best understood in terms of the impediments to living a virtuous life. Foremost is self-centeredness, which Confucius thought carried destructive consequences for others as well as oneself because humaneness is a virtue manifested in interpersonal relationships. Ignorance is another obstruction to humaneness; it might cause us to act rashly, to resort to violence, to speak an unkind word, or to neglect the humanity that connects us to one another. The practices of Confucian spirituality functioned to disable these obstacles and to train individuals in more wholesome ways.

As far as we know, Confucius never provided his apprentices with a step-by-step program for attaining moral perfection, but certain themes recur throughout the *Analects*. The fundamental practices endorsed by Confucius, and many other great teachers throughout history, focus on restraining desires. Confucius admonished his students to live simply, without ostentation or luxury. You will not find Confucius promoting hair shirts or self-flagellation, but he did think that a little discomfort kept the mind attentive to itself and sensitive to the wider world.

Confucius also promoted self-awareness through introspection, which he called **quiet sitting**. The purpose of such times was not to commune with the divine but to serve as opportunities for critical self-examination and

**Especially fond of music, Confucius often sang and played the *qin* with his followers.**

refining the faculty of **keen discernment**—forestalling reflexive actions to obtain a clearer understanding of one's limitations and abilities and to fine-tune one's listening and speaking skills. Without the self-awareness nurtured in introspection, thought Confucius, one is not fit to serve in government.

Where other great teachers may have called for a radical disregard for the things of this world, Confucius urged a radical engagement with them. Attending to such things as clothing, food, and even posture gave expression to one's respect for the social fabric and helped foster a greater awareness of the sacred dimension within all things. Confucius thought the whole of life ought to be conducted as a grand ritual. In all interpersonal relationships, human beings ought to comport themselves with the same poise and decorum appropriate to a sacred ceremony. Observing good manners means to act in a clearly prescribed way that is considerate of the feelings of others, and—this is the important part—to do so whether you feel like it or not. Confucius thought that continual practice of mannerly acts could engender sincere feelings in the one who performs them. You may not feel particularly humble, but after several thousand bows and prostrations, feelings of genuine humility begin to surface. As character is shaped by behavior, the performance of humane acts becomes natural and spontaneous.

A sophisticated enjoyment of music, poetry, and dance was also an important dimension of Confucian spirituality. Confucius thought that the cultured arts had the capacity to awaken and refine moral sensitivities. The *Analects* does not tell us exactly what it was about music that appealed to Confucius. Perhaps he valued music's ability to express and arouse moods and feelings appropriate for encouraging humaneness. We can also imagine how musical harmonies and coordinated dances would have reminded Confucius of the ideal of harmony between heaven and earth, ruler and subject, husband and wife. But Confucius also feared that music and dance could debase and disrupt humanity, particularly by inciting lust. Confucius therefore believed it was morally necessary to apply thoughtful control over the kinds of entertainments one attends.

In a more general sense, Confucius was concerned about the choices we make about our environment that might have an impact on our character. That concern extended to the people with whom we are friends: Those aspiring to be gentlemen should not enter the domain of someone who continually acted in an immoral way.

Confucian spirituality was nothing if not comprehensive. It involved disciplined attention to all aspects of life and concerned the person as an individual and the individual within a nexus of relationships. It sought to bring humanity to completion and harmony between heaven and earth. ■

## Important Terms

*dao*: The Chinese term for "path" or "way," as in a spiritual discipline.

**keen discernment**: The Confucian term for forestalling reflexive actions to obtain a clearer understanding of one's limitations and abilities.

**quiet sitting**: The Confucian term for introspection or meditative practice.

## Questions to Consider

1.  How comfortable are you with the idea of failure as a prerequisite to success on a spiritual path?

2.  What are your personal or cultural daily rituals, and how do they help or hinder your own spiritual development?

# What a Sage Does
## Lecture 8—Transcript

Confucius thought that becoming a sage was within the grasp of everyone. But he never said it would be easy. The path was long and hard, and there was no guarantee that one who aspired would in fact become a sage or even a gentleman. Confucius could not even promise there would be happiness at the end of the long road. At most, those on the way—or the rare individual who reached the destination—could enjoy the satisfaction of knowing that they had lifted themselves above the common lot and pursued the purpose for which humanity had been intended. Confucius knew the way was difficult and had to be traversed one step at a time. There were no shortcuts to humaneness.

We have spent much of our time up to this point looking at the conceptual dimensions of Confucius' philosophy, his ideas about Heaven and virtue and politics. That focus should not obscure the fact that he intended his teachings to be implemented and practiced, not merely pondered and evaluated. As we shall do for each of the other figures, we turn now to give consideration to the aspect of his teaching I have categorized as spiritual discipline. Under this rubric, I include those exercises and activities that these teachers promoted as ways of nudging their followers closer to what they considered human fulfillment, however that might be understood. Each of our four figures regarded these practical disciplines as essential to their teachings. These practices were not optional activities for those interested in extra credit but the very means by which each teacher sought to share his vision with others. In a very meaningful sense, therefore, we cannot completely appreciate what any one of them taught until we have actually taken the path he set forth and walked it to the end.

My choice of that metaphor, by the way, is deliberate. Confucius, the Buddha, Jesus, and Muhammad each referred to his spiritual practice as "the way" or "the path." Muhammad spoke of Islam as the "straight path"; Jesus called himself "the way and the truth and the life," and one of early Christianity's names for itself was simply "the Way"; the Buddha established the "Noble

Path" to nibbana; and Confucius urged people to follow the way, or *dao*, of Heaven. Each teacher believed taking his path required commitment and disciplined action.

I have come to love that word discipline, but my first associations with it were not happy ones. Discipline was what I got whenever I did something wrong, so I came to think of it as punishment. It hardly needs to be said, but that is not the sense in which we are using it here, although spiritual disciplines, like punishments, can sometimes be hard to bear. And like some punishments, spiritual disciplines serve a corrective or rehabilitative function. But unlike punishment—at least usually—spiritual disciplines are *voluntarily* undertaken. It is that voluntary aspect that can make spiritual discipline such a demanding, even grueling, experience. Discipline of the spirit means nothing if it is not willed for oneself. No one can force another to become enlightened or to seek perfect goodness. The motivation has to come from within, and that impetus is often very hard to muster, especially when there are so many diversions along the way.

The nature of the spiritual path, furthermore, is such that one is destined to fail before one succeeds. Failure, in fact, is essential to following any spiritual path. Confucius may have wanted people to attain perfect goodness, but they could only do so by failing to be perfect. Failure is required because the real strength of spirit is achieved when one has to find the gumption to get on the straight path yet again. The path of spiritual discipline may seem linear, but in reality it is a long process of starting over again and again and again. A lyric from the Mevlevi order of Sufism beautifully expresses this dynamic of discipline:

> Come, come, come again,
> Whoever you may be,
> A believer, an unbeliever, an infidel. Come.
> Ours is not the door of desperation.
> Even if you have broken your vows a hundred times,
> Come, come again.

The repetitive quality of starting over, of breaking vows and renewing them, is one of the reasons spiritual disciplines are called "exercises" and "practices" in some traditions. It is the practice that makes perfect. It is the continuous reaffirmation of the vows that makes the spirit strong.

The disciplines that Confucius recommended can perhaps be best understood when we first consider the impediments that prevent us from arriving at the goal of the virtuous life. At the top of the list would be self-centeredness or *hubris*, the tendency to believe and act as if one were the central item of reality. Now frankly, I have a hard time believing that I am *not* the central and most important feature of the cosmos. But I am told by others that the universe does not in fact revolve around me. Not only did Confucius think that believing oneself to be at the center of everything was a mistaken notion, he thought that it carried destructive consequences for others and for oneself.

The Buddha, Jesus, and Muhammad all said similar things. For Confucius, the problem with *hubris* was simple. If humaneness is a virtue manifested in interpersonal relationships, it is difficult to bring that quality to expression if one discounts the significance of another. Self-importance is the catalyst for ingratitude, arrogance, insincerity, dishonesty, anger, and a multitude of other defilements. Our list of obstructions to humaneness might also include ignorance, failing to know enough or to have sufficient self-awareness to act wisely in particular situations. Ignorance might cause us to act rashly, to resort to violence, to speak an unkind word, or neglect the humanity that connects us to one another. Confucius might single out ignorance of the past as a particular impediment to the virtuous life. How can we act virtuously when there are no contemporary models on which to base our behavior? Only in the past were there such worthy paragons.

The practices of Confucian spirituality functioned to disable these obstacles and to train individuals in more wholesome ways. Some of the practices were quite basic and common to a variety of spiritual paths; we'll begin with those. Others were more specific to the Confucian approach and relate to his deep appreciation of the value of ritual for regulating human life. As far as we know, Master Confucius never provided his apprentices with a step-by-step program for attaining moral perfection. But certain themes recur throughout the *Analects,* and it is upon those that we'll focus our attention.

The fundamental practices endorsed by Confucius, and many other great teachers throughout history, come as no surprise. They seem basic to all forms of self-discipline. We might simply call them exercises in restraining desires; Confucius called them "subduing oneself." If an overweening self is a major barrier to humaneness, then merely keeping the self in check goes a long way towards allowing us to practice virtue. Confucius admonished his students to live simply, without ostentation or luxury, as he did. He said: "A gentleman seeks neither a full belly nor a comfortable home. He is quick in action but cautious in speech." Not only was Confucius aware that pursuing wealth was no avenue to happiness or satisfaction; he believed possessing more than was necessary deadened the spirit.

China's sages have never really cared for the intense asceticism that one finds in the history of Indian religions and parts of Christianity, and Confucius was certainly among them. You will not find Confucius telling his protégés to wear hair-shirts or flagellate themselves. But he did think that a little discomfort was a good thing. A touch of asceticism was necessary to keep the mind attentive to itself and sensitive to the wider world, for both self- and other-awareness were vital to the way of virtue.

Self-awareness was cultivated through moments of introspection. Master Kong called these periods of reflection "quiet-sitting," "abiding in reverence," and "rectifying the mind." The purpose of such times was not to commune with the divine or experience extraordinary states of consciousness. More than anything, Confucius viewed these times of serenity as opportunities for critical self-examination. There was nothing exotic about the practice at all. It simply afforded the aspiring noble person time to remove him or herself from the din and distractions of daily life to attend to self-improvement. Quiet-sitting allowed the sage-in-training to look objectively, with ruthless honesty, at his or her own character and make changes as necessary. "When the gentleman makes a mistake," Confucius said on many occasions, "he is not afraid to correct it." Confucius' own habit of self-examination and the humility it required to undertake were among his most admirable traits. He told others, "When you see a noble person, think of equaling him; when you see an unworthy person, examine yourself inwardly"

Quiet-sitting contributed to the development of other characteristics of the noble one. It refined the faculty that Confucius called "keen discernment," by forestalling reflexive actions. When a student asked about "keen discernment," Confucius said, "When slanders that seep under the skin and grievances that cause pain do not drive you to an immediate response, you may be said to have keen discernment." No doubt introspective moments also gave a clearer understanding of one's limitations and abilities, the basis of what he called wisdom. In one of my favorite aphorisms, the Sage said: "If you understand it, say you understand it. If you do not understand it, say you do not understand it. This is wisdom" Introspection fine-tuned one's listening and speaking skills. It sharpened the proficiency to listen to others with an open-mind, free from preconceived opinions, and facilitated discretion in speech. Without the self-awareness nurtured in introspection, thought Confucius, one is not fit to serve in government.

We observed on several occasions that Confucian philosophy was decidedly oriented toward life in this world. Confucius never seemed to express a clear opinion about what he thought of the afterlife. In the depth of his heart, he may have believed in or hoped for or perhaps even denied a form of continued existence after death. But he certainly did not make that belief part of his teachings. Partly as a consequence of his this-worldly emphasis, Confucius gave paramount significance to the matters of ordinary existence.

Where other great teachers may have called for a radical disregard for the things of this world, Confucius urged a radical engagement with them. But he did not do so to promote a kind of Epicurean enjoyment of what life had to offer. Rather, he viewed everyday experience, including the most mundane things, with an eye to seeing their moral and spiritual significance. For Confucius, the commonplace details of life could become the signifiers of Heaven. Such things as clothing, food, and even posture were matters of great importance. The *Analects* reports that Confucius gave much attention to wearing the appropriate robes for each occasion, eating meats with the right condiments, and ensuring that the mat he sat on was properly aligned. All that fuss about the daily routine may strike us as rather wearisome and pointless. But to Confucius, attending to these everyday matters gave expression to one's respect for the social fabric and helped foster a greater awareness of the sacred dimension within all things.

As someone sensitive to the sacred aspect of the mundane world and to the transformative effects of ceremony, it should not surprise us that Confucius thought the whole of life ought to be conducted as a grand ritual. In an innovative move, Confucius extended the ancient role of *li* in Chinese statecraft and religion to include all aspects of human relationships. His perspective on life as a sacred rite was vital to his view of the world and was one of his major contributions to world religion and philosophy. The essence of this ideal was the belief that in all interpersonal relationships, human beings ought to comport themselves with the same poise and decorum appropriate to a sacred ceremony. According to the *Book of Poetry*, the spirits admired rituals that were conducted in a spirit of sincerity, close attention to detail, humility, respectfulness, and generosity. These were precisely the qualities Confucius valued in everyday life. Properly conducted state rituals and personal rites of passages such as marriages and funerals were the special areas where these qualities were cultivated and expressed. But in the everyday world, these qualities were formed and manifested in proper etiquette and manners.

Confucius was especially aware of the capacity of everyday etiquette to give shape to our potential for humaneness, thus evoking the best of what is in the human heart. The principle underlying this belief is fairly easy to understand. Observing good manners means to act in a clearly prescribed way that is considerate of the feelings of others, and—this is the important part—*to do so whether you feel like it or not*. So you really didn't care much for the Chia pet you received for your birthday. Your feelings notwithstanding, you know the mannerly thing to do is to express appreciation anyway. Fortunately, the words and gestures have already been formulated for you by society. "Wow, thanks, I always wanted one of these," you say, followed by a nice thank you note a few days later. Your benefactor is happy, and you feel good knowing you've done the right thing by preserving the harmony between you. And who knows, you might really learn to like that Chia pet—or maybe you won't. It doesn't really matter. What matters is that you express appreciation for another person's generosity. The simple expression of gratitude edges you a little bit closer to actually feeling it. You don't have to like the gift to be grateful for it.

Confucius thought that continual practice of mannerly acts could engender sincere feelings in the one who performs them. You may not feel particularly humble, but after several thousand bows and prostrations, feelings of genuine humility begin to surface. Humans are habitual creatures, and so repetitious actions can do amazing things to transform the character. Aristotle said, "We are what we repeatedly do." John Dryden, the English poet and playwright, also observed the dialectical relationship between behavior and character. He said: "We first make our habits, and then our habits make us." As character is shaped by behavior, the performance of humane acts becomes natural and spontaneous. It loses the artificial quality that may have attended it at first. For Confucius, this dialectical relationship between the external act and the internal disposition is the key to understanding how both ritual and decorum can make us more humane.

A sophisticated enjoyment of music, poetry, and dance was also an important dimension of Confucian spirituality. Like the practices of ritual, decorum, and introspection, Confucius thought that the cultured arts had the capacity to awaken and refine moral sensitivities. For Confucius, in fact, the principal value of these fine arts was moral rather than aesthetic. Music, poetry, and dance were of course important aspects of the rituals Confucius so highly prized, but he thought that they could be important quite apart from the ceremonial context.

Confucius was especially fond of music. The *Analects* quotes him as saying, "One is inspired by poetry, strengthened by rituals, and perfected by music." His followers noted that he loved to sing, and often did so with them. He also played the *qin*, a stringed instrument somewhat like a zither, to accompany the singing. Late in life, he learned to play the stone chimes. The songs he sang were usually from the classic called the *Book of Poetry*, from which we have quoted several times. An especially fine piece of music well-performed could send him into a state of ecstasy. Once, while visiting the province of Qi, Confucius heard "The Succession," a composition often played at state ceremonies. A student reported that for three months afterwards, Confucius did not notice the taste of meat. Unfortunately, we have no record of the melodies Confucius and his contemporaries may have heard, but archaeologists have recently uncovered some examples of the instruments on which they were played.

The *Analects* does not really give us enough information to know exactly what it was about music that appealed to Confucius or what precisely he thought refined the moral sense. There are passages that indicate that the lyrics to the songs he enjoyed expressed high ethical sentiments. But there must have been more than that, more than just the words, otherwise he would have been content simply with poetry. A bit of reflection on the nature of music might help us understand the Sage's infatuation with it. I am not particularly musical myself, but I have enough sensitivity to appreciate how particular forms of music can express and arouse specific moods and feelings. Certain moods such as reverence and pensiveness would have been especially appropriate for encouraging humaneness.

The powerful effect of music on the human spirit has been noticed throughout history. Muslim physicians in the Middle Ages, for example, used music to treat patients who had been diagnosed with mental illnesses. I can also imagine how musical harmonies would have reminded Confucius of the ideal of harmony between Heaven and Earth, ruler and subject, husband and wife. A perfectly performed musical piece, especially fitting the occasion and involving the coordination of dozens of musicians and singers, each playing his or her allotted role, would have been the consummate metaphor for his vision of the virtuous society. But even more than suggesting the ideal of a harmonious society, music can assist in making the ideal a reality. Anyone who has ever taken part in collective singing or listening to a concert understands the sense of unity and fellow feeling that can be experienced by those productions. For some of you, the point might be illustrated by a single word: Woodstock.

Just as he thought music, poetry, and dance had the potential for elevating the human spirit, Confucius believed they could also debase and disrupt humanity. He seems to have been especially concerned about the way music and dance could incite lust. He was particularly annoyed by the music from the province of Zheng. "Banish the music of Zheng," he said. "The music of Zheng is licentious." The ruler of Zheng, it seems, had a liking for music and parties that Confucius found offensive. This ruler was reported to have enjoyed late night drinking festivals in a large garden in which he had a pond filled with wine and invited men and women to cavort naked into the wee hours of the morning, all to the accompaniment of music. I don't think Confucius would have much cared for Woodstock.

Confucius also had firm opinions about dancing. Like music and poetry, he appreciated the potential of dance to embody and stimulate harmony and reverence. But he was also concerned with the possibility that dance, like music, could be used in nefarious ways. You'll remember two episodes from Confucius' life involving dancers, both of which illustrated that he considered dance serious business. In the first, he ordered the execution of troupe whose performance he found to be lewd and disrespectful to the dignity of the ruler. In the second, he resigned political office when the prime minister of Lu became enamored with dancing girls sent as a gift from a neighboring state.

Given the great power of poetry, music, and dance to affect the moods and dispositions of the heart, Confucius believed it was morally necessary to apply thoughtful control over the kinds of entertainments one attends. In a more general sense, he was concerned about the choices we make about our environments that might have an impact on our character. That concern extended to the people with whom we are friends. He recommended that those aspiring to be gentlemen should not enter the domain of someone who continually acted in an immoral way. The gentleman, he said, "draws near to those who possess the Way in order to be set straight by them."

Confucian spirituality was nothing if not comprehensive. It involved disciplined attention to all aspects of life, from the interiority of thoughts and feelings to the exteriority of actions and deeds. It moved throughout the sacred and the secular and diminished the distinction between them. It gave place to the worship of the spirits and to the folding of clothes. It concerned the person as individual and the individual within a nexus of relationships. It sought to bring humanity to completion and harmony between Heaven and Earth.

# Confucius and Confucianism

## Lecture 9

Two of the most important early Confucian philosophers, Mencius and Xunzi ... came to what appear to be diametrically opposite positions about the nature of human beings. Exploring the substance of their debate will help us appreciate the way the teachings of individuals like Confucius, the Buddha, Jesus, and Muhammad can be subject to such a range of understandings that often lead to sectarian divisions among their followers.

Preserving the memory and teachings of Confucius was not a simple matter of writing down what he had said and done. His students naturally had somewhat different recollections of his life and teachings and different senses about what his words and actions meant. Case in point, two of the most important early Confucian philosophers, Mencius and Xunzi, came to what appear to be diametrically opposite positions about the nature of human beings.

The 4th-century B.C.E. scholar Mencius was likely the most important Confucian thinker next to Confucius himself. He was most interested in the basic make-up of human beings. Confucius thought that all persons shared a common nature by birth but were molded in different ways. But Confucius did not say whether our common nature was naturally good or bad. Mencius, in response to philosophers such as Yang Zhu, who argued that all human actions are driven solely by self-interest, maintained that human nature was innately good. Our innate virtue, to Mencius, is like seedlings rooted in the fertile soil of human nature. Failing to care for and nurture these tender seedlings causes them to wither and die. People were not naturally evil, but they became evil when their upbringing and education neglected or thwarted moral cultivation.

Mencius also helped clarify some of the religious elements implicit in Confucius's teaching. Confucius had indicated that he considered himself commissioned by heaven to teach the way of virtue; Mencius took that idea one step further to suggest that heaven has endowed all human beings with virtue, and our proper response is to serve heaven by bringing our humane qualities to their fullness. Thus, following the way of heaven is the ultimate purpose of existence and empowers humans to participate in the very transformation of the universe.

Working with the same Confucian teachings and in the same context of rigorous philosophical dialogue, the 3rd-century philosopher Xunzi came to the opposite conclusion. He claimed that human beings were born with a tendency toward **waywardness**—an inclination to act in self-serving and self-pleasing ways. This is not

The Teaching Company Collection.

**Throughout his adult life, Confucius had a single and very lofty ambition: to restore moral vision and virtue to the world.**

evil per se but simply nonmoral, an outgrowth of the basic drive of self-preservation. Like Confucius and Mencius, Xunzi considered rituals and social etiquette to be the principal ways of fostering benevolence. But unlike Mencius and perhaps Confucius himself, Xunzi did not think of rituals and manners as expressions of human nature but as artificial constructs designed by the ancient sages to benefit people living in society. Nor did Xunzi believe that heaven willed for humans to be moral. Heaven was merely the natural world, which had no moral preferences whatsoever. The way was not mandated in heaven but in human societies that deemed morality essential to their survival and well-being.

Although Mencius and Xunzi held different understandings about the nature of the divine and human, both valued moral education that emphasized the study of tradition and ritual. Both also thought human beings were morally perfectible. The major difference was that Mencius considered education to be akin to nurturing a field of wild wheat, and Xunzi thought of it more like throwing a clay jar on a potter's wheel.

Generations of disciples who entered government service spread the ideals of Confucianism throughout the royal courts of China. Philosophers from other traditions began to offer their criticisms, as in the *Zhuangzi*, the great satirical classic of the Daoist tradition. But even as the authors of the *Zhuangzi* mocked Confucius, they sometimes used his character to give voice to the Daoist perspective. In other words, the Sage's reputation had grown to such an extent that other philosophers were using his good name to express their own points of view.

When the Qin dynasty came to power in 221 B.C.E., its rulers embraced Legalism and outlawed all other philosophical schools. Many Confucian texts were destroyed and well over a thousand Confucian scholars were tortured and killed. In 206 B.C.E., the Qin dynasty was succeeded by the Han dynasty, which made Confucianism the official state philosophy. The official canon of Confucian classics known as the Wu Jing formed the core curriculum for Chinese education and the basis for civil service exams from the mid-Han period until 1911, about 2,000 years.

In much of the modern era, the reputation of Confucian philosophy steadily declined. Many Chinese intellectuals blamed its conservatism for the tragic events of the 19th century. The Communist Party portrayed Confucius and Confucianism as quaint, backward, and antirevolutionary. Although Mao Zedong did much to eradicate Confucianism in China, in the post-Mao era, Confucianism seems to be enjoying renewed interest among Chinese and others around the world. ■

## Important Terms

**waywardness**: An inclination to act in self-serving and self-pleasing ways, born of one's innate drive of self-preservation.

***Zhuangzi***: The great satirical classic of the Daoist tradition that mocked Confucius but also featured him as a character espousing Daoist views.

1. Which do you find more convincing, Mencius's argument that humans are essentially virtuous or Xunzi's argument that humans are essentially amoral? What is your reasoning?

# Confucius and Confucianism
## Lecture 9—Transcript

In life, Confucius enjoyed modest renown at best; in death, however, his reputation flourished and his influence far exceeded anything he could have possibly expected. After Confucius died, his ideas and practices were kept alive and developed by his immediate protégés, many of whom went on to start their own schools and become teachers in their own right. These disciples began the process of preserving the Confucian legacy for future generations and disseminating his teachings throughout China. In our talk today, we will examine how that legacy fared in Chinese history. We will discuss the initial compilation and interpretation of his ideas, their influence in Chinese politics and education, and the gradual development of a religious practice centered on the Sage himself.

As we intimated in our discussion of the *Analects*, preserving the memory and teachings of Confucius was not a simple matter of writing down what he had said and done. His students naturally had somewhat different recollections of his life and teachings and different senses about what his words and actions meant. It was extremely easy to mesh one's own beliefs and ideas with what one thought the Master had said. There was nothing necessarily sinister or deliberate about that process. All of us sometimes attribute to someone we greatly admire the ideals or values that we ourselves hold dear. Certainly, those very human tendencies came into play as the Sage's students compiled the text of his sayings over a period of several generations. This of course is why much of Confucian scholarship is devoted to trying to extricate the authentic sayings of Confucius from the words and ideas of others. The difficulty of the task is symbolized by the clear lack of scholarly consensus about what is genuine and what is not.

But even if Confucius had authored a book of his own, explaining his philosophy carefully and systematically, his ideas would still be subject to diverse interpretations. No where is this point more clearly seen than in the divergent interpretations of two of the most important early Confucian philosophers, Mencius and Xunzi. Mencius and Xunxi came to what appear to be diametrically opposite positions about the nature of human beings. Exploring the substance of their debate will help us appreciate the way the teachings of individuals like Confucius, the Buddha, Jesus, and Muhammad can be subject to such a range of understandings that often lead to sectarian divisions among their followers. This exploration will also open us to a different level of thinking about Confucius himself. And, as if that weren't enough, the issue itself is intrinsically fascinating, regardless of what one thinks of Confucius. The question at stake is an ancient one: is human nature basically evil or basically good? With Confucius as their guide, Mencius and Xunzi came down on opposite sides of the issue.

Most scholars consider Mencius to be the most important Confucian thinker next to Confucius himself. He is the only other philosopher besides Confucius to whom scholars refer by a Latinized name. In Chinese, he is known as Mengzi, or Master Meng. Mencius lived in the 4th century B.C.E. and was born 18 miles from Confucius' hometown of Qufu about a century after the death of the Sage. Tradition claims that Mencius was a protégé of Confucius' grandson. Mencius was the first Confucian thinker of any real significance since Confucius, and as such, his understanding of the Master's thought became immensely influential in subsequent history. The relationship of Mencius to Confucius can be compared to that between Paul and Jesus. Paul was one of the first major interpreters of Jesus' life, and later Christians tend to see Jesus through the eyes of Paul. Likewise, many read the teachings of Confucius through the perspective of Mencius.

Mencius was concerned with all dimensions of Confucian philosophy and religion, but one area seems to have interested him more than any other: the basic make-up of human beings. You will recall from an earlier lecture that Confucius thought that all persons shared a common nature by birth but through upbringing and education they were molded in different ways, leading some to become good and others wicked. I suggested that Confucius thought of humans as "unfinished" beings who required socialization and self-cultivation to be complete. What Confucius did not say was whether or not he thought human beings were naturally good or bad. His reticence on this topic probably related to his aversion to speculative issues and to the practical orientation of his teachings. And it was simply not a question that philosophers of his day were asking.

But Mencius was working in a different intellectual environment from Confucius. For the most part, Confucius did not try to defend his position against rival points-of-view. The *Analects* essentially present his teachings as assertions rather than systematic arguments. Confucius did not feel compelled to provide a rational case for his ideas. Mencius, on the other hand, *did* feel obliged to respond to the questions and criticisms of other thinkers who were trying to advance their own philosophies. He was committed to the way of virtue espoused by Confucius but was aware that the Sage had not fully elaborated his perspective on many matters. Because he genuinely believed the Confucian way offered the best hope for China in an age on the brink of despair, he attempted to provide the comprehensive development and argumentation that Confucius' aphoristic teachings lacked. In the Period of the Warring States, when Mencius lived, one of the prominent points of discussion was the moral nature of human beings. The issue was not merely theoretical. Whatever position one might take could have important consequences for addressing the questions of governance and human harmony. If humans were by nature evil, for example, then it might be prudent for the government to curtail that inclination by any means necessary, including force or the threat of force. This in fact was the position of the school known as Legalism.

Mencius, however, maintained that human nature was innately good. He argued his case by means of a thought experiment:

> Suppose someone suddenly saw a child about to fall into a well: anyone in such a situation would have a feeling of alarm and compassion—not because one sought to get in good with the child's parents, not because one wanted fame among one's neighbors and friends, and not because one would dislike the sound of the child's cries.

Mencius does not argue that everyone would be *moved* to save the child, only that each person would experience a surge of fellow-feeling. That spontaneous reaction was the evidence, Mencius thought, of basic human goodness. Whether or not one acted on that impulse would be another matter. His argument seems to be specifically directed to challenge the position of another philosopher, Yang Zhu, who argued that all human actions are driven solely by self-interest. With his example, Mencius tries to show that at least *some* actions can be motivated by involuntary, selfless urges.

Mencius goes on to claim that such altruistic impulses are the defining quality of human beings:

> From this we can see that if one is without the feeling of compassion, one is not human. If one is without the feeling of disdain, one is not human. If one is without the feeling of deference, one is not human. If one is without the feeling of approval and disapproval, one is not human.

In short, Mencius locates the roots of the principal Confucian virtues in human nature. We come into the world with these basic qualities.

Yet, if human nature is fundamentally compassionate, how does Mencius explain the fact that compassion does not appear to be the prevailing characteristic of human existence? Mencius, after all, lived during a particularly brutal period in China's history. How can he account for that brutality and simultaneously argue that persons are essentially good? This was the same question that vexed the Christian theologian Augustine, who developed his theory of original sin to account for the discrepancy. The answer Mencius provided was different from Augustine's. The origin of human wickedness was not a primordial fall from god's good graces, as Augustine suggested, but the failure fully to cultivate and strengthen basic human goodness. Mencius compares innate virtue to seedlings rooted in the fertile soil of human nature:

> The feeling of compassion is the sprout of benevolence [that is, *ren*, or noble humanness]. The feeling of disdain is the sprout of righteousness. The feeling of deference is the sprout of propriety. The feeling of approval or disapproval is the sprout of wisdom.

Failing to care for and nurture these tender seedlings causes them to whither and die. In other words, persons are not naturally evil, but they become evil when their upbringing and education neglects moral cultivation or deliberately thwarts it. Mencius offers a story that provides an allegory of his understanding of human nature:

> The trees of Ox Mountain were once beautiful. But because it bordered on a large state, hatchets and axes besieged it. Could it remain verdant? Due to the respite it got during the day or night, and the moisture of the rain and dew, there were sprouts and shoots growing there. But oxen and sheep came and grazed on them. Hence, it was as if it were barren. Seeing it barren, people believed that there had never been any timber there.

According to this analogy, the prevalence of evil in the world does not disprove innate human goodness. Human wickedness only illustrates our failure to care for and develop the fragile qualities of our basic goodness.

Like Confucius, Mencius believed that education and domestic nurturance were vital to cultivating virtue. The practice of filial piety and the parental love for the child were essential for an individual to realize his or her potential for kindness. Mencius also envisioned a prominent role for government in this endeavor. Again like Confucius, he believed the ruler should govern by virtue rather than law. Because of our deep innate goodness, human beings are more responsive to displays of goodness than to demonstrations of force or the threat of punishment. It was crucial, he thought, for rulers to provide outstanding models of virtuous character, which their subjects would aspire to emulate. This idea was based on the Chinese concept of *de*, the belief that the accumulation of virtue has the power to awaken virtue in others.

Mencius also helped clarify some of the religious elements implicit in Confucius' teaching. Confucius had indicated that he considered himself commissioned by Heaven to teach the way of virtue; Mencius took that idea one step further to suggest that Heaven has endowed *all* human beings with virtue. Mencius sees this endowment as a gift, and our proper response is to serve Heaven by bringing our humane qualities to their fullness. Thus following the way of Heaven is the ultimate purpose of existence and the source of our deepest happiness. Mencius writes: "The ten thousand things are brought to completion by us. There is no greater delight than to turn toward oneself and discover Genuineness." Perfecting our moral natures, thought Mencius, brings us into accord with the will of Heaven and is the source of our greatest joy.

But not only does one's self-cultivation fulfill Heaven's will for our lives; it also empowers humans to participate in the very transformation of the universe. In an early Confucian text entitled *Centrality and Commonality*, we find this passage reflecting the Mencian viewpoint:

> Only that one in the world who is most perfectly [genuine] is able to give full development to his nature. Being able to give full development to his nature, he is able to give full development to the nature of other human beings and, being able to give full development to the nature of other human beings, he is able to give full development to the natures of other living things. Being able to give full development to the natures of other living beings, he can assist in the transforming and nourishing powers of Heaven and Earth; being able to assist in the transforming and nourishing powers of Heaven and Earth, he can form a triad with Heaven and Earth.

The benefits of moral self-cultivation, thought Mencius, reverberate throughout the entire universe.

Working with the same Confucian teachings and in the same context of rigorous philosophical dialogue, Xunzi came to the opposite conclusion from Mencius. Xunzi denied that humans were innately good. Xunzi lived most of his life in the 3<sup>rd</sup> century, and was probably born about the time Mencius died, so they never knew one another. But Xunzi knew of Mencius' work. Although they agreed on many other points about Confucian philosophy, on the question of human nature, they took what appear to be contrasting positions. This difference in views was the first major divergence within Confucian ranks.

At first glance, Xunzi seems to claim that human beings are born evil, with a tendency toward what he called "waywardness," an inclination to act in self-serving and self-pleasing ways. Because of this predisposition, individuals can become selfish and society can gravitate towards anarchy. Xunzi, however, probably did not intend to suggest that humans are evil to the core but that they have essentially *non*-moral natures. The tendency toward waywardness is simply an outgrowth of the basic drive of self-preservation, but fundamentally people are not naturally inclined towards moral or immoral behavior. In view of this basic moral neutrality, it is essential that persons receive deliberate and careful training in the cultivation of good behavior. Domestic nurturance and education are therefore vital to instilling morality, shaping amoral nature into human benevolence. Like Confucius and Mencius, Xunzi considered rituals and social etiquette to be the principal ways of fostering benevolence. But unlike Mencius and perhaps Confucius himself, Xunzi did not think of rituals and manners as expressions of human nature. Instead, he regarded them as artificial constructs designed by the ancient sages to benefit people living in society. Furthermore, unlike Mencius and Confucius, Xunzi did not believe that Heaven *willed* for humans to be moral. For him, Heaven was merely the natural world, which had no moral preferences whatsoever. Thus, for Xunzi, the Way was not mandated in Heaven but in human societies that deemed morality was essential to their survival and well-being.

Although Mencius and Xunzi held different understandings about the nature of the divine and human, the practical components of their teachings were in accord. Like the Sage who inspired them, both philosophers valued moral education that emphasized the study of tradition and ritual. With such training, both thought that human beings were morally perfectible. The major difference between them seems to be in the way they conceptualized the operation of education. Mencius considered education to be akin to nurturing a field of wild wheat and Xunzi thought of it like more throwing a clay jar on a potter's wheel. To extrapolate a larger point from this analysis, perhaps we can say that conceptual differences about metaphysics and anthropology need not preclude agreement on practical and ethical matters.

As I mentioned earlier, Confucius' protégés kept his memory alive not only by producing the *Analects* but also by opening their own schools. These academies produced generations of disciples who entered government service and helped spread the ideals of the Confucianism throughout the royal courts of China. As these new Confucians assumed official positions, the name of

Master Kong became more widely known and attracted both respect and derision. As we observed with Mencius and Xunzi, as the Confucian way became more prominent, philosophers from other traditions felt free to offer criticisms. Sometimes their disagreements took the form of satire, as in the *Zhuangzi*, the great classic of the Daoist tradition. But even as the authors of the *Zhuangzi* mocked Confucius, they sometimes used his character to give voice to the Daoist perspective. In other words, the Sage's reputation had grown to such an extent that other philosophers were using his good name to express their own points of view.

As the reputation of Confucius grew, so did opposition to his philosophy. During the Qin dynasty, which succeeded the Zhou period, that opposition became more than mere parody and academic disagreement. The Qin dynasty came to power in 221 B.C.E. when the state of Qin conquered the last of its rival kingdoms and unified China. The Qin rulers were not favorably disposed to the ideals of Confucianism; they embraced Legalism and its heavy-handed approach to governing, which partly explains their success in coming to power. The Legalists, as noted in an earlier discussion, advocated the centralization of authority and the strict enforcement of the law. The Qin rulers outlawed all philosophical schools except Legalism. Many Confucian texts were destroyed and well over a thousand Confucian scholars were tortured and killed.

Fortunately, the Qin dynasty lasted only 15 years. It was succeeded by the Han dynasty, which reigned about 400 years, from 206 B.C.E. to 220 C.E. The Han rulers not only reinstituted Confucianism; they made it the official state philosophy. By now there was an official canon of Confucian classics known as the Wu Jing, comprising five books, most of which we have already mentioned in the course of elaborating Confucius' life and teachings. They were the *Yi Jing*, the classic of divination; the *Book of History*; the *Book of Poetry*, the *Spring and Fall Annals*, and the *Book of Rituals*. This collection formed the core curriculum for Chinese education and the basis for civil service exams for government officials from the mid-Han period until 1911, just about 2000 years.

Han rule was critical to the perpetuation of Confucian philosophy; it was also instrumental in establishing religious practices dedicated to the spirit of Confucius. In 195 B.C.E., the Han emperor went to the tomb of Confucius in Qufu, where he offered sacrifices. This event was a key step in a gradual process whereby Confucius was given a succession of posthumous titles including "Duke," "Earl," "Venerable, Accomplished Sage," and "Emperor." His last official title was bestowed in 1906 when he was formally declared by imperial decree to be the "Co-Assessor with the deities of Heaven and Earth."

As his rank steadily rose by official proclamation, temples were built in his honor. Appropriately, educational institutions were among the first to sponsor Confucian temples. In the 5th century C.E., the first state temple to Confucius was erected in South China. In the 7th century C.E., the Tang Dynasty mandated that schools in all provinces of China should have a Confucian temple. At these shrines, sacrifices were offered the spirits of Confucius and many of his disciples. These offerings were part of the greater system of rituals conducted to honor and appease the other spirits and ancestors of the Chinese pantheon. But despite the efforts to give Confucius near-divine status, the cult of Confucius was never really popular among the vast majority of ordinary Chinese.

The Confucian way also developed new directions when it had to face the challenges posed by Mahayana Buddhism, which was introduced to China in the Han dynasty, and by Daoism, the other great indigenous Chinese tradition. During the Song Dynasty, the scholar Zhu Xi incorporated ideas from Buddhism and Daoism into his understanding of Confucianism. Zhu Xi's synthesis was largely ignored during his lifetime, but after his death his ideas became the new orthodox view of what Confucianism actually meant. Today, philosophers and historians believe that Zhu Xi developed a perspective significantly different from traditional Confucianism and hence call his philosophy Neo-Confucianism.

In much of the modern era, the reputation of Confucian philosophy steadily declined among the Chinese. Many intellectuals blamed what they considered the backwardness and conservativism of Confucianism for the tragic events in 19th century China, including the Opium Wars with the British

Empire. When the Communist party came to power under the rule of Mao Zedong, Confucius and Confucianism were portrayed as quaint, backwards, and anti-revolutionary.

Confucius' importance has grown and declined at various points in the last 2000 years, but overall he has received overwhelming admiration from the Chinese. His philosophy has been influential not only in China but in other countries with which the Chinese had significant contact, especially Korea, Japan, and Vietnam. Although Mao did much to eradicate Confucianism in China, in the post-Mao era, Confucianism seems to enjoying renewed interest among Chinese and others around the world.

In our next lecture, we leave Confucius for the moment and turn to his near-contemporary in another part of Asia, the Buddha, the great sage of ancient India.

# India at the Time of the Buddha
## Lecture 10

The new thoughts that disrupted Indian religion began to surface around 800 B.C.E., some 300 years before the birth of Siddhattha Gotama. Near this time, small coteries of intellectuals in northeastern India began to think seriously about death and its aftermath in response to increasing anxiety about the ultimate human destiny. ... The anxiety about death was prompted by the emerging sense of the self as an individual.

By 1500 B.C.E., the Āryans had started to migrate into the Indian subcontinent from Central Asia by way of Iran, bringing with them their vast oral tradition, the Vedas; their native language, Sanskrit; and a stratified social arrangement, the varna system. The early Āryans had not been not especially troubled by death; religious practices were intended to help secure the goods of the world that could make life here and now more comfortable and pleasurable. But by about 800 B.C.E., small coteries of intellectuals had begun to think seriously about death and its aftermath, prompted by an emerging sense of the self.

Gradually, one view of the afterlife began to dominate Āryan culture: The individual's death would be followed by another birth, then another life and death, and another birth, and so on. This transmigration of the soul, or **samsāra**, was a novel idea; the Vedas had suggested nothing like this. Conjectures about how and why this series of deaths and births occurred varied widely, but virtually everyone accepted that it did occur and that it was a highly *undesirable* situation.

Yoked with samsāra was the concept of **karma**, which ethicized the Indian view of rebirth. This ancient Āryan term originally referred to the mechanism by which rituals were understood to operate. It later came to mean action in a more generic sense, including any thought or word as well as any deed. But even more, karma referred to the consequences of the act. Karmic acts could be either good or bad, determined by whether or not they conformed to **dharma**, or truth, the duties incumbent on persons according to caste and gender. Fulfilling one's dharma was the way to produce positive karma; neglecting or violating dharma resulted in negative karma, and the consequences of karmic acts eventually returned to the agent in the form of good or bad events. The events of one's life were not predetermined by fate or a god; human beings determined their own destinies.

Since one does not always reap the consequences of one's actions in this life—after all, the wicked often prosper, while the good often suffer—ancient Indian thought extended the possibilities for karma's return into future lives. Good or evil acts led to favorable or unfavorable rebirths, raising or lowering one's place in the hierarchy of being. From the samsāric perspective, existence now had but one valid objective: to achieve freedom from the endless cycle of death and rebirth, from the suffering of an eternal parade of lives and deaths. The Hindus called this **moksha,** absolute and unconditional liberation. But attaining release from samsāra could not be accomplished merely by generating good karma. Even if one were the finest person possible, eventually one's store of good karma would be depleted, and one would at last face another death and rebirth. In the long run, rebirth itself would have to be brought to an end.

Born as Siddhartha Gautama in a princely family, the man known as the Buddha left his family's palace and took up the life of an Indian ascetic.

© iStockphoto / Thinkstock.

As this new understanding of human nature and destiny gained wide acceptance throughout northern India, it provoked a vast movement of individuals who decided to forsake their connections with the material world to seek final liberation from samsāra. They were called *samanas*, or strivers. They experimented with an immense array of disciplines and doctrines. Many wandered about northern India searching out new teachers and new spiritual techniques. Some isolated themselves in caves or deep within the forest. They all lived in self-imposed poverty, frequently owning only a bowl for begging food.

One scriptural legacy of the *samanas* is the sacred Hindu text called the *Upanishads*. This diverse collection of philosophical treatises and parables, written over several centuries, concentrates on three fundamental matters: the nature of the *ātman* (the self or soul), the nature of **Brahman** (ultimate reality), and the relationship between them. From its somewhat vague Āryan origins, the concept of *ātman* had developed into an eternal entity residing in but separate from the body and mind. Brahman was held to be a single, indivisible reality that could not be adequately explained or comprehended by ordinary means but could be partially known through the images of the many gods and goddesses of the Hindu pantheon. In the later *Upanishads*, the sages expressed their conviction that the soul and the ultimate reality were in fact, identical: Brahman-*ātman*. The source of human anguish on the wheel of samsāra was a consequence of ignorance, a complete misunderstanding about the true nature of the self and reality.

Such were the essential features of the intellectual religious world into which Siddhattha Gotama was born. He lived in a time of spiritual and religious questioning, when traditions were being reevaluated, and the basic questions of existence were receiving exhilarating new answers. ■

## Important Terms

*ātman*: The Hindu term for the self or soul.

**Brahman**: The name of the ultimate reality in Hinduism.

**dharma**: Literally, "truth"; in Hinduism, the duties incumbent on persons according to caste and gender.

**karma**: In Hinduism, action and its consequences, specifically their ethical dimension.

**moksha**: In Hinduism, release from samsāra, equivalent to nibbana in Buddhism.

*samana*: An ancient Hindu ascetic.

**samsāra**: Literally "meandering"; the Hindu term for the transmigration of the soul, suggesting an aimless, meaningless process.

## Questions to Consider

1. What do you think is the connection between an emerging cultural concept of the self and increasing interest in questions of death and the afterlife?

2. From what we have covered so far, compare and contrast the Confucian and early Hindu views on knowledge, desire, and metaphysics as they relate to the potential for human perfection.

# India at the Time of the Buddha
## Lecture 10—Transcript

The life of the Buddha was almost contemporaneous with that of Confucius. But they lived worlds apart. Siddhattha Gotama, the given name of the man who later earned the title "the Buddha," was born in ancient India just before the death of Confucius. Although they were vastly different, India and China 2500 years ago shared at least one thing: both were age-old cultures in the midst of great changes. But the Buddha's India was not disrupted by the kind of political turbulence that beleaguered ancient China; in fact, India was enjoying a period of remarkable political stability. But it was experiencing another kind of ferment, a profound transformation in thought. By the time Siddhattha Gotama was born, a slow but certain conceptual shift had been underway in India for several centuries. Just as the political situation in ancient China had prompted an outpouring of creative intellectual responses, the evolution of the Indian worldview likewise inspired a movement of impressive philosophical and spiritual innovation. Siddhattha Gotama was one of the many individuals who grappled with this transition that redefined the way Indians thought of themselves, their gods, and their world.

To set the Buddha's thought and practice in its historical context, we will spend this lecture investigating the nature of these changes and the new problems they summoned forth. Beginning with the earliest known inhabitants of the Indian subcontinent, we will trace the major cultural developments in this region up to the time of the Buddha, the middle of the first millennium B.C.E. We'll pay special attention to the deepening anxiety about death and the transient nature of the world and on the mounting hopes for overcoming these fears. This outline will be the background for our later discussion of the Buddha. It will also serve as a brief primer on classical Hinduism, for the Buddha's life and teachings emerge out of the same context that gave the Hindu tradition its distinctive character.

Long before the birth of Siddhattha Gotama, India had been the home of a great civilization that was every bit as sophisticated as the culture that existed at the same time along the banks of the Yellow River. By 3000 B.C.E., or perhaps even earlier, a remarkable society had begun to develop along the valley flanking the Indus River in the area now occupied by northwestern

India and Pakistan. We know little about this civilization apart from the archaeological remains that have been unearthed in the last 150 years. Its written language has never been deciphered, so we have no idea what its inhabitants called themselves. Today, it is simply known as the Indus Valley Civilization or the Harappan Culture, after one of its major cities. The archaeological artifacts from the Indus Valley Civilization indicate that its citizens lived a relatively peaceful life, based on an agricultural economy and some trade, and that they prized order and stability. Their religious practices focused on rituals for ensuring the continuance of life on earth, much like the religion of the Shang dynasty in China.

By 1500 B.C.E., however, this splendid civilization had nearly come to an end, and a new people had begun to dominate the region. These newcomers were the Āryans, who had started to migrate into the area from Central Asia by way of Iran. The Āryans brought with them a decisively different religious and cultural outlook than the Indus Valley inhabitants. They worshiped different gods, practiced different rituals, and lived a semi-nomadic existence based on a pastoral economy. They also brought a vast oral tradition they called the Vedas, borne by their native language, Sanskrit; and they brought a stratified social arrangement known as the varna system. Both the Vedas and the varna system became immensely important in the development of the Hindu tradition. The Vedas, which the Āryans regarded as revealed sacred knowledge, eventually became the highest scriptural authority for Hinduism. Varna became the basis of the caste system. Varna was the Āryan's name for the social classes, of which there were four. The highest varna was the Brahmans, who were the priests and educators; next was the varna of warriors and nobility, followed by that of the merchants and artisans. The lowest varna was the farmers and the manual laborers. Although the Buddha was a descendant of these Āryan migrants, he came to reject the validity of both the Varna system and the Vedas.

By the time of the Buddha, the Āryans had occupied northern India for around a thousand years. They had begun to expand into northeastern India, into the region known as the Gangetic Plain, the area surrounding the Ganges River and its tributaries. This was the area in which Gotama was born and spent his entire life. As they expanded eastward, the Āryans became more sedentary, establishing villages and towns and taking up farming and trade in addition to their traditional pursuits as pastoralists. With urbanization and a new economy, the Āryans began to enjoy material wealth as never before. At least a dozen small states governed by the warrior caste began to arise throughout the region.

As Āryan society evolved, traditional religious beliefs and practices, especially the rituals that had been exclusive domain of the Brahmans, came under question. Accordingly, the power and prestige of the priests diminished somewhat, abetted by the rise of the middle varnas, particularly, the warriors and merchants. This growing dissatisfaction with traditional religion, as well as an increasing restlessness among those with a philosophical bent of mind, was driven by several new ideas that were gaining widespread acceptance throughout the Gangetic plain.

The new thoughts that disrupted Indian religion began to surface around 800 B.C.E., some 300 years before the birth of Siddhattha Gotama. Near this time, small coteries of intellectuals in northeastern India began to think seriously about death and its aftermath in response to increasing anxiety about the ultimate human destiny. To appreciate the importance of this emerging concern, we have to recognize that the Āryans and their Indus Valley predecessors were not especially troubled by death. To these more ancient inhabitants of India, death was more or less accepted as a fact of life, a sad event to be sure, but nothing warranting great fear or terror. Religious practices were intended to help secure the goods of the world that could make life here-and-now more comfortable and more pleasurable. Not a whole lot of attention was given to what might lie beyond the cremation pyre.

But that attitude began to change in the centuries just before the Buddha. Death was now a subject exercising some of the brightest minds of the age. The anxiety about death was prompted by the emerging sense of the self as an individual. In a fascinating tale from the *Upanishads*, the great collection of philosophical reflection from this era, a young Brahman finds himself sent to the underworld where he confronts Yama, the god of Death. There, in death's own home, the young priest, whose name was Nachiketas, boldly pressed Yama to divulge the secrets of life after death. When Yama offered him a long life with many descendants and great wealth instead, Nachiketas refused, declaring that with death looming over existence, the pleasures of the world were ultimately meaningless. What this story revealed was the new intensity with which questions about death were being discussed among thoughtful Āryans. And along with the questions, there was, of course, no shortage of answers.

Gradually, one view began to dominate all others and over several centuries gained wide acceptance among the Indian populace. The consensus view was that the individual's death would be followed by another birth, then another life and death, and another birth, and so on. In what came to be called Hinduism, this process was called transmigration of the soul, because it was conceptualized as a spiritual entity traveling from one body to another. This was a novel idea; the ancient Vedas of the Āryans had suggested nothing like this. Conjectures about how and why this series of deaths and births occurred varied widely. But over time, virtually everyone accepted that it *did* occur and that it was a highly *undesirable* situation. This apparently vicious cycle was called samsāra, a word that meant "meandering," suggesting that the whole process was aimlessness and without meaning.

The idea of rebirth was yoked with another conception that made samsāra a unique idea in the history of world religions, the concept of karma. The doctrine of karma ethicized the Indian view of rebirth. In our discussion of Confucius, we observed that he ethicized the ancient practice of ritual by imbuing it with moral significance. In a similar way, the idea of karma added a moral dimension to the process of rebirth.

Karma was an ancient Āryan term that originally referred to the mechanism by which rituals were understood to operate. It later came to mean action in a more generic sense. In its fundamental meaning, then, karma was an act, and that included any *thought* or *word* as well as deed. But even more, karma referred to the *consequences* of the act; hence, one might have said that a particular action generated or produced karma. Karmic acts, furthermore, could be either good or bad. In classical Hinduism, the quality of any karmic act was determined by whether or not it conformed to dharma, the duties incumbent on persons according to their caste and gender.

Like karma, dharma is probably a term many of you are familiar with already. As we proceed with these lectures, you may hear slight variations in the ways I pronounce these and other words. For example, you may hear me say "dharma" and then, in other context, I will say "dhamma." That difference is deliberate. Dharma is a Sanskrit term; dhamma is a word from Pali, a language closely related to Sanskrit. I will use Sanskrit terms when I am discussing a Hindu concept because Sanskrit is the classical language of Hinduism. I will use Pali for Buddhist terms because Pali is the language of the earliest Buddhist writings. It is helpful to use these different languages because the words have different meanings in their respective contexts. Dharma and dhamma mean "truth" in both Hinduism and Buddhism, but they carry significantly different senses of what constitutes truth. You'll hear slight differences in other words, such as Siddhattha rather than the better known Sanskrit name Siddhartha; sutta rather than sutra; bodhisatta rather than bodhisattva.

Now, let's return to our analysis of dharma. As I was saying, dharma means truth in Hinduism, but also one's duty according to caste and gender. In this respect, dharma differs from Buddhism, which did not acknowledge caste and gender differences in it conception of truth. Hinduism did not embrace a universal ethic for all people at all times but thought that moral obligations were different for different kinds of people. It was the moral responsibility of members of the warrior caste to protect and defend their country and the moral duty of priests to sacrifice on behalf of others. Fulfilling one's Dharma was the way to produce positive karma; neglecting or violating Dharma resulted in negative karma. The Buddha accepted the principle of karma, but he rejected the idea that its moral quality was contingent on one's caste and gender duties.

The Buddha, however, did agree with the classical Hindu view on a very important point: that the consequences of karmic acts eventually returned to the agent. Simply stated, the one who acts will reap the good consequences of a good action and the negative consequences of an evil action. The return, or "ripening," of karma might not happen immediately; it might take a very long time for the consequences of an action to come back to the agent, but its return was inevitable. The good or bad events that occurred could be regarded as the result of the individual's actions performed in the past. One's so-called good or bad "luck" was not luck at all but simply the ripening of past karmas. The doctrine of karma meant that the events of one's life were not predetermined by fate or a god. For better or worse, human beings determined their own destinies. As the novelist George Eliot put it, "Our deeds still travel with us from afar. And what we have been makes us what we are."

The doctrine of karma significantly altered the conception of rebirth. Since it is not evident that one always reaps the consequences of one's actions in *this* life—after all, the wicked often prosper, while the good often suffer—ancient Indian thought extended the possibilities for karma's return into future lives. One's karma could come to fruition at rebirth and in the next life. Thus, the performance of good karmic acts conditioned a favorable rebirth; evil karmic acts, by the same token, led an unfavorable rebirth. Obviously, the expressions, "favorable" and "unfavorable," imply a standard for making these value judgments. A favorable rebirth was one that raised one's place on the hierarchy of being; an unfavorable rebirth lowered one's status. This hierarchy of being ranged from the divine realm of the gods to the human stratum, with its own ranking system based on caste, down to the animal, plant, and mineral levels. Potentially, one might be reborn at any place on this hierarchy, but always, it was self-generated karma that governed the process and dictated where one was reborn.

When the idea of rebirth acquired its ethical dimension, a new outlook on life began to color the Indians' view of the world. From the samsāric perspective, existence now had but one valid objective: to achieve freedom from the endless cycle of death and rebirth. The world of samsāra had its pleasures and satisfactions, to be sure, but in the long view, from the perspective of an eternal parade of lives and deaths, the world was a wearisome place, laden with pain and grief. Even the best sort of life was permeated with anxiety and suffering and would ultimately end at the charnel ground. Sooner or later, one would realize that complete freedom from samsāra was really the only thing worth seeking. The Hindus called this moksha, absolute and unconditional liberation. The Buddha called it nibbana, or "nirvana," the Sanskrit term more familiar to westerners.

Attaining release from samsāra could not be accomplished merely by generating good karma. Even if one were the finest person possible, performing only good deeds, it would not be sufficient to break free from samsāra's everlasting grind. Positive karmic acts might temporarily take one to the apex of the chain of being. But eventually, one's store of good karma would be depleted, and one would at last face another death and rebirth. As long one produced karma of any kind—good or bad—one was bound to the wheel of samsāra. Seeking a favorable rebirth could thus only be a short-term goal. In the long run, rebirth itself would have to be brought to an end.

As this new understanding of human nature and destiny gained wide acceptance throughout northern India, it provoked a vast movement of individuals who decided to forsake their connections with the world to seek final liberation from samsāra. They gave up their homes and possessions, their families and jobs, because they considered nothing as important as moksha. Men and many women, of all ages and castes, joined this movement, but persons from the middle castes were especially drawn to it. They were called samanas, or "strivers," to indicate their dedication to practicing religious austerities in pursuit of emancipation from rebirth.

The samanas were a common sight in the emerging villages and towns of the Gangetic plain, and ordinary people often sought their advice and teachings. These samanas often experimented with an immense array of disciplines and doctrines to seek a way to their goal. Many wandered about northern India searching out new teachers and new spiritual techniques. Some isolated themselves in caves or deep within the forest. They all lived in self-imposed poverty, frequently owning only a bowl for begging food. Some had even renounced clothing. Although the individuals in this movement varied greatly in their chosen paths and disciplines, they were united by a single ambition, to find relief from the anguish of samsāra. They were so dedicated to this cause that they were willing to give up the pleasures and comforts of the world to achieve it. Even more, they believed renouncing the world was *essential* to that purpose.

Some of these ascetics declared they had indeed discovered the path leading away from samsāra. Although we have no records of many teachings, we know a considerable amount about a few of them. The most prominent among the early teachings was offered by the *Upanishads*, that wonderful anthology from this age in Indian history, which later became one of the sacred scriptures of Hinduism. A brief exploration of this perspective will be helpful as we turn to examine the teachings of the Buddha. Because of the prominence of the Upanishadic philosophy, many of the Buddha's teachings were developed in direct response to this perspective.

The *Upanishads* was a fairly diverse collection of philosophical treatises and parables written over a period of several centuries. But most of the writings it contained concerned three fundamental matters: the nature of the self or soul, the nature of ultimate reality, and the relationship between them. The *Upanishads* offered several points of view on each of these issues, but it is possible to describe a consensus perspective.

We'll begin with the soul. The concept of *ātman*, or soul, had been a part of the Āryans' religion before they migrated into India. But in the Vedic tradition, this ancient concept was not clearly defined or well-developed. There seemed to be little agreement about where the soul came from, where it went upon death, or what exactly it was. At most, the Vedass understood the soul as a vague entity that animates life and keeps the body from being a mere corpse. By the age of the samanas, though, a more definite idea about the soul had come into view. According to this perspective, the soul was an eternal entity residing in, but separate from, the body. The authors of the *Upanishads* asserted that the soul was not created and never came into being at a particular time. It simply always had been. Furthermore, since it was not subject to birth, it could never die. The soul was immortal, beyond birth and death. While it is true the soul transmigrated, it was only the body that was born and died. The soul, which the *Upanishads* identified as the true self, the real self underlying all appearances, was imperceptible, beyond description, and distinguished from not only the body but the mind as well.

Just as the sages of the *Upanishads* sought to comprehend the nature of the soul, they also tried to grasp the ultimate reality, which they called Brahman. Again, the authors did not wholly agree about Brahman, but certain themes recurred, and these motifs had a profound influence on subsequent Hinduism. Among the most prevalent was the idea that Brahman was a single, indivisible reality that could not be adequately explained or comprehended by ordinary means. Although Brahman was the deepest reality underlying all things, it was unavailable to the five senses. It encompassed the whole of the universe, yet transcended it. It embraced both good *and* evil and yet was beyond them. Later Hindu thinkers would suggest that although Brahman was formless, it could be partially known through the images of the many gods and goddesses of the Hindu pantheon. Brahman itself transcended all the gods and yet empowered them.

In their search for overcoming samsāra, many Indian ascetics came to a startling conclusion that led them to believe that their quest of moksha might indeed have come to an end. In the later *Upanishads*, the sages expressed their conviction that the soul and the ultimate reality known as Brahman were in fact, identical, one and the same. The samanas did not simply declare that the soul was a *part* of Brahman; Brahman, after all, was indivisible. Rather, they suggested that *ātman* and Brahman were two names for the same reality. The true self *was* ultimate reality. Brahman-*ātman* was the only reality there was.

The samanas now understood the source of human anguish on the wheel of samsāra as a consequence of ignorance, a complete misunderstanding about the true nature of the self and reality. The failure to apprehend reality correctly encouraged the belief that the soul is an individual entity, separate from Brahman, separate from the rest of reality. This delusion is what caused persons to act in a self-obsessed manner, leading to the production of the karma that chained one to samsāra. Believing oneself to be an entity separate from all else bred the desire and hatred that led to the anguish of samsāra and ultimately caused the fear of death. The only way out of this morass was to realize completely the identity of the soul and the deepest reality. That realization came only at the end of a long road of intense spiritual discipline.

Here, as concisely as I am able to set forth, were the essential features of the intellectual religious world into which Siddhattha Gotama was born. I have not been able to present all the many subtleties and diverse viewpoints comprising this world. But this broad sketch will suffice to portray the social and religious environment of his life. He lived at time of spiritual and religious questioning, when traditions were being re-evaluated, and the basic questions of existence—What are we deep down? Where do we come from? Where are we going? What is the fundamental character of reality?—were receiving exhilarating new answers. The man called the Buddha will have his distinct voice to add to this conversation.

# Siddhattha Gotama
## Lecture 11

**None of the other three teachers in our course has even a remotely
similar biography. Confucius, Jesus, and Muhammad all started
out with little and accomplished their feats in spite of their humble
beginnings. Only the Buddha began with everything and chose to give
it all up.**

Prince Siddhattha Gotama was born and raised with every possible
advantage, but he was also sheltered. On the advice of his astrologers,
Gotama's father, King Suddhodana, made sure Gotama was shielded
from all that was distressing or unpleasant in this world, lest the soft-hearted
prince renounce his crown to become a holy man. But despite his father's
efforts, Gotama slipped away from his confinement. In short order, he saw
for the first time a sick person, an old person, and a corpse. Then he met
a *samana* who, despite his poverty and the ills of the world, was serene
and happy. Gotama thus decided to give up his life of privilege and seek
real happiness.

The stories of the Buddha's life and teachings did not appear in writing
until several centuries after his death, and like our other three sages, he left
no writings in his own hand. According to tradition, three months after the
Buddha's death, 500 of his senior students gathered in the town of Rājagaha
on the Gangetic Plain of India to decide how best to preserve his teachings
for future generations. The monk Ānanda, who had served as the Buddha's
personal attendant and was known for his astounding memory, was invited
to recite to the assembly his recollection of the Buddha's many discourses.
Another monk, Upāli, recollected the rules of community discipline that the
Buddha set out for his followers. After the recitations of both monks, their
declamations were validated by all present. From that moment forward, the
**sangha**, the community of monks and nuns, preserved the discourses and
rules of discipline by memorization.

These works were finally written down sometime in the 1st century B.C.E.
in the Pāli language, a vernacular closely related to Sanskrit but developed

specifically for the purpose of preserving the Buddha's teachings. This Pāli Canon is our best resource for historically reliable information about the Buddha's life. As with the *Analects* of Confucius, we cannot be absolutely certain that these texts report historical fact, but there is good reason to believe that the Pāli sources are founded on historical events and contain the substance of the Buddha's teachings.

**The story of King Suddhodana's over-protectiveness can be read as a cautionary tale about the dangers of ignorance.**

The Pāli Canon is large, a lot larger than the comparable sources we have for Confucius and Jesus. It is split into three divisions, or baskets. The first basket, called the **suttas**, claims to be the record of Ānanda's memories and contains well over 5,000 discourses. The second, called the **vinaya**, purports to be based on Upāli's recitation of communal regulations. The third is called the **abhidhamma**, a highly abstract and systematic presentation of the Buddha's philosophy.

Until recently, most scholars had set the Buddha's birth in or near 563 B.C.E. Today, they are inclined to place it closer to the death of Confucius, somewhere near 490 B.C.E. He was born into the warrior varna in an area occupied by the Āryan Sākyas clan in present-day Nepal, near its border with India. The legend of his birth—of which there were several versions—clearly moves the narrative into the realm of the mythic, touching on Gotama's various previous reincarnations, fable-like stories collected as the *Jataka* tales. In his penultimate life, he became a god in the Heaven of the Contented, where he dwelled for hundreds of thousands of years until deciding that the people of **Jambudvīpa**, an ancient name for India, would be receptive to the message of a Buddha. His conception and birth were attended by gods and celestial beings under auspicious stars, and he was born in full awareness, immediately taking seven steps and declaring that he had been born for the benefit of the world and would never experience birth again.

Obviously, most of this story is ahistorical and unverifiable. As far as his earthly experience, it is unlikely he was born a prince; at the time, the region was ruled by councils of elders, so his father was likely a high-ranking councillor, not a king. In the Pāli Canon, the Buddha did not say that his father tried to keep him confined and unsullied but did say he was well-to-do and pampered. The story's embellishments served an important purpose as literary expressions of the Buddha's teachings. They illustrate that the things almost all of us crave cannot possibly give us the kind of satisfaction and happiness we really want. ∎

## Important Terms

**abhidhamma**: The systematic presentation of the Buddha's teachings; part of the Pāli Canon.

**Jambudvīpa**: An ancient name for India.

**sangha**: The Buddhist community of monks and nuns.

**sutta**: A discourse of the Buddha; part of the Pāli Canon.

**vinaya**: The Buddhist monastic rule; part of the Pāli Canon.

## Question to Consider

1. Studies have shown that oral transmission of stories can be remarkably accurate in cultures without a written tradition. How well do you think the Pāli Canon could have survived the 400 years between the Buddha's death and its first written form? How does this affect your view of the materials it contains?

# Siddhattha Gotama
## Lecture 11—Transcript

The story of the Buddha is surely one of the great narratives in human history. A child born to the king and queen of an ancient realm in the foothills of the Himalayas, Siddhattha Gotama was brought up with every possible advantage. He was uncommonly handsome, a formidable athlete, and blessed with a brilliant mind.

As heir apparent, he was entitled to a career that would bring him great power and fame. Loved by all, he was surrounded by dear friends who sought to fulfill his every whim. His own heart was filled with compassion for all living things. But heeding a warning by his court astrologers, the king took extreme measures to shield his son from any form of suffering or distress.

The soothsayers had told King Suddhodana that the prince was so softhearted that he might renounce his right to rule and seek to become a holy man, if any unpleasantness were to upset his sensitive constitution. Responding to their advice, the father made sure that his son wore only the finest silks, ate the most delectable food, and was constantly entertained by the best musicians and dancers.

At 16, the prince married a ravishing princess, with whom he had a son. He and his young wife lived in three palaces, one each for the summer, winter, and rainy seasons. His excursions outside these palaces were carefully arranged by his father to guarantee that Prince Siddhattha would not encounter anyone or anything that might shatter his rose-colored view of the world.

It is hard to imagine what more could be added to this portrait to make his life seem any richer. Most people would be delighted to have just *one* of these things: good looks, physical prowess, great intelligence, devoted friends, political power and wealth, three luxurious homes, public adoration, youth. Siddhattha Gotama had them *all*.

Yet despite his father's ministrations, the young man slipped away from his confinement and caught a glimpse of the world as it was when it was not prettified for his benefit. In short order, the prince saw for the first time a sick person, an old person, and a corpse. Then he encountered another strange spectacle, one of the samanas of his time who had renounced the world and wandered about it with only a begging bowl in hand. With virtually nothing to call his own and amidst a world of disease, decay, and death, the samana wore a happy and serene countenance. Deeply disturbed by the suffering he saw—and yet heartened by the face of the holy man—Siddhattha Gotama decided he too must give up the life he knew and seek real happiness beyond the sham created by turning a blind eye to the world. On a warm summer night, he kissed his sleeping wife and child goodbye, and as the full moon lit his path, the 29-year-old Gotama walked away from all he had and gave it up forever.

There are not many stories like this one. The more popular narrative is one in which the individual starts out with little or nothing and with prodigious effort or good fortune attains some measure of success. Americans, especially, love such stories. We adore Abraham Lincoln, Andrew Carnegie, Rocky Balboa, Seabiscuit, and Cinderella. We're not so accustomed to the tale in which the hero starts out with everything imaginable and deliberately forsakes it. None of the other three teachers in our course have even a remotely similar biography. Confucius, Jesus, and Muhammad all started out with little and accomplished their feats *in spite of* their humble beginnings. Only the Buddha began with everything and chose to give it all up.

The tale of the Buddha was so compelling that early Christians even adopted it, and it became wildly popular in the Middle Ages. Before it was appropriated by the Church, though, the story received a good baptism. In the Christianized version, an Indian Maharaja named King Abenner so despised the Church that he began to persecute the Christians in his realm. Now, Christianity has a long history in India; tradition claims that Doubting Thomas, one of the 12 Apostles, introduced the faith in South India several years after the resurrection of Jesus.

When his son was born, the Maharaja consulted the astrologers, who predicted that the prince, whose name was Josaphat, would grow up and become a Christian. Needless to say, the forecast alarmed the Maharaja, and he went to great lengths to keep his son sheltered from outside influences, especially from anyone who might expose him to the teachings of Jesus. Yet one day, Josaphat ventured beyond his palace confines and confronted sickness, old age, and death, and met a Christian hermit by the name of Barlaam. Soon, the young man professed the Christian faith, and despite his father's unhappiness and pleas, Josaphat chose to remain a Christian. Eventually, the Maharaja himself became a Christian and abdicated in favor of his son. In the end, Josaphat himself left the throne to become a desert recluse.

There is no doubt that this Christian narrative is a retelling of the story of the early life of the Buddha. The name Josaphat has been traced back to "Bodhisatta," the Buddhist tradition's title for the Buddha before his enlightenment. The Eastern Orthodox Church still celebrates the feast day of Barlaam and Josaphat. In an odd way, the Buddha became a Christian saint.

If early Christians took the story of the Buddha and retold it to suit their purposes, is it possible that the Buddhists have done the same thing? Well, of course, and that is what very likely happened. But what parts of the Buddha's story, if any, are based on actual historical occurrences and what parts have been embellished for the sake of advancing the Buddhist worldview? Again, we face the issue we first met in our discussion of Confucius, and which we will meet again when we take up the other two teachers. And, again, the best way to tackle this matter is by first looking at the sources we have available for our understanding the life of the Buddha.

Like the Āryans who first migrated into India, their descendants who became followers of the Buddha preserved their sacred knowledge by oral means. The stories of the life and teachings of the Buddha did not appear in writing until several centuries after his death. The Buddha—like Confucius, Jesus, and Muhammad—left no writings in his own hand.

Nevertheless, according to Buddhist tradition, these texts accurately reflect the Buddha's own teachings both in spirit and letter. Three months after the Buddha's death, 500 of his senior students, gathered in the town of Rājagaha on the Gangetic Plain of India to decide how best to preserve his teachings for future generations.

At that time, so goes the tradition, the elder monk Ānanda, who had served as the Buddha's personal attendant, was invited to recite to the assembly his recollection of the Buddha's many discourses. Ānanda was reputed to have had an astounding memory. He began each of his recitations with the words, "Thus have I heard … ," followed by a statement of the Buddha's location and audience and a verbatim account of what the Buddha taught. Another elder monk, Upāli, recollected the rules of community discipline that the Buddha set out for his followers. After the recitations of both monks, their declamations were validated by all present. From that moment forward, the *sangha*, the community of monks and nuns, preserved the discourses and rules of discipline by memorization, and they often rehearsed them in community settings.

Because we have become so dependent on the written word, we moderns have a hard time believing that oral transmissions, especially of great length and over long stretches of time, could accurately maintain a body of knowledge. But such skepticism greatly underestimates the capacity of oral cultures to keep vast stores of information over time with little or no mutations. That ability is truly amazing, but it has been attested many times and in many places. In the case of the Buddhist material, the oral transmission was facilitated by numerous mnemonic devices such as numbered lists and the repetition of stock phrases, as well as by the awareness that the words held sacred significance.

The traditions of recited discourses and communal disciplines were finally committed to the written word sometime in the first century B.C.E., about 400 years after the Buddha. They were written in the language of Pāli, a vernacular closely related to the Sanskrit chanted by Brahmans during rituals and used for formal Hindu literature. Pāli was very close to, but probably not identical with, the language the Buddha himself spoke, which most scholars believe to be a dialect called Old Māghadhī. Pāli was developed specifically for the purpose of preserving the Buddha's teachings.

The oral tradition that began at the first Buddhist Council in Rājagaha now exists in writing as the Pāli Canon, which is probably our best resource for an historically reliable understanding of the Buddha's life. As a recent translator puts it, "if your aim is to get as close to 'the Buddha's idiom' as possible, the Pāli suttas are the logical starting point." The Pāli Canon is not the only collection of Buddhist scriptures, however. There is also a Chinese and a Tibetan canon, which replicate a great deal of the Pāli material, but these also add other materials not found in the Pāli. The Chinese and Tibetan versions were much later translations of Indian Buddhist texts. Furthermore, as Buddhism spread throughout Asia and diverged philosophically, new scriptures known as the Mahayana sutras were added to the collections of sacred literature. Unlike the Pāli Canon, however, it is not possible to trace the Mahayana sutras back to the Buddha through a lineage of oral transmission, although these texts do claim an ancient provenance.

Because of its proximity to the Buddha's own time and dialect, we will rely mainly upon the Pāli collection for discussing his life and teachings. As with the *Analects* of Confucius, we cannot be absolutely certain that these texts report historical fact; indeed, particular aspects of the Pāli Canon such as its accounts of past lives and the pantheon of gods, must be strictly excluded as verifiable facts according to modern historiographical principles. But there is good reason to believe that the Pāli sources are *founded* on historical events and contain the substance of the Buddha's teachings and probably many of his actual words. The remarkable internal consistency of the canon has convinced many scholars that these scriptures originated as the work of single mind.

The Pāli Canon is large, a lot larger than the comparable sources we have for Confucius and Jesus. In book form, it comprises about a yard's length of shelf space. The canon is split into three divisions, or "baskets." The first basket, called the suttas, claims to be the record of elder Ananda's memorized discourses of the Buddha's teachings. The suttas contain well over 5,000 discourses. The second, called the vinaya, purports to be based on Upāli's recitation of communal regulations. The third is called the abhidhamma, a highly abstract and systematic presentation of the Buddha's philosophy. Although the early tradition asserts that the abhidhamma dates back to the Buddha himself, this collection is almost certainly a later reworking of earlier material.

To develop our portrait of the historical Buddha, we will be concerned almost exclusively with the suttas. This basket of discourses is the one that presents the material most relevant to our interests, and it is the place where we find the greatest instances of the Buddha revealing his own life story. In sketching a portrait of the Buddha based on history, we are trying to set forth what we can reasonably know of the Buddha using the tools and principles of the historian's craft. I hasten to add that an historical image of the Buddha—or any of the other three figures—does not by any means exhaust his or their significance. Nor does such an image exhaust their histories. It merely states what can be said with some historical reliability. It does not—and cannot—report everything.

That said, let us begin. Up until a few years ago most scholars had set the date of the Buddha's birth on or near 563 B.C.E., based on a reckoning system from the Theravada, the oldest extant variety of Buddhism. That would have made the Buddha slightly older than Confucius. Today, most historians are inclined to place the Buddha's birth closer to the death of Confucius, somewhere near 490 B.C.E. No credible scholar, as far as I'm aware, has ever argued that the Buddha never existed.

The Buddhist tradition said that Siddhattha Gotama was born into the varna of the warriors and nobles in an area occupied by an Āryan clan known the Sākyas. There no reason to doubt this claim. His hometown was called Kapilavatthu, which modern scholarship locates in present-day Nepal near its border with India. The tradition, however, names his birthplace as Lumbini, a tiny place about 25 kilometers from Kapilavatthu. But this tradition cannot be authenticated and is probably part of the legend of the unusual circumstances surrounding Siddhattha's birth.

The legend of his birth—of which there are several versions—clearly moves the narrative into the realm of the mythic. The basic account goes something like this. It begins not with the birth of Siddhattha 2500 years ago but with the life of an individual named Sumedha, who lived untold eons ago in another world-system prior to the current one. Sumedha, who was a monk practicing spiritual austerities, was fortunate enough to meet the Buddha of that world, Dīpamkara. Sumedha was so impressed with the compassionate demeanor of Dīpamkara that he himself vowed to become a Buddha, one of those exceedingly rare individuals who attain the deepest understanding of reality by means of their own efforts.

Through hard work over incalculable lifetimes, Monk Sumedha edged closer and closer to the realization of his vow. He was reborn in a vast array of forms in the animal, human, and divine realms. The stories of his many lifetimes—particularly those of his animal rebirths—comprise an extremely popular genre of Buddhist literature known as the Jataka Tales. The stories are a bit like Aesop's fables and serve to teach Buddhist values, particularly to children. These stories are delightful—my four year daughter just loves them.

After so many lifetimes, the person who as Monk Sumedha vowed to become a Buddha had acquired enough merit, or good karma, to be born as a god in the Heaven of the Contented. This auspicious birth was to be his penultimate. He dwelled in the Contented Heaven for hundreds of thousands of years. When the time came for him to take rebirth, he surveyed the world and determined that the people of Jambudvīpa, an ancient name for India, would be receptive to the message of a Buddha. According to tradition, a Buddha appears only when the teachings of the previous Buddha have been forgotten and the world is amenable to hearing them again. Now was the time, and India was the place.

On the night he was conceived, the full moon shone in the clear sky and his mother, Queen Mahamaya, wife of King Suddhodana dreamt that a white elephant god touched her right side with a white lotus he carried in his trunk. The queen's pregnancy lasted for exactly ten lunar months. As her term neared the end, she felt a great longing to return to her native home. Along the way, she passed a pleasant grove near Lumbini and stopped to enjoy its beauty. As she reached up to touch the branch of a flowering sala tree, the Bodhisatta was born, while celestial beings looked on and auspicious stars shone in the heavens. The child was born, according to the story, in full awareness, with the luminosity of the sun. Immediately, he took seven steps and declared that he had been born for the benefit of the world and would never experience birth again. Seven days after giving birth to the Bodhisatta, Queen Mahamaya died, and she was reborn in the Contented Heaven, in recognition of the great merit she gained by bearing one destined for Buddhahood. After his mother's death, the prince was raised by her sister, Mahaprajapati, who was the king's second wife.

There is much about this story, of course, that excludes it from what the modern world considers historical. The discipline of history cannot verify or falsify claims about previous lives, celestial beings, and gods, and so would categorize most of this narrative as legendary or mythic. Modern historians even find it difficult to accept Siddhattha's royal status. On the basis of what we know from other sources about this region around the time of the Buddha, it is highly unlikely that he was born as a prince to a fabulously wealthy king and queen. At the time, the small states of the Gangetic Plain were governed by councils of elders, not autonomous monarchs. His father was probably a local chieftain or ranking member of the ruling council.

Little more about his early life can be established with confidence. The reports that he was a virtual prisoner of an overprotective father cannot be verified, and they were probably developed by the later tradition to highlight important features of the Buddha's philosophy. Interestingly, in the Pāli Canon the Buddha did not say that his father tried to keep him confined and unsullied by the realities of life. He merely indicated that he was well-to-do and pampered by all the attention lavished on him.

Looking back many years later, he described his youth to his followers:

> I was delicate, most delicate, supremely delicate. Lily pools were made for me at my father's house solely for my benefit. Blue lilies flowered in one, white lilies in another, red lilies in a third. I used no sandalwood that was not from Benares. My turban, tunic, lower garments and cloak were all made of Benares cloth. A white sunshade was held over me day and night so that no cold or heat or dust or grit or dew might inconvenience me. … I was entertained by minstrels with no men among them. … Though meals of broken rice with lentil soup are given to the servants and retainers in other people's houses, in my father's house white rice and meat was given to them.

This account confirms the traditional view that Siddhattha grew up as a privileged child, but it does not go so far as to claim that he had everything imaginable and was hermetically sealed off from the world. Later tradition seems to have added those embellishments.

But those embellishments serve an important purpose. Although they may not be historically accurate, they are precise literary expressions of the Buddha's teachings. The stories of the Bodhisatta's incredible wealth and his many talents and skills illustrate that the things almost all of us crave cannot possibility give us the kind of satisfaction and happiness we really want. The man who had them all discovered they were only an impediment to genuine freedom. Similarly, the story of King Suddhodana's over-protectiveness can be read as a cautionary tale about the dangers of ignorance.

Refusing to face the realities of life, in short, gets us nowhere. We can try to insulate ourselves from the truths about living and dying, and live a comfortable existence as if the rest of the world does not matter, but that is to accept a greatly attenuated existence. The best in human nature comes to expression not in beating a retreat from life's sometimes tough realities, but in accepting them. As we shall see, the Buddha came to believe that facing the truth, whatever it was, was the only way to freedom.

Sound trivial? The Buddha thought that all but a very few courageous individuals lived their lives in a cloud, preferring comfortable illusions and fantasies even though they perpetuate suffering and anguish. The truth about living and dying surrounds us and occasionally intrudes into our lives. For a moment, we awaken to this truth, but just as quickly, most of us hurry back to the warmth of our familiar fictions. Only a few step outside and investigate.

The Buddha was one. When we return, we will see what prompted the man who had it all to barter everything for a chance to find something more valuable than anything.

# The First and Second Great Awakenings
## Lecture 12

As it occurs, a dream seems real enough. Only when we awaken do we recognize that what we thought to be real was actually a fabrication of the mind. This was precisely the way the Buddha interpreted the human situation. All of us, excepting only rare, fully liberated persons, live in a self-generated fantasy, unable to distinguish reality from reverie.

The two events of the Buddha's life almost certainly rooted in history are traditionally called the Great Renunciation, when Gotama began the life of a *samana*, and the Enlightenment, when he realized the way to escape samsāra; we will call them the **First and Second Great Awakenings**. The title "Buddha" literally means "one who has awakened," suggesting that the pivotal experience of liberation is a coming to awareness rather than the acquisition of conceptual knowledge. Furthermore, it implies that those who have not yet awakened are living in a dreamlike state, unable to distinguish reality from reverie.

The Buddha's renunciation of his privileged life is not often thought of as an awakening, but doing so frames it as a positive moment of insight and clarity, not as an impulse of revulsion or disgust. The term also connects the two experiences: Without the first awakening, there would have been no second. It is important to recognize that the Buddha's transformation was not an instant but a process, the result of years of preparation—or eons, if you accept the stories of his past lives.

The legends present the Buddha's first awakening (also called the Four Sights) in a highly dramatic form. Interestingly, the Pāli Canon presents it differently; the Buddha says his insight was the outcome of careful and deliberate reflection, which lacks the drama of the later legend but has the greater ring of truth. What happened to Gotama was an awakening to the fact that there are no exceptions to the rule of aging and death. Until we come face-to-face with this fact, we all live sheltered lives.

The history of religions suggests that spiritual journeys often begin as the result of some disappointment or traumatic experience. Unlike his final awakening, Gotama's first epiphany brought him not peace but restiveness. Perhaps most of us would have retreated within the walls of illusion, refused to accept our mortality, or perhaps we would choose to "eat, drink, and be merry" with the time left. The Buddha chose neither of these, instead staking everything on the faintest of hopes that there was a better way to live his life.

Gotama's first order of business as a *samana* was to find a teacher. He began his studies under Ālāra Kālāma, a famed yogi, who taught him how to reach the meditative consciousness called the "sphere beyond materiality." He then went to Uddaka Rāmaputta, who taught him how to reach the sphere of "neither perception nor nonperception." Neither of these, he realized, were the highest attainments of spirituality as his teachers had claimed. Joined by five *samanas* who had been students of Rāmaputta, Gotama added the extreme asceticism to his practice. They systematically tried to bring their flesh as close to death as possible through fasting and not bathing. Eventually,

Corel Stock Photo Library.

**After years of struggle, Siddhattha sat down under a tree and "woke up" to the cause of suffering and to its final cessation.**

Gotama realized this would lead to death but with no spiritual gains. Just as he renounced his life of pleasure, he now renounced his life of pain. His companions, thinking he had abandoned the path to enlightenment, left him.

At a loss, Gotama rested under a tree and recollected that, as a child, attending to his breath made him more acutely aware of his surroundings and dispelled feelings of boredom and unrest. The path to nibbana might lie in this form of contemplation, so he decided to try this technique again. The Pāli accounts of what happened next are sparse. Later legends describe an onslaught of temptation and torment from the demonlike Mara, designed to sway Gotama from his goal. But Gotama would not be swayed, and Mara gave up. His confidence bolstered, Gotama's mind was expanding as he gained deeper insights into the human condition. Just as the morning star appeared in the sky before dawn, he became aware of the fact that he had finally discovered the ultimate truth. Henceforth, he was known as the Buddha. ■

## Important Terms

**First Great Awakening**: Siddhattha Gotama's rejection of his privileged life for a life of seeking nibbana; also called the Great Renunciation.

**Second Great Awakening**: Siddhattha Gotama's enlightenment, the moment he earned the title of Buddha.

## Questions to Consider

1. You have likely experienced an epiphany once or more in your life. Looking back, did the moment really come out of the blue, or was it the result of a string of other experiences?

2. Some Buddhists see Mara as an independent, malevolent entity, and others see Mara as a personification of Gotama's self-doubt. Which view is more amenable to you, and why?

# The First and Second Great Awakenings
## Lecture 12—Transcript

There is much about the traditional stories of the Buddha's life that cannot be verified by modern historical research. But two events were almost certainly rooted in history. They may not have occurred exactly as described by the Buddhist tradition, but I can see no way to dismiss them as complete fictions. The first took place when Siddhattha Gotama decided to leave the comforts of home at age 29 and join the samana movement that had attracted so many other Indo-Āryans of his era. The second occurred six years later as he sat under a tree, leading him to conclude he had discovered the way to end suffering and samsara. Without actual events grounding these two stories, the name Gotama would be unknown to the world, and there would be no religion known as Buddhism.

It is customary to refer to the first of these events as the Great Renunciation and the second as the Enlightenment, and these are perfectly acceptable names. For our purposes, however, I'd like to refer to them as the First and Second Great Awakenings, designations I'm actually taking from American religious history but using in a vastly different sense.

What many term the "enlightenment" was actually called the "awakening" by the Buddha. In fact, the title "Buddha"—and it is a title and not a name—literally means one who has awakened. This metaphor suggests that the pivotal experience of liberation is more a matter of coming to awareness rather than the acquisition of conceptual knowledge. Furthermore, it implies that those who have not yet "awakened" are living in a sleepy, dreamlike state. As it occurs, a dream seems real enough. Only when we awaken do we recognize that what we thought to be real was actually a fabrication of the mind. This was precisely the way the Buddha interpreted the human situation. All of us, excepting only rare, fully liberated persons, live in a self-generated fantasy, unable to distinguish reality from reverie.

I also want to use the metaphor of awakening to talk about the Great Renunciation, although it is not usually thought of in this light. My unconventional terminology underscores this event as a positive moment of insight and clarity, not as an impulse of revulsion or disgust. Using the same term, furthermore, connects the two experiences causally and qualitatively. Without the first awakening, there would have been no second. Without the second, we would have never known of the first.

It is important to recognize that there was a process involved in the Buddha's transformation; his ultimate awakening was the result of years of preparation—or eons, if you accept the stories of his past lives. It did not occur simply as the effect of one night of really strenuous meditation. Of course, it might sound a little strange to speak of *two* awakenings. If he needed a *second*, was the first really an awakening? To me, it doesn't seem odd at all; in fact, it happens every day. My first awakening occurs when my alarm clock sounds in the morning and the second takes place when my second cup of coffee kicks in. Wakefulness can be a matter of degree. But the second awakening for the Buddha was as awake as you can get.

The legends present the Buddha's first awakening in a highly dramatic form. We've already mentioned the basic elements of the story. The incredibly naïve and mollycoddled prince slips away from his gilded cage and is astonished to discover the world was not what he imagined. After seeing a sick person, an old person, a corpse, and a contented renunciant, he knew that he would have to leave behind the safety and security of home. The Buddhist tradition refers to this episode in the Bodhisattva's life as the Four Sights.

Interestingly, the Pāli Canon presents this experience in a different way. According to these early texts, the Buddha said that his insight into the tough realities of life came not as the result of outwitting his father's protective measures but as the outcome of careful and deliberate reflection. Since it reveals the methodical nature of his thought and conveys the flavor of the discourses, I'd like to quote his statement at length:

While I had such power and good fortune, yet I thought: "When an untaught ordinary man, who is subject to ageing, not safe from ageing, sees another who is aged, he is shocked, humiliated and disgusted; for he forgets that he himself is no exception. But I too am subject to ageing, not safe from ageing, and so it cannot befit me to be shocked, humiliated and disgusted on seeing another who is aged." When I considered this, the vanity of youth left me entirely.

I thought: "When an untaught ordinary man, who is subject to sickness, not safe from sickness, sees another who is sick, he is shocked, humiliated and disgusted; for he forgets that he himself is no exception. But I too am subject to sickness, not safe from sickness, and so it cannot befit me to be shocked, humiliated and disgusted on seeing another who is sick." When I considered this, the vanity of health left me entirely.

I thought: "When an untaught ordinary man, who is subject to death, not safe from death, sees another who is dead, he is shocked, humiliated and disgusted; for he forgets that he himself is no exception. But I too am subject to death, not safe from death, and so it cannot befit me to be shocked, humiliated and disgusted on seeing another who is dead." When I considered this, the vanity of life left me entirely.

The Pāli account clearly lacks the drama of the later legend. But the report in the Pāli collection, for all its philosophical thoughtfulness, has the greater ring of truth. I've always found it hard to believe that Gotama could have lived three decades without ever having encountered sickness, old age, or death. Nobody is *that* insulated from the world. Surely, it was no revelation to this young man that people get sick, get old, and die, as the story of the Four Sights would have us believe.

It matters little, of course, whether what occurred to Siddhattha happened outside the palace gates against his father's will or in the young man's mind as he soberly reflected on the nature of existence. Undoubtedly, *something* serious happened to Siddhattha Gotama that prompted his exit from a life of comfort and privilege. The real question is not *how* he came to leave his familiar world but why. It is in answering this question that the Pāli account may shed greater light than the more mythologized narratives.

The Pāli passage I just recited indicated that what happened to Siddhattha Gotama around the age of 29 was awakening to the fact that there are *no exceptions* to the rule of ageing and death. Even as children and youths, we know that people get sick, get old, and die. But at that tender age, our knowledge is merely abstract and vague, and we don't really believe it will happen to us. In the great Indian epic, the *Mahabharata*, the wise and pious Prince Yudhishthira was once confronted by a nature spirit, who demanded answers to a series of riddles, in a scene similar to Oedipus' encounter with the sphinx. The spirit asked: "What is the greatest wonder in the world?" To which Yudhishthira replied: "Every day, people see creatures die and depart to Yama's abode. Yet, those who remain still seek to live forever. Truly, this is the greatest wonder in the world."

The event that so profoundly disturbed Siddhattha's life of ease was not coming to know that sickness, old age, and death *existed*, but that they applied *to him* and to everyone he loved, without exemption. Until we come face-to-face with this fact, we all live sheltered lives, no matter how much experience we may have accumulated. You don't need to be locked up in a palace to be oblivious to this truth. And you don't have to be a kid either.

Coming to the awareness that the realities of life pertain to oneself can be intensely disillusioning. I still remember the disbelief I felt when I first looked into the mirror (around the age of 29 or 30) and noticed I was aging. "Wait a minute; this is not supposed to be happening to *me!*" I spent months denying the evidence before my very eyes and then months afterwards trying to hide it. This was disillusionment in the best sense of the word—an experience of being stripped of illusion. My disillusionment meant having to let go of the pretense that I was special, different from everyone else. I think something like this happened to Siddhattha Gotama. Without a similar disillusionment, he would have had no second awakening, no insight while calmly sitting under a tree.

The history of religions suggests that spiritual journeys often begin as the result of some disappointment or traumatic experience. Mahavira, the great hero of Jainism, set out on his path at age 28 when his parents died.

Jesus inaugurated his prophetic activity at the death of his mentor, John the Baptist. In Somerset Maugham's novel, *The Razor's Edge*, Larry Darrell forsakes his plans for a conventional life and leaves in search of spiritual adventure in India after he witnessed the devastation of the First World War. As Confucius succinctly put it, "No vexation, no enlightenment; no anxiety, no illumination.

Unlike his final awakening, Gotama's first epiphany brought him not peace but restiveness. It was enough to cause him to walk away from his life of ease and comfort. He could have easily stayed within the walls of illusion. He could have done what most of us do when we glimpse our frailties and mortality: just forget about it. With the aid of alcohol and other drugs, cosmetics and surgeries, amusements and sports, mindless consumption and acquisitions, we try to stop thinking about what we know to be true. We do it so well that we are usually not even aware we are doing it. Perhaps this has been the approach of choice for most humans throughout history. Our species has devoted an incredible amount of creative energy to discovering new methods to hide the truth from oursleves.

Siddhattha might have, on the other hand, adopted a kind of philosophical resignation: let's eat, drink, and be merry, for tomorrow we die. This ancient philosophy was first articulated in *The Epic of Gilgamesh*. It differs from our ordinary perspective by virtue of awareness. Those who adopt this outlook do not *deny* death; they simply choose consciously to live by the principle of pleasure in the face of it. At its best, this philosophy seeks to maximize pleasure by making rational choices; it is not necessarily a mindless hedonism, which seeks pleasure at any cost.

But the Buddha chose neither of these possibilities, either of which would have permitted him to stay at home. His first awakening was too deeply disturbing; returning to pleasure-seeking was just no longer an option. Siddhattha had awakened to the mystery of life. Like the young priest Nachiketas in the *Upanishads*, Gotama believed that the pleasures of life were meaningless with the Grim Reaper watching our every move. But leaving home—or "going forth into homelessness" as the Buddha called it— was also a risky venture. Gotama staked everything on the faintest of hopes.

There was no guarantee that he would succeed at exchanging everything he already had for something better. What if there *was* nothing better? No doubt many at the time thought that Siddhattha was crazy. Understandably, his father and mother tearfully pleaded with him to stay.

He left anyway. The legends describe how he rode far away from his parents' house and exchanged his fine silks and jewelry for a patchwork robe of orange, the identifying color of the samanas. He cut off his long hair, picked up a begging bowl, and started to learn how to fend for himself as a wanderer in the world. He walked southward into the central areas of the Gangetic plain where life in the new villages and towns was astir. He spent the rest of his days traveling throughout this region, never settling down for more than several months at a time.

His first order of business was to find a teacher to lead him to his objective, what he called "the supreme state of sublime peace." He began his studies under the tutelage of Ālāra Kālāma, a famed master of spiritual disciplines known as yoga. The Buddha himself reported that it did not take him long to learn everything Ālāra Kālāma had to offer. Under his direction, Gotama was able to reach a level of meditative consciousness called the "sphere beyond materiality."

But merely attaining a deep level of extraordinary consciousness was not what Gotama wanted. He found another renowned teacher, Uddaka Rāmaputta, who taught him how to reach the sphere of "neither perception nor non-perception," but that was not "the supreme state of sublime peace" either. He continued to regard the yogic practices he learned as important, but could not accept that these were the highest attainments of spirituality as his teachers had claimed. Gotama left Rāmaputta and began to drift towards the central part of the Gangetic Plain, near a town called Uruvelā. This time, five samanas who had been students of Rāmaputta went with him as his disciples.

Gotama and his followers now intensified his efforts. To their meditative practices, they added the extreme asceticism that many of the other samanas observed. They would dwell in haunted shrines, what the Buddha described as "awe-inspiring abodes ... which make the hair stand up" to steel themselves against the "fear and dread" of being in such scary places, the ancient equivalent of spending the night in a haunted house. Considering the body a hindrance to the highest spiritual achievements, they systematically and deliberately tried to bring the flesh as close to death as possible. They fasted for long stretches of time; when they ate, it was only a handful of rice or lentils. They allowed their hair and beards to grow long and matted. Their bodies accumulated thick layers of dust because they had forsaken bathing. Years later, the Buddha would tell his followers that he began to resemble a skeleton covered in decaying flesh. More than once, onlookers mistook him for a corpse. Had he continued much longer down that path, their perception would not have been a mistake.

Fortunately, the ascetic realized the way of self-mortification would only end in death, with no compensating spiritual gains. "By this grueling penance," he said, "I have attained no distinction higher than this human state, worthy of the noble one's knowledge and vision." The extreme practices of asceticism did not lead to "the supreme state of sublime peace." Just as he renounced his life of pleasure in Kapilavatthu, the samana Gotama now renounced his life of pain through religious austerities. He decided no longer to abuse his body in service to the spirit. He had tolerated as much pain as he thought anyone could take, and was not one whit better for it. He concluded that it would be necessary to look after the health of the body because the body would be required to sustain his continuing search for the sublime peace. Both denying the body's needs and indulging its appetites were errors, he decided. With this change of mind, he began to eat properly but moderately. Eventually his health returned. When his five disciples realized that he had abandoned the path of severe asceticism, they assumed he had lost his ambition to realize nibbana. They left him, just as he had left his teachers years before.

Having dismissed the way of worldly pleasures and the way of self-denial as both fruitless, the Bodhisatta was at a lost as to how to proceed. Having everything had not brought him the contentment he was seeking and neither did having nothing. But he *had* attained the empty openness that often precedes creative thought, an achievement, by the way, that should not be underestimated. It is not easy to reach this quality of mind. For Siddhattha

Gotama, it took following to their bitter ends the way of wanting and acquiring and the way of aversion and denial for him to find this fertile openness.

It is amazing what the mind can toss up when it is not following its well-worn neuropathways. As he rested under a tree, the Bodhisatta recollected an old memory from childhood. He recalled sitting under a rose-apple tree as a mere boy, as his father was plowing a nearby field. He found the whole experience terribly uninteresting and, with nothing else to do, he started to pay close attention to his breathing. He remembered that attending to his breath as a child made him more acutely aware of his surroundings and dispelled his feelings of boredom and unrest. As he remembered the pleasant feelings of calm attentiveness, he pondered whether or not the path to nibbana might lie in this form of contemplation. The experience under the rose-apple tree had once sharpened his sense of awareness and brought him a tranquility that the years of strenuous asceticism had not. He decided to try this approach again.

Near the little town of Gaya, close to Uruvelā, he found a congenial spot beside a quiet, clear river. There, on the full moon day of the month of Vesakha, he sat under a large peepul tree and vowed not to leave until he had attained complete awakening, even if it meant dying in the effort. The peepul tree later became known colloquially as the "Bodhi" or "Bo" tree, terms that mean wisdom, but more literally suggest wakefulness.

It is interesting to observe how trees appeared at three of the most significant moments of the Buddha's life. He was born under a flowering sala tree as his mother reached for a branch; he attained awakening under the Bo tree; and he died, achieving final nibbana as he lay between two sala trees. It is also interesting to note the appearance of the full moon at these critical junctures. His birth, awakening, and final nibbana were said to have all occurred at the time of the full moon in Vesakha, which usually occurs during the western months of April and May. Today, Vesak is the central holiday of the Buddhist world, and in some countries, like Sri Lanka, every full moon day is a holiday.

The story of the Buddha's second awakening is, of course, fleshed out in fascinating mythological detail by later tradition, but the Pāli accounts of what happened are sparse. The later legends emphasize his heroic qualities as he resisted the onslaughts of his great nemesis, Mara, a demon-like figure whose chief objective was to keep Gotama from reaching his goal. As the Bodhisatta deepened his meditation through the course of the night, Mara tried to entice him with visions of lovely, seductive women. When the allure of sensual pleasure failed, Mara tried to frighten Gotama with images of hostile armies seeking to destroy him. That too was futile. Then Mara attempted to make Gotama feel doubtful about his capacity to accomplish something as lofty as nibbana. After trying everything in his arsenal, and failing each time, Mara finally acknowledged defeat.

Mara was quite a fascinating figure in Buddhist literature. He functioned like Satan in the New Testament stories of Jesus, not so much as a god of evil but as a tempter and a nuisance. Although mythically, Mara is depicted as a separate being, Buddhist psychology also suggests that Mara is that aspect of our own personalities that tries to sabotage our happiness. It is interesting that Mara does not appear in the story of the Buddha until the moment he decides to seek enlightenment, just Satan only shows up to pester Jesus when begins his proclamation about the Kingdom of God. As long as the Bodhisatta lived in ignorance of the world, Mara had no need to trouble him. When one sets off to live the noble life, the trials begin in earnest. Long after the Buddha defeated Mara in his quest for awakening, the later legends say, the two actually became good friends and sometimes commiserated over tea about the hardships of fulfilling the roles allotted to them.

Back to the seconding awakening: With the conquest of Mara, the Bodhisattva gained confidence that his goal was within reach. His mind was expanding as he gained deeper insights into the human condition. Just as the morning star appeared in the sky before dawn, he became aware of the fact that he had finally accomplished what he had to do. He had indeed lived up to his name, Siddhattha: "he who reaches the goal." But henceforth, he would no longer be known by that name but by the title he had earned, the Buddha.

What the Buddha discovered during this night of insights was the basis for all that he subsequently taught. Many of the components of his philosophy, of course, he had learned in other contexts, such as the ideas of samsara and karma and the form of concentration he stumbled upon as a boy during a moment of boredom. But at his final awakening, he gained something even deeper and as well as the conviction of certainty. What he first accepted as belief, he now knew as truth, as the result of what he called "direct knowledge." In our next discussion, we will begin to explore the elements of the Buddha's vision. I will see you then.

# Knowing the World
## Lecture 13

**They should not accept anything simply because it was based on a claim of revelation; or because it was rooted in tradition or commonly repeated as fact; or because it came from scriptures; or because it conformed to logic and seemed rational; or because the teacher was competent and possessed a fine reputation. These grounds were not enough.**

The Buddha urged his students not to accept any dhamma as true until they had attained direct knowledge of it for themselves. He said the usual grounds on which most people accept something as true were insufficient for living the spiritual life. Much of what we call knowledge comes from second- and third-hand sources such as teachers, parents, friends, the news media, and the things we read. Usually this indirect knowledge is fine and even necessary. But the Buddha discouraged faith in matters of ultimate importance. To qualify as true, a doctrine or claim must be known by immediate experience.

Not only was the truth to be seen; it was to be embodied and lived out as well. The Buddha did his best to ensure that his dhamma was understood as a practical regimen leading to direct knowledge and not as a system of beliefs. During his 45-year teaching career, the Buddha instructed through philosophy, object lessons, thought experiments, even silence—simply refusing to answer questions put to him. To all, he presented his very life as the quintessence of his dhamma. "One who sees me," he said, "sees the dhamma."

The Buddha intentionally refused to speak on many metaphysical matters, such as the question of a created versus an infinite universe. These matters are called the *Avyakata*, which is usually translated as the "things that are not revealed" but which more literally means the "things that create unnecessary speech." There has been much debate about why he ignored such questions, but his own explanation was that the answers were irrelevant to ending suffering. Dwelling on such questions merely distracts us from the path.

The Buddha appears to have accepted the many gods of his culture as part of a vast cosmos populated with all kinds of beings, including humans, animals, ghosts, and hell-beings, all trapped in samsāra. They could help human beings in certain ways, but they could not help them attain the supreme state of sublime peace. That was something each being—human and divine—had to discover for him- or herself.

Did the Buddha have a place for "God"—the monotheist idea of a supreme being? No. But if the term "God" is used to refer not to an anthropomorphic being but an ultimate, transcendent reality, then we could say the Buddha embraced a functional analogue to this—namely, nibbana, the unconditioned absolute. The Buddha said very little about nibbana; he taught that understanding existence, the conditioned world, was the way to see the unconditioned, the nibbana.

The Buddha's **three marks of existence** were impermanence, insubstantiality, and insatiability. Impermanence, or **anicca** in Pāli, is significantly different from the simple idea that "things change"; rather, birth, growth, decay, and death occur at every instant in a manner difficult to discern without the skills of meditation, which makes it possible to sharpen perceptive attention to such a degree that one could have a direct knowledge of the momentary arising and passing away of all reality. The resemblance between successive moments is the result of what the Buddha called "conditioning," meaning that one event (or collection of events) greatly influences, but does not completely determine, the next. There is continuity but not constancy.

**The Buddha discouraged faith in matters of ultimate importance.**

The Buddha's understanding of change was so far-reaching, so thoroughgoing, that ultimately it meant that there were no "things" in the world at all. He did not think the universe was a complete illusion but that no item in our experience endured long enough or independently enough for us to say it was an entity with its own existence in space and time. Our minds, conditioned as they are by our language, tend to regard as "things" matters that are better understood as events or occurrences. Most of the time, it is perfectly acceptable that our minds do this. The danger arises when we forget that talking and thinking about "things" is a mere convenient contrivance.

To summarize his understanding of impermanence, let us say the Buddha did not think that things changed; he thought that change was the only thing there was. ∎

## Important Terms

**anicca**: The Pāli word for impermanence in the Buddhist sense—not simply the notion that things change but the idea that change is the only thing that truly exists.

*Avyakata*: The metaphysical matters that the Buddha refused to discuss; the word may be translated as "things that are not revealed" or "things that create unnecessary speech."

**three marks of existence**: In Buddhism, the three basic qualities of the material world: impermanence, insubstantiality, and insatiability.

## Questions to Consider

1. How does the Buddha's view on faith compare with the views other religious traditions you are familiar with? How does faith play a role in your life, in spiritual or other matters?

2. Some have noted similarities between the Buddha's concept of impermanence and concepts in modern physics, such as space-time unity and wave-particle duality. Does thinking of impermanence as a scientific, rather than metaphysical, concept help or hinder your understanding?

# Knowing the World
## Lecture 13—Transcript

The Buddha claimed his final awakening gave him profound insight into the nature of reality as well as the assurance that he had attained "the supreme state of sublime peace" for which he had long searched. "What had to be done has been done," he thought to himself as he recognized his achievement. He attributed this certainty to what he called "direct knowledge," understanding gained and confirmed by immediate, personal experience. When he began to teach his vision of the world to others, he urged them not to accept it as true until they too had attained direct knowledge for themselves.

This epistemology—that is, this approach to knowing—was especially important in the context in which the Buddha lived. The robust movement of samanas—the renunciants in search of liberation—and the urgency to address matters of ultimate concern had spawned a huge panoply of teachers, each of whom proclaimed his own dhamma, or truth. Amid so many claims, spiritual seekers and laypeople alike were genuinely perplexed about whose teaching—if any—was true. When the Buddha appeared on the scene with *his* dhamma, audiences wanted to know not only what distinguished his teaching from that of all the others, but also *how* they could know that his was the real dhamma as he claimed.

The Buddha offered them such a method. He told his listeners that the usual grounds on which most people accept something as true were insufficient for living the spiritual life. To one community called the Kalamas, who had heard more than their share of spiritual teachers, he enumerated these inadequate reasons. He told the Kalamas that they should not accept anything simply because it was based on a claim of revelation; or because it was rooted in tradition or commonly repeated as fact; or because it came from scriptures; or because it conformed to logic and seemed rational; or because the teacher was competent and possessed a fine reputation. These grounds were not enough, he thought, for a claim to pass muster as genuine knowledge.

Although we like to think differently about ourselves as modern people, much of what we accept as true is based on one or more of the grounds that the Buddha dismisses as insufficient. What we call knowledge usually comes from second- and third-hand sources such as teachers, parents, friends, the news media, and the things we read. We all claim to "know" the earth is a sphere, but how many of us have actually investigated that assertion and proven it to ourselves? Most of us "know" that atoms exist, but few of us have taken the time to study the evidence supporting the atomic theory. We "know"—or maybe I should say, we believe—these things because we trust the persons or sources that inform us. Much of the time, this indirect knowledge gained through trust is fine—and even necessary. We simply don't have the time, energy, and skill to prove *everything* to ourselves, and recognizing that limitation supports my point: most of what we consider "knowledge" in our everyday life is actually mediated to us by the faith we place in certain authorities.

But the Buddha discouraged faith in matters of ultimate importance. He wanted everyone to see the truth of his teachings for themselves and not to rely on his authority as a holy man or as a famous teacher or on what his followers said. Nor was it was enough for someone to consider his teaching true just because it seemed to make sense. He told the Kalamas:

> When you know *for yourselves* that these teachings are wholesome; that they are blameless; that they are praised by the wise; and that they, if undertaken and practiced, lead to benefit and happiness, then you should accept them and abide in them.

Within this compact statement, the Buddha sets out the standards for accepting a spiritual teaching as true. To qualify as true, a doctrine or claim must be known by immediate experience. Mere belief, according to the Buddha, was not enough when it comes to matters of ultimate significance. Mark Twain was once asked if he believed in infant baptism. "Do I *believe* in it?" he said. "Hell, I've seen it!" Twain's play on the word "believe," which reveals the ambiguous way the term is often used in the modern age, goes right to the heart of the matter for the Buddha. Belief is inferior to seeing for oneself.

Indeed, beliefs without direct knowledge can actually be dangerous, as later tradition suggested in an anecdote about Mara, the tempter who tried to derail the Buddha's awakening. As the story goes,

> Mara ... was traveling through the villages of India [one day] with his attendants. He saw a man doing walking meditation whose face was lit up with wonder. The man had just discovered something on the ground in front of him. Mara's attendants asked what that was and Mara replied, "A piece of truth." "Doesn't this bother you when someone finds a piece of the truth, o wicked one?" his attendants asked. "Not at all," Mara replied with a devilish smile. "Right after this they usually make a belief out of it."

Mara knew what the Buddha knew: that belief was not the same as personal experience and that direct knowing was the only way to secure liberation.

Although the Buddha's criteria for judging what is true depended on personal experience, this judgment was not merely subjective. Claims to truth also had to be measured against the standards of other wise individuals and must bear wholesome fruit in practice. Thus not only was the truth to be seen; it was be embodied and lived out as well. The Buddha did his best to ensure that his dhamma was understood as a practical regimen leading to direct knowledge and not as a system of beliefs.

The Buddha's teaching career lasted 45 years, from a few weeks after his enlightenment at age 35 until his death at age 80. During that long period, he instructed thousands of persons from all stations in life, men, women, and children of all castes, all occupations, and all levels of education and intellectual skill. As a masterful teacher, the Buddha was adept at addressing his audiences in a manner suited to their capacities to understand. For some, he spoke philosophy; for others, he gave object lessons or offered thought experiments based on ordinary life; for some, he taught by silence, simply refusing to answer questions put to him. To all, he presented his very life as the quintessence of his dhamma. "One who sees me," he said, "sees the dhamma."

Thus we have available to us a variety of ways to explore the Buddha's worldview. The most well-known approach to his vision is the very cogent outline known as the Four Noble Truths, which we will discuss in a future lecture. But today, we will begin exploring his teachings by a different route. The approach we'll be taking in this lecture aligns the Buddha's dhamma with the outline of topics we're considering for the other three figures. As with Confucius, our first subject in the study of the Buddha's teaching is metaphysics, his understanding of the basic nature and structure of reality.

To segue into that topic, and to bridge his metaphysics with our discussion of his epistemological views, I'd like to begin by noting the kinds of metaphysical issues that the Buddha intentionally *excluded* from consideration. Although he certainly made statements about the way the world is, he did not feel obliged to take positions on every possible question that might be raised about the nature of reality. For instance, he consistently refused to discuss questions about the temporal and spatial character of the world as a whole.

Did the universe came into being at a particular moment in time and will it come to an end, or has it always existed and always will? Is the universe extended infinitely in space or is it finite? About such matters, the Buddha declined to comment. These and other disregarded metaphysical matters are known in the Buddhist tradition as the *Avyakata*, which is usually translated as the "things that are not revealed" but which more literally means the "things that create unnecessary speech."

There has been a vigorous discussion about why the Buddha ignored these issues. Was it because he did not know the answers? Interestingly, he never said that. In fact, he often indicated that he knew a lot more than what he taught. Was it because answers to these questions were beyond the competence of language to articulate? That's quite possible, as the Buddha often found language inadequate to express his insights, which was one reason he insisted that his dhamma be personally realized. But his own explanation, which actually does not preclude these others, was rooted in practicality; knowing the answers to these kinds of questions, he said, was just not relevant to the sole objective of his teaching: to end suffering.

We can ask all sorts of questions about the world, and many of these are fascinating, riveting questions. As a kid, I couldn't stop thinking about these kinds of things. You know, questions like: If god created the world, who created god? Or if god did not create the world how did it come into existence? The Buddha thought that you do not need to know these things to attain human fulfillment and happiness. Dwelling on such questions merely distracts us from the immediate concerns of here and now and in its own way contributes to our suffering. As I recall, thinking about how god came into being usually left me with a pounding headache! Like Confucius, the Buddha tried to leave speculative issues alone.

If the Buddha refused to answer questions about the world's creation, we might wonder what he thought about the gods, since creation is often associated with the divine. To be sure, the Buddha lived in a culture in which creator-gods (and gods of all types) were commonplace, and the Buddha never seemed to doubt their existence. He often spoke about the gods, and in the legends, as I mentioned earlier, he was even portrayed as having been a god in previous lives. The Buddha appeared to have accepted gods as part of a vast cosmos populated with all kinds of beings, including humans, animals, ghosts, and hell-beings. As in classical Hinduism, it was possible for beings to be reborn into another category depending on their karma. So a human being might become an animal or a god might become a human in another life.

Obviously, the gods of the Buddha's world were not the same as the supreme being worshiped by Jesus and Muhammad; the gods were extremely powerful and lived enormously long lives, but they were nonetheless limited and subject to the same principles of karma and rebirth that governed the lives of all beings. Because the gods themselves were trapped in samsara, they too needed to take the path leading to nibbana. The ancient stories tell of the Buddha's journeys to the heavens to teach the divine beings his liberating dhamma. The gods therefore did not play a definitive role in the Buddha's teachings. They could help human beings in certain ways, but they could not help in the one thing that mattered most: attaining the supreme state of sublime peace. That was something each being—human and divine—had to discover for him- or herself.

Those were the gods. But what about God? Did the Buddha have a place for what many call God, capitalized in the singular? If by God, one means the monotheist idea of a supreme being, the answer is clearly and emphatically no. Never once does the Buddha even hint that he accepted belief in such an entity. He told of great gods known as Mahābrahmās who were very powerful but had an exaggerated sense of their own importance in the world. One of these great gods, Baka Brahmā, was once reborn alone in one of the many heavenly realms and assumed that he had caused his own existence and created his own realm, of which he was the sole supreme deity. But the Buddha simply maintained that such a claim was mistaken, arising out of a god's own conceit and limitations of knowledge. The implication of the Buddha's story is that he found untenable monotheist claims about a divine being with ultimacy, omnipotence, and singularity.

But if the term God is used in a different sense to refer to an ultimate reality that transcends the anthropomorphic god of monotheism, then it might be possible to say that the Buddha embraced a functional analogue to the concept of God. On such a view, God must be taken to refer to an unconditioned or absolute reality, not a being or entity. This is not the dominant view of God in the western religions, which clearly stress the personal, humanlike character of the divine. Yet there are places even within these western traditions where ultimate reality is regarded in ways that transcend personal conceptions. The not-so-well-known Christian theologians such as Meister Eckhart and Denys the Areopagite are two examples of religious philosophers whose understanding of God effectively denies divine personality in favor of an ineffable absolute beyond the human ability to conceive.

If such is the understanding of God, then the analogue to God in the Buddha's worldview was nibbana. Nibbana demarcated an important distinction in the Buddha's metaphysical world between the unconditioned absolute and the conditioned world of samsaric existence. He sometimes spoke of these dimensions using the metaphor of a river. Nibbana was the farther shore and samsara the nearer shore. His dhamma the Buddha regarded as the means for crossing to the other side. Significantly, the Buddha said very little about nibbana, although it was clearly the aim of everything he taught. In this respect, nibbana was similar to Eckhart and Denys' God: inconceivable and unutterable absolute. Although the Buddha spoke rarely about the farther shore, he had much to say about the world of existence. Understanding existence, the conditioned world, was essential, he thought, to seeing the unconditioned, the nibbana.

The Buddha summarized his understanding of existence in a simple three-part list that identified the salient characteristics of conditioned reality, or life as we know it. He called this statement the three marks of existence. The Buddha claimed that his understanding of these three qualities—like everything else in his philosophy—was based on direct knowing. In this sense, he denied that his metaphysical positions were speculative or indeterminate. Anyone who made the effort to see with complete attentiveness could confirm the truth of these qualities. But even the unenlightened person could conceptually grasp these ideas and see how they were supported by empirical evidence. Enlightenment added the depth, clarity, and certitude that could not be had by conceptual understanding alone

The three marks of existence were impermanence, insubstantiality, and insatiability. In the Buddha's understanding these three qualities were interrelated. Each implied the other two. We will take up each characteristic in turn and discuss its meaning and function in the Buddha's worldview. We will begin with impermanence. In our next lecture, we will take up the qualities of insubstantiality and insatiability.

Saying "things change" is such a cliché that for the Buddha even to point it out seems almost trite. Everyone knows the world and the things in it are constantly changing. Did it really require six years of asceticism and an experience of enlightenment for the Buddha to figure that out? Well, yes, as a matter of fact, it did, because the Buddha's understanding of impermanence, or *anicca* to use the Pali term, was significantly different from the run-of-the-mill idea that things they are a-changing. What distinguished the Buddha's vision of impermanence was its completely thoroughgoing nature. The Buddha applied the idea of impermanence to absolutely everything in existence, and he insisted that happiness depended on the direct understanding and unqualified acceptance of that fact.

For the Buddha, change was not merely what happens to an entity over the course of time. Change was not simply the birth, growth, decay, and death of an organism, the kinds of changes that are ordinarily perceptible. The Buddha saw that birth, growth, decay, and death also occurred at every instant in a manner difficult to discern without the skills of meditation. Meditative practice made it possible to sharpen perceptive attention to such a degree that one could have a direct knowledge of the momentary arising and passing away of all reality. When viewed this way, as the constant coming and going of transitory events, any perception of stability or permanence was only apparent. A deep, penetrating awareness of the world revealed that all things were concatenations of events happening so rapidly that they seem to be stable or changing only very slowly through time.

Although a tree appears to be a more or less stable thing in the world, in fact it is a grand parade of processes happening in swift succession at every level of the tree's existence. At any given moment, leaves may be engaged in the process of photosynthesis as chlorophyll interacts with the light of the sun; sap may be flowing through its xylem and phloem carrying nutrients from the soil throughout the tree's body; minute cells comprising its bark are dying and sloughing off as new cells are born to replace the old. And of course the atoms and their subatomic components that comprise these cells and systems are themselves in a wild, mind-boggling state of transformation. From this perspective, a tree is not—and cannot be—the same from moment to moment.

But neither is it completely different. The tree that appears at one moment in time bears a close resemblance to the tree at the moment just preceding it and to the tree at the moment just succeeding it. The resemblance between the successive moments of the tree's life is the result of what the Buddha called "conditioning." The tree at moment one conditions the tree at moment two, which conditions the tree at moment three, and so on. In this context, conditioning means that one event (or collection of events) greatly influences, but does not completely determine, the next. Moment three is what it is because of the character of moment two, which is what it is because of the character of moment one. Because of conditioning, there is *continuity* between the tree's successive moments in time, but there is not identity, constancy, or sameness.

Now, let's push this view even further. The Buddha's understanding of change was so far-reaching, so thoroughgoing, that ultimately it meant that there were no "things" in the world at all. I do not mean to say he thought that the universe was a complete illusion, a mere creation of some mind without objective reality; no, for the Buddha, the world was real enough. But he thought that no item in our experience—no thought, feeling, or physical object—endured long enough from one moment to the next for us to say it was a "thing." By "thing," I simply mean an entity that has its own existence in space and time.

Because change occurs so rapidly and so thoroughly, and because all items of experience are dependent on other items, like photosynthesis depends on the sun, it is misleading and technically wrong to call a tree a thing. There is nothing about a tree that warrants saying it has its own existence, since it depends on so much that is not-tree, like air, light, soil, and water, and since no particular form of it endures over time, not even a moment, however that would be defined. Imputing thinghood to these, these—I want to say "things"!—and that proves my point—these "aspects" of experience is a function of our language and thinking processes. That's what the Buddha wants us to see by means of this doctrine of impermanence. Our minds, conditioned as they are by our language, tend to reify, or regard as concrete things, matters that are better understood as events or occurrences.

Most of the time, it is perfectly okay that our minds do this. It is certainly more convenient to say, "Look at that tree over there" than to say "Look at that complex concatenation of successive events engaged in the processes of photosynthesis, the transport of nutrients, the death and birth of new cells, and the swirl of electrons. Isn't it beautiful?" The danger arises only when we *forget* that talking and thinking about "things" is a mere convenient contrivance. The true reality of the world of existence is something that cannot easily be captured by our thought and language.

To summarize his understanding of impermanence, let us say the Buddha did not think that things changed; he thought that change was the only thing there was. The attribution of thinghood to any aspect of our experience is merely a habit of thought, a function of language based on our need for convenience in negotiating this complex existence ours.

I hope our discussion has not been overly abstract or abstruse. If the point I am trying to make is not yet clear, perhaps our next discussion on no self, or insubstantiality, will help. In any event, please bear in mind that it took the Buddha himself lifetimes of preparation before he understood impermanence with direct knowledge!

# Can't Get No Satisfaction
## Lecture 14

Each of these worldviews holds a perspective on the self that the Buddha found untenable. He could find no reason to excuse any aspect of personhood from the principle of impermanence. Even more, he thought the tendency to deny the pervasiveness of change by sneaking permanence in through the back door with the idea of selfhood was the chief cause of human misery.

By observing the Buddha's vision of impermanence, we have already begun to make our acquaintance with insubstantiality, or **anatta**, the second of the Buddha's three marks of existence. Anatta literally translates as "no self" or "no soul." Human beings, he said, are not exempt from impermanence, yet almost every religious worldview, including the Hindu faith in which the Buddha was raised, posits an immortal soul or some core self. Even some modern views in psychology maintain the existence of a true self underlying the masks of our personality. But the Buddha could find no reason to excuse any aspect of personhood from impermanence and thought clinging to permanence through the idea of selfhood was the chief cause of human misery.

The Buddha was not trying to suggest that human beings do not exist; he merely refused to affirm the belief in an enduring, essential self or soul. It would be incorrect to say that the Buddha "believed in no-self"; rather, no-self means he declined to believe in the soul. He was convinced that the soul was an irredeemably flawed concept, an unwholesome and problematic way of thinking. To say the self "is" suggests that it is a thing—something fixed, unchanging, and separate from the rest of reality. Rather, a human is a compound of five processes called the **aggregates of being**: materiality, sensation, perception and apperception, conceptual constructs, and consciousness. These components are all rapidly changing processes, and none of them contains anything that could be identified as self, because we are not in complete control of any of these components.

For the Buddha, the problem with the concept of the self was not just that it was empirically unverifiable or unavailable to our experience, but that it gave rise to the third mark of existence, ***dukkha***, or insatiability. You might find *dukkha* translated elsewhere as illness, anguish, sorrow, unease, distress, unsettledness, lamentation, pain, grief, despair, or disappointment. It is the opposite of *sukha*, meaning happiness or contentment. At the root of *dukkha* is the fact that you can never get enough of what you don't really need.

Happiness for the Buddha meant not fleeting pleasure but the supreme state of sublime peace, the deep, abiding contentment that was not dependent on circumstances. It is possible whether one's sensations are pleasant or unpleasant. All beings seek *sukha*, which

© iStockphoto /Thinkstock.

**Of all the aspects of the Buddha's teaching, no-self has been the feature most prone to misunderstanding. The Buddha was not suggesting that human beings do not exist; rather, the Buddha declined to believe in the soul.**

the Buddha did not see as a problem per se, but he saw grave problems with how we seek it. Because of our failure to understand impermanence and insubstantiality, we inevitably pursue happiness in the very ways that thwart its fulfillment, and our thirst for satisfaction intensifies and worsens.

Most people seek happiness through acquisition and/or aversion. Acquisition can refer to material wealth as well as experiences, rewards, or relationships. So what's the problem with this? The ephemeral nature of reality. Deep, abiding contentment cannot be gained by glomming onto transient things. Aversion can refer to avoiding unpleasant situations, things, or people. As with acquisition, the problem with trying to find your happiness through avoidance is this thing called reality, which does not allow us to evade unwanted experiences. The whole approach to contentment through acquisition or aversion is fundamentally misguided.

Conditioned existence simply will not satisfy our deepest longings for happiness. When we awaken to the world "as it is," we discover, paradoxically, that the only way to find happiness is to relinquish these feverish efforts to protect and empower this mistaken belief we call the self. ∎

## Important Terms

**aggregates of being**: The five processes the Buddha considered the only components of human existence: materiality, sensation, perception and apperception, conceptual constructs, and consciousness.

**anatta**: Insubstantiality, the second of the Buddha's three marks of existence; literally, "no self" or "no soul." It does not deny the existence of people but the notion of a core essence that is the self separate from the aggregates of being.

*dukkha*: Insatiability, the third of the Buddha's three marks of existence. Sometimes translated as "unease," "pain," or "disappointment," is the opposite of *sukha*, contentment, and is driven by desire.

## Questions to Consider

1. Do you believe in the soul or some kind of essential self? Why or why not?

2. What do you understand as the difference between pleasure and contentment? Have you ever experienced the latter in the way the Buddha defines it?

# Can't Get No Satisfaction
## Lecture 14—Transcript

One of the many ways the Buddha explained his dhamma was by means of what he called the three marks of existence: impermanence, insubstantiality, and insatiability. These three qualities characterized the fundamental nature of conditioned reality as ascertained by the Buddha on the night of his enlightenment. He contended that direct understanding of these characteristics was readily available to anyone willing to see the world as it was, unclouded by preconceptions and beliefs. Our last discussion revealed how the Buddha's view of the first of these qualities, impermanence, was radical and unqualified. Our conversation today will take up the remaining two features of existence, insubstantiality and insatiability. We will see that the Buddha's understanding of these traits was as thoroughgoing and as uncompromising as his perspective on impermanence.

By observing the radical depth of the Buddha's vision of impermanence, we have already begun to make our acquaintance with the mark of insubstantiality. As we have seen, the transitory nature of existence led the Buddha to deny the existence of things, in the ordinary sense that we think of thingness. Because nothing maintained sameness or identity over successive moments or existed independently of other realities, the idea of a thing, an entity enduring through time and having its own existence, was just a misleading habit of the mind. This denial of thinghood, or what medieval philosophers called "quiddity," is the basic meaning of the quality of insubstantiality. When the Buddha said that insubstantiality is a mark of existence, he was simply saying there is no such thing as a thing.

Insubstantiality is the way I am interpreting the Pali term *anatta*, a word that literally translates as no-self or no-soul. No-self is the denial of thinghood or permanent substance or essence to what is ordinarily called the "self" or "soul." Human beings, in other words, are not exempt from impermanence; insubstantiality characterizes the *whole* of existence, including persons.

Suggesting that persons are no exception to the rule may sound unremarkable or hackneyed, but consider how often exceptions are actually made. Virtually all religions—and I can't think of one that does not—acknowledge the fact of change, but despite that recognition, almost every religious worldview posits an immortal soul or some version of a substantial self in which the personality has a core identity. No-self was directed specifically at the Hindu conception of the ātman, the immortal soul that the *Upanishads* claimed to be identical with the ultimate reality called Brahman. All things pass away, report the *Upanishads*, *except* this singular reality.

But other worldviews also hypothesize the existence of an essential or permanent self and are therefore vulnerable to the Buddha's critique. Certainly, the ancient Greeks believed in it, as did traditional Christianity, Islam, and other religions that suggest that an enduring soul faces eternal paradise or perdition after death or at the end of days. Even some modern views in psychology maintain the existence of a "true self" that underlies so many false selves or masks of our personality. Each of these worldviews holds a perspective on the self that the Buddha found untenable. He could find no reason to excuse *any* aspect of personhood from the principle of impermanence. Even more, he thought the tendency to deny the pervasiveness of change by sneaking in permanence through the backdoor with the idea of selfhood was the chief cause of human misery.

Of all the aspects of the Buddha's teaching, no-self has been the feature most prone to misunderstanding. It was a stumbling block to the first western interpreters of Buddhism who saw it as a token of nihilism. On the face of it, it may seem as if the Buddha was saying the human person did not exist or was unreal or was trying to deny something that seems to be, if you'll pardon the pun, self-evident. If *anything* seems real to us in this world, surely it is our own selves. The French philosopher René Descartes even said that everything in existence could be doubted except the doubting subject itself, which gave him the necessary leverage to make his famous claim, "I think, therefore I am." There seems to be something counterintuitive about denying the existence of the self. But the Buddha was not trying to suggest that human beings do not exist or that our souls are somehow annihilated when one dies or attains nibbana, the goal of the Buddha's practice.

Rather, the Buddha merely refused to affirm the belief in an enduring, essential self or soul. He was not proposing another concept in its place. No-self is a not concept; it has no content. Therefore, it would be incorrect to say that the Buddha "believed in no-self," as I sometimes hear it said. No-self means he declined to believe in the soul. After years of practice culminating in his awakening, the Buddha was convinced that the soul was an irredeemably flawed concept. This idea, he insisted, was an unwholesome and problematic way of thinking.

Like the rest of existence, what we conventionally call the "self" or the "I," the "me," clearly has reality, but our language and ordinary ways of thinking are incapable of adequately expressing that reality. We exist, the world exists, to be sure, but not the way we *think* they do. This failure of thought is in part a consequence of our native ignorance of the world and in part a consequence of the nature of language, which necessarily reifies, separates, and imputes substance to the flow of experience.

On one occasion, the Buddha explained why describing human personality was so difficult. He said:

> This world for the most part depends upon a duality—upon the notion of existence and the notion of nonexistence. But for one who sees the origin of the world as it really is with correct wisdom, there is no notion of nonexistence in regard to the world. And for one who sees the cessation of the world as it really is with correct wisdom, there is no notion of existence in regard to the world.

President Bill Clinton was actually quite correct when he said, "it all depends on what the meaning of is is." The Buddha's vision of "is" was simply inexpressible in the conventional duality supported by conventional language; his vision of reality was beyond the alternatives of being and not being. He would have regarded Hamlet famous question, "To be or not to be," as a false dilemma. The Buddha did not want to say the self "is." That would suggest that it is a thing, something fixed, unchanging, and separate from the rest of reality. At the same time, he was reluctant to say the self is *not*, which seems untrue to our experience and which can be interpreted as a kind of nihilism.

His strategy was to be silent if he thought his words might be misunderstood or to use language very carefully if the listener were prepared to comprehend what he had to say. If he thought his listener could correctly grasp it, he might deny the existence of the self, if it were clear that the self he denied was understood to be a mere fabrication, an illusion. Part of the problem was that people so completely identified with this fabrication that they thought a denial of selfhood was a denial of personhood, which is not at all what the Buddha intended. The great Buddhist philosopher Nagarjuna compared the concept of no-self and insubstantiality, to a poisonous snake. You must know how to handle it or you might be bitten and killed.

For the Buddha, the person is real, but, like all conditioned realities, is a concatenation of successive events, different from one moment to the next. We can examine this assertion more clearly by considering what the Buddha regarded as the component dimensions of the person. To the Buddha, the human being was a compound of five processes that he called the Aggregates of Being. The Aggregates were materiality, sensation, perception and apperception, conceptual constructs, and consciousness.

I'll explain each of these briefly. Materiality simply refers to our bodily natures, the fact that we inhabit the world in a physical form. I don't think there is much controversy about that assertion. Sensation means the feeling tone of our experience of the world. We are constantly judging our experiences as pleasant or unpleasant or occasionally as neither pleasant nor unpleasant. Perception and apperception refer to the process of perceiving the items of our experience in a certain way. I perceive this tall, hard, smooth, brown object here as a lectern.

Conceptual constructs are mental and volitional formations, the domain of intentions and desires. Finally, there is consciousness, the faculty and process of awareness.

Now we could spend a great deal of time expounding each of these five aspects of personhood, and if you are interested, the Buddhist tradition has a massive array of literature covering each of these aggregates in exhaustive detail. But for our purposes here, we need only note several important features about this compendium of human components.

First, these components are all rapidly changing processes. Like everything else in existence, the body, sensation, apperception, mental fabrications and intentions, and awareness are never the same from moment to moment. As with the rest of his teaching, the Buddha invited his listeners to examine their own experience and confirm this fact for themselves. Second, the Buddha maintained that these five processes were the complete constituents of the human being. There are no other aspects of personhood than what is denoted by these aggregates. Finally, none of these five processes or any combination of them contains a shred of substance or anything that could be identified as "self" or "soul."

The Buddha challenged his audiences to corroborate the absence of selfhood by introspection. He asked his listeners to consider systematically each of the five aggregates to determine whether or not it contained a self, soul, or directing agent. One-by-one, the Buddha asked if each component were under the control of the person, to which the answer was always no. Then he drew the inevitable implications:

If the body constituted a self, then it would not give us any trouble, and it would be possible to manipulate the body by making determinations such as *Let my body be this way, let my body not be that way*. So, because the body does not constitute a self, it *does* give us trouble, and it is *not* possible to manipulate the body by making determinations such as *Let my body be this way, let my body not be that way*.

If my body were my "self," I could will it not to be sick or to appear a certain way. As it is, I have extremely limited control over my body, and I have absolutely no control over its ultimate demise. The Buddha proceeded to make the same point about each of the other aggregates. Because we are not in complete control of any of the components of our being, he simply could not imagine a "self," in any meaningful sense, as being part of human personhood. He advised, therefore, that every aspect of what we are "should be seen with thorough understanding of what it is: *This is not mine, I am not this, this is not my self.*" There was simply nothing about what we conventionally call ourselves that corresponds to what is ordinarily meant by the self.

For the Buddha, the problem with the concept of the self was not just that it was empirically unverifiable or unavailable to our experience, but that it gave rise to the third characteristic of existence, insatiability. Insatiability is my translation of the Pali term *dukkha.*

*Dukkha* is one of those notorious words whose meaning, as they say, gets lost in translation. Usually translated into English as suffering or unsatisfactoriness, the meaning of *dukkha* is actually far richer than a single English word or even a cluster of English words can express. You might find it translated as illness, anguish, sorrow, unease, distress, unsettledness, lamentation, pain, grief, despair, and disappointment. Certainly all of these terms can be associated with *dukkha.* Today, however, I'm calling it insatiability; I don't intend that term as a replacement for these other words but rather to augment and represent them.

I selected insatiability not only because it nicely fits my alliterative scheme that includes impermanence and insubstantiality; but also because it nicely captures what I think is at the root of the experience of *dukkha* , and that is the fact that you can never get enough of what you don't really need.

Let me explain. In the Pali, *dukkha* is the opposite of *sukha*, a word that means happiness or contentment. Now, happiness and contentment are not to be confused with pleasure, which in the Buddha's view was a fleeting sensation or feeling. Happiness for the Buddha meant essentially "the supreme state of sublime peace," the deep, abiding contentment that was not dependent on circumstances. Happiness, he thought, was possible whether one's sensations were pleasant or unpleasant.

This kind of contentment, this happiness, was what all beings really, truly wanted. All beings, in their many and various ways, seek it. Perhaps everything we do can be traced back to this fundamental aspiration. The Buddha was not alone in this view. A great number of philosophers and spiritual teachers including Aristotle and Thomas Aquinas in the west have regarded the quest of happiness as the principal impulse of human activity. Aristotle said happiness was the one thing we seek for itself and not as a means to something else.

The Buddha certainly saw nothing problematic with the will to happiness *per se*, but he did see grave problems with how we go about trying to satisfy it. Because of our mistaken beliefs about the nature of the world and the human person, particularly our failures to understand impermanence and insubstantiality, we inevitably go about the pursuit of happiness in the very ways that thwart its fulfillment. Without awakening to the true nature of reality, we look for contentment in the wrong places, and because we can never find it, our thirst for satisfaction intensifies and worsens. It's like trying to put out a fire with gasoline.

Most people seek their happiness in two basic ways: through acquisition, which is the preferred method in the modern world, and through aversion, trying to avoid life's unpleasant situations. The quest for contentment through acquisition leads one to try to enhance the self by surrounding it with fine material possessions, fancy diplomas and trophies, and other markers of well-being and achievement. If you have ever gone shopping to cheer yourself up, then you know what I mean. (And obviously, *I* know what that's like, or I wouldn't be able to mention it as an example!) But acquisitiveness need not focus only on material things. One can seek happiness by having unique and interesting experiences—including spiritual experiences—or by holding the right religious or political beliefs or by identifying with an organization or a country or cause. One can seek happiness through the love of other beings, both human and divine.

There is no end to the ways we pursue contentment by means of getting and having. So what's the problem with trying to make ourselves happy in this way? Lots of things, really, but much of it has to do with the ephemeral nature of reality. Deep, abiding contentment cannot be gained by glomming onto transient things. Possessions break or decay, interesting experiences become mere memories, the persons we love leave or die or stop loving us. Even if acquiring something we really want satisfies for a while, it does not last. Soon, we start wanting something else.

Sometimes, we seek satisfaction by avoiding unpleasant situations or things or people. My doctoral thesis was over four hundred pages long, and every single page was composed with these three fingers. Why? I cannot type. Everything I've ever published has been written with these three fingers. They offered typing in high school, of course, but I was too afraid to take it. The course had a reputation for being extremely difficult, and I feared it would mar my grade point average. But allowing the fear of failing to rule over you, I discovered, is a poor strategy for a full engagement with life—or really for an education, even if it does yield up good grades. Fortunately, reality forced failure upon me in other areas of my life. After successfully escaping failure all throughout college and graduate school, I was finally able to screw up royally. I won't go into the details of my remarkable failures, but I can report from my own experience that without them, there is much about life I would have never known.

The life principally motivated by fear is not a happy one. As with acquisition, the problem with trying to find your happiness through avoidance is this thing called reality. Reality simply does not allow us to evade unwanted experiences. We might escape a few, like a class in typing, but we cannot avert them all, including the facts of life that impelled the Buddha on his journey to enlightenment: sickness, old age, and death. If our strategy has been to flee from unpleasant circumstances, when they come to meet us, as they surely will, our suffering will be great indeed.

The whole approach to contentment through acquisition or aversion is fundamentally misguided, the Buddha would say. You will recognize, of course, the way the Buddha's own biography informed his analysis. He was the man who had everything and the man who gave up everything. Both circumstances were unable to afford him any peace. Rather than bringing the satisfaction we so deeply want, acquisition and aversion only serve to frustrate us and increase our anguish and disappointment. Instead of questioning these methods themselves, in our unawakened state we foolishly think that we simply haven't acquired or averted the right thing. When one thing doesn't bring us happiness, we simply look for another. In other words, we are insatiable.

These situations I have been describing are encompassed by this rich Pali word, *dukkha.* That single term denotes this fundamental frustrating, insatiable quality to our unenlightened existence. The Buddha thought that *dukkha* did not merely characterize episodes or aspects of existence; rather, it was pervasive and insidious. Like impermanence and insubstantiality, there are no exceptions to *dukkha* in the conditioned world of life as we ordinarily know it.

In its most obvious forms, it manifests as simple suffering such anguish, fear, and grief. But clearly, all of life is not anguish, fear, and grief. It is important, therefore, to recognize the less apparent aspects of *dukkha* to grasp the Buddha's point fully. In its less obvious forms, it appears as frustration, annoyance, and irritation. Now the breadth of the concept becomes clearer. *Dukkha* names every aspect of experience in which there is the slightest twinge of anxiety, fear, or disappointment. With eyes wide open, the Buddha thought that anyone could see that all existence bore those qualities, even if it was nothing more than the awareness that the pleasantness one is now experiencing must eventually subside.

*Dukkha* is intrinsically related to the two other marks of existence. The failure to apprehend that the world and human persons are completely subject to impermanence and insubstantiality gives rise to *dukkha*, and the experience of *dukkha* in turn reinforces our misapprehensions. By attributing selfhood where there is none, we effectively believe ourselves to be separate, individual entities whose fragile existences must be propped up by possessions, achievements, beliefs, and relationships to convince ourselves that we are safe, protected from the vicissitudes of life. But this is an illusion. None of these things can give the security, the sense of well-being, the contentment that we really desire, and neither can trying to avoid unpleasant and unwanted things and situations. Conditioned existence simply will not satisfy our deepest longings for happiness. When we awaken to the world "as it is," we discover, paradoxically, that the only way to find happiness is to relinquish these feverish efforts to protect and empower this mistaken belief we call the self.

# Getting to the Farther Shore
## Lecture 15

**Language is grounded in human experience in the saṃsāric realm. Its vocabularies, metaphors, and grammars all refer to and derive from unenlightened experience in conditioned existence. How could it possibly suffice to explain that which is beyond this realm?**

The Buddha said very little about nibbana and described it mostly in negative terms; language, which is grounded in saṃsāra, was insufficient for describing the unconditioned absolute. He therefore resorted to **apophasis**, or saying by way of negation. He called nibbana the cessation of *dukkha*, the eradication of ignorance, the termination of the illusion of selfhood, the cooling of selfish desires, the end of attachments, the conclusion of rebirth, the deathless. It was clearly not a place nor a reality attained at death but an awakening to the end of suffering in life.

A person who has awakened is known as an **arahant**, one who has "laid the burden down." On death, the arahant enters parinibbana, the final nibbana. The distinction between nibbana and parinibbana is karma; when one awakens, *dukkha* ceases, but karma has not yet been spent. Nibbana entails the cessation of new karma, since all self-centered desires, the source of karma according to the Buddha, had been eliminated. But the ripening of old karmas has to take its due course. When all his or her karmic energies have been completely exhausted, the arahant attains parinibbana, free from the cycle of rebirth, never to be reborn again.

Specific countermeasures to *dukkha* are usually directed toward the cultivation of wisdom and compassion. Compassion, or **karuna**, means to sympathize with a being's suffering and to be strongly moved to alleviate it. Because human habits of self-centeredness are so deep and ingrained, Buddhist spiritual practice is a matter of gradual, gentle, disciplined reconditioning.

The Buddha taught that establishing sound moral conduct was foundational for spiritual advancement. Morality in the Buddha's worldview was not grounded in the commands of a god but in the quest to end suffering. Aspiration to moral behavior meant vowing to follow the **five precepts of wholesome action**, each of which sought to minimize harm and to dispel the illusion of the self by refusing to perform activities that perpetuate and reinforce it. The Buddha considered these ethical practices powerful enough to ensure a positive rebirth whether or not the practitioner followed any other aspects of the dhamma.

**Nibbana entails the cessation of new karma, since all self-centered desires, the source of karma according to the Buddha, had been eliminated.**

The Buddha encouraged various meditative practices toward different ends. Transformation of thought is the purpose of *metta*, or loving-kindness, meditation, which involves conjuring mental images of various persons in one's life and wishing for each of them freedom from illness, suffering, and fear and attainment of a sense of ease, contentment, and well-being. The practitioner usually begins by wishing for his or her own happiness, then moves to a loved one, then a stranger, then an enemy, and concludes by evoking this same wish for all beings. The intent of this exercise is to channel thought patterns toward kindness. Sitting meditation is intended to sharpen the mind and increase awareness. The practice involves finding a quiet place, stilling the body, and bringing concentrated awareness to the breath as an anchor for one's attention. When one becomes aware of the mind straying, one gently redirects it back to attending to the breath. The goal of this exercise is not to prevent thoughts or sensations from arising but to become aware of the moment they do and to learn to let them go. The continual observance of this technique gradually disciplines the mind and the body, helps sharpen the consciousness, and trains the practitioner in the art of relinquishing thoughts.

Although oriented toward different factors that contribute to *dukkha*, these practices all work together to loosen the bonds that inhibit ultimate freedom and clarity of mind. The Buddha's approach to spirituality was to enlist an arsenal of practices to remove incrementally the impediments that hinder us from being wise and compassionate. ■

**apophasis**: Saying by way of negation; this is how the Buddha usually described nibbana, which was beyond the power of language to describe.

**arahant**: In Buddhism, an awakened living being.

**five precepts of wholesome action**: In Buddhism, the foundational precepts of moral behavior—namely, refraining from harming sentient beings, from stealing and coveting, from sexual misconduct, from lies and false speech, and from using substances that impair the mind or body.

**karuna**: The Pāli word for compassion.

*metta*: Loving-kindness meditation, which involves wishing well on the self, a loved one, a stranger, an enemy, and all beings to train oneself in compassion.

**Question to Consider**

1. The metaphysics of Buddhism stand in stark contrast to most Western theologies. Do you find the same to be true of Buddhism's ethics and spiritual disciplines, or do you see more similarities there?

# Getting to the Farther Shore
## Lecture 15—Transcript

The Buddha likened the difference between samsara, the conditioned realm of existence, and nibbana, the unconditioned absolute, to the two banks of a river. Getting from this samsaric side to the farther shore of nibbana was a mighty task that required personal effort and discipline. He regarded his dhamma, his teachings, as a seaworthy craft for making the journey. But his vessel was more like a raft than a motorboat. It required the energy and careful attention of the voyager to make it to the other side. In no uncertain terms, he told his students, "The Buddha only shows the way. You must make the effort yourselves." Even more, when one has reached the farther shore, the Buddha said the raft should be abandoned. Once it has served its purpose, it is no longer necessary. Like everything else, the Buddha's teachings can be relinquished.

Up to now, we have focused our studies on the near shore. We have explored the Buddha's fundamental understanding of this world through its three key characteristics: impermanence, insubstantiality, and insatiability. Today, we set our sights on the farther shore and the means the Buddha offered for navigating the waterway between samsara and nibbana. Our conversation will take us into the Buddha's ethical and spiritual practices, for these observances constitute the way across to the other side. But we will begin our exploration not with the means to the end, but with the end itself. Starting with the destination might seem a bit unusual, but understanding the objective will greatly assist us in appreciating how the Buddha proposed we get there.

Although nibbana was the ultimate goal of his entire dhamma, the Buddha said very little about it, just as Confucius was reticent about his ultimate reality, Heaven. When he did speak, the Buddha described nibbana in mostly negative terms, which of course contributed to the west's early impression that Buddhism was a dour worldview. Yet there were very good reasons why the Buddha took a negative approach in his account of the ultimate reality. Once again, the matter concerned the nature of language. If the Buddha found the dualistic character of language insufficient for describing the conditioned reality of life as we know it, that inadequacy was even more evident when it came to discussing the unconditioned absolute. Language is grounded in human experience in the samsaric realm. Its vocabularies, metaphors, and grammars all refer to and derive from unenlightened experience in conditioned existence. How could it possibly suffice to explain that which is beyond this realm? Yet without language, how could the Buddha even indicate that there was a reality beyond samsara?

To resolve the tension created by this dilemma, he resorted to a rhetorical technique known in the western intellectual traditions as apophasis, or saying by way of negation. Accordingly, the Buddha's preferred way to speak of nibbana was to say what it was not, and this is what accounts for the negative tone of his description. He called nibbana the cessation of *dukkha*, the eradication of ignorance, the termination of the illusion of selfhood, the cooling of selfish desires, the end of attachments, the conclusion of rebirth, the deathless. Nibbana was not a negative reality; it was only expressed in negative terms because positive descriptions, the Buddha thought, could be misleading. On those relatively few occasions when he spoke of nibbana in more affirmative language, the Buddha called it "the supreme state of sublime peace," perfect clarity of mind, and unexcelled freedom and happiness. The Buddha said enough about nibbana to make it clear that it was not a place, although some of the metaphors he used might suggest that. The image of the "farther shore" was not an actual location, of course, but a concession to the limits of unenlightened mind.

Nor was nibbana a reality attained at death in the way some religious traditions that suggest human fulfillment comes only in a post-mortem existence. In fact, one "sees nibbana," to use a traditional phrase, while yet alive. The Buddha himself saw nibbana on the night of his final awakening; and everyone who awoke in this way was thought to have attained the end of suffering in their lifetimes. A person who had thus awakened was known as an "arahant," one who has "laid the burden down." Upon death, the arahant entered parinibbana, the final nibbana. The distinction between nibbana and parinibbana was a significant one, and it turned on the matter of karma. When one fully awakened to the world as it is, *dukkha* ceased; but the karmas that have driven existence to that point had not yet been spent. Nibbana entailed the cessation of new karma, since all self-centered desires, the source of karma according to the Buddha, had been eliminated. But the ripening of old karmas, the consequences of actions performed prior to enlightenment, had to take their due course. When all the karmic energies that had sustained conditioned existence had been completely exhausted, the arahant attained parinibbana.

Nibbana is thus the end of all the factors that condition insatiability. The illusion of a permanent, substantial, separate self is gone, and so is the craving and the attachments that arise to sustain and prop up this fantasy. When craving and attachments have been fully relinquished, one surrenders clinging to life or yearning for death. One is set free from the cycle of rebirth, never to be reborn again.

It is difficult for those of us on the near shore to imagine what life is like for the arahant on the other side because it is ultimately unimaginable. Our best clues come from the specific ethical and spiritual practices prescribed by the Buddha for those who would find an end to *dukkha*. Nibbana is essentially the perfection of these practices. By examining these exercises and understanding them as countermeasures to *dukkha*, we can better glimpse the nibbanic life for those who have successfully reached the farther shore.

Throughout the Pali and other canons, one can find a wide array of specific techniques and observances taught by the Buddha that qualify as ethical precepts and spiritual exercises. We will only be able to sample some of the most important of these. But our coverage of these topics is made simpler by noting that the practices the Buddha encouraged were directed towards the cultivation of wisdom and compassion, the two primary virtues of the dhamma. Perfecting wisdom and compassion, to put it as concisely as possible, is the way to nibbana and the end of suffering.

For the Buddha, wisdom meant to know the world as it is, as constituted by the qualities of impermanence, insubstantiality, and insatiability. As we have mentioned on several occasions, knowing these characteristics meant more to the Buddha than just grasping these ideas conceptually. It also entailed directly comprehending their thoroughgoing, radical nature and living life in light of their truth. With wisdom, in this sense, we have become quite well-acquainted.

Compassion, on the other hand, is a new term in our study of the Buddha's philosophy. Compassion, which translates the Pali word *karuna*, meant to sympathize with a being's suffering and to be strongly moved to alleviate it. Living compassionately meant to think and act without putting ourselves at the center of the universe, without believing that "It's all about me."

In the Buddha's view, wisdom and compassion were dialectically related to one another; each reinforced the other. When we see the world as it is, we cannot help but feel compassion for all beings. The more we recognize the depth and breadth of pain and anguish throughout the world, the more we see beings struggling and failing to overcome dukkha, failing to be free, the more we respond with a heartfelt willingness to see all creatures become happy. The *Karaniya Metta Sutta* compares this response with the love a mother has for her only child. At the same time, as we become more compassionate, we grow in wisdom, in our capacity to see reality more clearly. For the Buddha, the illusion of the self keeps us in bondage. The way out of this prison was through the practice of compassion, cultivating, in the words of the *Karaniya Metta Sutta,* "a limitless heart with regard to all beings" and "good will for the entire cosmos." This practice helps unfetter us from the delusion of selfhood, the principal of source of *dukkha*. Compassion for others helps us to see the world more clearly.

By the time we can be held accountable for our actions, we have already endured years of conditioning. We have learned to act and think in self-centered ways for so long that selfishness seems natural. Because our habits of self-centeredness are so deep and ingrained, the Buddha thought that persons needed a gradual, gentle discipline to reverse the effects of years (or even lifetimes) of conditioning. We cannot expect radical transformation to happen overnight, nor can we expect to be the persons we wish to be simply by willing. Willing must be accompanied by deliberate action. By acting compassionately and wisely, it becomes easier to will to be compassionate and wise; and the stronger our determination to be wise and compassionate, the easier it is act wisely and compassionately. Buddhist spiritual practice, therefore, is a matter of training and reconditioning: learning and acting to be the wise and compassionate persons we truly are.

In many ways and in many places throughout the written record of his teaching, the Buddha offered precise techniques for realigning the heart and mind to liberation. The classic statement of this training is the Noble Path of Eight Parts. The Buddha's spiritual disciplines were not limited to the practices contained in this statement, but all of his exercises, including the Noble Path, can be related to the goal of perfecting wisdom and compassion. Rather than attempt a comprehensive analysis of all of these techniques, I'd like to explore a select number of them to demonstrate how they serve to cultivate wisdom and compassion and how perfecting these virtues leads to the ultimate goal of nibbana. My selection follows a traditional threefold typology of spiritual practices in Buddhism. The first is training in moral conduct, and under that category I'll talk about what are known as the Five Precepts and the practice of generosity. The second division is known as mental cultivation. My choice as representative of these techniques is loving-kindness meditation. Finally, there are exercises that cultivate wisdom, seeing the world as it is, and here I'll mention sitting meditation. All three types of practices strengthen and mutually reinforce one another.

The Buddha taught that establishing sound moral conduct was foundational for spiritual advancement. One would be unable to develop the mind properly and gain insight into the true nature of reality without first mastering the rudiments of the ethical life. Advanced forms of spiritual practice required a basis of calmness and tranquility that cannot be experienced by anyone who routinely engages in immoral behavior.

Instilling moral behavior, of course, is a basic feature of most, perhaps all, spiritualities developed during and after the Axial Age. But unlike many other religions, morality in the Buddha's worldview was not grounded in the commands of a god who issues specific rules for human behavior, since there is no such god in Buddhism. Rather, the Buddha related moral behavior to the quest to end suffering, that is, to all beings' desire for happiness. Like Confucius, the Buddha thought that ethical conduct ought to be founded on the human desire to realize the good rather than on the fear of retribution. In this sense, moral behavior is also a spiritual practice in Buddhism because it is vitally connected to the ultimate objective of seeing nibbana.

Cultivating moral virtue takes the form of aspiring to noble conduct. At it most basic, aspiration to noble behavior, for the Buddha, meant vowing to follow the Five Precepts of wholesome action. In the beginning, one follows the precepts rather imperfectly. When one fails to live up to the ideal, he or she simply acknowledges the failure and endeavors to do better next time. Moral failure is not considered a sin. Gradually, by resolving to start afresh each time one falls short, the skill to adhere to the precepts becomes increasingly stronger, to the point where acting otherwise becomes unthinkable.

These foundational precepts follow the principle of non-harming, an idea that resounds throughout the world's philosophical and ethical traditions. These traditions recognize that at its most basic level moral behavior is not a matter of what one *does* but of what one *refrains* from doing. Confucius' formulation of the Golden Rule was expressed in this fashion: "What you do not want done to yourself, do not do to others." Imagine the kind of world we would have if everyone followed the simple principle to do no harm. The first precept of the Buddha's ethics states this principle in its basic form: "I promise to refrain from harming sentient beings." Sentient beings are creatures with the capacity to feel pain and pleasure. In short, the first step toward ending suffering is by refusing to inflict suffering on others, as well as on oneself. According to the law of karma, violence begets violence. Historically, some Buddhists interpreted this precept strictly and practiced vegetarianism, but not all did. The Buddha permitted his monks and nuns to eat meat or fish if it were offered as a gift and if the animal were not killed specifically for the monastics' benefit. It is not easy to live in the world without harming or killing some sentient life; when one finds it necessary to compromise this ideal, at least he or she can strive to minimize the amount of harm they do. Following this precept not only avoids the negative karmic effects of violence but also sharpens one's awareness of the magnitude of the world's suffering, a consciousness that arouses the deeper sense of compassion.

The other foundational precepts work in similar fashion and take a similar form: "I will refrain from stealing and coveting"; "I will refrain from sexual misconduct"; "I will not lie or use false speech"; "I will not use substances that impair my mind or body." Obviously, each of these vows serves to curtail the distress of others and oneself simply by limiting the infliction of harm. But each also serves to deepen wisdom and compassion. By intentionally determining not to harm, one develops a greater awareness of the vulnerabilities of all beings and of their desire to be happy. The precepts also help to dispel the illusion of the self by refusing to perform activities that perpetuate and reinforce it. I sometimes refer to these kinds of activities as "selfing" to indicate that certain behaviors help to convince us that the "self" is a reality rather than an illusion. Any behavior that serves this purpose— such as stealing, lying, and lust—is a form of selfing. The Buddha intended his ethical precepts to diminish the selfing function and bring the aspirant's life into greater alignment with reality.

As the practice of the precepts demonstrates, much is accomplished merely by doing nothing. But doing nothing is not so easy, since our lives have been so deeply conditioned into self-absorbed behavior. To help retrain the mind towards a wiser and more compassionate disposition, the Buddha suggested many other practices. One of these was *dana*, or generosity.

The virtue of *dana* is not difficult to understand. It essentially means to give to others without expectation of return, to give freely and liberally with no strings attached. Ordinarily, the observance of *dana* involves giving material goods, and it probably originated with the practice of the householders of the Buddha's day providing the basic necessities of life for the men and women who had gone forth into homelessness seeking the way to liberation. The samanas, of course, had no possessions or means of support other than what the ordinary folk provided them. The Buddha recognized this virtuous activity and encouraged it. Still, today one of the primary meanings of *dana* among Buddhist practitioners is to give to food, clothing, and other essentials to the monastics. But *dana* has a wider meaning than this. It pertains to any act of generosity performed in a compassionate spirit to benefit other beings. The Buddha said that an act as humble as throwing "the rinsings of a bowl or a cup into a village pond, thinking, 'May whatever animals live here feed on this,'" would qualify as an act of *dana*. The value of such practices in the Buddhist framework is readily apparent. The act of giving without expectation loosens the attachments we may have to our money and possessions, which relaxes the sense of self that money and possessions shore up. For the Buddha, the great benefit of acts of generosity is not principally the material transfer of goods to a needy person, as beneficial as that may be, but in the spiritual transformation of the mind. It *is* better to give than receive.

The Buddha considered these ethical practices powerful enough to ensure a positive rebirth whether or not the practitioner followed the other aspects of the dhamma or even a follower of the Buddha's dhamma at all. Anyone—Buddhist, Hindu, agnostic, atheist—benefits by the living the moral life. The Buddha taught claimed: "Another person has practiced the making of merit by giving as well as by moral discipline to a high degree; but he has not undertaken the making of merit by meditation. With the breakup of the body, after death, he will be reborn among humans in a favorable condition. Or he will be reborn in the company of the gods of the Four Great Kings."

Transformation of thought is also the purpose of *metta*, or lovingkindness, meditation, one of the practices of concentration. The lovingkindness contemplation involves conjuring mental images of various persons in one's life and wishing for each of them freedom from illness, suffering, and fear and a sense of ease, contentment, and well-being. The practitioner usually begins this contemplation wishing for his or her own happiness, with phrases such: "May I be healthy"; "May I be safe"; "May I experience no fear"; "May I live with ease." Then the exercise moves to thoughts about someone for whom the practitioner deeply cares. With an image in mind, the practitioner offers the same wishes for that person's happiness. Next, the meditator imagines another individual about whom he or she has no strong feelings, positive or negative—maybe the clerk at the grocery store—and pronounces the list of wishes with as much sincerity as they can summon. Then, the exercise focuses on a person for whom the practitioner has strong negative feelings, perhaps someone whose image evokes anger or hatred. And again, with as much earnestness as possible, the meditator wishes them great happiness. Finally, the practice concludes by evoking this same wish for all beings, with none excluded. The intent of this exercise in compassionate contemplation is obviously to work with the mind to help channel its patterns of thought into more wholesome and kindhearted ways. Over time, according to the

Buddha, this practice helps the mind to see the suffering of all beings with greater sensitivity and to develop a kinder disposition toward them all.

The Buddha encouraged meditative practice in a variety of forms towards different specific ends. Just as *metta* meditation was a means to shape a more compassionate mind, sitting meditation was intended to sharpen the mind and increase awareness. Sitting meditation is probably the spiritual exercise most often associated with Buddhism, since it is in this posture that the Buddha is most frequently depicted in Buddhist iconography.

The basic sitting practice taught by the Buddha was based on the technique he remembered using as a boy sitting under the rose-apple tree. That practice involved finding a quiet place, stilling the body with crossed legs and an upright spine, and bringing concentrated awareness to the breath as an anchor for one's attention. Inevitably, as one begins this practice, the mind begins to stray or the body and its feelings and perceptions demand attention. Almost reflexively and without awareness, the mind loses its concentration on breathing and begins to entertain a thought or focus on an emotion or sensation. Soon, the mind has completely forgotten about the breath and is instead thinking about what's for lunch or contemplating a vacation in Florida. That's the way the undisciplined mind works. It's an immensely powerful organ, but it is terribly unruly. The meditation practice begins when one becomes aware of the mind's waywardness and gently redirects it back to attending to the breath. The goal of this exercise is not to *prevent* thoughts or sensations from arising but to become aware of the moment they do and to learn to let them go. The continual observance of this technique gradually disciplines the mind and the body, helps sharpen the consciousness, and trains the practitioner in the art of relinquishing thoughts, the vast majority of which are not even worth the mental energy it requires to think.

The Five Precepts, *dana*, *metta* meditation, and sitting practice are four of the dozens of techniques taught by the Buddha for the development of wisdom and compassion, the two virtues that best represent the nibbanic life. Although oriented toward different factors that contribute to *dukkha*, the practices all work together to loosen the bonds inhibit ultimate freedom and clarity of mind. The Buddha's approach to spirituality was to enlist an arsenal of practices to remove incrementally the impediments that hinder us from being wise and compassionate—ignorance, cravings and aversions, attachments, and most especially the delusion of the self. Because each person's conditioning is different, the Buddha prescribed different techniques to assist each practitioner along the path to nibbana. The Buddha's skill in offering specific exercises suited to the needs of individuals was one of the traits that made him such an effective teacher. In our next lecture, we will examine the career of the Buddha as a teacher, which spanned 45 years of his life, from shortly after his enlightenment to his parinibbana at age 80.

# How the Buddha Taught
## Lecture 16

> Initially, [the Buddha] concluded that trying to teach his dhamma—
> his vision of reality and liberation—would be futile. … But he had a
> change of heart when one of the great gods suggested that some beings
> in the world have "only a little dust on their eyes" and are languishing
> because they do not know the way to freedom.

Out of compassion for those still suffering in samsāra, the Buddha decided to teach his Noble Path to those who might be ready to benefit from it. For 45 years, he traveled throughout the Gangetic Plain of India teaching others how to find the bliss of the nibbanic life, beginning with the five *samanas* who had abandoned him when he forsook asceticism. His first lesson as a fully awakened being was brief and to the point, philosophical, and particularly suited for longtime seekers. It was not a discourse for beginners. Yet it had been so carefully crafted that it became the touchstone of the Buddha's whole dhamma. The tradition calls this inaugural address "Setting the Wheel of Dhamma in Motion."

The Buddha explained that he had ascertained four essential facts about life he called the **Four Noble Truths**. The first truth is that *dukkha* is a fact of unenlightened existence. The second is that suffering comes from failure to apprehend impermanence and insubstantiality—in particular, attachment to the notion of self. The third truth is that beings can escape from *dukkha*. Finally, the fourth truth is that cultivating compassion and wisdom leads to freedom from *dukkha*.

According to the Pāli canon, at the very moment the Buddha completed this discourse, the news of the dhamma reached the realm of the highest gods. One of the five *samanas* was immediately enlightened; shortly afterwards, the other four became arahants. These first five recipients of the Buddha's dhamma formed the core of the sangha.

The Buddha then began to teach others—*samanas* and householders, men and women, and persons of all castes. Not all became monks; many continued to live as laypersons and helped support the monks and nuns. And not all who heard the teachings accepted them. The Buddha felt no urge to compel anyone to accept his teaching, but to those who were ready to receive his teaching, a personal encounter with the Buddha was transformative.

The Buddha's daily life was much like that of any of the other monks in the sangha. He wandered for nine months of the year, settling only during the rainy season. When possible, he preferred to sleep in the open. He arose early after a very brief sleep and practiced meditation. After daybreak, he would stroll the area and talk to those around him. Later in the morning, he would take his begging bowl to a home in the nearest village to receive food for his one daily meal. Sometimes he was offered nothing, and he moved on to another home. Sometimes he was invited in for an elegant meal, but he always ate moderately and washed his own bowl.

The Wheel of Dhamma, a symbol of the Buddha's first sermon. After his enlightenment, the Buddha set out on a life of teaching others, "setting the wheel in motion."

Corel Stock Photo Library.

After the daily meal, he would nap. Later, he would receive visitors and give instruction. When the others went to sleep, he sat in meditative silence—sometimes, the legends say, the gods would appear and ask him questions about the dhamma—until it was time to sleep again.

This quiet existence was, of course, punctuated by many noteworthy events, too many to list them all. Many of them were encounters with humans who were suffering greatly, where the Buddha uttered a timely and compassionate word that immediately transformed the sufferer. In each instance, his lesson was tailored to the particular needs of his listeners and delivered at a timely moment. The Buddha claimed that he only taught about suffering and the end of suffering; but in many respects, he also taught much about how to teach, revealing himself as an astute observer of the human condition and a skillful communicator of wisdom. ∎

## Important Term

**Four Noble Truths**: The core doctrine of the Buddha's dhamma—namely, that *dukkha* is a fact of unenlightened existence, suffering comes from attachment, beings can escape from *dukkha*, and cultivating compassion and wisdom leads to freedom from *dukkha*.

## Question to Consider

1.  Have you ever personally experienced or witnessed a transformation from the right message uttered at the right time?

# How the Buddha Taught
## Lecture 16—Transcript

"What had to be done has been done," thought the Buddha when he saw nibbana. The quest was over; all self-interested desires had been exhausted; perfect bliss had been achieved. What does one do when all that had to be done has been done? That's not a question that I expect to be pondering—at least not in this lifetime. But it is one that a Buddha must consider. One option is to do nothing but enjoy the fruits of one's labors. For several weeks after his awakening, this was exactly what the Buddha did. But as he contemplated his next step, he considered another alternative—sharing the fruits of his labors with others.

The Buddha gave the matter a great deal of thought. Initially, he concluded that trying to teach his dhamma—his vision of reality and liberation—would be futile. He said to himself: "This Dhamma that I have attained to is profound and hard to see, hard to discover ... if I taught the Dhamma others would not understand me, and that would be wearying and troublesome for me." But he had a change of heart when one of the great gods suggested that some beings in the world have "only a little dust on their eyes" and are languishing because they do not know the way to freedom. The Buddha thought of his former teachers, Ālāra Kālāma and Uddaka Rāmaputta, and agreed that perhaps they and others might be prepared to receive the instruction he could offer. So, out of compassion for those still suffering in samsara, he decided to teach his Noble Path to those who might be ready to benefit from it.

In our discussion today, we will look these last 45 years during which the Buddha traveled throughout the Gangetic Plain of India teaching others how to find the bliss of the nibbanic life. We'll try to get a sense of his personal characteristics by examining how he interacted with others and the impressions he made on them. Along the way, we talk about the various ways the Buddha taught. Like each of the other three figures of the course, the Buddha was regarded as a master teacher.

Shortly after resolving to teach others out of compassion for their well-being, the Buddha determined to seek out his past teachers and share his dhamma with them. He soon learned, however, that both had recently died. Then he thought about the students who left him when it appeared he had forsaken the ascetic way. Having learned that the five were residing in a Deer Park near the holy city of Benares, the Buddha set out on foot to find them. Still upset by what they regarded as his betrayal, the five samanas decided not to show him any of the usual courtesies when they saw him approaching. Yet as he got nearer, they could perceive a visible difference in his countenance and bearing. When at last he reached them, they were unable to abide by their agreement and practically stumbled over themselves to welcome him and make him comfortable. He told them that he had discovered the way to the farther shore and had come to share his findings. Judging by his serene appearance, they recognized that their former mentor had indeed undergone a profound transformation, and they invited him to speak. And so the Buddha began his first lesson as a fully awakened being.

His talk was brief and to the point. Its form was philosophical and particularly suited for longtime seekers of truth like the five samanas. It was not a discourse for beginners. Yet it had been so carefully crafted that it became the touchstone of the Buddha's whole dhamma. The tradition called this inaugural address "Setting the Wheel of Dhamma in Motion." The image of the wheel, which is the oldest icon in Buddhist art, would have called to mind the chariot wheel, long associated with the power of royalty. Just as a king set chariots in motion by declaring a war of conquest, so too did the Buddha commence the conquest of samsara by the force of his dhamma.

The Buddha explained to the samanas that he had ascertained four essential facts about life. He presented these facts not as propositions that could be debated or as faith statements that should be accepted as true, but as the discovery of incontrovertible realities, just as a physicist might discuss the four fundamental forces of nature. In other words, the Buddha regarded his "Four Noble Truths," as they are usually known, as having the same reality as we today attribute to gravity. Just as gravity is a universal governing force in nature that operates irrespective of our opinion about it, so too the Noble Truths were considered universal principles governing reality whether we recognize them or not. As with everything he taught, the Buddha expected his audiences to verify his claims for themselves by means of their own experience.

The basic form of the Four Noble Truths followed the medical model of diagnosing and treating a disease. The Buddha began with an objective description of the symptoms afflicting human beings and proceeded to explain their root cause. Then he offered a prognosis and continued by prescribing a treatment. In earlier lectures, we have become acquainted with the gist of the Noble Truths but in a different format, so much of the following exposition should seem familiar.

The first point of the Buddha's first discourse was that *dukkha* is a fact of unenlightened existence. To put the Buddha's assertion as succinctly as I can, let me state it this way: Disappointment and dissatisfaction pervade life as we know it. We all want happiness, but we cannot seem to find it. Dissatisfaction, disappointment, discontent—these are the manifest symptoms of what ails us.

The Buddha's second point identifies the source of our misery. Essentially, we suffer disappointment and dissatisfaction because we fail to apprehend the impermanent and insubstantial nature of all reality, especially what we call our "selves." Consequently, we act in self-centered ways and develop unhealthy attachments to persons, ideas, and all manner of things. When change occurs—as it always does—our attachments cause us to suffer. To be concise, our belief in self leads us to expect too much from the world, and that expectation leads to dukkha.

The third point is the good news that the prospects for our cure look bright. Although *dukkha* appears to be inherent in the way things are, it is not. There is an escape from *dukkha*, and it lies on the farther shore. Dissatisfaction, disappointment, and discontent are not necessary. Samsara can be overcome.

Finally, the Buddha offered a treatment for curing our distress. His prescription covered a variety of mutually supporting disciplines designed to diminish the harm we cause, cultivate moral conduct, sharpen awareness, weaken craving, and relax our white-knuckled grip on the many things that support our illusions about what we really are. Practicing these exercises brings wisdom and compassion and leads to ultimate freedom.

According to the Pali canon, at the very moment he completed his discourse, the news of the dhamma reached the realm of the highest gods. The universe "shook and quaked and trembled while a great measureless light surpassing the splendor of the gods appeared in the world." The entire cosmos recognized the significance of this event. The wheel of dhamma had begun to roll. At the same moment, one of the five samanas was immediately enlightened, simply by hearing the dhamma "well-proclaimed." Shortly afterwards, the other four became arahants, bringing the number of Awakened Ones in the world to six. These first five recipients of the Buddha's dhamma formed the core of the sangha, the monastic community that developed during the remainder of the Buddha's life and continued beyond it, to the present day.

After his Deer Park teaching, the Buddha began to teach others. His teachings were offered to samanas and householders, men and women, and persons of all castes. The dhamma was especially attractive to members of the lower castes and to women, in part because the Buddha believed that nibbanic life was available to anyone. In the Buddha's world, the usual marks of status— gender, class, wealth, ethnicity—meant nothing.

poignant story illustrating this egalitarian spirit involved a poor untouchable known as Sunita, who was a road-sweeper, or scavenger, as they are often called. Like many untouchables, Sunita was required to hide in the presence of persons of high caste lest his shadow fall upon them and make them unclean. Failure to so do might result in a beating. One day, as Sunita was sweeping a dirty road, the Buddha approached with a large retinue of monks and nuns. Finding no place to hide, the untouchable could only stand with his palms together in the traditional gesture of reverence as the Buddha walked toward him. The Buddha stopped and said, "Friend, would you like to leave this work and follow me?" Sunita was deeply moved and replied, "Sir, I have always received orders but never a kind word. If you will accept a dirty scavenger like me, then I will come." The Buddha ordained Sunita and accepted him as a full member of the sangha.

The first female to join the order was the Buddha's own aunt, Queen Mahaprajapati, the woman who had raised him when Queen Mahamaya died seven days after giving birth. Queen Mahaprajapati was later joined by Yasodharā, the wife of his youth, and many other women. His son Rahula, born shortly before Siddhattha's departure from his own father's house, had preceded his mother and grandmother as an ordained member of the sangha.

Of course, the monastic life was not for everyone. Many who heard and accepted the Buddha's dhamma continued to live as laypersons, or householders as they were called, and helped support the monks and nuns with their gifts of *dana*, or generosity. And not all who heard the teachings accepted them. As in the case of Confucius, Jesus, and Muhammad, many walked away from the Buddha's teaching unwilling to support his movement or his message in any way. The Buddha felt no urge to compel anyone to accept his teaching. If anyone criticized his dhamma, he responded calmly and politely and tried to explain why he did what he did and thought what he thought. He told his students: "If anyone should criticize me, the dhamma, or the sangha, do not be angry, resentful, or upset. For if you were, that would darken your judgment, and you would be unable to know whether what they said was right or wrong"

To those who were ready to receive his teaching, a personal encounter with the Buddha was transformative. Once one of his senior students met a man on the road whose face exuded serenity. The student said, "Householder, your senses are calmed, your complexion is clear and radiant. Have you talked today face-to-face with the Blessed One?" "How could it be otherwise, sir?" the man replied, "I have just now been sprinkled with nectar." Such was the charisma of the Buddha that simply to be in his presence and hear him speak was often sufficient to enable some listeners to see nibbana. A student described being in the Buddha's presence like this:

When he is teaching the Dhamma to an assembly, he does not flatter them or berate them; rather he instructs, uplifts, inspires, and encourages them. The sound that comes from his mouth has eight qualities: It is distinct and intelligible, sweet and audible, fluent and clear, deep and resonant. His voice does not extend beyond the assembly. After being instructed, uplifted, inspired, and encouraged, the assembly rises from their seats and departs reluctantly, keeping their eyes upon him, concerned with nothing else.

The Buddha's physical appearance was certainly no liability in keeping his audiences' attention. The suttas indicate that he was about six feet tall with coal black hair and a golden complexion. He was described by one Brahman as "handsome, good-looking, and pleasing to the eye. ... He has a godlike form and countenance."

But like everything else, the charisma that could help midwife liberation could also become an obstruction to spiritual progress. Once, a Brahman by the name of Vakkali became totally captivated by the Buddha's beauty. The Brahman followed him everywhere, just to gaze at him; I think today we'd call it a "man-crush." Finally, the Buddha had to confront Vakkali and command him to leave. The forced departure initially took the Brahman to the brink of suicide, but fortunately he came to his senses and, having broken his attachment to the Buddha's good looks, became an arahant.

Apart from his charismatic appeal, the Buddha's daily life seemed much like that of any of the monks in the sangha. Like other monks, he wandered about northeastern India for nine months of the year, and settled down only during the rainy season. When possible, he preferred to sleep in the open, often at the root of a tree. Occasionally he might take shelter in a potter's shed. During the rainy season, he took residence in one of the small huts that had been constructed for his use in various parks that had been donated to the sangha by generous patrons.

The Buddha arose in the early morning after, perhaps a brief sleep of only one hour, and practiced meditation. At daybreak, he strolled through his surroundings and often spoke with visitors or members of the order. Later in the morning, he took his begging bowl—one of the few things that he or any other monk owned—and walked to the nearest town or village to receive food for the one meal he ate each day. With his bowl held with both hands, he would stand silently at the door of a home to receive whatever the residents might offer. If he received nothing, he silently moved on to another place. Frequently, he was invited to a home for the daily meal, where the hosts would often serve elegant foods. But even during these occasions, he maintained his simple way of living: he ate moderately and washed his own hands and bowl afterwards. As is still customary in much of South Asia, he would take a brief nap after the midday meal. I fondly remember my own experience teaching in India when the faculty and students would all return to their rooms to have short rest after lunch before proceeding with classes. The world might be a nicer place, I came to believe, if we'd all observe the spiritual discipline of the afternoon nap. Later in the day, the Buddha received visitors and gave instruction to monks. At night when everyone else was asleep, the Buddha sat in meditative silence, and sometimes, the legends say, the gods would appear and ask him questions about the dhamma. When at last he slept, he assumed what was the called the lion posture [image from Polonnaruva], reclining on his right side, with one hand under his head and his feet placed on each other.

The Buddha loved solitude. But his position in the sangha and the demands made upon him as a teacher rarely afforded him time alone, except at the early hours of the day. When he was able, he slipped into seclusion for an extended period and only encountered those who brought him food and drink. In this respect, he was much like Jesus and Muhammad, both of whom sought long periods of solitude.

Such was the general pattern of the Buddha's life in the years after his awakening. This quiet existence was of course punctuated by many noteworthy events. It is not possible to discuss them all, of course, but I would like to mention a few remarkable occasions to help complete our portrait of the Buddha as a person and as a teacher.

One of the more unusual episodes in the Buddha's life involved a mass murderer by the name of Angulimala. As the story goes, Angulimala was a high-minded youth who excelled at his studies. His fellow students, however, were extremely envious of his skills and their teacher's fondness for him. They concocted a story about how Angulimala had attempted to seduce the teacher's wife. In anger, the teacher dismissed him as a student and demanded that he pay the tuition fee, which the teacher set as 1000 human fingers. Angulimala began to fulfill his teacher's request by murdering innocent victims and severing one of their fingers. He took the fingers and strung them to make garland, which he wore around his neck. The name Angulimala literally means "finger-necklace." It's not completely clear why the young man actually followed through on the teacher's outrageous request. Some texts suggest he was predisposed to violence as result of karma from a previous birth; others suggest he was simply honoring the vow to be unquestioningly obedient to his teacher. In either case, the mild-manner youth was turned into a raging bloodthirsty killer. As he was looking the 1000th victim, Angulimala saw the Buddha and ran toward him wielding a sword. The Buddha simply walked away in slow, measured steps. But Angulimala, running as fast as he was able, could not catch the Buddha. Astounded, the murderer demanded the Buddha to stop, at which point the Buddha turned and said that he *had* stopped and that Angulimala should also stop. When Angulimala asked for clarification, the Buddha explained that had stopped harming other beings and that Angulimala was still harming them. After hearing this, Angulimala changed his ways, joined the sangha, and soon attained arahantship. This story is another illustration of the Buddha's capacity to utter a timely and compassionate word in such a way that its transformative effects were immediate. But even more, the story emphasizes the power of the dhamma to liberate even the most hardened hearts. A person who has killed 999 others can still be freed from samsara.

In an earlier talk, I noted that throughout world religious history the spiritual quest is usually prompted by an experience of tragedy, loss, or disillusionment. Such was the case for Ubbiri, the wife of a ruler in the state of Kosala. Not long after giving birth to a beautiful daughter, whom Ubbiri named Jiva, the child died, and Ubbiri plunged into inconsolable grief. Each day she visited the river bank where Jiva's corpse had been cremated and grieved her lost daughter. One day, after these visitations had gone on for some time, the Buddha met her as she wept. Through her tears, she told him her story. After listening, the Buddha responded: "'Jiva, my daughter,' you cry in the woods. Come to your senses, Ubbiri. 84,000 daughters all named Jiva have been burned in that charnel ground. For which of them do you grieve?" The response of the Buddha was exactly what Ubbiri needed to hear. With a just few well-chosen words, he was able to open her eyes to the ubiquity of grief and the reality of impermanence. Awakened to these facts, Ubbiri was suddenly relieved of her sorrow. Later, she wrote these words, preserved in the *Therigatha*, a collection of poems from the earliest Buddhist nuns: "Pulling out—completely out—the arrow so hard to see, embedded in my heart, he expelled from me—overcome with grief—the grief over my daughter. Today—with arrow removed, without hunger, entirely Unbound—to the Buddha, Dhamma, and Sangha I go, for refuge to the Sage."

Ubbiri's story is not unique in the Pali Canon. There were many such accounts in which a woman was devastated by the death of a child. This was a time, of course, when the infant mortality rate was very high, and grieving mothers were not uncommon. In another instance, the Buddha met Kisagotami, a mother who carried around the corpse of her child, pleading for someone to bring him back to life. The Buddha offered to do so, if Kisagotami could bring him a mustard seed from a household that never knew grief. Kisagotami began her quest but eventually realized that there was no such home. She returned to the Buddha without the mustard seed but with the understanding that sorrow and death are universal and inevitable in conditioned existence. The knowledge was sufficient to soothe her sadness, and at last she allowed her child to be buried. She joined the Buddha's sangha and became an enlightened one.

In this all-too-brief overview of the Buddha's very long teaching career, we've sampled a variety of the ways the Buddha taught. In each instance, his lesson was tailored to the particular needs of his auditors and delivered at a timely moment. The Buddha claimed that he only taught about suffering and the end of suffering; but in many respects, he also taught much about how to teach.

For the samanas who heard the discourse that set in motion the wheel of dhamma, the Buddha spoke in systematic philosophical terms. His concise outline of the way to attain the supreme state of sublime peace was imparted to them with the authority and clarity of someone having direct knowledge of the subject. Perhaps such direct knowledge is not important in teaching some things; but for the sage who teaches wisdom and compassion, it is essential. As the Indian poet Kabir said, "I speak only the words of experience; anything else is untrue." The depth of the Buddha's knowledge is evidenced in the simplicity of the Four Noble Truths. The ability to make the complex simple—but not simplistic—is surely a mark of a great mind and, in this instance, a great teacher.

But not everyone learns by listening to philosophical discourses. Other temperaments require other approaches. Some respond to the simple display of compassion, as in the case of Sunita, the road sweeper, whose entire life was transformed by the Buddha's human touch and an invitation to envision a life of freedom beyond the restrictions imposed by society. Some whom the Buddha taught were so filled with fear and terror that neither philosophy nor kind invitations would have had any effect. For Angulimala, the depth of rage and torment was so great that only a display of an equal measure of fearlessness and calm could have disarmed him. And on occasion, the best lesson may be the one that seems the harshest, the least compassionate. Vakkali, the Brahman with the man-crush, could only make spiritual progress when he was commanded by the Buddha to leave the community. Sometimes it takes a sledgehammer to get through. But the lessons of the sledgehammer can be long enduring. Sometimes it only takes a gentle reminder of the facts of life to bring the lesson home. The grieving mothers Ubbiri and Kisagotami needed only someone to redirect their attention to the way things really are for them to see the truth. A gesture towards the charnel ground and an errand to fetch a mustard seed were sufficient. In each of these teaching moments, the Buddha revealed himself as an astute observer of the human condition and a skillful communicator of wisdom.

# The Buddha and Buddhism
## Lecture 17

Throughout his teaching career, the Buddha told his listeners, "All things in existence are subject to decay; everything that is born necessarily dies." ... Although he had attained the highest level of fulfillment of which any being was capable, the Buddha, too, was subject to this truth.

The last days of the Buddha's life are described in one of the great texts of the Buddhist tradition, the *Mahaparinibbanasutta*. According to this sutta, in his 80th year the Buddha increasingly felt the effects of aging and was afflicted by serious illnesses. Existence had become painful and tiresome, so he "renounced the life principle"—that is, he chose to allow the natural processes of decline to take their course. His final illness was from a meal of "hog's mincemeat"; his symptoms suggested dysentery or food poisoning.

Despite intense pain, the Buddha faced his illness in full awareness and complete equanimity. Lying down out in the open between two Sala trees with his monks and nuns gathered around him, he asked three times if they had any lingering questions about the dhamma. Three times there was silence. Satisfied, the Buddha uttered his final words: "All conditioned things are impermanent. Strive for liberation with diligence," then peacefully passed through the four states of deep meditation known as the **jhanas** and from there entered parinibbana. Like the crucifixion of Jesus, the Buddha's death was a lesson for his followers: For those who have awakened, death is nothing to fear. And if there is nothing to fear in death, then there is nothing to fear in life.

But what happens to a fully awakened being at the time of death? Does he or she still exist? The Buddha simply refused to answer this question because it is premised on dualistic thinking: the concept that something either exists or does not exist. The Buddha knew that any answer he might give would serve to reinforce this flawed pattern of thinking. As with seeing nibbana, the realization of parinibbana can only be described apophatically, with language that indicates what it is not. As you recall, the Buddha explained nibbana as the cessation of suffering, the end of ignorance, and the deconstruction of the illusion of the self. To these events, the parinibbana adds the final depletion of all energies that have sustained existence.

The body of the Buddha lay in state for six days after his death. On the seventh day, after the body was honored with perfumes and garlands, it was wrapped in oil-soaked cloth and burned on a pyre of aromatic wood at a sacred shrine near the site of the Buddha's parinibbana. Following the cremation, the ashes and other irreducible parts of the body were buried as relics in massive earthen mounds known as **stūpas**, which later became pilgrimage sites.

**Today, over one-half of the world's population lives in an area where Buddhism was or is a principal cultural force.**

For many years, Buddhism was merely one of many sects in ancient India. It was not until the missionary efforts of Emperor Aśoka the Great in the 3rd century B.C.E. that Buddhism attained the status of an international religion. Buddhism became a dominant cultural and religious force in India until the 12th–14th centuries C.E., when it became all but extinct in the country of its birth.

Buddhism experienced a number of doctrinal disputes in its early history. Today, Theravada, which means "the way of the elders," is the oldest surviving form, practiced mainly in Sri Lanka, Burma, Cambodia, Laos, and Thailand. Somewhere around the time of Jesus, the Mahayana, or "great vehicle," movement began in the monasteries of northern India, based on a collection of texts purported to contain teachings of the Buddha that had only been revealed to a select few of his students. Two developments in particular distinguish Mahayana from Theravada. First, Theravada had always maintained that Gotama Buddha was a human being; Mahayana believes him a transcendent reality known as the *dharma-kāya*, or the body of truth, giving him a more divine, godlike status. Second, in Theravada, bodhisatta was simply the title given to individuals prior to awakening, including the Buddha. In the Mahayana, the bodhisatta choose to forego entry into final nibbana and stay in samsāra to enable others to achieve awakening. Thus the

Mahayana began to take on the qualities of a savior religion. The Mahayana came to China during the Han dynasty in the early centuries of the current era and spread to Korea, Japan, and Vietnam, becoming the most popular variety of Buddhism over time and producing new schools such as Zen and Vajrayana. Through these traditional forms, Buddhism has traversed and influenced cultures throughout the entire continent of Asia. Meanwhile, an influx of Asian practitioners who have come to the West in the last few centuries and an increasing number of Westerners who have adopted Buddhism as their own are creating a new tradition. ■

## Important Terms

**jhana**: A deep meditative state.

**stūpa**: An earthen mound containing a relic of the Buddha.

## Question to Consider

1.  What is the difference between a religious leader and a spiritual savior? What aspects of the Buddha's life and teachings show him as one or the other?

# The Buddha and Buddhism
## Lecture 17—Transcript

Throughout his teaching career, the Buddha told his listeners: "All things in existence are subject to decay; everything that is born necessarily dies." This was a pre-eminent and ineluctable truth about the nature of reality. Although he had attained the highest level of fulfillment of which any being was capable, the Buddha, too, was subject to this truth. Having been born into existence, it was a certainty that he would decline and die. Death came to the Buddha in his 80th year, probably sometime around 410 B.C.E., 45 years after his enlightenment. Today, we will look at the events surrounding his final days of life, including his last years as a teacher of the dhamma and the development of the Buddhist tradition following his demise.

We have already examined many of the noteworthy events of the Buddha's post-awakening life, including his personal qualities and skills as a teacher. Before we move on to discuss his final nibbana, I'd to mention one more episode from this portion of his life—his relationship with his cousin Devadatta. We are not exactly certain when the events I'm about to describe occurred, but the texts intimate that they happened late in the Buddha's life.

Devadatta had grown up with young Siddhattha Gotama and from an early age tried to compete with the Bodhisatta. The legends tell several stories of Devadatta's efforts to embarrass or defeat Siddhattha. But despite—or perhaps *because* of—Devadatta's competitive spirit, he became a monk in the sangha shortly after the Buddha's enlightenment. In his early days, Devadatta was a good monk known for his abilities to use the extraordinary psychic powers that can be developed through meditation. But in spite of his meditative skills, he was unable to attain the ultimate goal of arahantship. Perhaps of out frustration, he became self-absorbed and sought worldly power and renown. Increasingly, he became envious of the respect and fame the Buddha received.

When he requested to be named the leader of the sangha, the Buddha flatly denied his request, and Devadatta vowed to destroy his cousin. Devadatta's first effort was to hire someone to kill the Buddha. But when the hired murderer approached the Awakened One, he lost the nerve, abandoned his weapons, and took refuge in the Buddha. Then Devadatta himself tried to kill the Buddha by pushing a huge boulder off a peak as the Buddha was walking below. As it careened downward, the rock struck another rock causing it to veer off course and miss the Buddha. Devadatta's third attempt involved feeding liquor to a fierce killer elephant until it was drunk. When the elephant saw the Buddha coming in the distance, it charged. The Buddha remained calm and generated feelings of compassion for the raging beast. Suddenly, the elephant halted in its tracks and became quiet and serene. The Buddha stroked its trunk and spoke softly. In a gesture of respect, the elephant removed the dust on the Buddha's feet with its trunk and scattered it over its own head. Once again, murderous rage proved no match for the Buddha's serenity and compassion.

The point of these stories is not really that the Buddha's self-composure saved his own neck, but how his peaceful radiance brought tranquility to others. According to the traditions, a Buddha acts solely out of compassion for others. Even Devadatta was saved by the Buddha's compassion. Shortly before he died, the would-be assassin repented of his misdeeds. The ripening of his evil karma, however, prevented him from seeing the Buddha to make amends. But before he died, he professed a commitment to the Buddha's teaching. That act, coupled with the merits he acquired as a young monk, ensured that Devadatta would eventually become an arahant in a future birth.

The last days of the Buddha's life are described in one of the great texts of the Buddhist tradition, the *Mahaparinibbanasutta*. According to this sutta, in his eightieth year the Buddha increasingly felt the effects of aging and was afflicted by serious illnesses. He knew his life was near the end. His foster mother, Mahaprajapati, Yasodhara, the wife of his youth, and his son Rahula had all pre-deceased him. He told his personal assistant, Ananda:

> I am now old and worn out ... one who has traversed life's path, I have reached the term of life, which is 80. Just as an old cart is made to go by being held together with straps, so the [Buddha's] body is kept going by being strapped up. It is only when the [Buddha] withdraws his attention from outward signs, and by the cessation of

certain feelings, enters into the signless concentration of mind, that his body knows comfort.

Existence had become painful and tiresome for the Buddha. When the writer Stewart Alsop was contemplating his own death from leukemia, he wrote, "A dying man needs to die, as a sleepy man needs to sleep, and there comes a time when it is wrong, as well as useless, to resist." This was the Buddha's recognition. When he had come to this awareness, the sutta tells us, he "renounced the life principle," that is, he chose to allow the natural processes of decline to take their course. He predicted he would take final nibbana within three months' time.

He continued to maintain his accustomed pattern of life until his shortly before his death. At that time, he accepted a meal from a blacksmith near the village of Kushinagara and soon became violently ill. It is not clear of what the meal consisted; the ancient texts call it "hog's mincemeat," which obviously suggests pork, but could also suggest the "food of pigs" or "pig's delight," which many scholars have interpreted as some kind of mushroom. The symptoms of his disease suggest that he may have contracted dysentery or food poisoning. In any case, it was clear that the meal was not intended to cause the Buddha harm. Indeed, as he approached the end of life, the Buddha made a special effort to reassure the blacksmith that he was in no way responsible for the Awakened One's death.

Despite his intense pain, the Buddha did not complain but faced his illness in full awareness and complete equanimity. As his death approached, he asked Ananda, to prepare a bed for him out in the open between two Sala trees. You will recall that the Buddha was born as his mother reached for the branch of such a tree in a grove near Lumbini. He positioned himself in the lion's posture, in which he customarily slept, and his monks and nuns gathered around him. He asked the members of the sangha if they had any lingering questions about the dhamma. Three times he asked, and three times there was silence. Satisfied that his followers had understood his teachings, the Buddha uttered his final words: "All conditioned things are impermanent. Strive for liberation with diligence." Then, he peacefully passed through the four states of deep meditation known as the jhanas and from there entered parinibbana, or the great final liberation. At once the earth began to tremble and thunder clapped, in recognition of the great being's passing. It was during the night of the full moon of the month of Vesakha when this occurred, the same time of the year when he was born and when he was enlightened.

The final nibbana is presented as a great, triumphant event. It was the Buddha's ultimate conquest of samsara. The legends indicate that the gods from throughout the universe made their way to Kushinagara to witness this event. Like the crucifixion of Jesus, the Buddha's death was a lesson for his followers. This is why the *Mahaparinibbanasutta* describes the end of his life in such great detail; the text is one of the longest in the Pali canon. The Buddha's dying lesson was that for those who have awakened to the reality as it is, death is nothing to fear. And if there is nothing to fear in death, then there is nothing to fear in life. The Buddha's death was as placid a departure as one could hope for.

But where did he go? Even some of the Buddha's own students wanted to know what would occur to a fully awakened being at the time of death. In the *Majjhima Nikaya*, the monk Malunkyaputta confronts the Buddha, complaining that Enlightened One never explained this matter in any of his discourses. Malunkyaputta threatened to leave the community unless the Buddha stated his position unequivocally. The monk gave the Buddha four choices and demanded that he explicitly indicate which was the case. First, was it the case that the Tathagata, that is, a perfectly enlightened being, exists after death? Or was it the case that the Tathagata does not exist after death? Or, does the Tathagata *both* exist *and* does not exist after death? Or does the Tathagata *neither* exist *nor* not exist after death? Those options would seem to cover all the possibilities, but apparently they did not. The Buddha simply refused to answer Malunkyaputta's point-blank questions. The monk's questions were premised on the same dualistic way of thinking that in an earlier lecture we witnessed the Buddha dismiss: the concept that something either exists or does not exist. Malunkyaputta's mind was still caught up in that web of thought and could not see beyond it. The Buddha knew that any answer he might give would serve to reinforce this flawed pattern of thinking.

As with seeing nibbana, the realization of parinibbana can only be described apophatically, with language that indicates what it is not. As you recall, the Buddha explained nibbana as the cessation of suffering, the end of ignorance, the deconstruction of the illusion of the self. To these events, the parinibbana adds the final depletion of all energies that have sustained existence. The five components of human life—physical matter, sensations, perceptions, mental fabrications, and consciousness—have been spent. Because the processes comprising samsaric existence are no more, rebirth no longer occurs. Samsara is over.

The image often associated with parinibbana is the extinguishment of a candle flame. The flame is a consequence of various elements: the wick, oxygen, and heat. When these constituents are exhausted—when the supply of oxygen is cut off, when the wick is burned out, when the heat has been cooled—the flame is gone. It makes as much sense to ask, "Where does the Buddha go after death?" as it does to ask "Where does the flame go?" The flame is not an entity that can "go" anywhere. The Buddha is simply not here.

Just before he died, the Buddha directed his followers to treat his remains in the same manner as a "Great Wheel Turner," or universal emperor. Accordingly, the body of the Great Master lay in state for six days after his death. On the seventh day, after honoring the body with perfumes and garlands, the Buddha's remains were wrapped in oil-soaked cloth and burned on a pyre of aromatic wood at a sacred shrine near the site of his parinibbana. Following the cremation, the ashes and other irreducible parts of the body, including a skull bone and some teeth, were collected and distributed to representatives from significant places in his life, including his birthplace; the site of his enlightenment; the location of his first teaching after enlightenment; and the site of his parinibbana. These artifacts were then taken back to these locations and buried in massive earthen mounds known as stūpas, a pre-Buddhist structure in which royalty were entombed.

The earliest stūpas were probably very simple constructions but the structures became more ornate as the significance of these reliquaries increased in Buddhist life. Stūpas soon became pilgrimage sites for those following the

Buddha's Middle Way. Monks, nuns, and ordinary householders began to travel great distances just to be able to glimpse these reliquaries and to come into physical proximity to them. The stūpa was a physical representation of the dhamma or the enlightened mind, functioning something like the way the crucifix or cross represents the gospel for Christians. As central part of their pilgrimage, Buddhists circumambulated the stūpa—in the same manner that Muslims walk around the Kaaba in Makkah as part of the Hajj. Coming to the stūpa and circling it came to be considered a meritorious action that could improve the circumstances of one's next birth. Some Buddhists even believed the bodily relics could confer release from suffering or promote actual healing.

If you were born into a religious tradition that venerates relics—such as Roman Catholicism or Eastern Orthodoxy—their allure for the religious mind is probably quite familiar. But if you were not brought up in such a tradition, the significance of relics and reliquaries may not be immediately apparent. You may even view such things with great suspicion. So let me try to demystify them a bit.

Matters of the spirit are by definition intangible, immaterial, and hence very difficult to conceive. The human mind, therefore, craves for something tangible, something physical that it can use as an aid to understanding, even if that thing is something that must ultimately be given up, as all good symbols should be. Images, icons, religious architecture, scriptures, the bread and wine of the Christian Eucharist all serve this function. Of course, there is no better mode of sacred tangibility than something closely associated with a great person who embodied the ideals of one's aspirations. And what can be more closely associated with such a person than fragments of his or her very body?

Consider for a moment the vast cults of celebrity throughout the world. Unfortunately, as societies, we today don't revere sages and noble persons as much as we worship television and movie actors and professional athletes. Think about the way one might prize an autograph or a piece of clothing from one of these celebrities—or even just a story-bought jersey with the name of a professional athlete embroidered on it. If you are ever in Memphis, the city where I now live, make sure you visit one of the United

States' most popular pilgrimage sites, Graceland, where you can view acres of Elvis memorabilia, including the jumpsuits he wore in his later year or the vials of sweat collected from his younger years. Elvis' mansion is a magnet for people all around the world who make a pilgrimage there to get close to the relics of the King that lie interred on the Graceland grounds in a location aptly named the Meditation Garden. Perhaps these analogies will help illuminate the role of relics in a more sacred context. Something of the charisma of the individual with which they are associated is believed to be mediated through such objects.

Within several months of the Buddha's parinibbana, 500 fully awakened monks met in the north Indian town of Rajagaha to confer about the future of the dhamma and the sangha. The Buddha did not appoint a successor to lead the sangha but directed his followers to allow the dhamma itself to guide the community. Thus, it was essential for the sangha to agree upon the content of the Buddha's teaching. It was here that his assistant Ananda stood before the assembly and recited the Buddha's discourses, establishing the oral tradition that later became the Pali canon. A few other councils were held to resolve a number of doctrinal and practical issues. Since the Buddha left governance and interpretation of the dhamma in the hands of the Sangha as a whole, disputes of this nature were almost inevitable.

Buddhism was not wildly popular in the immediate centuries following the life of the Buddha. For many years, it was merely one of many sects in ancient India. It was a demanding way of life and lacked many of the elements that would make it a more attractive religion for ordinary folk, such as belief in gods and community rituals. The cessation of suffering simply did not involve worship of the divine realm. The Buddha certainly never suggested that *he* should be the object of prayers or rituals.

It was not until the reign of Emperor Aśoka the Great in the 3rd century B.C.E. that Buddhism spread throughout the subcontinent and attained the status of an international religion. Aśoka's role in the history of Buddhism cannot be underestimated. Initially a ruthless conqueror, Aśoka converted to the Buddha's way after witnessing first-hand the massive atrocities caused by his insatiable quest for power and lands. In the aftermath of the Battle of

Kalinga, the horrifying spectacle of over 100,000 human bodies prompted him to renounce war and embrace the dhamma. Aśoka became as zealous a supporter of the Buddha's teaching as he had been a conqueror. Legend says he had the original stūpas opened to recover the relics and divided them to create 84,000 new reliquaries. Most significantly, he sent missionaries throughout India, Sri Lanka, the area now known as Afghanistan, and other parts of Central Asia. Under his patronage, Buddhism became a dominant cultural and religious force in India until the $12^{th}$-$14^{th}$ centuries C.E., when it became all but extinct in the country of its birth.

Like the development of any religious institution or school of philosophy, Buddhism experienced a number of disputes concerning the practice and the finer points of doctrine. At one time in the early history of Buddhism, there were at least 18 different schools that looked to the Pali canon as its definitive source. Today, of these 18, only the Theravada school remains, making it the oldest extant Buddhist tradition and probably the form closest to the way Buddhism was practiced around the time of the Buddha. Theravada, which means the way of the elders, is found mainly in Sri Lanka, Burma, Cambodia, Laos, and Thailand.

Somewhere around the time of Jesus, another Buddhist movement began to coalesce in the monasteries of North India. This development represented a much more significant division of thought than Buddhism had experienced in its first 500 years. The Mahayana, or the Great Vehicle as it came to be called, was based on a collection of texts purported to contain teachings of the Buddha that had only been revealed to a select few of his students. These Mahayana sutras, their advocates claimed, had been kept concealed until the time was appropriate for them for them to come to light, and they provided a superior understanding of the Buddha's teaching. From one point of view, the Mahayana texts furnished a considerably different understanding of the Buddha and his role in bringing liberation to the world; from another perspective, this understanding can be seen as the further development of ideas inherent in the earliest Buddhist schools.

Two developments in particular helped distinguish the Mahayana from the Theravada school. The first was its view of the Buddha. Theravada had always maintained that Gotama Buddha was a human being, who had by his own efforts attained the status of Buddhahood. According to the Mahayana, Gotama Buddha was the manifestation of a transcendent reality known as the *dharma-kāya*, or the body of truth. As the Buddha of this era, Gotama was a *nirmāna-kāya*, an appearance body of this cosmic principle. All Buddhas, in fact, were manifestations of the dharma-kāya. This conceptual development gave the Buddha a more divine, god-like status.

The second distinguishing mark of the Mahayana was its interpretation of the Bodhisatta. In Theravada, the Bodhisatta was simply the title given to the Buddha prior to his awakening. It was an epithet reserved only for Gotama and the other rare individuals destined for Buddhahood. In the Mahayana, the Bodhisatta—or Bodhisattva, to use the Sanskrit of the Mahayana school— was an enlightened being who choose to forego entry into final nibbana in order to stay within the world of samsara to enable others to achieve awakening. With this interpretation of the Buddha and the Bodhisattva, the Mahayana began to take on the qualities of a savior-religion. Interestingly, these developments took place at the same time another great savior-religion was taking shape in West Asia—Christianity.

The Mahayana was the form of Buddhism that was exported to China during the Han dynasty, in the early centuries of the current era. From there, Buddhism later spreads to Korea, Japan, and Vietnam. Over time, the Mahayana became the most popular variety of Buddhism and has so remained. Of course, it too has fragmented as new schools emerged from within it. One the Mahayana sects was Ch'an, which was later known as Zen.

The third major form of Buddhism, the Vajrayana, developed from the Mahayana around the 5th century C.E. in North India. This particular version of the Buddhist tradition contains elements of the Indian yogic practice known as Tantra, an esoteric practice of harnessing the body's energies to promote enlightenment. Vajrayana, or the Diamond or Thunderbolt Vehicle, was first taken to Tibet in 7th century C.E., where it was influenced by Bön, the indigenous Tibetan religion characterized by its interest in magic. Today, Vajrayana is still practiced in Tibet and Mongolia but also in Nepal, Bhutan, and India, the home of many Tibetan refugees, including Tenzin Gyatso, the 14th Dalai Lama.

Through these three traditional forms, Buddhism has traversed virtually the entire continent of Asia. Even when the inhabitants of these regions did not identify themselves as Buddhists, they were influenced by the perspective of the Buddha and his interpreters, in much the same way that westerners have been influenced by Christianity whether they consider themselves Christians or not. Today, over one-half of the world's population lives in an area where Buddhism was or is a principal cultural force.

Finally, I think it is worth mentioning the emergence of what appears to be a new form of the Buddhism arising in the western world. As yet, this evolving variety of the tradition has no specific name beyond perhaps "western Buddhism," but it seems to be taking a distinctive shape. This emerging Buddhism is the result of several older varieties of the tradition taking root in a new and very different culture, in the way Buddhism has done ever since Aśoka first sent missionaries beyond the borders of India. Western Buddhism's growth derives from an influx of Asian practitioners who have come to the west in the last few centuries and from an increasing number of westerners who have adopted Buddhism as their own.

With this cursory overview of the development of the Buddhist traditions, we bring to a close our study of the Buddha. We shall, of course, return to his life and teachings when we commence our comparative investigations of the four sages. In our next talk, we will take the sage with whom the Buddha is most often compared, Jesus of Nazareth. To conclude this portion of the course, let me quote Assaji, one of the five monks who heard the Buddha's first discourse, and who provided what is often taken as a concise summary of the dhamma:

To abstain from what is evil;
To do what is good;
To purify the mind:
This is the teaching of all the Buddhas.

# The Jewish and Roman Worlds of Jesus
## Lecture 18

> Almost from the beginning, the relationship between this god and his chosen people was tempestuous, to say the least. Poets and prophets likened it to a marriage—a marriage that was sometimes tender and loving, and sometimes on the verge of divorce.

Jesus of Nazareth lived at the intersection of two very different cultures: ancient Judaism and the Roman Empire, each of which decisively shaped his life and teachings. Ancient Judaism was more than our modern idea of a "religion"; it was a culture, touching every aspect of life. Judaism traces its roots to a nomad named Abram who responded to the call of the god Yahweh to leave his home in Mesopotamia (present-day Iraq) and journey to Canaan—later known as Palestine—where the state of Israel is now located. Over time, the 12 Jewish tribes living in Canaan were forged into the kingdom of Israel. But the cultural and political tensions between the groups became too great, and the kingdom was eventually split into the northern kingdom of Israel and the southern kingdom of Judah, from which the terms "Jew" and "Judaism" were derived. But the citizens of both kingdoms regarded themselves as the children of Abraham and as the chosen people of the god Yahweh. The people of both kingdoms likewise blamed their many misfortunes on their own lack of fidelity to their god.

Between the 8th and 1st centuries B.C.E., the people of Israel and Judah suffered under repeated invasions by the armies of the massive empires that surrounded them, including Babylon, Assyria, Persia, Macedonia, and finally Rome, which greatly changed their way of life. Religion in the Jewish homeland between the Babylonian Exile and the time of Jesus was not at all homogenous. The most prominent sects were the **Pharisees**, the **Sadducees**, and the **Essenes**. Pharisaism arose in the 2nd century B.C.E. as a movement among lay Jews who believed in the authority of what was called the Oral Torah (later preserved in writing as the Mishnah) and were resistant to the idea of the priesthood. They also believed in the resurrection of the dead, an idea that developed rather late in ancient Judaism. The Sadducees, in essence, held the opposite positions—supporting the priesthood and the written Torah and opposing the doctrine of resurrection. Rabbinic Judaism of today—Orthodox, Conservative, and Reform—is directly descended from Pharisaism. The Essenes were also active in this period, living in small, quasi-monastic, apolitical communities and focusing their practices on maintaining ritual purity. Each of these sects was a part of the world of Jesus.

**The Roman Empire was the latest in a centuries-long series of foreign conquerors of this tiny region.**

In 63 B.C.E., the Romans captured Jerusalem, and the Jewish homeland became a client state of Rome, with profound ramifications. Roman domination exacerbated the existing class divisions and tensions within Jewish society. The small, wealthy, privileged Jewish ruling class, on behalf of their Roman overlords, levied heavy taxes upon the tenant farmers, fishermen, craftsmen, and servants who made up 90 percent of the population. Peasant life was precarious, and life expectancy for a peasant was a mere 30 years. This tenuous existence became even more so under the reign of King Herod the Great, one of the client rulers appointed by Rome. Despite his Jewish heritage, he was not particularly sensitive to the plight of other Jews. He confiscated peasant lands, essentially forcing the population into serfdom. When Herod died in 4 B.C.E., revolts—some led by organized groups like the **Zealots** and **Sicarii**—erupted throughout the kingdom and legions of imperial soldiers were dispatched to silence the rebels. Two thousand insurgents were crucified in Jerusalem, but the resistance movement continued to grow.

After Herod's death, Palestine was ruled Roman governors, including the famous Pontius Pilate. The chief priest of Jerusalem and his associates, known as the elders, were appointed by Rome and asked to manage internal Jewish affairs and to maintain peace. Their position brought them great power and wealth, yet their status was extremely precarious. This was Palestine in the time of Jesus: a world full of tension, a world on edge. ∎

**Essenes**: A Jewish sect active between the 2$^{rd}$ century B.C.E. and 1$^{st}$ century C.E. whose members lived in quasi-monastic communities and were heavily concerned with maintaining ritual purity.

**Pharisees**: A Jewish sect that arose in the 2$^{nd}$ century B.C.E. and is the ancestor of modern rabbinic Judaism. Its members believed in the significance of the Oral Torah (later written down as the Mishnah), the primacy of scriptural study over Temple sacrifice, and the doctrine of resurrection of the dead.

**Sadducees**: A Jewish sect that arose in the 2$^{nd}$ century B.C.E. that promoted traditional Temple-centered worship and the authority of the priestly class over the scholarly (rabbinic) class.

**Sicarii**: A violent anti-Roman Jewish sect of the 1$^{st}$ century C.E. believed to be named for the daggers (*sica*) they carried. Judas Iscariot may have been a member of this group.

**Zealots**: An aggressively anti-Roman Jewish political sect active between the 1$^{st}$ century B.C.E. and 1$^{st}$ century C.E.

## Question to Consider

1. In what ways was the political world in the time of Jesus similar to that of Confucius? Of the Buddha? In what ways was it different?

# The Jewish and Roman Worlds of Jesus
## Lecture 18—Transcript

Jesus of Nazareth lived at the intersection of two very different cultures: ancient Judaism and the Roman Empire. Each of these contexts in different ways decisively shaped his life and teachings. Yet, he became convinced later in life that these two worlds were about to be replaced by an altogether new reality, the kingdom of god. In today's lecture, we will explore the nature and character of these Jewish and Roman cultures to set the stage for our examination of Jesus' life and his conviction that a wholly new age was on the horizon.

Ancient Judaism was a great deal more than what most people today mean by the word religion. It not only determined what one believed about god and what rituals one performed on holy days; it thoroughly inundated every aspect of life. It structured the daily routine, regulated one's diet, determined how people interacted with others, governed business transactions, defined criminality, shaped family relationships, and provided the fundamental concepts that formed the common worldview. So closely intertwined were what the modern world calls "religion" and everything else that the ancient Jews had no special word to designate the "religious" dimension of life. Religion and culture were identical.

What is today known as Judaism traces its roots to the persons and traditions described in the Torah, the first five books of the Tanakh, the most sacred collection of Jewish writings. According to these legendary accounts, the Jewish faith began when a nomad named Abram responded to the call of the god Yahweh to leave his home in Mesopotamia, in what is now present-day Iraq, and journey to a new land called Canaan—and later known as Palestine—where the state of Israel is now located. Yahweh promised to give this land to Abram and his descendants in exchange for allegiance to Yahweh as his god. Abram accepted the god's invitation, and thus began the long and complex narrative of the Jewish people's relationship with this god.

The ensuing saga includes many of the individuals and events that are well-known in western culture; they have become part of the common stock of our cultural literacy. Included in that story are the names of the great patriarchs and matriarchs who were the immediate descendants of Abram, or Abraham, as he was later called. Among them were Ishmael and Isaac; Jacob, who was given the name Israel, and his brother Esau; Joseph, the son of Jacob who was sold into slavery by his envious brothers and later reconciled with them in the land of Egypt. Generations later, there was Moses who, under the guidance of Yahweh, led the descendants of Joseph and his brothers out of Egypt and back to the land promised to Abraham. The story continues with the Israelites' struggles to establish a community in Canaan and to remain faithful to their god. They contended with the other peoples living in the Promised Land and with the temptations posed by the other gods of the land, who frequently seemed more accessible than the elusive Yahweh. Over time, what was initially a confederacy of 12 tribes living in Canaan was forged into the kingdom of Israel, united under the rule of Saul, David, and Solomon. But the cultural and political tensions between the groups became too great, and the kingdom was eventually split in two at the death of Solomon. The northern kingdom continued to be known as Israel, and the southern kingdom took the name Judah, after the dominant tribe of the realm. It was from the name Judah, which was later known as Judea, that the terms "Jew" and "Judaism" were derived. But the citizens of both kingdoms regarded themselves as the children of Abraham and as the chosen people of the god Yahweh.

Almost from the beginning, the relationship between this god and his chosen people was tempestuous, to say the least. Poets and prophets likened it to a marriage—a marriage that was sometimes tender and loving, and sometimes on the verge of divorce. The people found it hard at times to remain faithful to their commitment to Yahweh as their sole god, and they frequently went "whoring after other gods," to use the biblical language. Yahweh himself was often put out with his people, allowing them to suffer the consequences of their infidelity to him and threatening them with harsh punishments.

When the kingdom split into the northern and southern realms, it began to appear increasingly likely that that Yahweh was about to make good on his threats. Both kingdoms were tiny and highly vulnerable to the massive empires surrounding them. Prophets arose to warn the people of both territories to get right with god or face the unpleasant consequences. In the

8th century B.C.E., Israel, the northern kingdom, fell victim to the armies of Assyria and was destroyed. There would no longer be a political entity known as Israel until 1948. The southern kingdom, Judah, survived longer than Israel, but it too suffered a major blow at the hands of the Babylonians in the 6th century B.C.E. In both instances, the devastation wrought by these great empires was widely construed as the work of Yahweh exacting punishment on a people who neglected to live up to their side of the ancient agreement negotiated with Abraham.

In 587 B.C.E., the Babylonian army marched into Judah, took tens of thousands of Jews captive, and carried them back to Babylon in Mesopotamia. Many died on the nearly 1000 mile trek. This event, referred to as the Exile or the Babylonian Captivity, was a turning point in Jewish history, marking the start of the Diaspora, the dispersion of the Jews outside of Canaan.

It is during the Exile and afterwards that Judaism acquired many of the features that characterize it today. Prior to the deportation to Babylon, religious life centered on the temple in Jerusalem, which had been built by Solomon, King David's son. At the temple, members of the priestly caste offered animal sacrifices to Yahweh on behalf of the nation and performed various rituals for individuals. But the Exile temporarily brought that practice to an end. Solomon's Temple had been destroyed by the Babylonians, and the Jews living in the Diaspora would have been unable to worship there anyway. In response to their displacement, certain key features of Jewish practice were newly created and others altered. During this time, the institution of the synagogue was formed, which allowed Jews to worship their god while physically removed from the Temple in Jerusalem. The synagogue was an assembly of at least ten Jewish males over the age of 13, who constituted a *minyan*, or quorum. The development of the synagogue increased the importance of the rabbi, or the teacher. Worship of the god in the synagogue centered on reading and interpreting the Torah rather than the system of sacrifice that had characterized worship in Judaism's early history. It was during the Exile that the sacred writings began to be compiled and edited. By the time of Jesus, rabbinic Judaism centered on the synagogue was well-established in the Jewish homeland and was the form of Judaism that most profoundly shaped his life.

These developments did not mean, however, that sacrifice and worship at the Temple in Jerusalem was made obsolete. In 539 B.C.E., the Persians conquered the Babylonians and permitted the Jews to return to their homeland in 538. Most Jews stayed in Babylon, but some returned to Canaan. When the small contingent of former exiles arrived in the Promised Land, they rebuilt the temple, now referred to as the Second Temple, and tried to establish strict devotion to Yahweh and his Torah. Since they interpreted the Exile as the god's punishment for their failure to obey his commandments, they were zealously determined to maintain the traditions of the past, including animal sacrifice, and remain faithful to Yahweh to avoid a future catastrophe of this magnitude. Many of the individuals associated with the rebirth of temple insisted that it was *only* at the Jerusalem temple that Yahweh could be properly worshiped. Since the Persians who liberated the Jews from Babylon did not allow them to re-establish an independent monarchy, the priests, by default, emerged as the dominant authority. Consequently, the importance of the temple and the priesthood was amplified, generating tensions between the temple supporters and those living in the areas at a distance from Jerusalem, such as the Galilee and Samaria, the region located where the old Kingdom of Israel had once been.

In 333 B.C.E., two centuries after the return of the exiles from Babylon, the Jewish homeland was subjugated again, this time by the armies of Alexander the Great. Alexander's campaign of conquest, which extended as far as northern India, brought Greek culture and language throughout his empire. This expansion of Greek political and cultural influence is known as Hellenization. Many of the Jews welcomed Greek culture and adopted Greek philosophy, Greek dress, and the Greek language. A gymnasium was even built in Jerusalem, and some Jewish men tried to remove the marks of circumcision. But many resisted Hellenism and tried to remain loyal to the traditional customs and practices of the descendants of Abraham.

On the whole, Greek rule was initially benign. Alexander was a relatively tolerant ruler, who allowed conquered peoples a large measure of political and cultural autonomy. But after his death, his successors did not always adhere to that policy. One Greek king, Antiochus IV, was particularly cruel to the inhabitants of Palestine and was determined to force the Jews to give up their distinctive customs and traditions. Antiochus desecrated the Temple in Jerusalem and stole its sacred ritual implements; he forbade sacrifices to Yahweh; and, according to some stories, he compelled some Jews to eat pork, which they regarded as unclean. Antiochus' actions prompted a military response from a Jewish militia led by Judas Maccabeus. Under his leadership, the Jews overthrew Greek rule and established an independent nation governed by his family, the Hasmoneans. The Hasmoneans ruled an independent Jewish kingdom from the mid-2nd century until the mid-first century B.C.E. Judas Maccabeus reclaimed the Temple for the Jews and restored its sacred status. This triumph is still celebrated by Jews today during the festival of Hanukkah.

Although dedicated to a single god, religion in the Jewish homeland during Hasmonean rule and through the time of Jesus was not at all uniform or homogenous. In fact, the religion of the Israelites and Jews was probably *never* homogenous, despite the efforts of some to make it so. There were several major groups with differing opinions about what constituted correct practice of the faith. The most prominent of these sects were the Pharisees, the Sadducees, and the Essenes. When Christianity emerged in the middle part of the first century, it was simply regarded as another one of these other Jewish sects.

To the readers of the New Testament, the group known as the Pharisees will surely be familiar. They were often portrayed in the Christian scripture as the sanctimonious rivals to Jesus. But the Pharisees probably had more in common with Jesus than is ordinarily thought. Some scholars, in fact, have argued that Jesus himself was a Pharisee or had been a part of the sect at one time. Pharisaism arose in the 2nd century B.C.E. near the rise of the Hasmonean monarchy, as a movement among lay Jews—that is to say, Jews who were not part of the priesthood. The Pharisees believed in the authority of what was called the Oral Torah, a collection of traditions and commentaries that helped interpret the Written Torah. This oral tradition was eventually written down by rabbis and preserved as the body of writing called the *Mishnah* in the 2nd century C.E. The Pharisees were also resistant to the idea of the priesthood. They believed that all Jews were to be priests and that the nation was to be a "kingdom of priests," to quote the Tanakh. Laws that were originally intended for the priests, such as the regulations governing ritual purity, the Pharisees believed, should be observed by *all* Jews. The Pharisees also maintained a belief in the resurrection of the dead, an idea that developed rather late in ancient Judaism; it not mentioned in the earliest Jewish scripture. Rabbinic Judaism of today—Orthodox, Conservative and Reform—is directly descended from Pharisaism.

The Pharisees were opposed to the group called the Sadducees. Like the Pharisees, the Sadducees came into existence in the 2nd century B.C.E., but they were mainly associated with the ruling class and the temple priesthood rather than the laity. They rejected the authority of the oral tradition and insisted on a strict interpretation of Torah, whereas the Pharisees preferred a loose construction of the scripture. Because they viewed the Torah as the sole authority for faith, the Sadducees also denied the belief in the resurrection of the dead, which, as I mentioned, is not found in that text. Because of its close connection with the priesthood, the Sadducee sect disappeared after the Romans destroyed the Second Temple in 70 C.E.

Less popular than the Pharisees and Sadducees was a diverse group collectively known as the Essenes, who also began in the 2nd century B.C.E. The Essenes were not mentioned in New Testament, but they have received a fair amount of scholarly attention since the 20th century because of the Dead Sea Scrolls, which some have argued were part of the Essene library of texts. There is no consensus among scholars today as to whether or not that claim is true. But it is likely that some Essenes lived at Qumran, the location near the Dead Sea where the scrolls were discovered. The Essenes were not unlike later Christian monastics who also lived in small communities and practiced celibacy. They were decidedly apolitical and they were deeply concerned with maintaining ritual purity. They also objected to animal sacrifice, which put them at odds with the temple priesthood. Some historians have speculated that Jesus or John the Baptist may have been associated with the Essenes for a time, but there has been no convincing evidence to support that notion.

Each of these sects existed into the 1st century C.E. and was a part of the world of Jesus. Not all—probably not even most—Jews of his time were aligned with any one of these groups. But they are important to understand Jesus' life and teaching and to appreciate the divided context in which he lived.

The rule of the Hasmonean dynasty was brought to an end in 63 B.C.E., when the Roman general Pompey captured Jerusalem, and the Jewish homeland became a client state of the Rome. By the time Jesus was born around 4 B.C.E., Palestine, as the Romans called this region, had been under their domination for over a half century.

Roman control of and presence in Palestine had profound ramifications for the daily life of all its inhabitants. For one thing, the Roman Empire was the latest in a centuries-long series of foreign conquerors of this tiny region. The Jews had long become weary of being pushed around by alien behemoths. Frustration was on the rise. For another thing, Roman domination exacerbated the existing class divisions and tensions within Jewish society. A small fraction of the populace—no more than 1-2%—were charged by Rome with the responsibility of governing the region, which meant maintaining order and exacting heavy taxes to be paid to the Empire. The members of this small ruling class were beholden to Rome, which allowed them to live extravagantly at public expense, as long as they efficiently discharged their duties. The ruling elite were supported by another small class comprising about another 5% of the population. This group was composed of various government officials and bureaucrats, the religious hierarchy, the military leadership, and the businesspeople who furnished them goods and services.

By far the largest class, however, was the peasantry, who made up at least 90% of society in Roman-occupied Palestine. Most of the peasants were farmers. A few owned the land they worked but most were tenant farmers and day laborers. Also included in the peasant class were fishermen, craftsmen, and servants. Jesus of Nazareth was born into this class. Just below it was the very bottom rung of society: the destitute; the lepers, the blind, and the lame; those possessed by demons; prostitutes; and the ritually unclean. To borrow a word from the world of the Buddha's time, these were the "untouchables."

This social structure effectively constituted a caste system. At the top were the wealthy and powerful, who lived comfortably and often lavishly in the larger cities and towns, and down below were common folk, largely uneducated, who worked hard in the country and on the waters to eke out a livelihood that barely sustained them. As usually happens in such systems, the small top tier took a large portion of what the peasantry produced to fund their privileged lives and to pay the fees required by the Roman Empire. Some estimates suggest that the commoners had to forfeit one-half to two-thirds of their annual productivity to Rome and its Jewish collaborators. Peasant life was obviously precarious; a drought could easily thrust a peasant family into the lowest stratum of society, reducing them to begging for alms. The life expectancy for a peasant was a mere 30 years.

This tenuous existence became even more so under the reign of King Herod the Great, one of the client rulers appointed by Rome to govern Palestine. He ruled this region in the three decades before the birth of Jesus. Herod, who was half-Jewish, sought out and was given the title the "King of the Judeans" by the Roman senate. Despite his honorific title and Jewish heritage, he was not particularly sensitive to the plight of other Jews. Although he rebuilt the temple in Jerusalem to ingratiate himself with his subjects, he also sponsored campaigns to exterminate Jewish rivals and movements that resisted Roman rule. He even executed one of his own wives, who was a Hasmonean princess, and three of his own sons. During his regime, Herod confiscated peasant lands by means of foreclosure on debt and permitted other wealthy Jews to do so as well. Farmers were now required to work for large estates and grow crops determined by the landowners. No longer could the peasants raise their own food and barter their surplus with others; hence, they were no longer self-sustaining. As many of the peasant class lost their lands, they were forced into debt, which often resulted in imprisonment or indentured servitude. What was a hardscrabble life under the best of circumstances was made even worse by Herod.

Few tears were shed by the common people when Herod died in 4 B.C.E. Many of the Jews who suffered during his tenure used the occasion of his death to lodge protests against Roman rule. Widespread revolts erupted throughout the kingdom and legions of imperial soldiers were dispatched to silence the rebels. By now, the political resistance movement directly opposing Roman rule had become more organized and prevalent. Among the political insurrectionists were the Zealots and an even more extreme faction called the *Sicarii*, probably a Zealot splinter-group. This latter sect is particularly interesting for our study. The *Sicarii* were so-called because each carried a dagger, or *sicarius*, with which they stabbed their enemies:

the Roman occupiers and their Jewish collaborators. Some scholars have suggested that Judas Iscariot, the follower who betrayed Jesus, may have been a member of this group. They contend that the name "Iscariot" is a Greek transformation of the *sicari-ote*, that is, a member of the *sicarii*.

The uprisings that broke out after Herod's death were quickly snuffed. Two thousand insurgents were crucified in Jerusalem to express Rome's opinion of the insurrection. Because of its gruesome and public nature, crucifixion was almost always reserved for those convicted of sedition against the Empire. But despite the effort to provide a graphic deterrent to future rebellions, the resistance movement continued to grow and to prove itself a thorn in flesh of the Romans.

After his death, Herod's kingdom was divided by Rome into three smaller regions, each governed by one of his sons. The Galilee, in the northern part of Palestine, was given to Herod Antipas; and Judea, the Roman name for Judah, and the area called Samaria, between the Galilee and Judea, was given to Archelaus. The third son, Philip, was given a province northeast of Galilee. Archelaus' reign lasted only ten years. He was replaced by a number of Roman prefects, including the most famous, Pontius Pilate. During the rule of these Roman governors, the chief priest of Jerusalem and his associates, known as the elders, were appointed by Rome and given the responsibility to manage internal Jewish affairs and to maintain peace in the province. This arrangement meant that the chief priest and his colleagues both managed the temple, which was so important to Jewish life, and reported to the Roman prefect. Their position brought them great power and wealth yet their status was extremely precarious. One misstep and they could incur the ire of the Roman overlords or incite the masses to rebellion. They had ample reason to try to pacify both groups.

Jesus was born into a world full of tension, a world on edge. The strain existed on a variety of levels. On the political level, ordinary Jews living in Palestine resented the Roman occupation and suffered from it. They despised their fellow Jews who collaborated with the Empire. The Roman occupiers had virtually no interest in internal Jewish affairs but were centrally concerned with maintaining the *Pax Romana*—the Roman peace—and ensuring the abundant flow of tribute to Rome. On the economic level, the tension between rich and poor was greater than it had ever been. The rich kept getting richer at expense of the poor. On the cultural level, another conflict existed between those loyal to the ancient traditions of the descendants of Abraham and those who were attracted by ways of the Greeks and the Romans. At the religious level, there were quarrels between those who championed the centrality of the temple in Jerusalem, its priesthood, and its system of sacrifice and those who did not regard the temple as essential and who were resistant to the authority of the priests. There were also debates about the ways to interpret the sacred texts and apply them to daily life and differing beliefs about life after death.

Politically, economically, culturally, and religiously, ancient Palestine was stretched to the breaking point. Something had to give.

# The Son of Mary
## Lecture 19

We face difficulties in getting to the historical Jesus, the real individual who lived and died in human history. Our primary sources offer various portraits of the man, and the ways we and others since his time have construed those literary portrayals are profoundly shaped by our preconceptions.

Few persons in history have been subject to such a wide range of interpretations as Jesus, for clear reasons. The only texts that relate historically relevant material about his life are the four Gospels in the Christian New Testament and the noncanonical Gospel of Thomas, each presenting different viewpoints on who he was and what he taught. But perhaps more importantly, for Christians, who have been the sources of most explications of his life and teachings, Jesus functions not only as a savior or as the incarnation of the god of the Jews but as the personification of ideal humanity. Because of this, those who interpreted his life were apt to impute their own values and beliefs to the man.

What can we say with reasonable certainty about the life of Jesus? Virtually all credible scholars believe he was a real person who grew up in the village of Nazareth in the Galilee. Sometime within the last three years of his life, he began to work publicly as an itinerant teacher, preacher, and healer, garnering a modest following, and was executed as an insurrectionist against the Roman Empire. Beyond this, scholars debate which words and events reported in the Gospels can be taken as authentic and which might be embellished or invented.

Most historians believe that the **synoptic Gospels**—Mark, Matthew, and Luke—contain more historically reliable material than the Gospel of John, which is mainly theology told as biography. Mark was likely the first Gospel, written down around 70 C.E., near the time of the Roman destruction of Jerusalem. Matthew and Luke were written a decade or two later and clearly use Mark's narrative as a source, along with a lost text called *Q*, short for *Quelle*, the German word for "source." About 75 percent of the noncanonical

Gospel of Thomas is also found in the synoptics. But these books are by no means identical, nor do they always relate historically precise material.

Invented or historically doubtful material was intended not to deceive but to make important theological statements. For example, the narrative of Jesus's birth in Matthew connects him to the lineage of King David, places his birth in Bethlehem, and matches in detail the prophecies in the book of Isaiah, linking Jesus to Jewish expectations of the messiah (*chrīstos* in Greek). Herod's Slaughter of the Innocents likely

© Photos.com/Thinkstock.

**Unlike in popular Nativity stories, which have the wise men arriving near the time of Jesus's birth, Matthew indicates that they arrived two years later.**

never occurred (it appears in no other sources, Christian or otherwise) but is consistent with Herod's historical character and triggers the Flight into Egypt, which recalls the story of Moses—a comparison that continues throughout Matthew's Gospel. Luke, on the other hand, traces Jesus's lineage all the way to Adam and places the story in a Roman, not a Jewish, political context, underscoring Jesus's universal importance. The importance of Mary in the story, the contrast to Augustus, and the presence of the shepherds in Luke's account associate Jesus with the commoners and the disenfranchised.

Do those differences really matter? We should at least acknowledge that the authors' choice of details is shaped by their theological presuppositions and intentions. It is more plausible to say that these are different stories, addressed to different audiences, and told to convey different ideas about who Jesus was. Neither author is interested in objectively reporting events.

In Jesus's own lifetime, those who knew him had a great many ideas about who he was and what he meant when he taught and performed mighty deeds. A half-century later, when the Gospels were being written down, the diversity of viewpoints about his life and teachings remained. Since that time, the interpretations have only continued to amass. ∎

## Important Terms

*chrīstos*: The Greek translation of the Hebrew term "messiah," meaning "anointed one."

*Q*: A lost source text used by the authors of the Gospels of Matthew and Luke.

**synoptic Gospels**: The collective name for the Gospels of Matthew, Mark, and Luke.

## Question to Consider

1. If you are a member of a faith tradition (particularly one of those founded or inspired by one of our four sages), how important is the historical accuracy of scripture to your faith?

# The Son of Mary
## Lecture 19—Transcript

Few persons in history have been subject to such a wide range of interpretations as Jesus. The array is so diverse that it almost seems as if everyone has their own "personal Jesus," to quote the title of a song by Depeche Mode.

There are clear reasons for this broad spectrum of views. One concerns the nature of the sources we have for understanding Jesus. The only texts that relate historically relevant material about his life are the four gospels in the Christian New Testament and the non-canonical Gospel of Thomas; yet, each of these accounts presents different viewpoints on who he was and what he taught. Sometimes the dissimilarities are minor, and sometimes they are substantial. But the careful reader of these writings cannot mistake the variations in perspective, style, and occasionally, the presentation of facts. From the very beginning of his public activity, Jesus was seen and understood in disparate ways by those who knew him, and he was aware of this difference of opinion.

But another—and perhaps more important—reason for these countless interpretations is the role Jesus has played in human history, and in particular, western culture. For Christians, who have been the sources of most explications of his life and teachings, Jesus functions in a unique way. Almost from the start of what can be called "Christianity," many followers of Jesus regarded him not only as a savior or as the incarnation of the god of the Jews; they also understood him to be the very personification of ideal humanity. Jesus was—and is—considered by those in the Christian traditions as manifesting the supreme qualities of what a human being should be. He was "perfect in manhood," to cite a phrase from the Chalcedonian Creed. When Christians looked at Jesus, they saw the image of what *their* lives should be. This dynamic had a profound bearing on the way Jesus has been interpreted throughout the years, especially in recent centuries in which scholars have attempted to gain access to the "historical Jesus," the individual who lived in 1st century Palestine apart from the many layers of tradition that accrued after his death. Because Jesus functioned as the representation of ideal humanity for many, those who interpreted his life were apt to impute their own values and beliefs to the man. In every era for the last 2000 years, and in every culture that finds him meaningful, Jesus has been envisioned in ways that fit that society's or that individual's understanding of what is ideal. There is little wonder the life and teachings of Jesus have been so diversely understood.

As with Confucius and the Buddha, we face difficulties in getting to the historical Jesus, the real individual who lived and died in human history. Our primary sources offer various portraits of the man and the ways we and others since his time have construed those literary portrayals is profoundly shaped by our preconceptions, whether those are known to us or not. Even the most optimistic academic Jesus scholar today is cautious about drawing sharp and firm conclusions about the life of this teacher. There is much about the historical Jesus we just do not know, and much that we simply cannot know with the resources we have available currently.

So what *can* we say with reasonable certainty? First, virtually all credible scholars believe there actually was a person living in ancient Palestine whom modern people now know as "Jesus." Few historians doubt that he existed.

But this individual was not known to his contemporaries by the name Jesus. "Jesus" is a relatively recent rendering of a number of other names by which he has been known. In 1629, the King James Version of the Bible began to spell his name as J-E-S-U-S and the corresponding pronunciation "Jesus" soon followed and remained the standard in the English-speaking world. But the original version of the King James Bible, first published in 1611, followed the Latin tradition of spelling his name I-E-S-U-S, which would have been pronounced "ye-soos." "Iesus" was actually a bit closer to the way his name was probably pronounced in the 1st century, but not quite. The Latin spelling relied on the Greek, which added an "s" to the end of his name because all masculine names in Greek ended in "s." In Greek, his name was "ee-ay-soos." But this was still not the pronunciation of his name in Aramaic, the language Jesus and his contemporaries spoke. In Aramaic, the name would lack the "s" on the end, and so could be pronounced as Yeshú, Eeshó, or Eshoo. There were many dialects of Aramaic, so it is difficult to know which pronunciation is exact. "Eshoo" was the Aramaic version of the

Hebrew name, Yeshua, a shorten form of Yehoshua or Joshua as the English has it today. Yehoshua is a venerable old Hebrew name meaning "god is salvation" or "god saves." But by whatever name history has known him, there was a real person behind it.

There are just a few other things we can say with some confidence. Jesus was born into the peasant class and may have worked as a *tekton*, a common laborer who made things like doors and window frames. Based on archaeological discoveries about 1st century peasant life in Palestine, we can say that he was probably about five feet tall and 110 pounds. But beyond this, we have no idea what he looked like. The gospels do not consider it important to describe his appearance. He would have been considered an adult around the ages of 13-15 and had a life expectancy of 30 years, although he lived to be around 33. We are uncertain whether he was literate or had any formal education.

He grew up in the village of Nazareth in the Galilee, a province ruled by Herod the Great's son, Herod Antipas. Nazareth was only four miles from the largest and most important city of the Galilee, Sepphoris. An ancient Christian tradition maintains that this city was the hometown of the Virgin Mary and her parents, Anna and Joachim. Interestingly, Sepphoris is not mentioned in the Bible at all, yet it was within an hour's walk of Jesus' hometown. What makes this omission so curious is the fact that Sepphoris was a wealthy, thriving city with such amenities as a 4,000-seat amphitheatre probably built at the time of Jesus' youth. The proximity to Nazareth suggests that Jesus almost certainly visited the city. In Sepphoris, he would have been exposed to the forms of Greek and Roman culture and to a cosmopolitan life that would have been unavailable in Nazareth. But how growing up so close to this important cultural center affected Jesus is not clear.

Sometime within the last three years of his life, he began to work publicly as an itinerant teacher, preacher, and healer. His public career garnered him a modest following and eventually led to his execution as an insurrectionist against the Roman Empire.

Beyond these bare biographical details, the story of Jesus' life and teachings rests on a less certain historical basis. Critical academic scholars debate which words reported in the gospels can be taken as authentic, and there is no absolute consensus about these. There are also debates about which events reported in the New Testament actually occurred and which have been embellished or invented to make particular theological points. As I have done for Confucius and the Buddha, I will note the areas where I think the historical grounding is solid and the places where it seems less so.

When it comes to deciding what is and is not historical about Jesus' life, one of the first distinctions we need to make concerns the gospels themselves. Most historians believe that the so-called synoptic gospels—Mark, Matthew, and Luke—contain more historically reliable material than the gospel of John. Most scholars view John's account of Jesus' life as mainly theology told as biography. In other words, the significance of John is its theological message, not its historical accuracy, which most historians think is slight. The synoptic gospels, on the other hand, appear to be rooted in traditions that contain some authentic memory of Jesus' life and teachings.

Based on philological analysis, most biblical scholars think the gospel of Mark was the first gospel and was written down around 70 C.E., near the time of the Roman destruction of Jerusalem. Matthew and Luke were written a decade or two later and clearly use Mark's narrative as a source. Both Matthew and Luke quote whole sections of Mark verbatim or with slight changes. Matthew and Luke also appear to have used another common source that no longer exists. Scholars call this theoretical text "Q," short for Quelle, the German word for source [graphic of the Q hypothesis]. A fifth gospel, that of Thomas, was not included in the Christian canon of scriptures, yet about 75% of Thomas is also found in the synoptics.

Thus, Mark, Matthew, Luke, and Thomas relate similar aspects of the life of Jesus. But these gospels are by no means identical; nor does their similarity mean that they always relate historically precise material about the actual life of Jesus. Much of these texts is almost certainly based on the historical Jesus, but much is also fabricated by the authors or the oral traditions on which they relied. Invented sayings attributed to Jesus or historically doubtful events in these gospels are intended not to deceive, of course, but to make important theological statements.

To illustrate this point, let us examine the stories of Jesus' birth. This study will serve two purposes. First, it will allow us to appreciate the differences between the various sources we have for constructing our portrait of Jesus and thereby help us understand part of the reason he has been subject to such wide-ranging interpretations throughout history. Second, it will provide us with material about Jesus' heritage and birth, which we will later consider in comparison with our other figures in the course.

Every year, children around this country and other parts of the perform adorable Christmas pageants at their churches, retelling the story Christians know so well. That story describes how Mary is visited by an angel who tells her she will give birth to a son; sometime later, she and her betrothed husband Joseph travel to Bethlehem and, unable to find a room for the night, take lodging in a stable. That night, Jesus is born, placed in a manger, and visited by shepherds and three wise men from the East bearing gold, frankincense and myrrh. Then a heavenly host descends and fills the world with angelic singing.

I love that Christmas drama and have very fond memories of performing in it. It's not quite the biblical story, however. The Christmas pageant retelling is actually a blending of elements from two very different stories in Matthew and Luke, the only two gospels in the New Testament that tell about Jesus' lineage, conception, and birth. Let's look at each of these stories separately.

Matthew's account of Jesus' nativity begins with a genealogy that traces Jesus' ancestry from Abraham through King David to his earthly father Joseph. Then the narrative turns to describe how Mary, a young virgin engaged to marry Joseph, came to be pregnant by god's holy spirit. When he discovered his fiancée was expecting a child that he knew was not his, Joseph decided to break off the engagement quietly. But before he could, he was visited by an angel who counseled him against the plan, and Joseph relented.

The author of Matthew then concludes: "All of this has happened so the prediction of the Lord given by the prophet would come true." Then he quotes a passage from the prophet Isaiah, words familiar to all Christians:

Behold, a virgin will conceive a child
And she will give birth to a son
And they will name him Emmanuel (which means "God with us").

This quotation is the first of many passages from the Tanakh that Matthew cites as ancient predictions of the "messiah," the anointed one sent by god to restore his people. Matthew's intention is evident. He is attempting to show that Jesus fulfills Jewish expectations of this anointed one, the *chrīstos*, as he was called in the Greek translation of the Tanakh.

On the angel's instruction, Joseph married Mary believing that her child was of divine origin. In due time, Mary's son was born in the town of Bethlehem in the province of Judea, and Joseph named him Eshoo, or Jesus. What is missing in Matthew's account is the story of Mary and Joseph's trip to Bethlehem from their hometown of Nazareth in the northern province of Galilee. The gospel lacks this journey episode because it assumes that Mary and Joseph were *from* Bethlehem. We learn just a few verses after the announcement of Jesus' birth that Mary and Joseph are living in a house. Apparently, this is where Jesus was born, according to Matthew. There is no mention of a stable, as there is in Luke, or a cave, as later tradition believed.

The next scene in the narrative involves the *magi*, the famed wise men from the East who showed up in Jerusalem inquiring about the new "King of the Judeans." These wise men were astrologers who had discerned from the stars that a child of great significance had been born, and they wanted to honor him. The text does not indicate that there were *three* wise men as popularly believed; it gives no number at all. When King Herod the Great heard about the astrologers he summoned them and carefully interrogated them. He found out the exact time the special star associated with the new king appeared in the sky. Then Herod consulted with his advisors who informed him that the prophets predicted the messiah would be born in Bethlehem, about four miles from Jerusalem. So Herod sent the astrologers to the village, and there they discovered Jesus, living with his parents in a house. They presented him with their gifts, paid their respects, and returned home without reporting back to Herod as he had asked.

When Herod realized that the *magi* had deceived him, he was enraged and issued a command that all boys under the age of two in Bethlehem and vicinity should be put to death. Herod's monstrous response obviously indicated that he was gravely threatened by the birth of the new "King of the Judeans." After all, the Roman senate had named *him* "King of the Judeans." The age of Herod's intended victims is worthy of note. Since he ordered the killing of children two years of age and younger, and since he knew the precise moment the new king was born according to the astrologers calculations, we can infer that the visitation of the magi took place about two years after Jesus was born, not on the night of his birth as the Christmas pageants tell us. It was a great relief for me to figure this out, by the way. Growing up, I could never understand how these wise men could get to Bethlehem from "the East"—wherever that was—in a single night. I could only imagine they had some superfast camels.

Fortunately, it is highly unlikely that this horrifying slaughter of the innocents that Matthew describes actually occurred. There is no mention of such an event elsewhere; even Luke's birth narrative fails to mention it. More probably, the tale serves as a literary contrivance. It certainly reveals something of the character of Herod. Although this particular episode probably did not happen, it is consistent with what we know of him. He had his *own* sons executed for treason, after all! But the story is intended to suggest more than just Herod's paranoia; it also recalls a similar episode from the Tanakh: the time when Pharaoh in Egypt ordered the murder of the baby boys of the Israelites to keep the slaves from becoming too powerful. Moses, you will recall, survived the massacre because of his mother's resourcefulness and the compassion of the Pharaoh's daughter, and went on to become Israel's deliverer.

Matthew's comparison of Jesus and Moses is deliberate. This intent is confirmed in the next episode of the story in which the angel appeared again to Joseph and told him to flee with his family to Egypt to evade Herod's persecution. Joseph did as he was told—again, as Matthew says—to fulfill a prophecy. The story concludes with Mary, Joseph and Jesus returning from Egypt to the Promised Land after Herod's death and settling in Nazareth in Galilee rather than their original home in Bethlehem. And again, the parallels with Moses and the Exodus are purposeful. Throughout Matthew's gospel, Jesus is portrayed as a New Moses. He is even depicted as delivering a new law to the Jews—the Sermon on the Mount—just as Moses delivered the old law from Mt. Sinai.

Luke, however, has another story to tell. In Luke's gospel, the angel announces the pregnancy to Mary, not Joseph. In fact, in Luke, Mary's role is central and Joseph's is peripheral—just the opposite from Matthew's perspective. Luke's genealogy of Jesus is also quite different from Matthew's, and the line is traced back past Abraham, all the way to Adam. In distinction to Matthew's emphasis on Jesus' Jewishness, as suggested by a pedigree that includes Judaism's most illustrious figures, Luke highlights Jesus' universal significance by invoking the name of humanity's first father.

Even the political background of Luke is different from Matthew's. Rather than setting the story of Jesus' birth in the context of Judea and the reign of Herod, Luke places the story against the backdrop of the Roman Empire and reign of Emperor Augustus. Luke's setting serves to underscore the universal importance of Jesus and to provide a striking contrast to the humbleness of Jesus' origins. Caesar Augustus was not just the ruler of the known world; he was also a son of god, an incarnation of the divine. His many titles included "the One who Brought Peace to the World," the lord, and the savior—some of the very titles Luke reserves for Jesus. But in the eyes of Luke, the baby born to peasant parents in a barn in a cultural backwater—not the imposing emperor in Rome—is the world's true ruler and benefactor. That contrast foreshadows an important theme throughout Luke: Jesus' coming means the overturning of conventional values.

Caesar's call for a census was the occasion for Mary and Joseph to leave their hometown—which Luke thinks is Nazareth—to travel to Bethlehem. Importantly, both Matthew and Luke agree that Jesus was born in Bethlehem, the city of David. But in point of fact, most scholars think Jesus was probably born in Nazareth, his boyhood home, and that the story of a birth in Bethlehem is an addition to support the claim that he was the messiah. In any event, it was there in Bethlehem, amidst animals and fodder, that Luke says Jesus was born and laid in a feeding trough, quite a different setting from the home-birth of Matthew.

The visitors that night were not the wise men but common shepherds, who had been visited by an angel and informed of the savior's birth. The presence of the shepherds in the Luke's account accents the theme of humility and lowliness. Shepherds were regarded as among some of the lowest members of Judean society. From the very beginning, Luke associates Jesus with the commoners and the disenfranchised. In view of the role of women in this patriarchical society, the prominence of Mary and her cousin Elizabeth, the mother of John the Baptist, also reinforces this Lucan theme.

After Jesus' birth, Luke mentions his ritual circumcision and an incident at age 12 when he was discovered conversing with teachers and scholars in the temple at Jerusalem. This is all the New Testament has to say about his early life. The next we hear of Jesus in the Bible is at the time he begins his public activity of healing and proclamation, around the age of 30. The relative lack of information about the first 30 years of his life obviously indicates that the first Christians thought his greatest significance was in his teaching and, most especially, his death and resurrection, two events that all four gospels report.

Our comparison of Matthew and Luke's birth narrative should suffice to make it clear that there are, at the least, substantial differences of emphasis in the two accounts. The only common elements in both stories are the idea of a divine conception, the names of Jesus' parents, a birth in Bethlehem, and Nazareth as Jesus' boyhood home. Beyond these details, the stories are quite dissimilar.

Do those differences really make a difference? One might argue that the differences are inconsequential because the accounts are reconcilable. Just because Luke does not mention the *magi* or Matthew does not mention the shepherds does not mean the authors are telling different stories. The authors just report what they think is essential about one single story. If that is true, then we should at least acknowledge that what they think is vital is shaped by their theological presuppositions and intentions. In other words, they are not simply relating an objective description of what happened. The gospels are selective in what they report; else Matthew and Luke's account would be much closer in detail. Yet, there are still problems with arguing that the stories are reconcilable. Matthew regards Mary and Joseph as residents of Bethlehem and Luke sees them as visitors. They can't both be right. And how could one author omit a matter the other considered crucial? How could Luke fail to mention something as momentous as Herod's massacre of the children or the family's flight to Egypt? How could Matthew neglect Jesus' birth in a stable?

It is more plausible to say is that these are different stories, addressed to different audiences and told to convey different ideas about who Jesus was. They may have been based on the same oral traditions about the early life of Jesus such as his birth in Bethlehem and his childhood home in Nazareth, but the authors cannot really be saying the same things. Neither account is interested in objectively reporting events as they actually occurred; each is a mixture of historical fact as recounted by oral tradition and imaginative embellishment. Matthew's account focuses on Jesus' Jewishness: the gospel sees him as fitting ancient predictions about an anointed one and suggests ways he parallels another Jewish deliverer and law-giver, Moses. It would be logical to infer that Matthew intended his story for a Jewish audience. Luke, on the other hand, stresses Jesus' universal significance and aims to undermine the political theology of the Roman Empire. It would make sense to suggest that his story was written primarily for a non-Jewish audience. Matthew plays up Jesus' kingship; Luke highlights his humbleness.

In Jesus' own lifetime, those who knew him had a great many ideas about who he was and what he meant when he taught and performed mighty deeds. A half-century later, when the gospels of the New Testament were being written down, the diversity of viewpoints about his life and teachings remained unabated. Since that time, the interpretations have only continued to amass.

# The First 30 Years
## Lecture 20

**What did Jesus look like? What was he like as a child? How did he treat his parents and other family members? Was he educated? Could he read and write? Did he live in Nazareth up until he began his public work? Was he married and, if so, why do the Gospels fail to mention his wife? ... We simply do not know enough based on the evidence we now have available.**

There is very little that we can say about Jesus's first 30 years. Beyond the stories of his birth, we have only the biblical mentions of Jesus's circumcision and an incident at the Temple in Jerusalem when he was found astonishing the scholars with his wisdom. Our curiosity naturally urges us to wonder about many things that concerned some of the earliest Christians as well. In the absence of information, the human imagination, of course, steps in.

Tradition has been very happy to suggest answers to our natural questions. The Infancy Gospel of Thomas (different from the previously mentioned Gospel of Thomas) briefly describes Jesus during his first 12 years, about which the Bible is completely silent. This collection of about a dozen tales was probably written in the latter half of the 2nd century C.E. and features tales of the preteen Jesus performing miracles, including raising a friend from the dead, some of them childishly impulsive or ethically questionable. In essence, they attribute to the boy the powers of the man but add the element of immaturity. Scholars think these stories contain little historical fact, subordinating history to theology.

One persistent idea has been that as a young man, Jesus traveled to India, where he studied under Hindu and Buddhist gurus, and then returned to Palestine to preach a Judaized version of these religions. Advocates of this view point to the remarkable parallels between Christianity and Mahayana Buddhism, which also developed in the first centuries C.E. A different version of this story suggests that Jesus escaped death on the cross and made his way to Kashmir, where *he* taught the Buddhist and Hindu scholars. Modern scholars think both stories are highly unlikely.

In recent years, the question of whether or not Jesus was married has become a matter of public discourse and has stirred up a good deal of controversy. What is interesting is the way the suggestion of a married Jesus meets with such resistance and horror by many. Perhaps people find something so troubling about the whole sexual dimension of human experience that they regard it unworthy of the one they consider truly god and truly human. Once again, we see how preconceptions about divinity and humanity can inform and perhaps even skew an interpretation of Jesus.

**There are hints, however, that John's relationship to Jesus was more than simply that of a herald or harbinger.**

Any real knowledge we have about the historical Jesus does not start until the debut of his public activity near the age of 30, near the point at which Mark, the oldest Gospel, begins. The New Testament Gospels all regard John the Baptist as Jesus's forerunner and all identify John with a figure from the book of Isaiah who "shouts in the wilderness: Make ready the way of the Lord." He performed ritual cleansings—baptisms—in the Jordan River, in the wilderness of Judea, where he lived an ascetic life, which has led some to speculate that he was an Essene.

It was only after John's arrest and imprisonment that Jesus began his own work, and his message was the same as John's: Repent, for the Kingdom of God is near. We could therefore speculate that John was not just Jesus's precursor but also his mentor and teacher. After Jesus's death and resurrection, his earlier relationship with John became a bit of a problem: If Jesus were the messiah, his baptism and discipleship with John might seem an embarrassment. Perhaps later traditions recast John as Jesus's forerunner to keep him subordinate.

Scholars agree that the coming of God's kingdom was the substance of Jesus's message, but there has been much debate about the details. What exactly did Jesus mean by "the Kingdom of God"? Was this kingdom earthly or heavenly? What did Jesus mean by "at hand"? What changes would the coming entail? How did he understand his own role? Jesus never addressed these issues directly. Instead, he tried to illustrate his meaning by parable and paradox and to demonstrate it by acts of healing, exorcism, and flouting religious customs. According to the Gospels, even his closest associates did not always grasp his meaning. ■

## Questions to Consider

1. Is filling in the gaps in Jesus's biography merely an academic exercise, or could this information have theological repercussions for Christians?

2. Does the idea of Jesus having a mentor affect your opinion of claims about his divinity?

# The First 30 Years
## Lecture 20—Transcript

Our last discussion made several important points about the study of Jesus. First, the resources we have available for understanding his life and teachings can present very different portraits of the man. Matthew and Luke, who in many respects offer very similar narratives about Jesus, nonetheless have different purposes and perspectives in mind when they relate his story. Second, the historical accuracy of these the biblical texts about Jesus are questionable. There is a bare-bones plot to Jesus' life that seems indisputable, but on other matters, including the content of his teaching or the facticity of actions attributed to him, there are doubts about the gospels' reports. Third, contemporary interpretations of Jesus' life are clearly colored by often unconscious beliefs that interpreters have about ideal human character. Thus, descriptions of who Jesus was are commonly shaped by the interpreters' own beliefs and values. Finally, there is very little that we can say about Jesus' first 30 years. I have suggested that neither Matthew nor Luke is wholly reliable in their reports about his early life, and most of what they relate about this period is very slim. Beyond the stories of Jesus birth, we have only the mention of his circumcision and an incident at the Temple in Jerusalem when he was found astonishing the scholars with his wisdom.

Our curiosity naturally urges us to wonder about many things. What did Jesus look like? What was he like as a child? How did he treat his parents and other family members? Was he educated? Could he read and write? Did he live in Nazareth up until he began his public work? Was he married and, if so, why do the gospels fail to mention his wife? These were questions that concerned some of the earliest Christians as well. Ultimately, these questions must remain unanswered. We simply do not know enough based on the evidence we now have available. It's possible some new archaeological find might unearth a cache of texts that would answer these questions to our satisfaction; but that find has not been made.

So in the absence of information, the human imagination, of course, steps in. Tradition has been very happy to suggest answers to our natural questions. We will spend a few moments looking at some of the responses to the gaps in historical knowledge about Jesus' early life. In each instance, these responses are mainly conjecture, usually told to advance a particular point of view. I know of no serious Jesus scholar who takes these speculative stories as historically factual.

Let us begin with a fascinating set of stories about Jesus as a young boy growing up in Nazareth. The Infancy Gospel of Thomas is one of almost 20 gospels that we know of that were not included in the New Testament canon. This gospel is different from the Gospel of Thomas I mentioned in the previous lecture as containing some historical material about Jesus. The Infancy Gospel briefly describes Jesus during his first 12 years, the time about which the Bible is completely silent. This short collection of tales was probably written in the latter half of the 2nd century C.E., well over one hundred years after the death of Jesus. Clearly they were written to satisfy a curiosity among Christians about Jesus' early life. What makes the stories so interesting is that they take seriously both the divinity and humanity of Jesus as affirmed in the Christian creeds by imagining what divine nature would look like in a pre-teenager. In other words, think about what your typical boy would be like if he had god-like powers.

In one story, Jesus is helping his father Joseph to build a bed for a rich patron. After cutting two pieces of lumber that were supposed to be of a particular length, Joseph realized one piece was shorter than necessary, and he was perplexed as to what to do. Jesus told Joseph to hold one end of the shorter board while he held the other end. Then Jesus pulled on the board and stretched it until it was the exact length as the other. Joseph, of course, was astounded about the miraculous feat.

According to another story, when Jesus was five, he and some other boys were playing in a stream on the sabbath day. Jesus took some mud and molded it into 12 sparrows. When a villager saw what Jesus had done, he went and told Joseph: "Your boy is at the stream and has taken mud and made 12 birds with it, and has violated the sabbath." Joseph immediately went to Jesus and asked him "Why are you doing what's not permitted on the sabbath?" Jesus didn't answer but simply clapped his hands and shouted: "Be off and fly away, and remember me!" And the sparrows took off and flew away.

In another story, a boy running through the village accidentally bumped Jesus on the shoulder. The jostling angered Jesus, and he cursed the other boy, who instantly fell down and died. The villagers who saw the incident were shocked and wondered, "Where did this boy come from?" When the parents of the dead boy learned what Jesus had done, they came to Joseph and blamed him and begged him to teach Jesus how to bless rather than curse. So Joseph confronted Jesus and scolded him, but Jesus was obstinate and said "these people must take their punishment," at which point the parents of the dead boy became blind. Then everyone in Nazareth became fearful of Jesus' powers. Joseph got angry and pulled Jesus' ear very hard; then Jesus became enraged and said to Joseph, "Don't anger me! Don't you know that I do not belong to you?"

There are over a dozen such stories in the Infancy Gospel. The last one I'll mention involves Jesus and a friend playing on the roof of a house when the other boy accidentally fell off and died. Given his reputation in the village, the parents of the dead boy arrived and accused Jesus of killing him. Jesus, of course, insisted on his innocence. Then he sudden jumped down from the roof and shouted at the dead boy: "Zeno, get up! Did I throw you down from the roof?" Suddenly Zeno returns to life and says, "No, you didn't push me down, but you raised me back up."

Obviously, stories like these attribute to the boy Jesus the powers he was believed to have as an adult, and they show how others were awed by his deeds. The stories draw upon some features we read about in the New Testament gospels but then add to that the element of immaturity. This is how the stories take Jesus' humanity seriously. They describe him as a real five or six year boy who at times can be sweet and helpful and at times an absolute menace who can't control his temper. I remember enough of my own life at that age to be grateful that I did not have divine powers!

As I said, scholars think these stories contain little historical fact—except the setting of Nazareth and naming Joseph as Jesus' father. What is important to note here is the apparent process by which the Infancy Gospel was written. It is evidently an imaginative tale based on a few historical details and then elaborated in a way consistent with the author's understanding of who

Jesus was. The author made almost no effort to be historically accurate; the important feature of the text was its theological affirmation of Jesus' divinity and humanity. The gospel subordinates history to theology. Yet, the image of the boy Jesus may have been just a little too human to be included in the New Testament.

Throughout the last 2000 years, others have speculated about Jesus' life during the 30 year span between his birth and the beginning of his public proclamations. One persistent idea has been that as a young man Jesus traveled to India, where he studied under Hindu and Buddhist gurus, and then returned to Palestine to preach a Judaized version of these religions. Advocates of this view point to the remarkable parallels between Christianity and the form of Buddhism that was beginning to develop in the first centuries C.E., the Mahayana. You will remember in our discussion of the Buddha that in the development of the Mahayana, the Buddha began to be viewed as having more divine qualities and functioning more as a savior to assist others in reaching the end of suffering. A different version of this story suggests that Jesus escaped death on the cross and made his way to Kashmir in northern India. There, *he* taught the Buddhist and Hindu scholars, who Indianized *his* theology. Still today, one can visit the reputed tomb of Jesus in the city of Srinagar in Kashmir. Modern critical scholars of Jesus think both versions of the Jesus-India connection are highly unlikely.

One final area of speculation that's worth mention is one that has received a good deal of renewed attention in the last half century: whether or not Jesus was married. In recent years this question became a matter of public discourse as the result of the releases of Martin Scorsese's film "The Last Temptation of Christ" and the popular novel The Da Vinci Code and the movie based on it. These releases indicate that Jesus was in fact married to Miriam of Magdala, or Mary Magdelene. And that idea stirred up a good deal of controversy. But these recent works were not the first time there has been a suggestion of a married Jesus. In 1970, a Bible scholar named William E. Phipps published *Was Jesus Married?* in which he argued that it was highly probable that Jesus was married since the Bible mentions nothing to the contrary. Phipps proposed that marriage was taken as such a matter of normal behavior in ancient Judaism that had Jesus not been married, the New Testament would surely have to explain it. If he were married, there would have been no reason to make mention of it. Phipps' contention was an argument from silence. The New Testament has absolute nothing to say about Jesus' marital status. It neither affirms nor denies that Jesus was married. Phipps had a point; it would have been highly unusual for Jesus to have been a bachelor all his life. It is possible that he was widower by the time he began his public work. But the argument from silence is a weak one and hasn't convinced most scholars. Bachelorhood may have been rare, but it was not impossible. The idea of a marriage between Jesus and Mary Magdalene is even less convincing. But what is interesting to me about the whole idea of a married Jesus is the way the suggestion meets with such resistance by many. They find the notion that Jesus may have been married to be repugnant, as evidenced by the controversies generated by the "The Last Temptation of Christ" and "The Da Vinci Code." Why? I think these controversies have less to do with the issue of marriage and more to do with sexuality. There's nothing particularly problematic with the idea that Jesus may have participated in an ancient and honorable human institution. But the hint that he may have had sex upsets a good many people because it clashes with their idea of divinity, and perhaps ideal humanity. In other words, many people find something so troubling about the whole sexual dimension of human experience that they regard it unworthy of the one they consider truly god and truly human. Once again, we see how preconceptions about divinity and humanity can inform and perhaps even skew an interpretation of Jesus.

Any real knowledge we have about the historical Jesus does not start until the debut of his public activity near the age of 30. This in fact is near the point at which Mark, the oldest gospel, begins. Mark disregards any mention of Jesus' life prior to the start of his ministry. The inauguration of his work as a teacher, preacher, and healer is closely connected with John the Baptist. The New Testament gospels all report that Jesus and John had a special relationship, but the four accounts discuss that association in slightly different ways from one another.

The New Testament gospels all regard John the Baptist as Jesus' forerunner. They all identify John with a figure from the Book of Isaiah who "shouts in the wilderness: Make ready the way of the Lord." On the basis of this identification, they describe John as someone whose role is to prepare people for the coming of Jesus. In this role, John called the people of Palestine to repent of their ways and submit to baptism, a ritual symbolizing the washing away of sins. John performed his baptisms in the Jordan River, in the wilderness of Judea, where he lived an ascetic life, wearing a camel hair shirt and eating raw honey and locusts. The Baptist's unconventional lifestyle has led some to speculate that he may have been one of the Essenes, who observed similar practices. But it also placed him in line with some of ancient Judaism's greatest prophets who preached fiery messages of repentance.

There are hints, however, that John's relationship to Jesus was more than simply that of a herald or harbinger. According to Luke, Jesus told his followers, "Among those born of women none is greater than John." Luke also suggests they were second-cousins, but that claim is doubtful. No one else indicates they had a familial relationship. Each of the four gospels says that John began his public activity before Jesus began his. John had a message to proclaim. According to Matthew, John's proclamation was concise: "Repent, for the kingdom of heaven is at hand." That message brought Judeans out of the city and the countryside to hear John and to accept his baptism. Mark and Matthew indicate that Jesus himself went to John and was baptized by him. Some time after Jesus' baptism, John was arrested by King Herod Antipas, because John was critical of Herod's marriage to his brother's ex-wife, a violation of Jewish marital laws. It was at the moment of John's arrest and imprisonment that Jesus began his own work as a preacher and healer. Matthew writes: "Now when Jesus heard that John had been arrested, he withdrew to Galilee. He left Nazareth and made his home in Capernaum by the sea." "From that time Jesus began to proclaim, 'Repent, for the kingdom of heaven is at hand.'"

It is important to observe that Jesus does not begin his public work until John is unable to continue his. Furthermore, when Jesus *does* begin to preach, his message, according to the earliest gospels, is precisely the same as the Baptist's: the Kingdom of Heaven—or the Kingdom of God—is near and everyone one needs to live their lives in accord with this fact. These observations suggest that John was not just Jesus' precursor but was also his mentor and teacher. On this view, Jesus was first a disciple of John's and then took up where John left off when he was arrested.

This interpretation of Jesus' relationship to John helps to clear up a baffling event in Jesus' life: his baptism. John called the Judeans to submit to baptism as a sign of their repentance to receive forgiveness for their sins. But why did Jesus go to John to be baptized if he were, as the later Christian tradition asserts, the sinless son of god? I remember pondering this very question as a ten-year-old theologian, and I never received a convincing answer. Mark's gospel does not try to answer the question at all, but Matthew indicates that Jesus' acceptance of the ritual was to do "what is fitting and right," a rather vague and not very satisfying answer. Luke suggests that Jesus was baptized, but perhaps by someone other than John; the identity of Jesus' baptizer in Luke is unclear. Like Mark, Luke does not try to explain the baptism. The Gospel of John does not mention Jesus' baptism at all. What's going here?

I think it is likely that Jesus was one of many in Palestine who were attracted by John's message about the coming of the kingdom of god. He was baptized by John and became one of the Baptist's disciples. When John was imprisoned by Herod, Jesus took over his work and began to proclaim the message of the kingdom. Jesus' own disciples, some of whom may have originally been with John, continued the custom of baptizing, as indicated by the New Testament. Later, particularly after his death and resurrection, when Jesus' significance was greatly magnified in the eyes of his followers, his earlier relationship with John became a bit of a problem. If Jesus were the messiah or the sinless son of god or god incarnate, to cite a few of the Christian claims about him, his baptism and discipleship with John might seem an embarrassment. So, the later traditions, including the four New Testament gospels, cast John as a forerunner, a precursor, a herald of Jesus, not his mentor, in order to keep John's role subordinate to that of Jesus'. Thus the baptism is simply neglected in the Gospel of John, perhaps performed by someone else in Luke, or done because Jesus declares it is "appropriate" in Matthew. These treatments are ways of mitigating the potential claim that John's baptism implied his superiority over Jesus.

To be clear, I offer this interpretation not as historical fact but as a theory, a way to try to make sense of the various reports about Jesus and John's relationship. I'm obviously not reading the gospels at face value; the tensions among the gospel texts invite us to look for a deeper reading. This theory tries to provide a plausible explanation of why Jesus submitted to baptism, why he waited until John's arrest to begin his public activity, and why their messages were the same. Viewing John as Jesus' mentor clarifies each of these questions.

But however we understand the nature of their relationship, the synoptic gospels—Mark, Matthew, and Luke—report that Jesus and John both proclaimed the coming of god's kingdom. But despite how simple it is to say that, the meaning of that declaration is anything but simple. Scholars of Jesus agree that the coming of god's kingdom was the substance of Jesus message, but there has been much debate about the details of that message. Among the issues that have been discussed are these: what exactly did Jesus mean by the kingdom of god? Was this kingdom an earthly or a heavenly reality? What did Jesus mean when he said the kingdom is "at hand"? Did he think it had arrived or was coming shortly? What changes would the kingdom entail? How did he understand his own role in the coming of this new reality? Was he simply warning people about its inevitable arrival or did he think that he himself was doing something to bring it about? These are far from easy questions to answer because Jesus never addressed them directly. Rather than provide straightforward explanations, Jesus tried to illustrate the meaning of god's kingdom by means of parable and paradox and to demonstrate it by acts of healing, exorcism, and flouting the religious customs of his culture, such as ignoring its purity laws. Even his closest associates did not always grasp what he was trying he communicate when he offered a parable to help them understand god's kingdom. Frequently, the gospels depict his followers coming to him in private asking for a clearer interpretation of one of his stories. Sometimes he would try to spell it out for them; sometimes he just would lament how dense they were.

When we return, we will devote our next lecture to trying to come to a better understanding of what Jesus meant by the kingdom of God by exploring the nature of his teachings and his deeds. I look forward to seeing you then.

# The Kingdom of God
## Lecture 21

For Jesus, the Kingdom of Heaven was not a place where the streets were paved with gold and Saint Peter guarded the pearly gates. ... The important thing to bear in mind is that for Jesus, the Kingdom of God was not a location. ... The kingdom, for Jesus, was an invisible or intangible reality.

There is little disagreement among biblical scholars that the reign of God was the focus of Jesus's life's work. The debates arise when these scholars try to determine what exactly Jesus meant by this phrase. In the Gospels of Mark and Luke, we find the Greek term *Basileia tou Theou*; Matthew, however, uses slightly different words: *Basileia tōn Ouranōn*, the "Kingdom of Heaven." Matthew probably used the word "heaven" as a euphemism since his Gospel was addressed primarily to a Jewish audience and the Jews customarily avoided using God's name. (You might also recall how in ancient China "heaven" and "god" were sometimes used interchangeably.) But neither "Kingdom of Heaven" nor "Kingdom of God" should be understood as a physical location at all.

The kingdom, for Jesus, was an invisible or intangible reality. Although it is not localized to a particular place, it is understood to be an earthly reality. It is not territorial, but it is terrestrial. Contrary to the popular mythology of later Christianity, Jesus never spoke of human beings going to heaven but said that the Kingdom of Heaven would come to earth. Everything Jesus said about it suggests that God's kingdom would be an earthly utopia, a blessed state of affairs free of suffering and poverty, in which justice and harmony flourish. Jesus's descriptions of and analogies for the reign of God seemed to suggest that it was the exact opposite of the reign of Caesar.

One of the best-known descriptions of the kingdom is the **Beatitudes**, which appears in different forms in Luke and Matthew. Reading or hearing this passage from the perspective of a politically oppressed, economically struggling community, the political overtones of the message become obvious; certainly they were not lost on his listeners. The juxtaposition of

these blessings and curses in Luke intimates the paradoxical character of God's dominion, contravening the common values of the world.

Paradox abounds throughout the teachings of Jesus, particularly in his parables. For example, in the story of the Good Samaritan, the real point is not that people should be compassionate but the sense of surprise—and even shock—that it induced in Jesus's audience through the selfish behavior of the "good" characters and the compassionate behavior of the "bad" character. It is hard to forget such a story; the mind mulls it over and over. And it reminds the listener that the Kingdom of God will not be what you expect. Jesus's message was also conveyed through his actions,

**As an adult, Jesus preached in largely rural areas of Galilee.**

particularly his healings, exorcisms, and miracles (what the Gospels refer to as "signs" and "powerful acts"). The story of the wedding celebration at Cana, for example, contains many inversions and paradoxes: Jesus seems to refuse his mother's request for help but helps out anyway; the best wine is served last, when it ought to come first; even the atmosphere of joy and celebration is far removed from everyday life in that time and place.

Jesus's fame in his lifetime depended mainly on his reputation as a healer and exorcist. The healing stories have been variously interpreted throughout

© Photos.com / Thinkstock.

Christian history. Ordinarily, they were taken as indicative of Jesus's divine power. But stories of healings, exorcisms, powerful acts, and miracles are not unique to Jesus. Even stories of resurrections are not so unusual in the Bible and in literature worldwide. (That is not to say he was not divine, only that the miracle stories do not suffice to prove it.) What the miracles do suggest is that Jesus was foreshadowing life in the coming kingdom, where human suffering would be banished and the division of pure and impure would be obliterated, along with the categories of rich and poor, powerful and weak, sick and healthy. Jesus acted as if he were abolishing these distinctions by his very words and deeds. ■

## Important Terms

***Basileia tōn Ouranōn***: A Greek phrase from the Gospel of Matthew usually translated as "Kingdom of Heaven."

***Basileia tou Theou***: A Greek phrase from the Gospels of Mark and Luke usually translated as "Kingdom of God."

**Beatitudes**: A passage found in similar forms in the Gospels of Matthew (5:3–12) and Luke (6:20–23) wherein Jesus describes how people will live in the Kingdom of Heaven, each line beginning with the phrase "Blessed are… ."

## Questions to Consider

1.  Jesus's concept of the Kingdom of Heaven can be interpreted as highly political, especially in the context of the early Roman Empire. To what political uses has his message been put, historically and to the present day? Do these uses seem to correspond to Jesus's intent as presented in the Bible and other ancient texts?

2.  What parallels do you see between Jesus's teaching by paradox and techniques used by our other sages?

# The Kingdom of God
## Lecture 21—Transcript

The heart of Jesus' message was the kingdom of god. The earliest gospels are emphatically clear on this point. "I must proclaim the good news of the kingdom of God," Jesus told a crowd, "for I was sent for this purpose." There is little disagreement among biblical scholars that the reign of god was the focus of Jesus' life's work. The debates arise when these scholars try to determine what exactly Jesus meant by this phrase. Just as the kingdom of god was basic to Jesus' teaching, disputes about the meaning of the kingdom of god are central to modern Jesus scholarship. Today we will try to get a clearer understanding of what Jesus meant by the kingdom of god.

To start, let's begin with the phrase itself. In the gospels of Mark and Luke, the expression "kingdom of god" translates the Greek term *Basileia tou Theou*. Matthew, however, uses slightly different words, *Basileia tōn Ouranōn*, which is usually rendered as the "kingdom of heaven." Both expressions mean the same thing. Matthew probably used the word "heaven" as a euphemism for "god" since, as we saw in an earlier lecture, this gospel was addressed primarily to a Jewish audience, and the Jews customarily avoided using god's name. You might also recall how in ancient China "heaven" and "god" were sometimes used interchangeably. In any event, neither "kingdom of heaven" nor "kingdom of god" should be understood as "heaven," if by heaven one means the abode of god and his angels. For Jesus, the kingdom of heaven was not a place where the streets were paved with gold and St. Peter guarded the pearly gates. In fact, the kingdom was not a place at all.

In the Greek, *basileia* is defined by rule or power not territory. In this sense, "kingdom" is a misleading translation. Biblical specialists have been aware of this problem for quite some time and have tried to come up with more suitable expressions. Some of these include the "reign of god," "the dominion of god" and "god's imperial rule." These phrases have the benefit of removing the territorial connotations of "kingdom," but they still carry the disadvantage of referring to a form of governance that most of us no longer experience. Hence the metaphor lacks the evocative power that the word "kingdom" had for Jesus' listeners. But not having a completely satisfactory alternative, I'll continue to use the word kingdom, with "reign" or "dominion" thrown in occasionally for variety. I do that as much for sentimental reasons as anything. My grandmother used the expression all the time. She used to say things like: "I don't care if you cry till kingdom come; it won't do you any good."

The important thing to bear in mind is that for Jesus, the kingdom of god was not a location. When members of the Pharisee sect asked him when the kingdom would come, Jesus told them: You won't be able to observe the coming of God's imperial rule. People are not going to be able to say, 'Look, here it is!' or 'Over there!' On the contrary, God's imperial rule is right there in your presence." The kingdom, for Jesus, was an invisible or intangible reality. In the gospel of Thomas, Jesus told his followers: "If your leaders say to you, "Look, the [Father's] kingdom is in the sky," then the birds of the sky will precede you. If they say to you, "It is in the sea," then the fish will precede you. Rather, the [Father's] kingdom is within you and it is outside you."

Jesus' statement in Thomas intimates another characteristic of the kingdom. Even though god's reign is not localized to a *particular* place, it is understood to be an earthly reality. It is not territorial, but it is terrestrial. Contrary to the popular mythology of later Christianity, Jesus never spoke of human beings going to heaven. He said nothing about souls being transported to the celestial regions after death. He did, however, indicate that the kingdom of heaven would come to earth. It was here that god's reign would be realized, not somewhere beyond the skies. The point is evident in the well-known words of the Lord's Prayer: "Thy kingdom come; thy will be done on earth as it is in heaven." The kingdom comes to people; people do not go to the kingdom.

Everything Jesus said about it suggests that god's kingdom was a utopia, a blessed state of affairs free of suffering and poverty, in which justice and harmony flourish. To put it in the language of Jesus, the kingdom was the state in which god's will for the world prevails. It was *shalom*, the condition of peace, plenty, and well-being. It is hard *not* to think of Jesus' use of the phrase "kingdom of god" as a deliberate affront to the kingdom of Rome, or what we might call for the sake of parallelism, the kingdom of man. As we noted in our discussion of the birth narratives, the Roman Empire, as manifested in the reign of King Herod and Augustus Caesar, was the imposing backdrop against which the life of Jesus began and the power by which it ultimately ended. Rome's occupation of Palestine was a ubiquitous reality that caused deep and extensive suffering for the vast majority of Judeans and Galileans. Jesus' descriptions of and analogies for the reign of god seemed to suggest that it was the exact opposite of the reign of Caesar.

One of the best-known descriptions of the kingdom is the passage known as the Beatitudes, which appears in different forms in Luke and Matthew. In this classic piece of world literature, Jesus tells his listeners what the kingdom will be like. Try to hear these words with the ears of those whose lives had been brought low by the imperial power and its local collaborators. I'll use a different—and more accurate—translation than what you are probably accustomed to to help you hear it differently. In Luke, Jesus declares:

> Congratulations, you poor!
> God's domain belongs to you.
> Congratulations, you hungry!
> You will have a feast.
> Congratulations, you who weep now!
> You will laugh.

To those being crushed by Roman power, Jesus' proclamation would have indeed been received as gospel, that is, as good news. Luke adds a complementary pronouncement of curses just after this series of blessings.

> Curse you rich!
> You already have your consolation.
> Curse you who are well-fed now!
> You will know hunger.
> Curse you who laugh now!
> You will learn to weep and grieve.

Again, it is hard to neglect the political overtones of Jesus' message; certainly they were not lost on his listeners.

The juxtaposition of these blessings and curses in Luke intimates the paradoxical character of god's dominion as Jesus understood it. I am using the word "paradox" in its original sense as something contrary to expectation or received belief. The kingdom of god contravenes the common values of the world. In the eyes of the world, you may be poor and wretched, but when the kingdom comes, it will belong to you, *not* to those whom the world considers rich. You may be grieving now, but when god's dominion arrives, you'll be laughing. On the other hand, those who are complacent and well-fed, who are don't give a second thought to anyone but themselves, those who are rich and powerful, will get their comeuppance. From the perspective of the kingdom of god, what the kingdom of man calls wealth, prestige, fame, success, and power is nothing.

Paradox abounds throughout the teachings of Jesus, particularly in his parables, the brief, engaging stories he told to communicate the meaning of the kingdom. Take for instance one of the best known parables, the story of the Good Samaritan. Let me briefly remind you of the plot. On the road to Jericho, a Judean was accosted by robbers who beat him, stripped him, and left him for dead. A priest and later a Levite traveling the same way saw the beaten man and each crossed to the other side of the road to avoid him. But at last a Samaritan saw the man and had compassion for him. The Samaritan administered first-aid, put the victim on his own donkey, and took him to an inn and nursed him. The next day, the Samaritan gave the innkeeper some money and asked him continue to care for the beaten man in his absence. The Samaritan promised to reimburse the innkeeper for any extra expense he might incur. End of story.

For such a concise narrative, this parable is rich in significance, as almost all of Jesus' parables were. And hence it has been subject to a myriad of interpretations. I won't even begin to try to do it justice with a comprehensive reading. Let me only point out what makes this a characteristic parable and an effective teaching device. The real point of this story is not that people should *be* compassionate to one another, although that of course is implied. Simply to derive a "moral" from the tale as if were a fable of Aesop flattens a parable and reduces its impact. The deeper significance of a parable lies in the response it provokes in the listener, the sense of surprise—and even shock—that it induces, and it is that response that likens the story to the kingdom of god.

To the 1st century listener, the surprises of the Good Samaritan story would come in several ways. The first is the way the priest and Levite completely ignore the robbers' victim. Not only were these two Judeans—that is, fellow countrymen of the fallen man—they were also specialists in the Judean religion. How could they possible ignore him? Most likely, the priest and Levite shunned the wounded man to preserve their ritual purity. To touch a dead body or blood was to become polluted and would require a ritual restoration of cleanliness. Better to turn a blind eye. These are men who have allowed their devotion to institutions and religious beliefs get the better of their compassion.

The second surprise comes when the beaten man's true benefactor arrives: a Samaritan, a citizen of the region between the Galilee and Judea, and a descendant of the inhabitants of the ancient kingdom of Israel that was destroyed by Assyria 700 years earlier. Although the Samaritans professed to worship the god of Abraham, Isaac, and Jacob, they believed that Yahweh chose Mount Gerizim in their country rather than the Temple at Jerusalem as the center of worship and sacrifice.

In the time of Jesus, the Samaritans were regarded as impure and were despised by the Judeans. Jesus' listeners would have been astounded—and perhaps incensed—that Jesus told a story in which the hero turned out to be a Samaritan. This reaction would have contributed to the story's effectiveness. It is hard to forget such a story; the mind mulls it over and over. Imagine a story about an American soldier wounded in World War II who was ignored by fellow Americans who feared risking their lives to save him. Instead, a member of the Gestapo put *his* life on the line to save the fallen soldier and nursed him back to health. The Good Samaritan is that kind of story. The parable disrupts conventional beliefs and expectations. Those who would have been assumed to assist the beaten man walk right on by, but the detested Samaritan stops to render aid. This is how it will be in the kingdom of god: things as they are will be upended; what the world calls power will be revealed as weakness; the losers will be declared winners; customary hierarchies will be shaken up; the first shall be last. The kingdom of god will not be what you expect.

Let's consider another of Jesus' stories, the parable of the mustard seed. You'll recall that we discussed another mustard seed parable in our study of the Buddha. Jesus' story is much different. In fact, it is not much of a story at all; it is more of an expanded simile. Jesus said: "What is God's imperial rule like? What does it remind me of? It is like a mustard seed that a man took and tossed into his garden. It grew and became a tree, and the birds of the sky roosted in its branches."

This is a baffling saying. Perhaps its most obvious meaning is that the kingdom of god starts out as something small, even insignificant, like a mustard seed, one of the smallest of seeds, and develops into something great. On that level, it's a nice story. Insignificant beginnings yield immense results. Some interpreters have taken this anecdote as a metaphor for the growth of the Christian church throughout history, but I doubt that is what Jesus had in mind. Here's what complicates this story. Jewish law recorded in the *Mishnah* actually forbade growing mustard seeds in a garden. Mustard was a highly invasive weed; it did not actually grow into a tree but a shrub and was extremely difficult to eradicate, like bamboo. Planting it in a garden would be foolish, as well as illegal. It would soon take over the garden and overpower the vegetables. Then, it would provide shelter for the birds of the sky.

Nice image, but who wants *birds* in their garden? I believe that is why they invented scarecrows. Finally, mustard was wild and grew everywhere. Why would *anyone* actually cultivate it? These points would not be lost on the peasants who listened to Jesus. Imagine *their* responses to the story. First, think of their surprise at comparing the reign of the King of Universe to a common weed. "Hey Jesus, we were expecting something a little more like the Garden of Eden, not a garden that needs weeding!" Then imagine how they might ponder the violation of the law. Does he mean the kingdom comes in defiance of our regulations and the authority of our teachers? But even if there were no laws against it, what person in his or her right mind would actually *introduce* weeds and birds into a garden. Does this mean the kingdom comes in foolishness?

This is the way Jesus' parables worked. They implicitly invited those who heard them to contemplate their significance. Rarely did a parable have a single, simple meaning. Their intention seems to be deliberately to provoke unconventional, unaccustomed thinking, to stimulate the imagination, to envision new possibilities, and to disrupt habit. Certainly some of Jesus' listeners must have just walked away from one of his sermons shaking their heads, thinking the man must crazy. Others may have sat there with their mouths agape, trying to figure out these bewildering sayings. Even some of his closest associates would approach him later and ask Jesus to explain the meaning of his parables. Sometimes the gospels report that he would accede and provide his disciples with some allegory, but I suspect these allegories were added by the gospel writers to help dispel the parable's mysteriousness. When the writers try to explain the story, it becomes flat and loses its evocative and imaginative power. It's like telling a joke and then having to explain what it means when gets no one gets it. The explanation is never as effective as the joke itself.

Jesus' message of the god's kingdom was conveyed not only in parables and anecdotes but also in his actions. His deeds were a way of expressing his understanding of what the reign of god would be. His healings and exorcisms were all ways of dramatizing the message of the kingdom, as were what is sometimes called his "miracles," but what the gospels call "signs" and "powerful acts."

Let's examine one of these powerful acts, the well-known story of turning water into wine at a wedding celebration at Cana. According to John's account, shortly after Jesus began his public activity, he and his disciples attended a marriage feast in the village of Cana. This was not simply the ritual in which the marital vows were solemnized. This was the party that took place after the ceremony. Sometimes the celebration would last for a week. Such feasts were very important occasions in the lives of the peasants of Palestine. Weddings provided welcomed relief from their hard lives, a holiday in which the food and wine was plentiful, work was temporarily forgotten, and music and dance abounded. At some point during the festival, the wine ran out and Jesus' mother, who was also attending, asked Jesus to do something about it. For some reason, Jesus responded to her rather brusquely, "Woman, what is it with you and me? It's not my time yet." But she let his rather disrespectful comment pass and directed the servants to do whatever he said. Jesus told them to take the huge stone jars that were used for ritual purification and fill them with water. After doing so, Jesus instructed servants to give some of the water, now become wine, to the caterer, who tasted it and was astonished at how good it was. Then the caterer called the groom aside and asked why the best wine has been served last, contrary to usual practice.

Like one of Jesus' parables, this story has many levels of meaning and admits of divergent interpretations. In recent years, the story has sometimes been cited to show that Jesus endorsed marriage as the union of one man and one woman in order to challenge the idea of gay marriages. In the past, particularly during Prohibition, it was used to argue that Jesus approved of drinking alcohol. But to focus on these ancillary aspects of the story tends to detract from the way it illustrates the coming of the kingdom. God's reign will be like a feast, a holiday, with music and dance and plenty to eat and drink. In fact, Jesus ensures that the party keeps going, avoiding pre-emption by running out of provisions. Jesus' idea of the kingdom was earthy; there were no angels floating around strumming harps of gold. And it all happens contrary to expectation: the best wine comes at the end; Jesus is abrasive with his mother, but does what she asks; and he performs his mighty deed using, of all things, the jars that contained the foot-washing water. This is a plot with several twists and a happy ending.

Like the parables and his powerful signs, Jesus' healings and exorcisms served to reveal the character of god's kingdom. The New Testament gospels relate the stories of dozens of such cures. His fame in Palestine, in fact, depended mainly on his reputation as a healer and exorcist. The masses seemed to flock to him to experience his healing power. Jesus even referred to himself as a physician, yet he occasionally seemed to get a little annoyed by all the requests for cures. The texts report that in addition to casting out demons, he cured a wide variety of ailments, including blindness, deafness, fever, leprosy, paralysis, seizures, and chronic hemorrhaging. The New Testament also mentions three occasions when Jesus brought individuals back to life after they had died.

The healing stories have been variously interpreted throughout Christian history. Ordinarily, they were taken as indicative of Jesus' divine power. The 17th century English philosopher John Locke argued that Jesus' healings and miracles constituted empirical proof of Jesus' divinity. Many today would argue the same point, just as others would dismiss such an argument on the assumption that spontaneous healings and acts like transforming water into wine simply cannot occur because they violate our scientific understanding of the world. Interestingly, Locke made his argument *because* he believed these miracles were scientific evidence for Jesus' supernatural origins and thus verified Christianity.

Whatever one may conclude about the historical facticity of the accounts of these events, I think it is hard to dispute that many persons experienced a healing power in Jesus' presence. The real issue is what *significance* we attribute to Jesus' remarkable powers. Did they mean that Jesus was divine, that he was god incarnate as the later Christian tradition asserted? Personally, I find it difficult to draw such conclusions for one simple reason: stories of healings, exorcisms, powerful acts, and miracles are not unique to Jesus. Even the stories of resurrections were not so unusual. There are such accounts throughout the Bible and in literature from across the centuries and cultures. There were even miracle-workers in Galilee at the same time as Jesus, such as Rabbi Chanina ben Dosa, who was credited with numerous healings and nature-miracles. I can think of no principle by which to dismiss other reports of powerful deeds as false while accepting those about Jesus as true. In other words, it is hard for me to think that the stories of Jesus' extraordinary powers confirm claims about his unique oneness with god. That does not mean I deny the claim, only that miracles do not suffice to prove it.

What the miracles *do* suggest is Jesus' understanding of the reign of god. When the kingdom comes, the world will be a very different place. The demons and illnesses that afflict us will be banished. Pain and suffering will be no more. The end of suffering does not just imply the well-being of individuals; it portends a new kind of relationship among people. In Jesus' day, illnesses and demon-possessions were not merely unfortunate events that happened to individuals. They often implied impurity and untouchability.

Compounding the pain of leprosy or hemorrhaging was ostracism from society. The sick and demon-possessed had to endure the sense of shame that came with being a social outcaste. In the new age that Jesus proclaimed, the division of pure and impure would be obliterated, along with the categories of rich and poor, powerful and weak, sick and healthy. Jesus acted as if he were abolishing these distinctions by his very words and deeds. He ignored the purity practices by touching the untouchables; he promised that the hungry would be fed and the poor would be vindicated; he cast out demons and cured the afflicted; and he kept a party going by making sure there was plenty of wine to drink.

# Back to the Future
## Lecture 22

**The ultimate reality for Jesus was, of course, the god of ancient Judaism, the same deity worshiped by Abraham, Isaac, and Jacob. There is little, if anything, in Jesus's teaching to suggest that he departed in any way from the Jewish traditions in his thinking about God.**

The first part of Jesus's message was to announce that the reign of God is near. The second part was an admonition to live our lives accordingly. In fact, Jesus wanted his followers to live as subjects of God's reign even before it arrived in its complete manifestation.

Jesus believed that the god of the Jews was the world's creator and king, that he was profoundly moral and interested in the welfare of his people, that he often intervened in the affairs of human beings, and that he formed relationships with persons. It is evident that Jesus understood his own relationship with God as an intimate one; calling God his father, or **Abba**, is one thing that scholars are virtually certain was an authentic practice of the historical Jesus. Although using the metaphor of a father for God is hardly unique in the history of the world's religions, it is relatively uncommon in ancient Judaism. Such a sense of God's nearness was likely based on profound experiences that Jesus identified as holy.

Some might argue that Jesus, as God incarnate, came into the world with a vivid god-consciousness. But the synoptic Gospels suggest quite the opposite. Whatever the case, Jesus invited his followers to regard the divine in the same intimate way that he did.

Jesus's convictions about human nature and the problems besetting humanity were not out of the ordinary for someone shaped by ancient Judaism, particularly by its prophetic tradition. Jesus seemed to think that people had gotten absorbed by trivialities and an inordinate concern for themselves, which led to the tremendous suffering he saw all around. The world's anguish was self-inflicted, because human beings had departed from God's way. For Jesus, life in God was more important than anything. If it meant giving up everything else—including one's life—to participate in that reality, it would be worth it.

Reorienting one's life was not a one-time event. Jesus himself regularly practiced disciplines of spirituality, prayer in particular, which was not an opportunity to request God's assistance but a discipline for subordinating human desires to divine wisdom. Although Jesus prayed publicly, his preference was to do so in solitude, with an economy of words, and perhaps even silence—what some Christians today call **contemplative prayer**. Such departure from daily routine can bring a deeper awareness of one's own life and the world surrounding it.

**If the basic problem with human beings was their failure to care about the things God cared about, then the obvious solution was for them to reorient their lives to God.**

Jesus also promoted the communal practice of taking meals. Like Confucius and the Buddha, Jesus regarded eating as an activity with profound spiritual significance. The banquet was the symbol *par excellence* of God's reign. Jesus refused to discriminate among his mealtime companions, deliberately flouting Jewish purity laws, which he saw as a human contrivance. Meals also symbolized and fostered the sense of community that was a hallmark of the kingdom. Sharing common food represented common dependence on the same earthly elements for sustenance.

Jesus's teachings and spiritual disciplines were oriented to sharpening persons' awareness of the divine reality and galvanizing the will to care about the things God cared about. And what God cared about, Jesus thought, was human fulfillment and happiness, abundant life for every human being, and justice. Life in the kingdom therefore meant acting in some extraordinary ways, ways that were unconventional and dangerous. Three principles stand out as especially important: nonviolence, antimaterialism, and forgiveness, which ironically seem to go against the grain of much of Western social and religious convention. ■

**Abba**: An Aramaic word translated as "father"; one of the few Aramaic words that the Greek New Testament preserves in its original form.

**contemplative prayer**: The Christian practice of prayer in solitude and silence, not unlike the Buddhist practice of meditation.

## Questions to Consider

1. What sort of selfish trivialities occupied the people of Jesus's world? Were these similar to the issues in the cultures of the other sages? In our culture today?

2. Eating (or a similar way to obtain energy) is a basic biological need of all life forms. Why do you think this everyday occurrence has taken on such religious and ethical importance in so many cultures?

# Back to the Future
## Lecture 22—Transcript

The first part of Jesus' message was an announcement: the reign of god is near. The second part of his message was an admonition: begin to live your lives accordingly. As Matthew's gospel reports, Jesus urged his listeners, "Change your ways because Heaven's imperial rule is closing in!" The coming of the new world demanded a response. But exactly what kind of response did Jesus expect? In what ways did Jesus want his listeners to change? The answer was simple enough: think and act as if the kingdom were *already* here. Jesus wanted his followers to live as subjects of god's reign even before it arrived in its complete manifestation.

But what did living in the kingdom really mean? To explore this question requires that we move deeper into our understanding of Jesus' teachings and practices. For this discussion, we will return to the fundamental categories that guided our study of Confucius and the Buddha and will inform our consideration of Muhammad: the ideas of ultimate reality, anthropology, spirituality and ethics. These topics will help shape our image of Jesus' vision of life in the approaching new age.

The ultimate reality for Jesus was of course the god of ancient Judaism, the same deity worshiped by Abraham, Isaac, and Jacob. There is little, if anything, in Jesus' teaching to suggest that he departed in any way from the Jewish traditions in his thinking about god. We can find parallels to everything Jesus taught in the teachings of other Jewish sages. Jesus certainly believed that the god of the Jews was the world's creator and king, that he was profoundly moral and interested in the welfare of his people, and that he often intervened in the affairs of human beings, directing the course of history in ways that suited his purposes. All of this is implied in Jesus' proclamation of god's kingdom.

Like other Jews, Jesus also believed that god formed relationships with persons. Earlier, we mentioned how ancient Israel conceived of its relationship with its god as a marriage: the Israelites thought of themselves as Yahweh's bride. In the Tanakh, God usually dealt with his people collectively rather than as individuals, but occasionally, he established close relationships with exceptional persons such Abraham, Jacob, and Elijah. Moses was also one of these. The Book of Exodus declares that "the Lord used to speak to Moses face to face, as one speaks to a friend." Both the corporate and individual forms of divine relationships contrast with the formal and distant way the Chinese approached their gods, as we saw in our study of Confucius.

It is evident that Jesus understood his relationship with god as an intimate one, of the sort attributed to Moses. But Jesus thought of god not as a friend but as a father. Calling god father is one thing that critical scholars are virtually certain was an authentic practice of the historical Jesus. "Abba," one of the terms translated as father, is one of the few Aramaic words that the Greek New Testament preserves in its original form. That is one clue that the word goes back to Jesus himself. In the synoptic gospels, Jesus addresses or refers to god as father over 40 times. Using the metaphor of father for god, however, is hardly unique in the history of the world's religions. But it was used relatively infrequently in ancient Judaism, which preferred images such as lord, creator, king, and judge for the divine reality. The synoptic gospels alone have twice as many references to god as father than the entire Tanakh.

Jesus' usage of the parental trope emphasizes his sense of radical dependence on god as well as the close nature of their relationship. The use of the English word "father," in fact, may not fully convey their intimacy as Jesus understood it. Today, father often carries a more formal tone than the word Jesus used. Some of the other words we use to address our fathers may actually be closer to Jesus' sense of his relationship to god. "Daddy" or "papa," words that are structurally similar to abba, would probably be closer to Jesus' meaning than "father." Abba is almost baby-talk.

Such language suggests that Jesus thought of god as very close, almost palpable. For Jesus, god was not remote or disinterested. Such a sense of god's nearness, it seems to me, could only be based on profound experiences that Jesus identified as holy. The Tanakh, as well as the history of human religiousness, relates many such personal experiences of the divine. Whatever one may think about such experiences—whether they are purely psychogenetic or actual encounters with some transcendent dimension of reality or something else entirely—they are quite vivid and convincing to those who have them. They are also quite transformative. Such religious experiences often yield momentous changes, not unlike the way the Buddha's awakening to the realities of existence prompted him to walk away from his comfortable life to seek an end to suffering.

The New Testament gives us few clues as to when Jesus' religious experiences led him to conceive of god in such intimate terms. Some might argue that Jesus came into the world with a vivid god-consciousness. As god incarnate, they might say, Jesus was born with fullness awareness of god and his own divine mission. Not only do the synoptic gospels *not* say this, they suggest quite the opposite, that Jesus' spiritual and intellectual development, like his physical growth, was a gradual process. Luke writes: "And Jesus *increased* in wisdom and stature, and in favor with God and others."

It is quite possible that Jesus' sense of intimacy with god was connected to his discipleship with John the Baptist. Perhaps Jesus left home sometime in his 20s to join John in the Judean desert to fulfill a yearning for deeper spirituality. The ancient Jews often encountered their god in the wilderness, whether they were seeking him or not. We cannot be certain about what influence, if any, John's mentorship had on Jesus' religious experiences, but it is interesting to observe that Mark and Matthew report one of these experiences just after Jesus' baptism. The heavens open, the spirit of god descends like a dove, and he hears the voice of god announcing his approval.

What is clear from the New Testament accounts of Jesus' religious experiences is that he understood god as present reality. Jesus believed he shared an intimate connection with his god and invited his followers to regard the divine in the same way. Because Jesus' theology was informed by these profound experiences, his followers sensed in him the sacred presence of which he spoke. As many remarked on numerous occasions, they were astounded at his teaching because he taught as one having authority, not as one of their religious scholars. Such authority is grounded in existential experience, not mere belief or hearsay.

Like Jesus' understanding of god, his convictions about human nature and the problems besetting humanity were not out of the ordinary for someone shaped by ancient Judaism, particularly by its prophetic tradition. Jesus did not spend much time articulating his beliefs about human existence in the abstract. But from his words and actions, it is clear that he thought something was terribly askew in the human situation of his day. To put it as simply, he believed people no longer cared about what god cared about. Jesus seemed to think that people had gotten absorbed by trivialities and an inordinate concern for themselves. This disordering of values was manifested in the tremendous suffering he saw all around, from the Jewish purity system that graded people like cuts of meat to the Roman occupation that stole food from people's mouths to satisfy the palates of the well-to-do. The world's anguish was self-inflicted, because human beings had departed from god's way.

If the basic problem with human beings was their failure to care about the things god cared about, then the obvious solution was for them to reorient their lives to god. This seems to be the whole point of Jesus' endorsement of the summary of the Torah: "You shall love the Lord your God with all your heart, and with all your soul, and with all your strength, and with all your mind; and your neighbor as yourself." If anything qualifies as a synopsis of how Jesus thought one should prepare for the kingdom, this statement would be it. For Jesus, life in god, life in the kingdom, was more important than anything. If it meant giving up everything else—including one's life—to participate in that reality, it would be worth it. He said: "the kingdom of heaven is like a merchant in search of fine pearls; on finding one pearl of great value, he went and sold all that he had and bought it." The first step towards the life in god's domain was a radical commitment to the things god cares about.

But as the Buddha and Confucius also knew, making promises were of little value unless those pledges were enacted and reaffirmed continually. Reorienting one's life in god was not a one-time event. Jesus himself regularly practiced disciplines of spirituality to maintain and foster his sense of intimacy with the divine and focus on life's most important matters.

Foremost among these spiritual exercises was prayer. As a Jew, Jesus' fundamental approach to prayer would have been shaped by the traditions of ancient Judaism. In his day, it was customary to pray at dawn, in the evening, before meals, and at synagogue on Shabbat, the sabbath. But Jesus' prayers were not limited to these times. The gospels indicate that he prayed frequently, at various times, according to diverse needs and circumstances. Jesus seemed to view prayer principally as a discipline for subordinating his desires to divine wisdom rather than as an opportunity to enlist god's assistance in fulfilling a personal wish-list. As he anticipated his impending death, Jesus prayed, "*Abba* all things are possible for you! Take this cup away from me! But it's not what I want that matters, but what you want." Even the Lord's Prayer, the model prayer Jesus provided for his disciples, petitions god for the basic requisites to align one's desires and deeds to those of god. Daily bread, forgiveness, and deliverance from evil—these were no more than the necessary things for living in the kingdom.

Although Jesus prayed publicly, his clear preference was to do so in solitude, with an economy of words, and perhaps even silence. He advised his listeners:

> But whenever you pray, go into your room and shut the door and pray to your Father who is in secret; and your Father who sees in secret will reward you. When you are praying, do not heap up empty phrases as the Gentiles do; for they think that they will be heard because of their many words.

The New Testament relates that Jesus, like the Buddha and Muhammad, craved solitude and used every opportunity to steal away from the crowds to be alone. We know nothing, of course, of the content of his prayers during these periods of isolation, but we can imagine that much of his time was spent in complete silence, in what some Christians today call contemplative prayer. Contemplative prayer is the practice of simply allowing the mind to settle and become quiet and receptive by focusing on a phrase or the breath. It is not too dissimilar from the form of sitting meditation taught by the Buddha.

On at least one occasion, and perhaps on others not recorded, Jesus retreated into solitude deep into the wilderness and fasted for an extended period. The gospels state that one such instance occurred just after his baptism. After 40 days of prayer and fasting, Satan appeared to Jesus for the first time and attempted to disrupt his spiritual quest. Just as Mara, the Buddhist tempter figure, tried to lure Siddhattha Gotama into forsaking his goal of complete enlightenment, so too did Satan aim to upset Jesus' aspiration to center his life in god. First, Satan suggested that Jesus try to satisfy his hunger by turning stones into bread. When Jesus refused, Satan whisked him away to the highest point of the Temple and dared him to jump to see whether god would protect him. Again Jesus declined. Finally, Satan produced a vision of all the kingdoms of the world in their glory and offered them all to Jesus in exchange for worshiping the Prince of Darkness. For the third time, Jesus rejected the offer, and Satan accepted defeat for the moment.

In each instance, Satan's temptation was an invitation for Jesus to indulge his own desires: to give in to his wish for food, to assuage the doubts he may have had about god's endorsement of his mission, and to accept the easy glory of the kingdoms of man rather than the arduous path to the kingdom of god. This retreat, and perhaps others like it, served the purpose of heightening Jesus' awareness of god and fortifying his spirit against the onslaughts of selfish desire, represented by the figure of Satan.

I once visited the place where tradition claims that Jesus spent his 40-day retreat after his baptism. Today, Christians call it Mt. Temptation, just west of the ancient city of Jericho. There was something so intriguing and compelling about the sight of that desolate and barren place that decided to have a taste of that experience of solitude and hunger for myself. Some years later, I spent three days and nights alone in a desert canyon in the panhandle of Texas, without food or companion. There are many things about that time that I could comment upon, but the observation that impressed me most was the way stripping away all the familiar markers of my life heightened my awareness of space, time, and self. With no one talk to, no meals to look forward to, and no newspapers, internet, or other distractions to occupy my attention, my sensation of the external world was sharper than it had ever been. My sense of time slowed to a snail's pace. And my mind penetrated deep into forgotten nooks and crannies. I became conscious of how much my daily routine had insulated me from a deeper awareness of my own life and the world surrounding it. I can easily understand why the sages loved the solitude of nature to intensify their experience of living.

Jesus observed the disciplines of prayer, fasting, and retreat as an individual; but another practice was decidedly communal: taking meals. Like Confucius and the Buddha, Jesus regarded eating as an activity with profound spiritual significance. For Confucius, eating in certain ways expressed one's respect for self and others and the rules of decorum. For the Buddha, taking only one meal a day and consuming it in quiet mindfulness was essential to maintaining the Middle Way. For Jesus, meals represented something quite different. It was an enactment of the kingdom to come.

Jesus apparently loved feasts. We've already mentioned his pivotal role at the wedding celebration in Cana. Many of Jesus' powerful deeds involved food, such as the occasion in which he fed over 5000 listeners with five loaves of barley bread and two fishes. Many of his parables and aphorisms were drawn from the experiences of growing, preparing, and eating food. Jesus' fondness for feasting also became a bone of contention for those who sought to criticize him. They referred to him disparagingly as a glutton and a drunkard. But Jesus was unmoved by their complaints; the banquet was the symbol *par excellence* of god's reign. The Christian church still remembers that with its sacrament of the Eucharist.

The practice of taking meals was important to Jesus' vision of the kingdom for many reasons. Foremost was the inclusive nature of his eating customs. Jesus adamantly refused to discriminate among his mealtime companions. Anyone—from the wealthy elites to the "sinners and tax collectors"—was welcome. This practice scandalized those who of his culture who were strict about maintaining the rules of ritual purity. They could not grasp how someone who professed to be on such close terms with god would allow himself to be contaminated by eating with the unclean. From Jesus' perspective, the distinction between pure and impure was a humanly contrived system. Not only did god not recognize it, he positively opposed it, and Jesus made the point by deliberately flouting purity laws.

Meals also symbolized and fostered the sense of community that was a hallmark of the kingdom. By sharing common food that will be incorporated into their individual bodies, the meal represents a bond among people and their common dependence on the same earthly elements for sustenance. We all must eat to live. Eating together has a way of breaking down many of the barriers we impose among ourselves. If you have ever seen the fine Danish film, "Babette's Feast," based on a story by Isak Dinesen, you may have some sense of the point I'm trying to make. Babette is a French housekeeper working for two elderly sisters who belong to a rather strait-laced Christian sect on Jutland. After many years in their employ, Babette suddenly comes into a tidy sum of money, and she decides to splurge the whole of her small fortune on preparing and serving a single exquisite banquet, the likes of which the Danish sisters could not even imagine. They and their guests, mostly members of the same puritanical religion, agree to participate in the meal but determine to resist enjoying its sensual pleasures. But Babette's extraordinary gifts as a chef dissolve their distrust and apprehensions. Soon the diners begin to enjoy the exceptionally fine food and wine, and a new spirit of life settles over the table. Old grudges are forgotten and old loves are rekindled. The dreaded supper becomes a banquet of joy. That's the way Jesus imagined god's dominion.

Jesus' teachings and spiritual disciplines were oriented to sharpening persons' awareness of the divine reality and galvanizing the will to care about the things god cared about. And what god cared about, Jesus thought, was human fulfillment and happiness, abundant life for every human being, the prevailing of justice. Life in the kingdom therefore meant acting in some extraordinary ways, ways that were unconventional and dangerous. I think this is part of the reason Jesus' teaching were oriented to surprising and shocking the listener and why his spiritual disciplines functioned to take the practitioner out of the routine and familiar. As I said before, the kingdom of god was not what you expect.

Of the many remarkable features of Jesus' ethics for the kingdom, three principles stand out to me as especially important. Each of them is striking in the way it contrasts with our ordinary proclivities. I have in mind non-retaliation; generosity and non-possessiveness; and forgiveness. Let me say a few words about each.

I don't know if I was born with it or conditioned into it; it may have been something in the water of Texas. But for as long as I can remember I have had a reflexive impulse to punch the lights out of anyone who insulted me, hurt someone I cared about, or tried to steal something that was mine. Jesus thought I shouldn't do that. He said: "we were once told, 'An eye for an eye' and 'A tooth for a tooth.' But I tell you, Don't react violently against the one who is evil." Jesus was right. He says do not react *violently* to evil, but he does *not* say do not react. There is nothing in Jesus' teachings that suggest humans ought in any way to cooperate with evil or allow it to flourish. He did not, however, think it was necessary to answer evil with evil or violence with violence. The surprising nature of god's kingdom meant that new possibilities were available and that persons attuned to creative thinking were bound to discover them.

Jesus also had a lot to say about wealth and possessions—a lot! And what he taught was not the "gospel of prosperity" that many television preachers attribute to him today. Jesus was quite clear that wealth was a serious impediment to participation in god's kingdom. On numerous occasions, he urged those with wealth to give it all away and those without it to be happy with what they had. Contemporary interpreters in the affluent west seemed to have a dozen ingenuous ways to mitigate the severity of Jesus' denunciation of wealth. The gospels are clear that Jesus preached non-possessiveness and generosity. He taught others not acquire possessions and to give away lavishly and extravagantly: "if anyone wants to sue you and take your coat, give your cloak as well; and if anyone forces you to go one mile, go also the second mile. Give to everyone who begs from you, and do not refuse anyone who wants to borrow from you."

Finally, there is forgiveness. Forgiveness means relinquishment. To relinquish something is to release whatever power it holds over us. If I forgive someone for a wrong done to me, I no longer allow that event to determine how I treat the other person. I may remember the wrong or I may forget it, but either way I have disarmed it. It no longer determines my actions, thoughts, or words. Forgiveness in this sense is rarely easy or quick. Because of its difficulty, forgiveness has to be practiced. It is less an act than a way of living, a discipline, a cultivated skill. I think this is why Jesus told his students to forgive "70 times 7." True forgiveness often comes only at the end of an inner struggle. We forgive to be free, to be liberated from the destructive power of anger and hatred. Of course, it's a lot easier to nourish the thoughts of indignation. It's hard to surrender the delicious feeling that we've suffered unfairly. But ultimately that sense does us no good.

All my life, I've heard people talk about how Jesus helped them get their lives in order, which generally meant they gained social respectability. But I often wonder if taking Jesus seriously wouldn't more likely turn somebody's life upside down, since it so much of his teachings and practice seems to go against the grain of social and religious convention.

# Jesus's Christology
## Lecture 23

**We have observed that Jesus's teaching and actions centered on the coming of God's reign; our first approach to Jesus's christology, then, is to consider how he understood his role in this new order. Did he think of himself as simply a messenger warning others of the approaching new age or did he believe he was playing—or would play—a role in making it an actuality?**

Christology is the branch of Christian thought that seeks to understand the nature and deeds of Jesus, which began shortly after his death and resurrection and continues to this day. We will attempt to answer what might seem to be an odd question: What was *Jesus's* christology? How did he understand his role in the new order of God's reign?

One of the most hotly debated areas of modern Jesus scholarship is when and how Jesus thought the kingdom would come. Since the last century, most critical scholars have thought that Jesus believed God's rule would be established within a few years of his lifetime, based on evidence from the Gospels of Mark, Matthew, and Luke and Paul's letter to the Thessalonians. This idea helps explain certain beliefs and practices of the earliest Christians, such as the urgency of spreading Jesus's message and the practice of celibacy. This is called the **impending model**. Because the kingdom did not appear on time, the church had to revise its understanding of Jesus and his teachings. Another interpretation suggests that Jesus believed the kingdom was a present reality, already available to anyone willing to be a part of it. In this perspective, Jesus's mission was to teach others how to see and live in the kingdom because the full manifestation of God's reign on earth depends on the human willingness to accept it. This is called the **involvement model**.

The title by which Jesus has been most commonly known throughout history is the Christ, or the messiah, meaning "anointed one"—someone divinely appointed to a sacred task. Throughout Jewish scripture, numerous individuals are called messiahs, including King David and King Cyrus of

Persia. But by the time of Jesus, "messiah" had come to refer to a hero—not a divine being—who would restore the kingdom of Israel to its former greatness, and a slew of persons were claiming to be the Christ. Did Jesus make this claim for himself? In the Gospel of John, he makes this claim several times, but critical biblical scholars have doubts about the historicity of that book. In the synoptic Gospels, *others* assert that Jesus is the messiah, but Jesus seems hesitant to accept the title. Perhaps he was concerned that his followers might misunderstand what messiahship truly meant, or

More than a prophet figure, Jesus was a healer, exorcist, and wonder worker. In his presence, people sensed a sacred, restorative power.

what Jesus considered true messiahship could not be revealed until his death and resurrection. Or perhaps he did not consider himself the messiah.

The title of son of God is much better attested in the synoptic Gospels, but discerning Jesus's understanding of this title is not easy. Throughout biblical literature, this phrase could refer to angels, humanity as a whole, or particular noble individuals. Notably, outside Jewish tradition, Augustus Caesar was called a son of god as well. There is little definitive evidence about whether Jesus thought of his sonship as a unique relationship to God.

One of the most frequently used expressions for Jesus in the synoptic Gospels is the son of man. Many Christians today believe this phrase indicates Jesus's humanity versus his divinity. Historian Geza Vermes believes it was not really a title but just a polite way in which people referred to themselves.

But according to the book of Daniel, at the end of the world, a figure known as the Son of Man would descend from heaven to rule the earth. It is quite possible that this was Jesus's meaning. ∎

## Important Terms

**Christology**: The branch of Christian thought that seeks to understand the nature and deeds of Jesus.

**impending model**: The belief of early Christians (and possibly Jesus himself) that the coming of the Kingdom of God was imminent, within their own generation.

**involvement model**: The belief of later generations of Christians that the coming of the Kingdom of God was not a scheduled event but depended on human action to bring it about.

## Question to Consider

1. Which of the titles used by or given to Jesus are complementary, and which are contradictory? Which of them seems to best harmonize with his stated message?

# Jesus's Christology
## Lecture 23—Transcript

Christology is the branch of Christian thought that seeks to understand the nature and deeds of Jesus. The systematic study of the person of Jesus did not actually begin until after his death and resurrection, although his first disciples were certainly trying to comprehend who he was from the very beginning of their relationships with him. After he was gone, the efforts to understand his significance intensified and became more sophisticated. Ultimately, these christological endeavors culminated in the great creeds of the church that pronounced Jesus as fully god and fully human, the second person of the Trinity. Yet, christology did not end with these statements of faith. The work of understanding who Jesus was and what his significance is continues to be a vital part of Christian theology today. Christians still seek to know Jesus.

As a theological enterprise, christology has always been the work of Jesus' followers. But today we will pose and attempt to answer what might seem to be an odd and certainly anachronistic question: What was *Jesus'* christology? In other words, what did Jesus think about himself? Did *he* regard himself as the messiah, or the Christ, to use the Greek term? Did he think he was god or the son of god? Why did he refer to himself as the son of man? What, if anything, did he think his death on the cross would accomplish? These are the issues that we'll begin to explore together in this talk.

We have observed that Jesus' teaching and actions centered on the coming of god's reign; our first approach to Jesus' christology, then, is to consider how he understood his role in this new order. Did he think of himself as simply a messenger warning others of the approaching new age or did he believe he was playing—or would play—a role in making it an actuality? To answer this question requires that we delve into one of the most hotly debated areas of modern Jesus scholarship: when and how did Jesus think the kingdom would come?

Since the last century, most critical scholars have thought that Jesus believed god's rule would be established within a few years of his lifetime by a spectacular event initiated and directed by god himself. These theologians took seriously Jesus' proclamation that the kingdom of god was "near" or "at hand." In the Gospel of Mark, for example, Jesus declared, "Truly I tell you, there are some standing here who will not taste death until they see that the kingdom of God has come with power." Later in the same gospel, Jesus predicted:

> ... in those days ... the sun will be darkened, and the moon will not give its light, and the stars will be falling from heaven, and the powers in the heavens will be shaken. Then they will see "the Son of Man coming in clouds" with great power and glory. Then he will send out the angels, and gather his elect from the four winds, from the ends of the earth to the ends of heaven. ... Truly I tell you, this generation will not pass away until all these things have taken place.

Matthew and Luke record similar statements. Even the apostle Paul, writing to the Thessalonians in the mid-1st century, believed that the kingdom would arrive before some of his fellow Christians had died.

The belief that Jesus taught that the rule of god would soon appear helps explain certain beliefs and practices of the earliest Christians. For instance, it would account for the great sense of urgency that inspired Jesus' followers to spread his gospel throughout the empire and for the fact that it was almost a half a century before Jesus' story was committed to the written word. It would help clarify Paul's exhortation for Christians not to marry and to practice celibacy. If the new world were truly near to hand, what need would there be to change one's marital status or risk being consumed with lust? Why record Jesus' story if god's dominion were about to dawn? It would be far better to focus all efforts on preparing for the kingdom.

Theologians called this outlook an "interim ethic," a way of life appropriate for persons expecting the complete transformation of the earth at any moment. He also contended that later developments in Christian theology and practice were prompted by the fact that the spectacular coming of the kingdom did not occur as Jesus anticipated. Jesus, in other words, was wrong about its timing, and the church had to revise its understanding of Jesus and his teachings to cover up the mistake.

As I said, this has been the dominant view among most liberal biblical scholars for at least a hundred years. But of course, there have been other interpretations. One such reading suggests that Jesus believed the kingdom was a *present* reality, already available to anyone willing to be a part of it. In other words, the kingdom would not arrive in a dramatic display of god's cosmic powers but would rather quietly and almost imperceptibly appear as more persons committed themselves to living as subjects of god's rule.

Advocates of this view cite such passages as the one in which Jesus declares "the kingdom of God is among you." Here it seems that Jesus is suggesting that the kingdom is here; one only needs to change one's way of perceiving in order to see it. In this perspective, Jesus' mission was to teach others how to see and live in the kingdom because the full manifestation of the god's reign on earth depends on the human willingness to accept it. Jesus' healings, exorcisms, and powerful acts were all ways to demonstrate participation in this new reality. Not only did Jesus perform these acts, he also commissioned some of his disciples to go out and do the very same things he did: healing, casting out demons, and proclaiming god's dominion. When Jesus urged his listeners to follow him, he intended for them to respond by helping him to make the kingdom a reality. Without human cooperation, the rule of god could not be established. But by collaboration, human beings could bring the kingdom into being at this very moment.

It is difficult to adjudicate between these interpretations of Jesus' view of the kingdom. At first glance, they seem at odds with one another. In the first view, which I'll call the "impending" perspective, Jesus would have believed that his principal calling was as a prophet or messenger to urge his contemporaries to prepare for the glorious transformation of the world to be produced by god at any moment. Those who failed to change their ways and get right with god were liable to find themselves excluded from the new world. The second view, which I'll call the "involvement" perspective, suggests that Jesus' primary role was to inspire and enable others to see the possibilities of a new way of living free from the sufferings and disappointments of life as we now know it. As more people shared this vision and participated in it, the more god's reign would become an actuality.

As frameworks for interpreting Jesus, both the impending and involvement perspectives have their merits and drawbacks. Both have support from the earliest texts we have about the historical Jesus. Advocates of either view can bring forth passages from the gospels to support their argument. The impending view seems to fit well with apocalyptic expectations of the time and is consistent with the preaching of John the Baptist. The involvement view may seem more appealing from a Christian theological perspective. It avoids having to say that Jesus was mistaken about the kingdom's timing and gives modern Christians a focus for their faith by encouraging the continuation of Jesus' advocacy of justice.

Is it possible that *both* viewpoints are true, that Jesus preached a kingdom that was both coming and yet already in some sense here? This was the thesis of several prominent New Testament scholars of the last century, who argued that as a result of Jesus' life, death, and resurrection god's reign on earth had been initiated but still awaited its final consummation at some point in the future. Today, most evangelical scholars support this point of view. This outlook is attractive because it obviates the need to emphasize some of Jesus' sayings over others. Yet, it is not clear how it resolves Jesus and the early Christians' belief that the kingdom would be fully manifested within their generation.

What one decides about Jesus' understanding of the coming of the kingdom will in large measure determine what one believes about his christology. The impending viewpoint suggests that Jesus regarded himself mainly as a prophet of the end-times. The involvement model implies that Jesus saw himself more as a teacher whose role was to educate others about a new way of life. Throughout the New Testament, he is referred to in both ways. While certainly these titles were appropriate, the gospels are also quite clear that these were not the *only* ways that Jesus was thought of—or that he thought of himself. Examining these other designations might shed light on Jesus' understanding of his role in god's dominion and illuminate his own christology. We'll consider the most of prominent of these titles: messiah, son of god, and son of man.

The title by which Jesus has been most commonly known throughout history is the Christ, or the messiah. So closely associated have been the words "Jesus" and "Christ" that the terms are often used interchangeably. Many people today are unaware that "the Christ" is a title applied to Jesus just as "the Buddha" was given to Gotama. The fundamental Christian affirmation is that Jesus of Nazareth was the Christ. But what is the Christ and did Jesus understand *himself* that way, as his followers obviously did?

The word messiah derives from Hebrew and Aramaic terms that mean "anointed one," and an anointed one was literally someone on whom holy oil had been ritually applied. This ritual of anointment symbolized divine appointment to a sacred task. Throughout the Tanakh, the Jewish scripture, numerous individuals are called messiahs, including King David and King Cyrus of Persia, the emperor who liberated the Jews from their Babylonian captivity.

But by the time of Jesus, "messiah" came to acquire a more specific meaning. Under the domination of Greek and then Roman rule, many Jews in Palestine began to expect or yearn for a new messiah who, like King David and King Cyrus, would be an exceptional military hero and who would restore the Kingdom of Israel to its former greatness. This hope was partly based on passages from the apocalyptic book of Daniel that refer to an approaching anointed prince, a descendant of King David, who would lead his troops "to restore and rebuild Jerusalem." The expectation did not necessarily involve the idea that the messiah was god or divine, only that he was designated by god for a special purpose. This may not have been the only way the new messiah was envisioned, but it was the dominant view. There seems to have been an extensive belief in Jesus' time that matters had gotten so dire that the messiah would appear very shortly. Perhaps in response to the common hope, a whole series of persons appeared in the 1st century claiming to be the Christ. Was Jesus of Nazareth one of them?

Let me be clear: I am not asking, *was* Jesus the messiah? I am merely asking, did the historical Jesus *claim* to be the messiah? I am sure others will disagree with me, but I do not believe that how we answer the second question necessarily determines how we answer the first.

For some readers of the New Testament, perhaps even most, the answer is as plain as day. Of course Jesus declared himself to be the Christ. The Gospel of John reports a well-known story about Jesus' encounter with a Samaritan woman at a public well. After a conversation, the woman challenges Jesus about one of the issues separating the Judeans and Samaritans—the appropriate place to worship god. Jesus responds by telling her, "the time is coming—in fact, it's already here—for true worshipers to worship the Father as he truly is, without regard to place." "The woman continues, 'All I know is that the Messiah, the one called Anointed, is going to come; when he does, he'll tell us everything.' Jesus says to her, 'You've been talking to the Anointed all along; I am he.'" We could pull out several other passages from John to make the same point. Indeed, John's gospel goes even further to suggest that Jesus more than just god's anointed. He was the word of god made flesh.

Critical scholars, as I've mentioned before, have grave doubts about the historicity of most of John's gospel. Very few aspects of John can be certified as historically probable according to the standards of modern historiography. We haven't the time to discuss these issues in detail, but let me mention a few factors that contribute to this judgment. First, John's gospel was written later than the synoptics, at the end of the 1$^{st}$ or beginning of the 2$^{nd}$ century; by that time, christological developments that had been in process for 60 or 70 years. As we've seen with the Buddha and Confucius, as time proceeds, the biographies of charismatic individuals tend to acquire greater legendary qualities.

Second, John neglects to mention most of the events and teachings contained in Mark, Matthew, and Luke. John contains no parables, no reports of exorcisms, and no discussions of the end-time. John only mentions the kingdom of god twice. It's hard to account for these omissions if John had access to the same historical material that the synoptics used. There are other factors involved, of course, but the consensus among academic biblical specialists who apply the methods of modern historical study is that John contains little historical fact and few, if any, authentic sayings of Jesus. Accordingly, most critical scholars doubt that the historical Jesus actually identified himself as the Christ as the gospel of John describes.

But what of the synoptics? Mark, Matthew, and Luke are generally believed to contain material that came from Jesus himself. Is there evidence in these texts that Jesus laid claim to the title messiah? In these earliest written gospels Jesus refrains from declaring outright that he was the Christ. On a few occasions, however, *others* make that assertion. But he himself appears hesitant to accept the title. This motif is referred to by scholars as the "messianic secret." The most noteworthy expression of this theme occurs in Mark:

> Jesus went on with his disciples to the villages of Caesarea Philippi; and on the way he asked his disciples, "Who do people say that I am?" And they answered him, "John the Baptist; and others, Elijah; and still others, one of the prophets." He asked them, "But who do you say that I am?" Peter answered him, "You are the Messiah." And he sternly ordered them not to tell anyone about him.

The other gospels report similar events or other occasions during which Jesus gives ambiguous answers to questions about his identity. If indeed the messianic secret is historically accurate, that is factually goes back to Jesus' life, what could possibly explain it? One plausible answer is that Jesus was concerned that his followers might misunderstand what messiahship truly meant. If the common hope was for a political hero along the lines of King David, then Jesus did not want the masses attempting to coerce him into that role.

As we noted, there were other messianic claimants at the time, many of them associated with violent revolutions. Perhaps Jesus wanted to avoid these connotations to forestall distractions to his genuine mission. Another possibility is that what Jesus considered true messiahship could not be revealed until his death and resurrection. In short, he urged his followers not to speak of him—and perhaps even to *think* of him—as the messiah until his crucifixion and resurrection disclosed the true nature of messiahship. A third possibility has to be that Jesus never actually claimed to be the messiah. The messianic secret was a literary device used by the synoptic gospels to explain why Jesus never made messianic claims even though Christians were claiming he was the Christ.

In the final analysis, is hard to state with confidence that Jesus unequivocally accepted the title the Christ. Even if it were clear that Jesus had embraced that designation, it is not altogether evident what he would have meant by it.

Let's consider another title often attributed to Jesus: the son of god. With respect to this appellation, the attestations in the synoptic gospels seem clearer, and it seems likely that Jesus *did* think of himself as god's son. One fairly obviously example is the way Jesus constantly referred to god as father, particularly in prayer. In Mark's gospel, whenever Jesus' performs an exorcism, the demons typically call him son of god. But despite these attestations, discerning Jesus' understanding of this title is not easy.

Throughout the biblical literature and the Mediterranean area, various permutations of the expression "son of god" conveyed many different meanings. In the Tanakh, son of god or sons of god could refer to angels, to humanity as a whole, or to particularly noble individuals. But there are suggestions, especially in non-canonical Jewish texts, that the anticipated messiah would also be called the son of god. Furthermore, as we observed in our discussion of the stories of Jesus birth, Augustus Caesar was called "son of god," as well as "god," "god from god," "redeemer," "liberator," and "savior of the world." Unfortunately, the lack of primary sources in Aramaic about the life of Jesus makes it impossible to determine whether he himself or others referred to him in that language as "a son of God" or as "the Son of God." Almost certainly, Jesus thought of himself as a son of god, but there is little definitive evidence to compel us to say that he thought of sonship as a unique relationship that only he had with god.

One of the most frequently used expressions for Jesus in the synoptic gospels was the son of man. It may also be one of the most obscure. There is little doubt that Jesus actually used this term to refer to himself; there is none of the ambiguity that we find with messiah or son of god. In Mark, for instance, Jesus called himself the son of man when he referred to his own fate: "The Son of Man is to be betrayed into human hands, and they will kill him, and three days after being killed, he will rise again."

Many Christians today believe "son of man" indicates Jesus' humanity, as compared with his divinity. Historian Geza Vermes believes that "son of man" was not really a title but just a polite way in which people referred to themselves. These interpretations may both be correct, but it is also true that in the Tanakh and the New Testament, the expression could have a more technical meaning.

According to the Book of Daniel, at the end of the world, a figure known as the Son of Man would descend from heaven to play a decisive role in the annihilation of evil and to return the world to the path of righteousness. Daniel writes of his vision:

> I saw one like a [Son of Man] coming with the clouds of heaven. And he came to the Ancient One and was presented before him. To him was given dominion and glory and kingship, that all the peoples, nations, and languages should serve him. His dominion is an everlasting dominion that shall not pass away, and his kingship is one that shall never be destroyed.

Was this what Jesus had in mind when he called himself the son of man? It is quite possible he did. Shortly after he told his followers that he would die and rise again, Jesus told them: "Then they will see 'the Son of Man coming in clouds' with great power and glory." Or as Matthew tells, Jesus said: "The Son of Man is to come with his angels in the glory of his Father, and then he will repay everyone for what has been done. Truly I tell you, there are some standing here who will not taste death before they see the Son of Man coming in his kingdom."

As we near the end of this lecture, let me observe that we have hardly reached any conclusions. Indeed, we've raised more questions than provided answers.

My purpose has been to provide a glimpse into the diversity of perspectives that characterize current scholarship on Jesus and the complexity of the issues involved. Soon, I'll begin to put these puzzle pieces back together again. But before I do, we'll need to consider one final aspect of Jesus' life: his death and resurrection.

# The Last Days in Jerusalem
## Lecture 24

> The apostle Paul ... based his entire theology on Jesus's crucifixion and resurrection without ever mentioning his teachings. ... Although other Christians have certainly given far more attention to Jesus's life and teachings than Paul did, on the whole they have still concurred with Paul's belief in the centrality of the death and resurrection.

Jesus's death and resurrection were without doubt the most important events of his life according to the New Testament. All four Gospels relate detailed stories of these occurrences. The apostle Paul based his entire theology on these events, and for two millennia, Christianity has followed his lead. But rather than view these events as a divinely planned transaction conferring the forgiveness of humanity's sins, let's consider them in relation to the central message of Jesus's life.

When Jesus journeyed to Jerusalem during the **Passover** festival, he may have intended to dramatize his message of the coming kingdom and to bring it to its final fullness. Jerusalem was the symbolic center of ancient Judaism and the home of the priests and elders who collaborated with Rome, and Passover was the time when the Jews celebrated their freedom from Egypt. As Pontius Pilate and his Roman troops paraded into the city at the start of the holiday to remind the Jews of Roman presence and power, Jesus entered the opposite end of the city alone, on a donkey, a humble king founding a peaceable kingdom.

During the days following his entry into the city, Jesus continued to speak of the Kingdom of God and perform acts to symbolize it. When Jesus declares that the Temple has become a "den of robbers," a phrase from the book of Jeremiah, he seems to be referencing not the money changers but the priests and Temple authorities who benefited from the Roman occupation. Jesus also instituted the ritual meal that would become the Christian sacrament of the **Eucharist**, the meaning of which would become the subject of fierce debate among Christians for centuries to come. It was during this meal that Judas Iscariot left to inform the Temple authorities of

Jesus's whereabouts, an act the Gospels all struggle to explain. But he was hardly the cause of Jesus's death. The stories suggest that Jesus was fully aware of what might happen to him by taking his message to Jerusalem during the Passover.

**Because it was excruciating and public, crucifixion was reserved for those convicted of sedition against the state.**

In the Garden of Gethsemane, Jesus struggles to accept what he believes is God's will but offers no resistance to the Temple police who come to arrest him. Jesus was taken to Caiaphas, the high priest, and asked point-blank, "Are you the messiah?" Jesus gives an ambiguous answer but seems to accept the alternate title son of man. It was enough for the high priest to declare Jesus a blasphemer and for the council to judge him deserving of death. But executing such a sentence was the sole prerogative of Rome.

The priests brought Jesus before Pilate, where he again evaded the question of whether or not he was the messiah, a silence that could be seen as contempt for Roman authority. Pilate thus ordered Jesus's **crucifixion** on a charge of insurrection. Crucifixion was a slow, painful, humiliating death reserved for enemies of the state. According to Mark, Jesus's death was accompanied by celestial darkness and a Roman centurion's declaration that "Truly this man was God's Son!" The historicity of these events is doubtful, but they reinforce the importance of Jesus's death to his message.

The four Gospels all offer different accounts of what happened on the Sunday morning after Jesus's death. Mark, the earliest Gospel, ends abruptly with an open tomb and a message that the disciples would see Jesus again in Galilee. (The stories of Jesus's appearances that follow are later additions to the text.) Matthew ends his Gospel with Jesus appearing and commanding his disciples to spread his message. Luke tells the story of Jesus revealing himself during a meal with two of his followers and disappearing. Common Christianity has long taken these episodes to indicate Jesus's divinity, but was this really the Gospel writers' meaning, or is there another significance? ∎

**crucifixion**: Execution on a cross; in the Roman Empire, this form of punishment was reserved for crimes of sedition and insurrection.

**Eucharist**: The Christian sacrament that commemorates the Passover meal Jesus shared with his followers in the Gospels (Matthew 26:17–29; Mark 14:12–25; Luke 22:7–38) shortly before his execution.

**Passover**: The Jewish festival commemorating the escape from Egyptian domination. At the time of Jesus, parallels between the Egyptian and Roman domination of the Jews raised Romans' fears of riot and revolt during the festival.

## Question to Consider

1. Consider the stories of the release of Barabbas and the two criminals executed alongside Jesus. What are the theological implications of these incidents? What are the political implications? Do these two views complement or contrast with each other?

# The Last Days in Jerusalem
## Lecture 24—Transcript

Jesus' death and resurrection were without doubt the most important events of his life according to the New Testament. All four gospels relate detailed stories of these occurrences. The apostle Paul, whom I consider the chief founder of Christianity, based his entire theology on Jesus' crucifixion and resurrection without ever mentioning his teachings. For two millennia, Christians have followed Paul's example. Although other Christians have certainly given far more attention to Jesus' life and teachings than Paul did, on the whole they have still concurred with Paul's belief in the centrality of the death and resurrection.

The emphasis on this aspect of Jesus' life is directly related to his function in Christianity. Jesus is considered by Christians to be the atonement for human sinfulness and the means by which salvation is made possible. As Paul wrote, Jesus "was handed over to death for our trespasses and was raised for our justification." That has been the dominant view of the meaning of Jesus' crucifixion and resurrection among Christians for centuries.

But in our discussion today, I want to develop another understanding of these events, one focusing on what we know of their historicity and their significance for the message Jesus proclaimed: the coming of god's kingdom. I will not suggest that my interpretation and the dominant interpretation of Christians are necessarily incompatible. I simply intend to demonstrate the continuity of the crucifixion and resurrection with the rest of Jesus' life and teaching as we've studied it thus far. From that vantage point, I want to discuss these events in the same manner as we have considered the parables, the healings and exorcisms, the miracles, and his prayers and feasts: as enactments of life in the kingdom. Rather than view Jesus' death and resurrection as a divinely planned transaction conferring the forgiveness of humanity's sin, for a moment, let's think about them in relation to the central message of Jesus' life.

Jesus urged his contemporaries to prepare for the kingdom of god and begin living as if it were a present reality. He believed god's reign would disrupt the values and priorities of the current state of affairs and bring a new age to the world characterized by a radical commitment to the things god cared about. In this new way of life, there would be plenty of resources for everyone and freedom from every kind of bondage. The world would be at peace and the qualities of fairness, compassion, and imagination would prevail. When Jesus decided to leave the relative safety of Galilee, where his public activity had centered, and journey to Jerusalem during the Passover festival, it was with the intent, I believe, both to dramatize this message of the kingdom and to set in motion the events that would signal its coming in final fullness.

The choice of both place and time were deliberate. Jerusalem was, of course, the symbolic center of ancient Judaism, the location of its Temple and its traditions. It was also the home of the high priests and the council of elders and the heart of Judean collaboration with the Roman Empire. The Passover was one of major celebrations of the Jewish people, one of three festivals in which Jews from all over Palestine made pilgrimage to Jerusalem. Passover, of course, commemorated the Israelites' exodus from Egypt, specifically the night Yahweh spared the children of Abraham from the tenth and final plague, the killing of the firstborn.

Jesus chose to go to Jerusalem at the time the Jews were celebrating their freedom from Egyptian domination, surely an occasion in which they were particularly cognizant of the contrast between liberation from Egypt and their virtual enslavement to Rome. Jesus would also have known that Jerusalem would have been especially crowded. Perhaps he saw that as an opportunity to reach a greater audience with his message. But he could not have been unaware that the city would also be packed with Roman soldiers, who would have been dispatched for crowd-control. Passover would have been a prime opportunity for a rebellion to erupt, the last thing the Romans wanted; they would take extra precautions to ensure that order was maintained. In fact, Jesus was surely aware that the Roman prefect, Pontius Pilate, and the Roman reinforcements would parade into the city at the start of holiday from his headquarters on the coast to pointedly remind the Jews of Roman presence and power.

I feel confident that Jesus was aware of the Roman procession because he staged another, very different parade at about the same time. From the opposite end of the city, Jesus entered Jerusalem riding on a donkey, symbolizing another power and another kingdom. Jesus' entry, celebrated by the church each year as Palm Sunday, was a dramatic allusion to the words of the prophet Zechariah:

> Rejoice greatly, O daughter Zion!
> Shout aloud, O daughter Jerusalem!
> Lo, your king comes to you;
> triumphant and victorious is he,
> humble and riding on a donkey,
> on a colt, the foal of a donkey.
> He will cut off the chariot from Ephraim
> and the warhorse from Jerusalem;
> and the battle-bow shall be cut off,
> and he shall command peace to the nations;
> his dominion shall be from sea to sea,
> and from the River to the ends of the earth.

Jesus' procession into Jerusalem enacts the entrance of a humble king to mark the start of his peaceable kingdom, in glaring contrast to the ostentatious march of the Roman military in all its glory.

During the days following his entry into the city, Jesus continued to speak of the kingdom of god and perform acts to symbolize it. One of the memorable incidents occurred within the Temple precinct when Jesus drove out the sellers and buyers and overturned the tables of the moneychangers and dove-sellers so that no one could carry anything through the Temple. Then he began to teach to those present. He declared: "Is it not written, 'My house shall be called a house of prayer for all the nations'? But you have made it a den of robbers." I think it would be a mistake to read this story as an indictment of mixing commerce and religion, as it is usually interpreted. That doesn't mean, however, that I endorse the way so many have made a big business out of religion! It's just that I don't think that's quite what the story is about.

When Jesus declares that the Temple has become a "den of robbers," I do not think he is directing his condemnation to the moneychangers and dove sellers, who, after all, were providing an essential service for pilgrims to the Temple and may not have been making all that much money. Briefly bringing temple business to a halt by overturning the tables was simply a way for Jesus to stop the commotion and get attention to state his message, which was intended for the priests, those who were in charge of the Temple and who were the chief collaborators with the Romans. The phrase "den of robbers" is taken from the prophet Jeremiah, who was deeply critical of the ancient Jews for failing to live up to god's standard of social justice by oppressing foreigners in their midst, allowing the orphans and widows to go uncared for, and for shedding innocent blood. For Jesus, the real robbers were the priests and Temple authorities, who benefited by the Roman occupation and refused to resist the imperial exploitation of the poor and destitute. Mark says that just after this incident, the chief priests and scribes—*not* the moneychangers and dove-sellers—began to look for a way to kill him.

On Thursday evening of Passion or Holy Week, as the church now calls it, Jesus celebrated his last meal with his disciples. The New Testament reports that two important events occurred at this last supper. First, Jesus instituted the ritual of the Eucharist, or Lord's Supper, by offering bread and wine to his companions. The meaning of that ritual, of course, would become the subject of fierce debate among Christians for centuries to come. The second event was Judas Iscariot's departure during the meal to inform the Temple authorities of Jesus' whereabouts. Judas' role in Jesus' death is an enigma.

The gospels struggle to explain his motivations. Luke can think of nothing better to say than the devil made him do it. John suggests he was motivated by money—30 pieces of silver. Neither is a satisfying answer. More recent interpretations suggest that Judas became disappointed when he discovered that the kingdom Jesus had in mind was not the one that Judas wanted. Others have thought he was cowardly and sought to avoid the consequences that Jesus appeared headed for. The recently released translations of the non-canonical Gospel of Judas propose that Judas and Jesus conspired to arrange Jesus' arrest so he might complete his mission on earth. In this interpretation, Judas was Jesus' closest and most important disciple. Whatever was historically the case with Judas, it is clear that early Christians couldn't decide how best to explain him. The books of New Testament do not even agree on how he died. Matthew says he hung himself, and the Book of Acts says he fell in a field and spilled his guts. Regardless of his motives and demise, the gospels do agree that he played a central role in Jesus' arrest. But he was hardly the cause of Jesus' death. The stories suggest that Jesus was fully aware of what might happen to him by taking his message to Jerusalem during the Passover.

It was late in the night when the temple police arrived at the Garden of Gethsemane at the foot of the Mount of Olives to arrest Jesus. He had been praying there with some of his followers since supper. The New Testament relates a very heart-wrenching scene in which Jesus struggles to accept what he believes is god's will. Luke says "his sweat became like great drops of blood falling down on the ground." When the Temple guards arrived, Jesus offered no resistance and allowed himself to be taken into custody. His followers, however, abandoned him.

What happened after the arrest is unclear. The gospels report that Jesus was taken to Caiaphas, the high priest, and a hearing was conducted before the Temple authorities. Several witnesses were brought forth, but they were unable to present consistent testimony against Jesus. Finally, the high priest simply asked point-blank: "Are you the messiah, the son of the blessed one?" Jesus' answer was far from lucid. Most English translations of Jesus' response in Mark's gospel report his answer as "I am." But that phrase in Greek could just as correctly be rendered as "Am I?" Matthew and Luke's gospel preserve the ambiguity with "You have said so" and "You say that I am." Then Jesus said a curious thing. Mark expresses it this way: "you will see the Son of Man seated at the right hand of the Power, and coming with the clouds of heaven." Jesus gives an ambiguous answer to the question about his messiahship, but seems to accept for himself the title Son of Man.

As we noted in our discussion of Jesus' christology, these appellations were ordinarily understood to mean two very different figures: one, a military hero; the other, a figure appearing from the heavens at the end-time. In any event, it was enough for the high priest to declare Jesus a blasphemer and ask the council for a recommendation. They judged him deserving of death.

At dawn on Friday, Jesus was taken to Pilate, who was staying at Herod the Great's former palace. It is likely that the Temple authorities were not allowed to condemn to death. That would have been the sole prerogative of Rome. Hence, it was necessary to get the prefect's approval to put an end to Jesus' life. Pilate asked Jesus if he were the king of Judeans. Pilate's question was probably full of sarcasm as he looked upon the bound and beaten Galilean: "Are *you* the King of the Judeans?" Jesus gave a curt, evasive answer: "You so say," again, not exactly a resounding affirmation. In Mark, the chief priests make other accusations, but Jesus remains completely silent until he is crucified; Jesus' silence at this time has always seemed to me a gesture of contempt for Roman authority.

The New Testament suggests that Pilate did not want to execute Jesus and tried to get out of the situation gracefully without stirring up a riot. Mark tells how Pilate tried to escape his predicament by offering to release Jesus in accord with a Roman custom of freeing one prisoner at Passover. But the crowd chose Barabbas, a convicted insurgent, over Jesus. The whole Barabbas episode is highly unlikely. It is hard to believe that the Romans would really release a man convicted of insurrection at a time when rebellion could erupt in a flash. The story is more likely a literary device to show how the Judeans preferred the path of violent insurrection to the non-violent resistance represented by Jesus. Whether the Barabbas story is a fiction or not, it is true that Pilate ordered Jesus' crucifixion as an insurrectionist against the empire, probably as a matter of expediency. Better to kill one man than risk an uprising.

Jesus was turned over to the Roman soldiers who began to treat him without mercy. They picked up on the charge that Jesus claimed to be the King of the Judeans, and they mocked him accordingly, giving him a purple robe and a crown of thorns, and prostrated themselves before him. After they have had their amusement, they forced him to march up to Calvary, a very public location just outside the city wall, carrying the wooden crossbeam of his cross. There, he was stripped naked, nailed to the crossbeam, and hoisted up to the vertical post on which the horizontal crossbeam rested.

Crucifixion was meant to be both painful and humiliating. Those who were crucified ordinarily died a slow death; it often took days for the victim to succumb. Death could have been caused by blood loss, exposure, dehydration, asphyxiation, infection, or a combination of these. Because it was excruciating and public, crucifixion was reserved for those convicted of sedition against the state and for chronically disobedient slaves. Obviously, it was intended as a deterrent to future acts of defying authority.

According to Mark, Jesus was crucified around 9:00 in the morning, between two Judean insurgents. At noon, a great darkness began to cover the earth. This literary symbol should be interpreted in the same way as the great lights and earthquakes that accompanied significant moments of the Buddha's life, namely, as the cosmic recognition of the significance of these events. By mid-afternoon, Jesus was approaching his death. At the moment of his death, around 3:00 in the afternoon, a Roman centurion who watched him die said, as Mark tells it, "Truly this man was God's Son!"

It is doubtful that the centurion's announcement was an historical event, but there is tremendous theological significance here. First, there is the immense irony. The symbol of Roman might and oppressiveness is the mouthpiece by which Jesus' identity is revealed to the world. But equally important is the moment at which the announcement is made. It was only when the soldier "saw that in this way he breathed his last," to quote Mark, that he was moved to declare Jesus' relationship with god. We are led to conclude that there was something in the way Jesus died that prompted the pronouncement, but Mark isn't clear about what it was. Perhaps it was the courage and nobility revealed in the way he faced death that touched the centurion. Perhaps it was Jesus' willingness to proclaim a message of justice in the face the Roman and Judean authorities—even though it meant his death—that impressed the soldier. But whatever the reason, the declaration serves to reinforce the idea we mentioned at the beginning of our talk, that Jesus' death was one of the two most important aspects of his life, according to the later Christian tradition.

Jesus' body was removed from the cross and placed in a tomb shortly before sunset on Friday, which would have been the start of Shabbat. Once the sun had set, the corpse would have had to remain on the cross until the end of the sabbath. The arrival of Shabbat meant that the usual preparations for burial could not be undertaken before the body was entombed. That is why the women who followed Jesus to Jerusalem and had cared for him in the Galilee had gone to his tomb early in the morning on Sunday. Their plan was to cleanse and anoint his body, which they had been unable to do on the day of his death.

The four gospels all offer different accounts of what happened on that Sunday morning. The earliest gospel, Mark, presents a terse description with an abrupt ending.

> When the sabbath was over, Mary Magdalene, and Mary the mother of James, and Salome bought spices, so that they might go and anoint him. And very early on the first day of the week, when the sun had risen, they went to the tomb. They had been saying to one another, 'Who will roll away the stone for us from the entrance to the tomb?' When they looked up, they saw that the stone, which was very large, had already been rolled back. As they entered the tomb, they saw a young man, dressed in a white robe, sitting on the right side; and they were alarmed. But he said to them, 'Do not be alarmed; you are looking for Jesus of Nazareth, who was crucified. He has been raised; he is not here. Look, there is the place they laid him. But go, tell his disciples and Peter that he is going ahead of you to Galilee; there you will see him, just as he told you.' So they went out and fled from the tomb, for terror and amazement had seized them; and they said nothing to anyone, for they were afraid.

There are several puzzling aspects of this account. To begin, it is rather curious that the women consider the obstacle of the stone only *after* they were on the way to the tomb. We they arrive, they only encounter a young man who tells them that Jesus is not there but instructs them to tell the other followers that Jesus will meet them in Galilee. But the whole event scares them, and they flee and do not tell anyone. This is the point at which the original gospel of Mark ends. Apparently, later Christians found this conclusion unsatisfying because much later they added an alternative ending, with stories of Jesus appearances. But critical scholars are fairly certain that the original text ends with the women fleeing the empty tomb and determined not to tell anyone.

The stories of Matthew and Luke differ significantly from Mark in detail. The most important difference is the account of Jesus' appearances. In both Matthew and Luke, some of his disciples see Jesus after his resurrection. In Matthew, the women who had gone to the tomb encounter Jesus *en route* to tell the other disciples of the empty grave. Immediately, they fell at his feet and worshiped him. Later, the remaining 11 apostles visit a mountain back in Galilee and they too see Jesus. Matthew concludes his story with these words from Jesus:

> Go therefore and make disciples of all nations, baptizing them in the name of the Father and of the Son and of the Holy Spirit, and teaching them to obey everything that I have commanded you. And remember, I am with you always, to the end of the age.

Matthew's account of Jesus' appearance adds one very interesting detail: "When they saw him, they worshiped him; but some doubted." In other words, even seeing Jesus after his death was not sufficient to convince some apostles that he had indeed been raised by god.

Luke tells of other stories in which Jesus' followers see him. Interestingly, Luke does not mention the women seeing him as Matthew does. When the women returned to the apostles with the news, the men refused to believe them. Then Peter ran to the tomb and discovered that it was indeed empty. Later, Luke reports what I think is the most interesting of the appearance stories. On Resurrection Sunday, two followers of Jesus were walking away from Jerusalem to a village called Emmaus, and Jesus suddenly began to walk along side them. They were discussing Jesus' death and the story of the empty tomb. Jesus conversed with them for quite some time, and yet they did not recognize him. As they approached the village, they invited Jesus to share a meal with them, which he accepted. Then, as Luke tells the story: "When he was at the table with them, he took bread, blessed and broke it, and gave it to them. Then their eyes were opened, and they recognized him;

and he vanished from their sight." There are two important features of this story. First is the fact that Jesus was not immediately recognized by these disciples, even though he walked with them and spoke with them at length. Second is the setting during which they finally *do* identify Jesus: at a meal, one the great symbols of the kingdom. But just as soon they recognize him, he vanished from their midst.

What are we to make of the stories? Did Jesus *really* appear to his followers or did the gospel writers make that up? What do these resurrection stories really mean? Can we take them as evidence of Jesus' divinity or do they perhaps indicate something else? When return for our final talk on Jesus we'll address these questions and try to wrap these many loose ends.

# How Jesus Became Christ

## Lecture 25

**There is little agreement among the sources as to what occurred and to whom. But that *something* happened seems hard to deny. It is difficult to account for the fervent movement that began to coalesce among Jesus's followers without positing some powerful experience that convinced them that their teacher had been vindicated by God and lived on, in some fashion, despite his death.**

The extraordinary and varied stories of Jesus's empty tomb and his appearances to his disciples that end each of the canonical Gospels invite us to inquire into their historical basis and their significance for those who accepted them as true. The simplest and most plausible explanation of this experience is that some of the disciples saw Jesus or perceived his presence after his death, but the exact nature of these perceptions cannot be determined. Nor can we assume they believed that the selfsame individual who died on Good Friday was *physically* brought back to life the following Sunday morning. The Gospels themselves indicate that the post-Easter Jesus was different from the Jesus they had known as their teacher and mentor.

Whether or not human beings collectively would be raised from the dead at the end of time was a matter of considerable debate during Jesus's time. Neither the Pharisees nor the Sadducees seemed to think that "resurrection" was an individual, historical phenomenon. The fact that the early Christians used the term resurrection suggests they considered what happened to Jesus as an **eschatological**, end-of-days event. Paul called the resurrection of Jesus the "first fruits of those who have died," consistent with the early Christian belief that Jesus would return from heaven shortly. Paul's experience of the post-Easter Jesus—a spiritual encounter, not a physical one—appears to have shaped his theology, which as it spread transformed Jesus of Nazareth into Jesus Christ, the Son of God, and eventually God incarnate.

The substance of the message of the historical Jesus was the coming of God's kingdom and the necessity to live life in light of this new reality. Paul's message, as expressed in his letter to the Romans, was that "Christ died for our sins in accordance with the scriptures, and that he was buried, and that he was raised on the third day in accordance with the scriptures." The messages are not necessarily incompatible, but they are not the same.

The final answers to the questions of Jesus's identity and self-understanding are not now—and may never be—available to us, but we can build a "theory of Jesus."

We know Jesus was a Galilean Jew born of peasant parents in Roman-occupied Palestine near the beginning of the 1st century C.E. He grew into adulthood with a keen sensitivity to the presence of the God of the Jews as well as matters of social justice and human suffering. Jesus found a teacher and role model in John the Baptist, although Jesus's skills and spiritual

After his conversion to Christianity, Paul became the faith's best-known missionary.

acumen probably transcended those of John, and he used those skills to help others see the truth for themselves. Jesus was also a healer, exorcist, and wonder worker. In the most historically reliable accounts, Jesus tends to resist the title Christ, or messiah, but almost certainly thought of himself as *a*—if not *the*—Son of God. Jesus also likely thought of himself as the Son of Man, viewing his own impending death not as a human sacrifice to effect the forgiveness of sins but as preparation to return to earth at the end of time. Jesus died a martyr's death, bearing witness to the failings of the kingdom of man in contrast to the Kingdom of God. Did Jesus think he was God? Almost certainly not. The idea that Jesus was a divine incarnation appeared many decades after his death, probably under the influence of Greek and Roman religious beliefs.

All of this might appear to undermine the central claims of the Christian tradition, but that is not necessarily so. Although there was a predominant expectation among Jews as to what this messiah would be, there was no official definition or job description. Christians had as much right to reinterpret the concept as anyone. Jesus may not have regarded himself as the messiah, yet in the way his followers came to judge his significance, the title was warranted. Jesus may not have thought of himself as God, but his followers may have discovered the divine through him to such a degree that it seemed fitting to call him God's incarnation. ■

## Important Term

**eschatological**: Pertaining to the end of days or the ultimate destiny of humankind.

## Questions to Consider

1. Paul's preaching to the Roman world outside of Palestine brought early Christianity into direct contact with Greek and Roman religious culture. From what you may know of Greco-Roman myths and religious practices, how do you think they may have affected the early development of Christianity?

2. This lecture presents an argument that Jesus, just like Confucius and the Buddha, was a man, not a god. If this were true, how would it affect the practice of Christian groups you are familiar with? How much does it matter to the practice of the faith?

# How Jesus Became Christ
## Lecture 25—Transcript

Within three days of his ignominious crucifixion, many of Jesus' closest followers became convinced that he had overcome death. Their conviction was both experienced and interpreted in a variety of ways. In the Gospel of Mark, the empty tomb appears to have been a sign from god that Jesus had transcended the bonds of the grave. But Mark's gospel does not tell us what exactly happened to him, simply that he was no longer in his tomb. Matthew and Luke both report that some of Jesus' disciples saw him in various settings. Matthew says that the women who went to the tomb to prepare his body for burial were the first to see him and that later the 11 remaining apostles saw him on a mountain in the Galilee. Luke indicates that the first persons to see Jesus were not the women or the 11 apostles, but two otherwise unknown followers who walked with him to a village called Emmaus and recognized him only after they began to share a meal with him. Luke also says that shortly afterwards, Jesus appeared to the 11 while they were gathered in Jerusalem, not the Galilee as Matthew tells it. At first, they "thought they were seeing a ghost," to quote Luke, until Jesus invited them to touch him and feel his flesh and bones.

During the entire experience, the apostles felt terror, joy, disbelief, and wonder. Luke ends the story by describing how Jesus was carried up to heaven in an event known in the Christian tradition as the ascension. In John's gospel, Jesus first appeared to Mary Magdalene, who mistook him for the caretaker of the garden where the tomb was located. Later in the day, Jesus appeared to the apostles, except for Thomas, who was not among them. A week later, Thomas saw Jesus and actually touched him, dispelling the skepticism that had earned him the title "Doubting Thomas." John continues to describe several other occasions on which Jesus' followers saw and interacted with him.

These extraordinary stories of Jesus' empty tomb and appearances to his disciples invite us to inquire into their historical basis and their significance for those who accepted them as true. Let us begin with the question of history. What really happened in the days after Jesus' death?

As our overview of the gospel accounts suggests, there is little agreement among the sources as to what occurred and to whom. But that *something* happened seems hard to deny. It is difficult to account for the fervent movement that began to coalesce among Jesus' followers without positing some powerful experience that convinced them that their teacher had been vindicated by god and lived on, in some fashion, despite his death. In my view, the simplest and most plausible explanation of this experience is that some of the disciples—perhaps individually, perhaps collectively—saw Jesus or perceived his presence after his death. The exact nature of these perceptions—whether dreams, visions, audible voices, mass hallucinations or some other phenomenon—cannot be determined. But I see no reason to deny that the crucified Jesus was seen, heard, and even felt by several of his closest companions after his entombment. Experiences of this sort, while not completely understood scientifically, are widely attested both in history and our own era. In Hinduism, for instance, sightings of the god Krishna are relatively commonplace, as are visions of the Virgin Mary in Roman Catholicism. There is no good reason to dismiss such reports as merely pathological or pure fabrications. Such experiences are often had by individuals who are no more neurotic than the average person. Therefore, I am quite comfortable affirming that the stories of Jesus' resurrection appearances are rooted in actual historical events—namely, the disciples' experiences of him following his crucifixion.

That does not mean, however, that I would be willing to affirm that the selfsame individual who died on Good Friday was brought back to life the following Sunday morning and then visited with his disciples until he was taken up into heaven. The gospels themselves indicate that the post-Easter Jesus was different from the Jesus they had known as their teacher and mentor. In several accounts of his appearances, Jesus was not immediately recognized, indicating that the experience was not a simple resuscitation of a dead individual. Jesus was perceived as somehow transformed in a profound way. Yet at the same time, what they saw and heard was sufficiently familiar for the disciples to identify him as *Jesus* and not an angel or someone else. The apostle Paul, writing before the gospels were written, called the resurrected form a "spiritual body" and distinguished it from a "flesh-and-blood" body. The idea of a spiritual body is almost oxymoronic, and it is not immediately evident what Paul intended by it. But it is clear that this concept was distinct from the traditional Greek view of the immortality of the soul. The early Christians believed that resurrection entailed a raised body, but a body that had been transformed in some substantial manner. It was no longer the identical body that belonged to the individual prior to death.

However we might understand what "really" happened on Easter Sunday, it is significant that Jesus' followers referred to the event as a "resurrection." Whether or not there was such a reality as resurrection was a matter of considerable debate during Jesus' time. The Pharisees and Sadducees argued about it. The issue at stake was whether human beings collectively would be raised from the dead *at the end of time*. Neither the Pharisees nor the Sadducees seemed to think that "resurrection" was an *individual* person brought back to life during the normal routine of history. The general resurrection of humanity at Judgment Day would have been the predominant understanding of the concept in Jesus' time. The fact that the early Christians used the term resurrection suggests that they considered what happened to Jesus as an eschatological event, that is to say, as an occurrence associated with the end of days. The apostle Paul seems to have construed Jesus' post-Easter appearances in just this manner. He called the resurrection of Jesus the "first fruits of those who have died," indicating that god's raising of Jesus was the inauguration of events that would culminate in the resurrection of all the dead and the final establishment of the kingdom of god. Paul's view was consistent with the early Christian belief that Jesus would return from heaven shortly and that god's reign would bring an end to all suffering and want and destroy humanity's ultimate enemy, death itself. As Paul writes in his first letter to the Corinthians:

> What I am saying, brothers and sisters, is this: flesh and blood cannot inherit the kingdom of God, nor does the perishable inherit the imperishable. Listen, I will tell you a mystery! We will not all die [before the kingdom comes], but we will all be changed, in a moment, in the twinkling of an eye, at the last trumpet. For the trumpet will sound, and the dead will be raised imperishable, and we will be changed. For this perishable body must put on imperishability, and this mortal body must put on immortality. When this perishable body puts on imperishability, and this mortal

body puts on immortality, then the saying that is written will be fulfilled:

Death has been swallowed up in victory.'
Where, O death, is your victory?
Where, O death, is your sting?'

The sting of death is sin, and the power of sin is the law. But thanks be to God, who gives us the victory through our Lord Jesus Christ.

The name of Paul signals a new stage in the development of christology. In Paul, we have a person who seems to have regarded Jesus in a way significantly different from the way Jesus thought of himself. Because of the substantial christological shift represented by Paul and because of his decisive influence on the evolution of thinking about Jesus, I have suggested that he is rightly considered the chief founder of Christianity. Paul's own experience of the post-Easter Jesus appears greatly to have shaped his theology. At first a persecutor of the nascent Jesus-movement, according to the Books of Acts, Paul is suddenly blinded by a bright light while traveling on the road to Damascus and hears the voice of Jesus saying:

I have appeared to you ... to appoint you to serve and testify to the things in which you have seen me and to those in which I will appear to you. I will rescue you from your people and from the Gentiles—to whom I am sending you to open their eyes so that they may turn from darkness to light and from the power of Satan to God, so that they may receive forgiveness of sins and a place among those who are sanctified by faith in me.

Although he had never met the pre-Easter Jesus, Paul now believed that he too, like some of Jesus' original followers, had a personal encounter with the resurrected Jesus, probably several years after Easter Sunday. From that moment onward, Paul took as his appointed mission to take the gospel to the Gentiles, the non-Jews. It is largely through Paul's efforts that the Christian movement eventually became overwhelming Gentile.

The gospel that Paul took to the Gentiles was, however, significantly different from the gospel proclaimed by Jesus. Examining the nature of these differences will help us appreciate the developments that transformed Jesus of Nazareth into Jesus Christ, the Son of god, and eventually god incarnate.

The divergence between Jesus and Paul can best seen in their respective proclamations. As we have observed in earlier lectures, the substance of the message of the historical Jesus was the coming of god's kingdom and the necessity to live life in light of this new reality. Paul's gospel was expressed differently:

> For I handed on to you as of first importance what I in turn had received: that Christ died for our sins in accordance with the scriptures, and that he was buried, and that he was raised on the third day in accordance with the scriptures, and that he appeared to Cephas, then to the 12. Then he appeared to more than five hundred brothers and sisters at one time, most of whom are still alive, though some have died. Then he appeared to James, then to all the apostles. Last of all, as to someone untimely born, he appeared also to me.

Many scholars regard the core of this statement as the oldest part of the New Testament, reflecting perhaps the earliest creedal formulation of Jesus' followers. The key elements of this proclamation were incorporated into later Christian creeds: that Christ died for human sins, was buried, was raised from the dead, and appeared to his followers.

The message has clearly shifted. Whereas the historical Jesus promised a new state of affairs centered in god's reign, Paul declared the forgiveness of sin centered in Jesus, who is now called the Christ. Jesus urged his listeners to amend their ways and live in accord with the new reality being enacted in his words and deeds and coming imminently in its fullness; Paul told his listeners to believe in Christ Jesus to be saved from the wrath of god that would be directed against the ungodly when Jesus returns to earth to establish his kingdom. Paul writes: "if you confess with your lips that Jesus is Lord and believe in your heart that God raised him from the dead, you will be saved." The messages of Jesus and Paul are not necessarily incompatible with one another, but they are *not* the same message.

As we move toward concluding our discussion of Jesus, it is time now to try to provide a concise summing up of his life and teachings and their influence on his immediate followers. In so doing, I want to offer what I will call a "theory" of Jesus. What I mean by theory is exactly the same thing meant by that term in the natural sciences: a coherent explanation to account for a set of phenomena. In this instance, the set of phenomena comprises what we have learned in our analysis of the life of the historical Jesus and the development of interpretations of that life by his earliest followers. The term theory is appropriate, I believe, because the final answers to the questions of Jesus' identity and self-understanding are not now—and may never be— available to us.

Many of the elements of this theoretical explanation of have already been presented in previous lectures, but other aspects have yet to be provided. Thus far, we have seen that Jesus was a Galilean Jew born of peasant parents in Roman-occupied Palestine near the beginning of the 1st century C.E. About the first 30 years of his life we know virtually nothing, except what can be reasonably conjectured based on what we know of others in his social, economic, and cultural situation 2000 years ago and on the way his life eventually unfolded. Jesus grew into adulthood with a keen sensitivity to the presence of the god of the Jews as well as to matters of social justice and human suffering, an abiding concern of the Jewish god, according to many interpreters. Both traits put Jesus within the Jewish prophetic tradition that includes such figures as Jeremiah, Isaiah, and Amos. Both characteristics were probably decisive in leading Jesus to John the Baptist. In John, Jesus found a teacher who shared his passion for god and the possibilities of creating a righteous and wholesome society. John also provided Jesus with the paragon of a meaningful life. John demonstrated great courage in criticizing the immoral behavior of King Herod Antipas, a virtue that led to his imprisonment and eventual execution. It is very likely that John helped shaped Jesus' theology and spirituality and inspired his bravery in confronting the political powers of his day.

But it is also quite probable that Jesus' skills and spiritual acumen transcended those of John. Jesus was more than just John's lieutenant who took over when the Baptist was beheaded. Jesus was apparently an individual of marvelous intellect and imagination whose creativity and wit made him a charismatic teacher. In his parables and aphorisms, we see clear evidence of these traits. Jesus used his creative abilities to craft intriguing stories and sayings designed to stimulate the hearer's own imaginative capacity to envision a better life beyond the present one. In ways like the Buddha, Jesus tried to enable others to see the truth for themselves and break out of habitual patterns of thought. His imaginative and often paradoxical messages are part of what has made Jesus subject to such a wide range of interpretations and why he remains so elusive.

Jesus was also more than just a prophet-figure. Unlike John, he was a healer, exorcist, and wonder-worker. In his presence, people sensed a sacred, restorative power. It is difficult to accept many of the stories of Jesus' "mighty deeds" at face value, such as his raising of Lazarus from the dead or calming a raging storm on the Sea of Galilee. I can only read such accounts as fictions intended to express the extraordinary qualities that Jesus possessed. It is not difficult for me to believe that Jesus *was* an individual with extraordinary qualities, including a deeply compassionate nature that provided many with a sense of wholeness and acceptance.

But what did Jesus think of himself? In an earlier discussion, we examined some of the titles by which he has been known, particularly messiah, Son of God, and Son of Man. We noted that in the most historically reliable accounts, Jesus tends to resist the title Christ, or messiah, and we offered some possible reasons for that reluctance. We also noted that Jesus almost certainly thought of himself as a son of god but whether or not he considered himself *the* son of god was an open question.

My own opinion is that during the course of his public activity, Jesus came to regard himself as the Son of Man who would play a key role in the final act of the inauguration of the kingdom of god. This is the title he used most frequently to refer to himself in the earliest gospel, and it is almost assuredly authentic to the historical Jesus. The hypothesis that Jesus thought of himself as or becoming the Son of Man provides a compelling explanation of his decision to leave Galilee to teach his subversive message in Jerusalem at a highly volatile moment. Jesus probably knew full well that his presence in Jerusalem during Passover would eventuate in his execution, but also I think he believed that his death would be necessary to initiate the complete manifestation of the kingdom. It is quite possible that Jesus viewed his impending death not as a human sacrifice to effect the forgiveness of sins, as Paul and other Christians would later regard it, but as a vital part of his task as the Son of Man. According to the prophecies, the Son of Man would descend from heaven on clouds to establish god's reign and eliminate evil for good. His death and assumption into heaven, he may have thought, would prepare him to return to earth at the end of time. This belief may have contributed to the disciples' widely held expectation that his return was imminent. There is also an important sense in which Jesus' execution in Jerusalem made a bold statement about the nature of god's kingdom. Like other non-violent resisters, Jesus willingly allowed himself to suffer humiliation and death at the hands of Rome and its collaborators to dramatize graphically the oppressive nature of their rule. Throughout his teaching career, Jesus made a point of illustrating by his deeds the destructiveness of human neglect of justice and mercy as well as the possibilities of life when lived in accord with the will of god. Jesus died a martyr's death, bearing witness to the failings of the kingdom of man. I think Jesus considered his crucifixion his final statement to the world before what he thought would be his glorious return as the Son of Man.

Did Jesus *think* of himself as the Christ? Probably not. The concept of the messiah was simply too laden with militaristic and violent overtones for the historical Jesus to embrace that idea as referring to himself. The idea of the messiah, as generally understood at the time, was not consistent with Jesus' ideals and comportment. If he did think of himself as the Christ, it was in very different terms than what most Jews were expecting. Yet regardless of whether Jesus considered himself the Christ, it is quite clear that his followers *did* and that they chose this title as their principal way to refer to him. It is equally clear that the disciples understood this title to mean something other than the standard interpretation. Exactly what they intended when they called Jesus the Christ, however, is not completely evident. Perhaps they were suggesting that the true path to Israel's restoration lay in the way of the cross, the willingness to resist evil in a non-violent manner. But it is not all together obvious why his followers would use a title that Jesus did not seem to accept outright and that was commonly understood as symbolizing a way to freedom that Jesus forthrightly rejected.

Did Jesus think he was god? I think the answer to that question is almost certainly no. Even if he had considered himself to be the *son* of god or the messiah, those titles would not necessarily have amounted to a claim of divine incarnation. The Romans were comfortable with the idea of that a god could assume human form, but that notion is essentially alien to Judaism. The historically reliable gospels never portray Jesus claiming to be god, and as a devout Jew it is hard to imagine that Jesus ever thought of himself that way. The idea that Jesus was a divine incarnation is a christological development that appears many decades after Jesus' death, long after the Christian movement had gained a foothold in other parts of the Roman world. It is probable that his followers began to think of Jesus as a divine incarnation only under the influence of Greek and Roman religious beliefs.

It might appear that if Jesus never thought of himself as the messiah or as god the central claims of the Christian tradition are undermined. But as I indicated earlier, I do not see that that necessarily must be the case. The messiah was a concept generated within ancient Judaism. Although there was a predominant expectation among Jews as to what this messiah would be, there was no official definition or job description. Christians had as much right to reinterpret the concept and declare Jesus the Christ as others had to declare their favorites the messiah or to deny Jesus' Christhood because he did not fulfill the common hope for what the messiah would do. By posthumously declaring Jesus as the Christ, the disciples were acting in the same manner as when the church declares an individual a saint. Such a person might not think of him or herself as a saint while he or she is living; he or she might deny such a label altogether. Yet, in the judgment of others, the title saint is appropriate, perhaps even necessary. In the same manner, Jesus may not have regarded himself as the messiah, yet in the way his followers came to judge his significance, the title was warranted.

A similar consideration obtains when we evaluate the Christian assertion of Jesus' divinity. Jesus may not have thought of himself as god, but his followers may have discovered the divine through him to such a degree that it seemed fitting to them to call him god's incarnation. But that claim of divinity need not imply that Jesus was omniscient or omnipotent. It need not imply that Jesus was incapable of making mistakes, such as miscalculating the timing of god's kingdom. He was, after all, a human being and Christianity expressly affirms that, although it has sometimes had a hard time taking its own affirmation seriously. In such instances, Christianity has allowed preconceptions of what god is determine how it understood who Jesus was, when in fact the tradition indicates that the process ought to move in the opposite manner: It is *Jesus* who reveals the true nature of god.

In making these statements, I am neither affirming nor denying the traditional Christian assertions about Jesus. I am only suggesting that what we know about the historical Jesus need not threaten those claims outright. History can neither prove nor disprove those claims. Affirming or denying Christianity's declarations about Jesus must be made on other grounds.

The stories of Jesus leave us in this rich, ambiguous territory. Like one of his parables, the meaning of the life of Jesus is hard to pin down. The significance of Jesus is elusive and subject to multiple interpretations. Perhaps Jesus' life is itself a parable, a story told to stimulate our imaginations, to envision new possibilities, to break our patterned ways of thinking of our existence and the ultimate reality.

In out next lecture, we begin our study of Muhammad, a prophet like Jesus, but one who was never subject to claims about his divinity and yet one whom Islam considers even greater than Jesus.

# Arabia in the Days of Ignorance
## Lecture 26

> Although al-Lah was still recognized as the god supreme, he had now become one of many. Only a small remnant of monotheists, called the hanifs, remained faithful to Abraham's religion and worshiped al-Lah alone. Muslims refer to this age of polytheism and religious iconography as al-Jāhiliyyah—the days of ignorance.

Like Jews and Christians, Muslims trace their spiritual lineage to the great patriarch Abraham, or Ibrāhīm. According to Islam, Ibrāhīm was not a Jew but a devoted worshiper of the one true god, **al-Lah**. He and his son Ishmael, or Ismā'īl, established the **Ka'ba**—the House of God—in the city of Bacca, later called **Makkah**. But gradually, the Ka'ba became the home of the Arabian pantheon, housing the physical representations of over 300 local deities. Only the **hanifs** remained faithful to Ibrāhīm's religion and worshiped al-Lah alone. It was during this period—called **al-Jāhiliyyah**, or the days of ignorance—that the Prophet Muhammad was born.

Outside of Muslim sources, not a great deal is known about Arabia prior to the 7th century C.E. The sources are restricted to a handful of artifacts and written material from Egypt, Persia, Greece, and the Roman Empire. Pre-Islamic Arabia was an oral culture; the Qur'an was essentially the only written Arabic work of any significance. Recollections of the pre-Islamic period were put in writing after Islam's ascendancy and thus reflect a Muslim perspective.

Life in ancient Arabia was so hard that the great empires of the region had no ambition to conquer it. Its reputation as an uncivilized territory was shaped by its social structure and culture, comprising large, autonomous tribes and smaller subgroups of clans. There was no central authority or government. The scarcity of goods fostered sharp competition and outright hostility; the tribes were at constant war with one another. Ethical and religious culture centered on the supreme importance of the tribe, and a deeply ingrained custom of tribal vendetta prevented any possibility of unification.

The tribal ethic also included a number of virtues, particularly hospitality, generosity, and promise keeping. Tribal survival depended deeply on the virtue of *murūwah*, commonly translated as "manliness" but meaning to have courage, resilience, a willingness to avenge a wrong against the group, and a readiness to defend the weak and oppose the powerful.

Muslims remember al-Jāhiliyyah as an age of depravity, particularly racism and ethnic bigotry, usury, female infanticide, and sexual licentiousness. But these moral shortcomings, according to traditional Islamic interpretation, were merely symptomatic of a deeper problem—the worship of false gods.

The precise history of the Ka'ba prior to the advent of Islam is not known. In the 6th century C.E., it was the focal point of Arabian religion. Images of the gods were kept in the inner sanctum, and the exterior may have been covered in symbols of demons, angels, and jinn (or genies). It was a center for pilgrimage, and so Makkah was not only the religious center of Arabia but its commercial center as well. This custom of pilgrimage, known as the Hajj, was retained by Islam.

**Moral shortcomings, according to traditional Islamic interpretation, were merely symptomatic of a deeper problem—the worship of false gods.**

Like the religious culture of Confucius's China, pre-Islamic Arabian religion was decidedly this-worldly. Like other ancient religions that are loosely described as pagan, it had no creed, scripture, or defined practices. It had no developed priesthood or hierarchy, although *kahins* functioned as priests at local shrines, performing sacrifices and offering prayers. They were able to fall into ecstatic trances and reveal divine communications through poems of rhyming couplets. They came from every social and economic stratum in Arabia, and included some women as well as men.

Any description of the religious landscape of ancient Arabia would be incomplete without mention of Judaism and Christianity. By the time of Muhammad, the Jews had been almost completely assimilated into the culture of pre-Islamic Arabia. Their religious practices were loosely based on traditional Jewish beliefs and customs, but they also participated in aspects of the popular religion of the Arab pagans, such as the use of magic, charms, and divination. There were also some Arab tribes that practiced Christianity, such as the Nestorians (now known as the Assyrian Church of the East) and the Syrian Orthodox. Muhammad felt a great affinity for the Jews and Christians of ancient Arabia because he considered al-Lah the same god described in the Jewish and Christian scriptures. According to Qur'anic tradition, Muhammad was a hanif and never followed contemporary polytheistic practices. He preferred instead to retreat to the hills for periods of quiet contemplation and prayer, apart from the din and clamor of the world below. It was on one of these retreats that he received a message from al-Lah that would profoundly change his life and forever alter the course of human history. ■

## Important Terms

**al-Jāhiliyyah**: Literally, "the days of ignorance"; the Muslim term for the period that began when the Arabs turned away from the religion of Abraham toward polytheism and ended with the founding of Islam.

**al-Lah**: Also spelled Allah; the name of the single god of Islam. According to Muslim tradition, this is the same being as the Judeo-Christian Yahweh/Jehovah.

**hanif**: A pre-Islamic Arabian monotheist; according to tradition, the Prophet Muhammad was raised in this faith.

**Ka'ba**: Literally, "the House of God"; the shrine at the center of the Great Mosque of Makkah, the holiest site in the Muslim faith. It dates to pre-Islamic times, when it was used to worship over 300 different gods or godlike beings, including Jesus Christ and the Virgin Mary.

*kahin*: A poet-priest (or priestess) and oracle of pre-Islamic Arabian religion.

**Makkah**: Also spelled Mecca; the birthplace of the Prophet Muhammad and the holiest city in Islam.

***murūwah***: Often translated as "manliness"; the Arabic cultural virtue encompassing courage, resilience, a willingness to avenge wrongdoing, and defense of the weak.

## Question to Consider

1. Like many of the texts we have discussed so far, our sources for pre-Islamic Arabic religion were written long after the decline of its practices. How would you expect this to affect the accuracy of our information? What can we really know about this world?

# Arabia in the Days of Ignorance
## Lecture 26—Transcript

Like Jews and Christians, Muslims trace their spiritual lineage to the great patriarch Abraham. According to traditional Islamic belief, Abraham was neither a Jew nor a Christian but simply a devoted worshiper of the one true god, known in the Arabic language as al-Lah. The Qur'an relates that Abraham and his son Ishmael established the Ka'ba—the House of God—in the city of Bacca and brought to Arabia the pure monotheistic faith. As the centuries passed, Bacca, which was later called Makkah, became a center of pilgrimage for the many Arabs who embraced the religion of Abraham. But gradually, Arabia lapsed into a dark age of religious bewilderment and moral confusion. Enchanted by allure of tribal gods and goddesses, all but a few Arabs abandoned the ancient monotheism of Abraham and Ishmael. Eventually, the Ka'ba became the home of the Arabian pantheon, housing the physical representations of over 300 local deities. Although al-Lah was still recognized as the god supreme, he had now become one of many. Only a small remnant of monotheists called the hanifs remained faithful to Abraham's religion and worshiped al-Lah alone.

Muslims refer to this age of polytheism and religious iconography as *al-Jāhiliyyah*, the days of ignorance. It was during this era that the Prophet Muhammad was born. But by the time of his death in 632 C.E., the age of religious bewilderment had been drawn to a close, and the faith of Abraham had been restored to the Arabian Peninsula. Our study of Muhammad thus begins with an examination of the *Jāhiliyyah*, his immediate cultural context and the world in which Islam was proclaimed.

Apart from Muslim sources, not a great deal is known about Arabia prior to the 7th century C.E. when Islam was established, or re-established, as the tradition would have it. The sources available to the historian for understanding this period are restricted to artifacts gathered in a few modern archaeological excavations and to written material from Egypt, Persia, Greece, and the Roman Empire. Arabic literature written before the Islamic era is quite meager, limited to a small number of inscriptions from the area of Yemen and a handful of poems found inside the Ka'ba. Pre-Islamic

Arabia was a decidedly oral culture. The Qur'an was essentially the first work written in Arabic of any significance. Recollections of the pre-Islamic period were put in writing after Islam's ascendancy and thus reflect Muslim perspectives on the state of affairs in Arabia prior to Muhammad.

Although the Arabian Peninsula is considered a rich land today, due to its vast oil and gas reserves, the contemporary sources from the ancient world tell us that it was regarded by other nations as a desolate wasteland—and with good reason. The land was mostly arid desert and very difficult to cultivate for food. Starvation and malnutrition were constant threats to the well-being of its inhabitants, particularly for the nomads who lived in the peninsula's interior caring for their livestock. The sedentary agriculturalists who lived near springs and oases fared only somewhat better than their nomadic cousins. Lacking adequate resources, the Arabs depended heavily on trade, bartering what few items the region was able to produce—dates, wheat, and resins for incense and perfume—in exchange for other necessities of living. Life in ancient Arabia was so hard that the great empires of the region, Persia and Byzantium, had no ambition to conquer it. The land was considered inhospitable and its occupants wild barbarians. For the most part, the world simply ignored Arabia.

Its reputation as an uncivilized territory was shaped by its social structure and the culture it produced. Arab society comprised large, autonomous tribes and smaller subgroups of clans based on kinship. These collectives were extremely close-knit, and loyalty to one's kinship group was essential to the individual's well-being. In the harsh environment of Arabia, the individual would easily perish without the protection of the larger group. There was no central authority or government enforcing a common law to regulate tribal or intertribal affairs. Each group was responsible for caring for its own and promoting its own welfare. The tribal chief ensured the equitable distribution of the sparse resources to care for the weaker members.

The scarcity of goods for life fostered sharp competition and outright hostilities among the tribal groups. The tribes, in fact, were at constant war with one another. Raiding caravans or the settlements of other tribes was a common practice and, in the words of one scholar, a "national sport." Stealing from social groups other than one's own was not regarded as immoral or wrong; theft was only unethical when it was committed against a member of one's own group. Because of the intense rivalries, tribes would often create alliances with other tribes for mutual protection. Such covenants were frequently secured by marriages between members of the allied groups. Nonetheless, social associations were in constant flux; alliances between clans and tribes were like the shifting sands of the Arabian Desert.

The structure of Arabian society and the absence of a central governing authority stimulated the development of a unique ethical and religious culture based on the supreme importance of the tribe. Without pan-Arabian kings or councils, each tribe was left to enforce its sense of justice. Crimes committed against the tribe were requited by the tribe, a practice known as blood vengeance. If a tribe were to suffer the slaying of one of its members, for example, it would in turn kill a member of the killer's tribe. It was not necessary to exact justice on the actual killer. To satisfy the demands of blood vengeance, a tribe need only kill a *member* of the killer's tribe. Failure to avenge an injury would weaken the image of a tribe and render it vulnerable to future attacks by other tribes. This deeply engrained custom of tribal vendetta made the cycle of violence vicious and prevented the social groups from uniting and working together to solve their mutual problems.

The tribal ethic also included a number of important virtues that individuals were expected to uphold. Among the most important of these were hospitality and generosity. The poems of this era frequently extolled the noble merits of taking care of one's guests. Some stories tell of magnanimous hosts who sacrificed their own well-being to provide for a guest, even a stranger. The best hosts always ensured that their visitors were given plenty of food and beverage, especially wine. In Arabic, one of the words for "grapes" and one for "generosity" are derived from the same root and pronounced and spelled almost identically.

Although Islam did not continue the ancient custom of lavish drinking, it did retain the great virtues of generosity and hospitality. Promise-keeping was another. Abiding by one's promises and covenants was closely associated with one's sense of self-worth and integrity. Failure to keep one's promises was to incur a deep sense of shame and dishonor. Legends relate how certain individuals would sooner accept the death of their children or the destruction of their households than break a covenant. Finally, tribal survival depended deeply on the virtue of *murūwah*, which is commonly translated as "manliness." In pre-Islamic Arabia, *murūwah* specifically meant courage in fighting adversaries, endurance in bearing adversity, a willingness to avenge a wrong committed against the social group, and the readiness to defend the weak and oppose the powerful. These ethical ideals seem to have significantly informed the development of Islamic morality. Some Muslim commentators have even suggested that the prevalence of these virtues was a chief factor in al-Lah's selection of the Arabs as the people to whom he entrusted his final revelation.

Be that as it may, Muslims also remember the days of ignorance as an age of depravity, a time in which Arabs lacked the moral compass of the one true god. During this period, say the Muslim interpreters, the worship of local gods and goddesses led the Arabs into an ethical morass that Islam was later compelled to repudiate. Among the prevailing sins of *al-Jāhiliyyah*, Muslims include racism and ethnic bigotry, as reflected in the tribal structure of society, the practice of usury, or charging exorbitant interest rates on loans, female infanticide, and sexual licentiousness. Concerning the charge of sexual immorality, we know very little about practices of the pre-Islamic culture that Muslims later found objectionable.

In the Qur'an, al-Lah commands the wives of the Prophet: "And make not a wanton display like the lewd displays of the times of ignorance" In this instance, Muhammad's wives were counseled to dress modestly, which suggests that part of what was judged as sexual immorality was provocative clothing. It is instructive to observe that some Muslims in the modern age have begun to refer to the lifestyles of the western world as *Jāhiliyyah*. This new usage of the concept illustrates that the days of ignorance represent more than just a bygone era for Islam; it can also be regarded as a psychological or cultural state of godlessness and decadence. This understanding yields insight into the disposition of many Muslims towards the west, which some regard as racially and ethnically biased, obsessed with money and the material world, and sexually permissive, precisely the grievances against the Arabs in the original time of ignorance.

But these moral shortcomings, according to traditional Islamic interpretation, were merely symptomatic of a deeper problem inherent in the *Jāhiliyyah*— the worship of false gods. According to tradition, as we noted earlier, the days of ignorance commenced when the Arabs began to forsake the exclusive worship of al-Lah and started to devote themselves to local, tribal deities. Although these Arab "pagans," as they are usually called, never denied the existence of al-Lah, they apparently found him increasingly remote and ultimately irrelevant to their daily concerns; so they turned to the gods they found more accessible.

In the days of ignorance, al-Lah was understood to be the creator and supreme deity. He was a powerful god to invoke when swearing an oath, but never a god to trouble for ordinary matters. Only in times of great peril would he be called upon for help. On most other occasions, it was more expedient to turn to his underlings, the lesser gods and goddesses of the pantheon. Perhaps the most important of these subordinate divinities were the three goddesses known as the "daughters of al-Lah." They were al-Lāt, or simply "the goddess"; al-Uzza, whose name means "the mighty" and who was probably a manifestation of the Egyptian goddess Isis; and Manāt, the goddess of fate. These goddesses had no mythologies, so it is unclear why they came to be regarded as al-Lah's daughters. Each of these deities had her image inside the Ka'ba as well as her own shrine in the vicinity of Makkah. They functioned as mediators with al-Lah and were very powerful in their own right. It was to these goddesses that the Arabs prayed when they needed rain, when they were sick, and when they were about to engage in battle or embark on a dangerous journey.

In addition to the daughters of al-Lah, the interior of the Ka'ba bore witness to a host of other pre-Islamic deities, many of them adopted from cultures surrounding Arabia. Among them were Hubal, the god of the moon who was probably introduced to Arabia from Mesopotamia and who was a favorite of the Quraysh, the tribe into which Muhammad was born and the custodians of the Ka'ba. Even the images of Jesus and his mother Mary were enshrined there. Tradition suggests that, in all, there were 360 divine images housed in the Ka'ba, representing all of the gods of the peninsula. Because of its correspondence to the days of the year according to some reckoning systems then in use, that number almost certainly had astrological significance for the ancient Arabs. Many of the gods kept there were in fact associated with various planets and astral bodies. Although al-Lah was widely regarded as the creator and highest god, he was not represented by a physical image in the Ka'ba, and Islam fervently maintains this iconoclastic stance.

Besides the various gods and goddesses, the spirit world comprised innumerable demons, angels, nature spirits, ancestors, and a class of beings called the jinn. The jinn, or "genies" as they are better known in the West, were spiritual creatures made of smokeless fire who were believed to possess free will and thus able to perform good or evil deeds. They were also intelligent creatures, although less intelligent than humans, and very powerful. Because of their capacity to do evil and lead humans astray, the jinn were often feared by the Arabs, who made a point of avoiding their desert haunts.

In the 6th century C.E., during which the Prophet Muhammad was born, the focal point of Arabian religion was the Ka'ba. In those days, the Ka'ba was a simple cubic structure made of granite stones and mud and sunk into the sand. Its four walls were probably much lower than they are now. At its base, there were two small doors, which allowed entry into the inner sanctum where the images were kept. Some sources indicate that the exterior of the Ka'ba was covered in symbols representing the myriad demons, angels, and jinn that were prominent inhabitants of the spirit world.

Long before the time of Muhammad, the Ka'ba had been a center for pilgrimage. Each year during the Arabian holy months, all tribal warfare was temporarily halted and pilgrims from all over the peninsula came to Makkah to worship their deities and pray for health and prosperity. During these holidays, Makkah swelled with visitors, and great bazaars and fairs sprang up in the area surrounding the sacred precincts. Makkah was not only the religious center of Arabia but its commercial center as well.

At the Ka'ba, the Arabs conducted their sacred rituals, which included the recitation of poetry, dancing, offerings, and a practice whose origins are obscure—circumambulating the Ka'ba seven times. Some scholars have suggested the original intent of this observance may have been to imitate the motion of the heavenly bodies, symbolizing the belief that the Ka'ba was the center point of creation just as the earth was at the center of the universe. This pre-Islamic custom of pilgrimage, known as the *Hajj*, was retained after the Ka'ba was restored to what Islam considered it pristine function, the worship of al-Lah as the only god. The seven circumambulations of the Ka'ba is still the primary ritual of the annual *Hajj*.

The precise history of the Ka'ba prior to the advent of Islam is not known. Some ancient legends say the shrine was constructed by Adam, the first man, and then destroyed by the Great Flood described in both the Bible and the Qur'an. Afterwards, it was rebuilt by Noah and his sons and then forgotten for centuries. The patriarch Abraham discovered its foundations while visiting his son, Ishmael, and Ishmael's mother Hagar, whom Abraham had banished at the behest of his chief wife, Sarah. The book of Genesis describes their expulsion from the Canaan as the result of Sarah's jealousy of Ishmael's firstborn status when her own son, Isaac, was born. Ishmael and Hagar wandered in the wilderness until they came to the region that was later called Makkah. When he visited with them in the Arabian wilderness, Abraham discovered the ancient sanctuary and restored it according to al-Lah's instructions. The Qur'an says:

As Abraham raised the foundations of the shrine, together with [Ishmael] (*they prayed*): "Our Lord, accept this from us. You are the Hearer, the Omniscient. Our Lord, make us submitters to You, and from our descendants let there be a community of submitters to You. Teach us the rites of our religion, and redeem us. You are the Redeemer, Most Merciful. Our Lord, and raise among them a messenger to recite to them Your revelations, teach them the scripture and wisdom, and purify them."

Muslims believe that in the life of the Prophet Muhammad, Abraham and Ishmael's prayer for a messenger to the Arabs had been answered.

Modern history is unable to verify these stories about the origins of the Ka'ba. Because of the lack of literary records from the pre-Islamic period, critical historians cannot state with any certainty who initially built the Ka'ba or even determine how long it has been in existence. There is no doubt, however, that the shrine long antedates Islam and that it has been repaired and rebuilt many times both before and after Muhammad.

Like the religious culture of Confucius' China, pre-Islamic Arabian religion was decidedly this-worldly. The Arabs had no concept of an afterlife or a sense of individual destiny beyond this existence. The tribe, not the individual, was the highest value; immortality meant the endurance of the tribe. Religious concerns of the day were much more immediate: Which god will make it rain or bring us to water? Who can be relied upon to protect us from our enemies among the other tribes? What deity can cure our afflictions?

Ancient Arabian religion hardly constituted an orderly system of beliefs and practices. Like other ancient religions that are loosely described as "pagan," it had no creed or scripture or a uniformly defined forms of practice. It also had no developed priesthood or hierarchy. There were, however, individuals known as *kahins* who functioned as priests at local shrines. The *kahins* performed sacrifices and offered prayers, as priests do, but they also functioned as soothsayers and oracles. They were able to fall into ecstatic trances and reveal divine communications through poems of rhyming couplets. The *kahins* did not communicate directly with the gods but gained accessed to them through the jinn and other spirits.

These poet-priests came from every social and economic stratum in Arabia, and included some women as well as men. Through their ecstatic trances, the *kahins* interpreted dreams, found lost animals, foretold the future, and settled arguments. Many Arabs believed that the *kahins'* clothing, hair, and saliva contained a potent curative power, and hence they were sought out for their healing skills. The *kahins* also provided protection against the dreaded evil eye. The concept of the evil eye was—and still is—a widespread belief throughout the Middle East, the Mediterranean region, Africa, and South Asia. Those who fear the evil eye believe that the envious looks from certain persons can have detrimental consequences for the person he or she envies. The Qur'an tells its listeners to "take refuge" from "the ill of the envious when he envies." Various cultures have devised assorted ways of warding off the evil eye. The *kahins* probably used amulets and spells to neutralize the effects of the evil eye. Although the Qur'an recognizes the phenomenon,

Muslims are forbidden to use such charms and are advised to call upon al-Lah to avert the effects of the evil eye.

Any description of the religious landscape of ancient Arabia would be incomplete without mention of Judaism and Christianity, both of which played important roles in the early history of Islam. Some scholars trace the Jewish presence in the peninsula to the Babylonian Exile in the 6th century B.C.E., the beginning of the Jewish diaspora. It is likely that were also other, and probably more significant, migrations after the Roman destruction of Jerusalem in 70 C.E. and the Bar Kokhba rebellion in the 2nd century C.E. By the time of Muhammad, the Jews had been almost completely assimilated into the culture of pre-Islamic Arabia. Throughout the peninsula, there were Jewish traders and nomads, Jewish agriculturalists and warriors. They adopted Arab names and Arab dress and spoke Arabic as their primary language. The religion they practiced was loosely based on traditional Jewish beliefs and customs, but they also participated in aspects of the popular religion of the Arab pagans, such as the use of magic, charms, and divination. There was even a Jewish counterpart to the Arabian *kahins* known as the *kohens*, who also functioned as priests and soothsayers. The words *kohen* and *kahin* are obviously related. *Kōhēn* is the Hebrew word for priest and the basis for the popular Jewish surname, Cohen.

There were also some Arab tribes that practiced Christianity. In the Hijaz, the coastal region bordering the Red Sea, the majority of Christians were of the Nestorian sect, now known as the Assyrian Church of the East. The Nestorians believed that Jesus Christ existed as two separate persons, the man Jesus and the divine Son of God rather than as divine and human natures in one person. That may seem to be theological hair-splitting, but it was enough to get the Nestorians condemned as heretics by the Roman Catholic Church. In Yemen, on the southern side of the peninsula, the Christians were Syrian Orthodox. In the 6th century C.E., shortly before the birth of Muhammad, Christianity in the region of Najran in southwestern Arabia was prominent enough to have a bishop, monks, nuns, and priests, and, interestingly, it was ruled by a Jewish king.

Muhammad felt a great affinity for the Jews and Christians of ancient Arabia because of their devotion to al-Lah, whom he thought of as the same god described in the Tanakh and the New Testament. Both Arab Jews and Christians referred to their god as al-Lah, which simply means "the god." According to Qur'anic tradition, Muhammad was a *hanif*, a member of the remnant still devoted to the faith in one god established by Abraham and Ishmael. Thus the tradition asserts that throughout his life Muhammad never followed his contemporaries in their polytheistic practices and their infatuation with divine images. He preferred instead to retreat to the hills for periods of quiet contemplation and prayer, apart from din and clamor of the world below. It was on one of these retreats that he received a message from al-Lah that would profoundly change his life and forever alter the course of human history.

# The Trustworthy One
## Lecture 27

**The stories of Muhammad's birth and early life, like those of Confucius, the Buddha, and Jesus, portend his future greatness. ... They are told not to set forth historical information but to create a portrait of the individual who most embodies the spirit of Islam and whose very life offers to Muslims an unparalleled example of faith.**

Most stories of Muhammad's life cannot be verified according to the standards of modern history, but there is sufficient material for constructing a reasonable account of him. Although he is mentioned by name only four times in the **Qur'an**, the scripture offers insight into Muhammad's life and the issues with which he struggled as the Islamic community, or *ummah*, evolved. Of immense importance to the faith, but of less value for historical purposes, are the **Hadith**, quotations and vignettes of his life from the oral tradition, written down over a century after his death.

Because the Islamic calendar is lunar, it is hard to pinpoint the day and month of Muhammad's birth on the modern Western calendar, but the year is traditionally reckoned to 570 C.E. As with our other sages, the biographies of Muhammad ascribe to him a noble lineage. He was born in Makkah into the Banu Hashim clan, which was part of Arabia's leading tribe, the Quraysh. Although once very powerful, by the time of Muhammad's birth, the clan had fallen on hard times and had begun to lose some of its earlier prestige. Again, as with the others, legends suggest supernatural aspects to Muhammad's conception, birth, and early childhood. He lost his father before his birth, his mother at the age of six, and his grandfather at the age of eight; he was raised by his uncle, Abu Talib, and his uncle's wife, Fatimah. Muhammad's childhood acquaintance with poverty, vulnerability, and loss would heighten his sensitivity to the weaker members of society, especially the parentless, the poor, and women. Like Jesus and the Buddha, Muhammad spent long periods alone in nature, often receiving there the revelations that would comprise the Qur'an.

We know virtually nothing about Muhammad's formal education—if any. Islamic tradition insists that Muhammad was unable to read or write but possessed a fine memory and excellent speaking skills. Some Western scholars, however, assert that Muhammad probably had a basic literacy needed in his adult work as a trader.

In adolescence, Muhammad was examined by a Christian hermit named Bahira, who interpreted a growth of skin between the boy's shoulder blades as "the seal of prophethood." Around the year 590 C.E., Muhammad attended an important tribal meeting convened by the forward-thinking tribal chief Abdallah ibn Ja'dan. There Muhammad witnessed the creation of the Alliance of the Virtuous, one of the world's first human rights statements. The virtues of fairness and honesty, perhaps instilled in that tribal meeting, were to guide Muhammad throughout his life. Those who knew him called him the "Trustworthy One."

The Qur'an offers insight into Muhammad's life.

Early in adulthood, Muhammad worked as a shepherd. Later, he became a trader, where his reputation for honesty attracted the attention of a caravan owner and wealthy widow named Khadijah bint Khuwaylid. She hired him to lead her caravans and eventually sought to marry him. They lived together as husband and wife for about 25 years, until her death. Khadijah was Muhammad's confidante and was the first to embrace Islam when he began to receive revelations. According to the Sunni sources, they had six children—four daughters and two sons, both of whom died young. Shi'a sources contend that Khadijah and Muhammad had only one daughter, Fatimah, and that the other three were adopted. All traditions indicate that Muhammad greatly enjoyed family life and found much fulfillment as a husband and a father.

As Muhammad neared middle age, his stature as a devoted family man, an honest merchant, and as individual with sound judgment increased. By the time he was 35, many supposed that he would assume leadership of the Banu Hashim. Then, during a desert excursion for prayer and solitude, Muhammad had an experience that would forcefully thrust his life in a new direction. ■

## Important Terms

**Hadith**: Quotations and vignettes of Muhammad's life written down about a century after his death. Different branches of Islam accept different groups of Hadith as authentic and give different levels of importance to them.

**Qur'an**: The central sacred text of Islam, accepted by all its traditions as the revealed word of al-Lah to Muhammad.

## Question to Consider

1.  We have noted that all four of our sages come from noble lineages, most of them fallen on hard times. Do you think this is coincidental or significant to their lives and works? Do you find it easy to believe, or somewhat suspect?

# The Trustworthy One
## Lecture 27—Transcript

The stories of Muhammad's birth and early life, like those of Confucius, the Buddha, and Jesus, portend his future greatness. Many of these stories, of course, have a legendary quality, telling of events that cannot be confirmed by modern historiography. But their significance concerns beliefs about the Prophet and his role in Islam that transcend mere factual details. They are told not to set forth historical information but to create a portrait of the individual who most embodies the spirit of Islam and whose very life offers to Muslims an unparalleled example of faith.

Although many stories of his life cannot be verified according to the standards of modern history, there is sufficient material for constructing a reasonably sure account of the historical Muhammad. The most reliable source is the Qur'an, the holy book revealed to Muhammad over a period of 23 years. Although he is mentioned by name only four times in this scripture, the Qur'an offers much insight into his life and the issues with which he struggled as the Islamic community, or *ummah*, evolved. Of immense importance to the faith, but of less value for historical purposes, are the *hadith*, the reports about his sayings and vignettes of his life that were kept in oral tradition by his followers and written down over a century after his death. The actual historical value of this source is the subject of considerable debate in the contemporary scholarship on Muhammad. Some researchers claim that the traditions contained within the collections of *hadith* are all inventions of later Muslim writers, in the way most of the *Analects* of Confucius is believed to be the work of later Confucians. Other scholars maintain that many of the *hadith* contain a core of historical material even if many of them are spurious. Within Islam itself, particular collections of *hadith* are asserted to be valid in their entirety and are used as important supplements for understanding the Qur'an.

Nevertheless, Muslims have never accepted all putative *hadith* as historically authentic. Because of the importance of *hadith* in Islam, some less-than-scrupulous individuals have been known to create their own "traditions of the Prophet," such as the self-serving onion seller who amazingly "discovered" a *hadith* that promoted the benefits of buying onions. As a consequence of such abuses, the tradition has insisted that only *hadith* that can be traced back to Muhammad through a trustworthy chain of transmission can be accepted as legitimate. But this safeguard has not been foolproof, since even links to reliable authorities can be and have been counterfeited. There are several major collections of *hadith*, the most important of which, at least for most Muslims, is called *Sahih Bukhari*, which was compiled by Muhammad al-Bukhari in the 9th century. Al-Bukhari whittled down over 300,000 *hadith* to a set of just over 2600 that he regarded as authentic. The Sunnis, members of the largest branch of Islam, consider the nine volumes of the *Sahih Bukhari* to be the most important book next to the Qur'an itself and a principal guide to the life of Muhammad and the practice of the faith.

Historians also depend on the early biographies of the Prophet. Such biographies began to be written relatively early in Islam. There were at least two dozen texts written within three centuries of the Prophet's death that narrate all or part of his life-story. The earliest biography comes from Ibn Ishaq, who composed his *Life of God's Messenger* about a century and a half after Muhammad's death. Ibn Ishaq reputedly relied on oral traditions that went back to the Prophet and his acquaintances. Original copies of Ibn Ishaq's biography no longer exist, but it has been transmitted through history in a version edited by Ibn Hisham in the 9th century. We are unable to know, however, just how accurately Ibn Hisham transmitted the original. And since there are no non-Muslim sources from near the start of Islam that mention Muhammad, there is no external confirmation or disconfirmation of Islamic interpretations of the Prophet's life. As with the study of the other sages we have discussed in our course, scholars are cautious about what facts and interpretations about Muhammad can be authenticated. As I have done with the others, I will indicate the places where the narratives of the Prophet's life seem most firmly rooted in history and where legend seems to have influenced the story.

Ibn Hisham reports that Ibn Ishaq determined that Muhammad came into the world on a Monday evening on the 12th day of the third month of the "year of the elephant." Because the Islamic calendar is based on the rhythms of the moon rather than the sun, it is hard to pinpoint the day and month of his birth on the western solar-based calendar. The "year of the elephant," refers to a time in Arabian history when a ruler from the southern part of the peninsula marched on Makkah with a massive army and a white elephant, intent on destroying the Ka'ba. But the elephant refused to enter the sacred precincts and simply knelt down, as if worshiping at the shrine. Unable to make the elephant move forward, the army was forced to return home unsuccessful. The year of the elephant is traditionally reckoned to correspond to the year 570 C.E. But today, historians generally believe it occurred nearer to 560 C.E. It is probably true that Muhammad was born in or around 570, but in not in the year of the elephant as Ibn Ishaq maintained.

Like the stories about Confucius, the Buddha, and Jesus, the biographies of Muhammad ascribe to him a noble lineage. He was born in Makkah into the Banu Hashim clan, which was part of Arabia's leading tribe, the Quraysh. The Banu Hashim had been a highly respected family, especially among the other Quraysh. Although once very powerful, by the time of Muhammad's birth, the clan had fallen on hard times and had begun to lose some of its earlier prestige.

Again, like Confucius, the Buddha, and Jesus, legends suggest unusual circumstances surrounding Muhammad's conception. There are slightly different versions of the narrative, but the basic story involves Muhammad's father Abdallah, his mother Aminah, and another woman. One telling of the story has Abdallah on his way to consummate his newly arranged marriage with Aminah. En route, he is accosted by the other woman who tries to detour him into her own bed. Since it was his wedding day, after all, Abdallah declined the invitation, but promised to return on his way home the next day. He proceeded to Aminah's house and stayed the night, during which Muhammad was conceived. On his way back to his own home the next morning, he stopped by the residence of the woman who had waylaid him the day before to see if the invitation was still in effect. This time, the woman refused him, saying that earlier there had been a bright light blazing between Abdallah's eyes, but now, it was gone. In some versions, the woman goes on to interpret the light as a sign of the coming of the Last Prophet. When she notices the light has disappeared from Abdallah's face, she realizes that another woman has taken the honor of conceiving the new messenger. The major difference among the variant narratives is the other woman's identity. In one, she is unnamed; in another, she is Abdallah's chief wife; in a third, she is the sister of the one of the prominent *hanifs*, the monotheists of Arabia. Regardless of who she was, the story's purpose is clear: to suggest divine intention in Muhammad's birth, a prominent theme in the accounts of Jesus' birth as well. But notice how strikingly these stories contrast in their views on sexuality!

Muhammad never knew his father and was technically considered an orphan at birth. Abdallah died on a trip to Yathrib—later known as Madinah—when Muhammad's mother Aminah was two months pregnant. Her pregnancy, according to Ibn Ishaq, was accompanied by numerous "strange signs" and the birth was remarkably easy. After seeing a vision that announced the child would be the master of his people, Aminah gave her son the name Muhammad, which means "he who is worthy of praise." Ibn Ishaq claims Muhammad was a very unusual name at the time. In this same vision, Aminah was also instructed to place the infant under the protection of the one god to shield him from the evil eye. His paternal grandfather Abd al-Muttalib was overjoyed at the birth and recalled an oracle from a *kahin* who had told him that one his descendants would rule the world. Immediately, he took the baby to the Ka'ba as an act of gratitude.

As was the custom in Makkah at the time, children were entrusted to Bedouin families who would raise them in the nearby desert, acquainting them with nomadic life, before returning them at a later age to their parents in the city. Desert life, as we have noted in our previous lecture, was difficult and precarious, and this practice was intended to accustom children to facing the rigors of Arabian life. Muhammad stayed with his Bedouin family for four years before he was returned to Aminah. Halimah, his Bedouin foster mother, reported unusual occurrences that led her to believe that Muhammad was a special child. On one occasion, she related how her own son witnessed two men in white laying the four-year-old Muhammad on the ground, splitting open his chest, and removing something from inside it. Muhammad himself confirmed the story. Fearing for his life, Halimah returned the boy to his mother in Makkah. Interestingly, Aminah was not surprised by the story and in fact recounted similar events. Years later, Muhammad says that the men had removed a black clot from his heart in an act of spiritual cleansing.

Muhammad remained with his mother for only two years. When he was six, Aminah died, leaving the child bereft of both parents. His grandfather Abd al-Muttalib, who was now 80, immediately brought his grandson into his own household, but then two years later, Abd al-Muttalib himself died. But before he did, Muhammad's grandfather charged his son Abu Talib— Muhammad's uncle—to continue to raise and care for the boy. Apparently, Abu Talib discharged his responsibilities as a foster father admirably. Muhammad would later reflect fondly on the care he received from the uncle and his wife Fatimah.

These early experiences seem to have decisively shaped Muhammad's outlook on life. His childhood acquaintance with poverty, vulnerability, and loss made him familiar with the tenuous nature of life and in adulthood would heighten his sensitivity to the weaker members of society, especially the parentless, the poor, and women. In one of the shortest chapters of the Qur'an, al-Lah pointedly reminds the Prophet of these childhood experiences and draws a moral that Muhammad took to heart:

Did God not find you an orphan and give you shelter and care? And He found you wandering and gave you guidance. And He found you in need, and made you independent. Therefore, do not treat the orphan with harshness, Nor repulse the one in need; But the bounty of the Lord—rehearse and proclaim!

At a time when children most need to feel the secure presence of the adults in their lives, the young Muhammad had to negotiate a world in which his caretakers were frequently changing. This early experience may have kindled within him a deep longing for a source of constancy beyond his ever-shifting circumstances.

His time among nomads was also an important element in shaping his character. Bedouin culture was steeped in a rich oral tradition, and the members of the nomadic tribes were renowned as poets and master story-tellers. No doubt Muhammad's facility with language was refined by his exposure to this tradition and its bearers. In later life, his mastery of spoken Arabic would be put to use in his struggles to articulate in words the revelations he received, many of which came to him through intense experiences barely on the edge of language.

Desert life seems also to have influenced his relationship with the natural world. Like Jesus and the Buddha, Muhammad spent long periods alone in nature, and it was during these times that he often received the revelations that would comprise the Qur'an. For Muhammad, nature was also a revelation of another sort. He viewed nature as a cipher of the divine. The Qur'an speaks of the created order as rich with the marks of the creator for those perceptive enough to recognize them: "He has made subject to you the Night and the Day; the sun and the moon; and the stars are in subjection by His Command: [truly] in this are Signs for [ones] who are wise."

Nature appears to have taught Muhammad the value of silent contemplation and the observation of objects and events to understand their deeper significance. Later in his young life, Muhammad became a shepherd tending flocks just outside Makkah where his skills of mindfulness and discernment were further cultivated.

Beyond assumptions we might make about his experience with his Bedouin foster family, we know virtually nothing about his formal education—or even if he received a formal education. Islamic tradition insists that Muhammad was unable to read or write but possessed a fine memory and excellent speaking skills. Many Muslims consider this point important to validate the claim that the Qur'an is an authentic revelation and not derived in any way from other sources. Some western scholars, however, question this tradition and assert that Muhammad probably had a basic literacy since he would he need rudimentary skills in reading and writing in his adult work as a trader.

By now, Muhammad was entering adolescence. Two events during this period of his life are often told to foreshadow his call to be the Last Prophet to humanity. At age 12, Muhammad accompanied his uncle Abu Talib on a caravan to Syria. As it approached the ancient town of Busra, about 100 miles south of Damascus, the caravan was observed by a Christian hermit named Bahira, who saw what appeared to be a cloud hovering over the procession and protecting it from the sun. Intrigued, he invited the members of the caravan to stop for a meal, and they accepted. Bahira was inexplicably drawn to the boy Muhammad and took him aside to get to know him better. After asking about his family and his early experiences in life, Bahira asked to see his back. Muhammad complied with the request. Bahira reported that he saw a growth of skin between the boy's shoulder blades, which the monk interpreted as "the seal of prophethood." Like the stories about the physical marks discovered on Prince Siddhattha, this legend suggests that signs of Muhammad's spiritual achievements were inscribed on his very body.

Another account from this stage in Muhammad's life concerns his attendance at the negotiation of an important tribal alliance around the year 590 C.E. As we noted in the previous lecture, the tribal arrangements characteristic of pre-Islamic Arabia were taking their toll on the well-being of Arabian society. Groups appeared locked in a wearisome cycle of intertribal warfare and constantly reconfiguring social alliances. In an effort to curtail the violence and establish some semblance of order, as well as to promote commerce, the chief of one prominent tribe, the forward-thinking Abdallah ibn Ja'dan, summoned all interested parties to meet for the purpose of establishing a covenant of justice that would transcend tribal affiliations. The result of that meeting was an agreement known as the Alliance of the Virtuous. In it, the participating tribes committed themselves to respect universal principles of fairness and to intervene collectively to establish justice in intertribal disputes. The pact was written and placed inside the Ka'ba to signify its sacred status and place it under the protection of the gods. Today, the United Nations considers the Alliance of the Virtuous one of the first human rights statements and one of the antecedents for its own Universal Declaration of Human Rights. The event made a lasting impression on the young Muhammad. In later life, he favorably recalled the agreement not only because he valued its fundamental principles of fairness and equity but also because it acknowledged the possibility a system of ethics that all persons, regardless of ethnic or religious affiliations, could affirm.

The virtues of fairness and honesty were to guide Muhammad throughout his life. As he entered young adulthood, he became widely known for these qualities. Those who knew him called him the "Trustworthy One." A well-known story about this time in his life is often told to illustrate how profoundly he embodied these traits. When he was a young man, the Quraysh, the custodians of the Ka'ba and the tribe to which Muhammad belonged, decided to refurbish the sacred shrine by razing it to the foundations and reconstructing its walls. As the construction was taking place, the time came to reset the holy Black Stone that had formed part of one of the exterior walls. The Black Stone had long been an important feature of the Ka'ba and was believed by many to have fallen from heaven in the days of Adam and Eve. Indeed, scholars today believe the stone is a meteorite. During their circumambulations, pilgrims would stop and kiss the stone, which was placed in the wall about five feet above ground. Legends say the stone was originally a brilliant white but over the years turned black because it absorbed the sins of humanity. When it was time to secure the Black Stone in the newly constructed wall, a dispute arose among the clans as to which would have the honor to put it back in place. The conflict was about to erupt into violence when Muhammad entered the precincts and was asked to settle the quarrel. After listening to the arguments of the clans, he asked for a cloth, put the stone upon it, and invited all the clan chiefs to carry the stone together and lift it in place by holding the edges of the fabric. In this way, the honor of each clan was upheld, and all parties were satisfied.

By now, Muhammad had left his job as a shepherd to work as a trader. His reputation for honesty had attracted the attention of one of the prominent caravan owners in Makkah, a wealthy widow named Khadijah bint Khuwaylid, one of his distant relatives. According to tradition, Khadijah was 40 when, at the recommendation of Abu Talib and others, she hired the 25-year-old Muhammad to lead her caravan to Syria. Although Muhammad had little business experience, his honesty and skill in fair-dealing served him well, and he returned to Makkah with twice the profits Khadijah had expected. Khadijah was so pleased with Muhammad's accomplishment that she asked him to accompany a second caravan to Yemen the following winter.

Over time, Muhammad continued to impress her. Her interests in him became more than simply commercial in nature, and, eventually, she sought to marry him. Marriage was not easy decision for her to make. Khadijah had been married twice, and each time lost her husband during the intertribal wars. Until she met Muhammad, she had no intention of marrying a third time, although she had received proposals from many highly respected men throughout peninsula. That she overcame this reluctance and set aside the offers of more prominent men attests to the great impression Muhammad made on her. She sent a friend as an emissary to Muhammad to see how he felt about marriage in general and Khadijah in particular. Muhammad told the friend that he was too poor to contemplate marriage. When she mentioned Khadijah's name, Muhammad indicated he was very interested, but again, he could not imagine how he could even consider such a relationship given his lowly status. Without telling him that she had been sent by Khadijah herself, the emissary assured Muhammad that she would discreetly act on his behalf. When Khadijah was informed of Muhammad's openness to marriage, she invited him to her home and proposed. And Muhammad accepted. After consulting their uncles about the propriety of the arrangement, the two were married.

They lived together as husband and wife for approximately 25 years until her death. Apparently, their marriage was one of great love and devotion. During his time with Khadijah, Muhammad took no other wife. She became his confidante and was the first to embrace Islam when he began to receive revelations from al-Lah. After her death, he took many other wives, but he always remembered Khadijah with great affection and wistfulness, which occasionally stirred up no small resentment among his newer wives.

Together, according to the Sunni sources, Muhammad and Khadijah had six children, four daughters and two sons. Both sons, however, died early in their lives. Because of the number of children they had, some scholars have questioned whether Khadijah was actually 40 at the time of her marriage to Muhammad, as tradition maintains. Some have suggested that she may have been closer to 30. Sources from the Shi'a branch contend that Khadijah and Muhammad had only one daughter, Fatimah, and that the other three were nieces or orphans whom they adopted. If that were case, then the age of 40 seems less problematic. In any event, there is no doubt that Khadijah was older than the Prophet.

The sources from all traditions indicate that Muhammad greatly enjoyed family life and found much fulfillment as a husband and a father. Not only did he father many children of his own, he also adopted several, including his young cousin Ali, whose father—Muhammad's uncle, Abu Talib—was suffering some financial difficulties. When he was only ten, according to some sources, Ali was the first male to embrace Islam. Later, Ali became Muhammad's son-in-law when he married Fatimah, Muhammad's daughter by Khadijah. Muhammad also adopted a young man named Zayd, whom Khadijah had given to him as a slave. Muhammad gave Zayd his freedom and accepted him as a son.

As Muhammad neared middle-age, his stature as a devoted family man, an honest merchant, and as individual with sound judgment increased. By the time he was 35, many supposed that he would assume leadership of the Banu Hashim. But at the time, Muhammad had little interest in civic affairs. He preferred to spend his time with his family and in occasional retreats into the wilderness surrounding Makkah, where he could enjoy his solitude and pray. But during one of these desert excursions, Muhammad had an experience that would forcefully thrust his life in a new direction and ultimately lead him to the place where evading leadership was no longer an option. That experience will be the starting point of our next discussion.

# "I Am Only a Messenger"
## Lecture 28

"Sometimes it comes to me like the reverberations of a bell, and those are the hardest on me; the reverberations stop when I am aware of their message. And sometimes the Angel takes the form of a man and speaks to me, and I am aware of what he says."
—The Prophet Muhammad, *Sahih Bukhari*, I.3

Muhammad began receiving revelations in the month of Ramadān in the year 610 C.E. during one of his regular retreats to the wilderness for prayer and solitude. Awakened by an overwhelming presence, he heard the command, "Read!" When he responded that he could not read, he felt as if he were being violently squeezed to the point that he could barely breathe. The force subsided, and the process was repeated twice more. Then Muhammad was told: "Read, in the name of your Lord. ... He teaches man what he never knew" (Sura 96:1–5). Muhammad began to repeat the words he heard. Khadijah, who immediately believed his revelations were from God, went to see her cousin Waraqa bin Nawfal, an old and revered Christian, who said Muhammad was being called as a prophet to the Arabs. Muhammad struggled with this idea for a long time and told no one else about the experience.

After a few more revelations, the messages stopped for two years, causing Muhammad great despair. When they began again, al-Lah reassured him: "Soon your guardian Lord will give you what shall make you content" (Sura 93:5). He received more than 100 revelations over the next 20 years. Sometimes the voice was accompanied by a vision of the angel Gabriel, but very often, the revelation came as indistinct and overpowering sensations that required great effort to render into language.

Historically, many scholars from outside Islam have sought a naturalistic explanation for Muhammad's revelations, such as epilepsy, a deep meditative state, or dreaming. None of these natural explanations necessarily means that Muhammad was disingenuous; it is difficult to believe he would have risked his life and his followers' lives for something he knew to be a sham. Nor is it incompatible with a divine origin of the revelations. There is no reason that al-Lah could not use epileptic seizures or the unconscious mind as media through which to communicate.

Others have sought to discredit the revelations by noting their similarity to the principles and precepts of other religions. Indeed, Muhammad never claimed novelty for his message; he insisted the message was ancient, as old as Adam. The novelty was the messenger. God had at last sent a prophet to the Arabs.

> **Muhammad never claimed novelty for his message. To the contrary, he insisted the message was ancient, as old as Adam, humanity's first prophet. The novelty was the messenger.**

Whenever Muhammad received a revelation, he committed the words to memory and recited them to others. Only after his death were they completely transcribed, perhaps as early as 20 or as late as 300 years later. The Qur'an comprises 114 chapters, or **suras**, of over 6,000 verses, arranged from longest to shortest. In Islam, the Qur'an serves the role that Jesus does in Christianity—God's word made manifest. More precisely, it is the words, not the book; the Qur'an is most meaningful in spoken form. Some Muslims use a separate term—**Mushaf**—to designate the printed Qur'an and **al-Qur'an** for the recitation in Arabic.

Initially, the Islam movement was small, limited to Muhammad's closest friends and family. Eventually, Muhammad came to understand that he had been called to be not simply a *nabi*—an ordinary prophet—but a *rasul*—a messenger, the bearer of al-Lah's last revelation to humanity. The *shahadah*, the Muslim profession of faith, says: "I bear witness that there is no god but God and that Muhammad is His Messenger."

As his understanding evolved, and despite the rejection of his message by tribal elders, whose power was threatened by these ideas, Muhammad never departed from the basic message of the earliest revelations: the oneness of al-Lah and the principle of human equality. Gradually, the revelations began to speak of a last day at which the dead would be resurrected and all souls would be judged as individuals by al-Lah. Resurrection was a novel idea to the Arabs, and the idea that one's communal associations would mean nothing on that day was seen as absurd.

Despite the rejection and ridicule he endured from older and more powerful Makkans, Muhammad's movement grew. Some early followers misunderstood the stringency of Muhammad's monotheism. When Muhammad made it clear that Islam precluded the worship of the al-Lat or other goddesses, many renounced the faith. The most powerful members of the Quraysh asked Muhammad's uncle Abu Talib to withdraw his protection of the Prophet, but Abu Talib refused. The clan chiefs then tried to bribe Muhammad to stop preaching, but of course, he also refused. This recalls similar attempts in the lives of the Buddha and Jesus to lure them from their paths.

When those opposing the Prophet were unable to deter *him*, they began to persecute his followers. Finally, a husband and wife were tortured and killed for refusing to renounce their faith, and Islam had its first martyrs. ■

## Important Terms

**al-Qur'an**: The recitation of the Arabic Qur'an text, considered its most meaningful form by the Islamic faithful.

**Mushaf**: The printed Qur'an.

***rasul***: The Arabic word for "messenger"; in the context of Islam, an important prophet.

***shahadah***: The Muslim profession of faith: "I bear witness that there is no god but God and that Muhammad is His Messenger."

**sura**: A verse of the Qur'an.

1. Muhammad is the first of our four sages to show doubt about his own mission, at least at the outset. What, if anything, do you think this says about Muhammad as a person?

2. Jesus and Muhammad, as far our sources indicate, suffered more political persecution than Confucius or the Buddha. Do you think this is because of their different cultures, some difference in their messages, or some other factor?

# "I Am Only a Messenger"
## Lecture 28—Transcript

Muhammad was not certain about what was happening to him when he began to receive the revelations that comprised the Qur'an. According to the traditional account, they started in the month of Ramadān in the year 610 C.E., when Muhammad was 40, during one of his regular retreats to the wilderness for prayer and solitude. He was abruptly awakened from his sleep in a small cave in one of the mountains surrounding Makkah by what seemed to be an overwhelming presence. Then he heard the command, "Read!" When he responded that he could not read, he felt as if he were being violently squeezed to the point that he could barely breathe. When the force bearing down on him subsided, the voice again commanded him to read; again he said he was unable; again, he felt himself being crushed. This exchange was repeated for a third time, after which Muhammad was told:

> Read, in the name of your Lord, who created, created the human from a clot of blood. Read, and your Lord is most generous, who taught the use of the pen. He teaches man what he never knew.

Frightened for his life and not knowing what else to do, Muhammad began to repeat the words he heard. He later reported he thought he was being possessed by a jinni and was becoming a *kahin*, one of the entranced pagan soothsayers. One biographer even suggests that the thought of becoming a *kahin* filled Muhammad with such despair that he attempted to throw himself from the mountaintop but was prevented from doing so by the sight of an angel standing on the horizon. Instinctively, he turned and rushed home to Khadijah. Trembling, he begged her, "Cover me, cover me!" and she wrapped him with a cloak and held him until he regained his composure. After telling her of the experience, Khadijah tried to assure him that he was not possessed. From the very moment she heard his story, Khadijah was confident that the voice he heard spoke words from god.

Shortly after Muhammad's return, Khadijah went to see her cousin Waraqa bin Nawfal, an old and much revered Christian. Some accounts say she went alone and others say Muhammad accompanied her. In any event, when Waraqa was told of the experience, he replied: "This is 'Namus,' the angel entrusted with divine secrets whom al-Lah sent to Moses." Waraqa interpreted the incident as a sign that Muhammad was being called as a prophet to the Arabs. At the Ka'ba, sometime later, Waraqa told Muhammad that he would suffer great hostility from the Makkans, a prediction that in fact came to pass. A prophet, as Jesus said, is never welcome in his own hometown.

Eventually, Muhammad would accept Waraqa's conviction that god had called him to be a prophet. But Muhammad struggled with the idea for a long time before he was able to accept it. Meanwhile, he told no one else about the occurrence on the mountain. He received a few other revelations shortly afterward, but no one knows precisely how many. Then, suddenly, they stopped. It would be about two years before Muhammad heard the voice of the angel again. This was a period of grave self-doubt and even suicidal despair. He interpreted the abrupt absence of revelations as an indication that god had decided he was unworthy to receive the divine message. At last, he heard the voice speak words of reassurance that dispelled his uncertainty:

> By the glorious morning light,
> And by the night when it is calm,
> Your guardian Lord has not forsaken you, nor is he displeased:
> hereafter will be better for you than what has been before.
> Soon your guardian Lord will give you what shall make you
>     content.

Thenceforth, Muhammad had no uncertainties about the source of his revelations or his mission. The revelations continued sporadically over the next 20 years and were usually occasioned by specific situations in his life that required divine insight.

Muhammad had well-over 100 such experiences, although we are unsure of the exact number. The voice did not always speak with the clarity and distinctness of the first revelation that woke him from his sleep. In one of the *hadith*, Muhammad describes the nature of the revelations: "Sometimes," he said, "it comes to me like the reverberations of a bell, and those are the hardest on me; the reverberations stop when I am aware of their message.

And sometimes the Angel takes the form of a man and speaks to me, and I am aware of what he says." The Qur'an identifies this angel as Gabriel. As Muhammad's description indicates, sometimes the aural experiences were accompanied by a visual perception of Gabriel, but very often, the revelation came as indistinct and overpowering sensations that required great effort to render into language. In these cases, the process of articulating the revelation was not unlike the way a poet might struggle to find just the right words to give expression to deep feelings that lie below the surface of consciousness. One of the Qur'anic passages comprising an early revelation admonishes Muhammad to attend carefully to the complete depth of the experience and allow the words to come to expression in their own good time. He was once quoted as saying, "Never once did I receive a revelation without thinking that my soul had been torn away from me." Even today, some Muslims think there is a bit of Muhammad's soul in the Qur'an. Thus, Muhammad occasionally experienced the divine voice as coming from without and occasionally as coming from within. But either way, Muhammad always identified the source of the revelation as a reality beyond his individual self.

Historically, many scholars from outside Islam have felt compelled to provide a naturalistic explanation of Muhammad's revelations. One such theory suggests that Muhammad suffered from epilepsy, which would account for the trance-like states and occasional loss of consciousness he underwent during these moments of inspiration. Other analysts contend that he lapsed into states of greater sensitivity to the contents of his unconscious mind such as occurs during dreaming. Both hypotheses imply that the source of the revelations was none other than his own mind, but neither necessarily means that Muhammad was disingenuous in claiming that the revelations came from outside him. In other words, the argument goes, Muhammad may have genuinely believed the words of revelation were from Gabriel even if they originated in his own mind. Considering the intense opposition he later faced, it is difficult to believe that Muhammad would have been willing to risk his life—and those of others close to him—for the sake of something he knew to be a sham.

A naturalistic explanation for Muhammad's experiences, however, need not be incompatible with the traditional Muslim conviction that al-Lah is the ultimate author of the revelations. There is no reason why al-Lah could not use epileptic seizures or the unconscious mind as media through which to communicate. In "Saint Joan," George Bernard Shaw's play about the life of Joan of Arc, the heroine tries to persuade Robert de Baudricourt to lend her his men so she might raise a siege against Orléans. When Robert asks her about the source this plan, she tells him: "I hear voices telling me what to do. They come from God." Robert replies: "They come from your imagination." "Of course," responds Joan. "That is how the messages of God come to us." It is a mistake to assume that tracing the source of an idea to the human mind rules out the possibility of divine inspiration.

Just as some have tried to discount the authenticity of Muhammad's revelations by offering a purely naturalistic explanation, others have sought to discredit them by noting their similarity to the principles and precepts of other religions. There is no doubt that many of the revelations Muhammad articulated bear strong resemblances to stories and images in the Bible. As one scholar puts it, there was "nothing new" about the revelation on Mountain of Light, the place where Muhammad first heard the voice of Gabriel. And, indeed, Muhammad never claimed novelty for his message. To the contrary, he insisted the message was ancient, as old as Adam, humanity's first prophet. The novelty was the messenger. God had at last sent a prophet to the Arabs. In the Islamic view, the sanctity of Muhammad's revelations had less to do with the manner in which he received them and more with the fact that millions found—and continue to find—a living truth in them. Regardless of the mode of reception or the originality of its ideas and values, the Qur'an appeared to provide a framework for resolving many of the deep social tensions of Arabian society in Muhammad's day. In so doing, the revelations enabled the Arabs to break through to a new level of consciousness and establish a more just and equitable society.

Whenever Muhammad received a revelation, he committed the words to memory and recited them to his companions later. Several of these companions would also memorize them. Each year, during the month of Ramadān, he would repeat each of the revelations that he had received to that point and in that way fixed them in an oral tradition. Muslims believe that Muhammad did not alter the revelations by a single word. Islamic tradition maintains that some of the revelations were preserved in writing during the

Prophet's lifetime, but it was only after his death that they were completely transcribed and put together as a physical book. The full text in the form it now exists may have been completed as early as 20 years after Muhammad's death, although some scholars argue for a later date, sometimes as late as the 10th century. The book comprises 114 chapters, or suras, of over 6000 verses. The suras are not placed in the order in which they were received by the Prophet but generally by length, from the longest to the shortest, a manner specified by Archangel Gabriel to reflect the order of the Qur'an as it exists in heaven. The length of the complete Qur'an is comparable to that of the New Testament.

Although the Qur'an is similar to the New Testament in size, the texts do not compare in terms of their function as scripture. In Christianity, the Bible is generally regarded as the written witness to god's revelation, which for Christians is Jesus himself. Traditionally, Christianity has asserted that Jesus is god's word made manifest; the Bible serves as a testament to that revelation. In Islam, the Qur'an serves the role that Jesus does in Christianity. The Qur'an is god's word made manifest, not as a human being but as a book. Yet, the Qur'an is not just a book in the sense of a written text; more precisely it is an oral and aural book.

The words of the Qur'an are most meaningful in spoken form. Some Muslims use a separate term—*Mushaf*—to designate the Qur'an in its textual form. "Al-Qur'an" literally means the recitation, and it is in spoken Arabic, Muslims believe, that the rich significance and beauty of the Qur'an is most fully conveyed. Indeed, a translation of the Qur'an into any language other than Arabic is not truly the Qur'an. Much of the transformative power of the book is surely attributable to the evocative quality of the words as they are chanted in a way that borders on music. The traditions tell of many individuals who converted to Muhammad's faith upon merely hearing the Qur'an recited. Umar ibn al-Khattāb, whom some biographers say planned to kill the Prophet, embraced Islam when he heard a recitation of the revelations. "When I heard the Qur'an," he said, "my heart was softened and I wept, and Islam entered into me." Even for those who are not proficient in Arabic, as most Muslims today are not, the verses of the Qur'an seem to touch a resonant chord within their hearts and lift them to a transcendent world.

Anyone who appreciates the beauty of Gregorian chant may understand how the ethereal recitation of words—even in a foreign tongue—can move the spirit.

After coming to terms with the trauma of the first revelations, and as the revelations began again following the period of silence, Muhammad became more willing to share the substance of the message with his family and friends. Khadijah, as we have noted earlier, readily accepted his experiences as genuine communications from the god. Now others began to embrace Islam as the Prophet quietly taught his message to those closest to him. His cousin and foster son Ali was among the first new converts, as was Abu Bakr, one of Muhammad's longtime friends. But to his regret, Muhammad's beloved uncle, Abu Talib and other senior members of his clan were not willing to relinquish the old traditions to subscribe to Muhammad's monotheism. Nevertheless, Abu Talib remained Muhammad's protector, affording him much needed security as the disenchantment with the prophet's message grew, just as Waraqa predicted. Initially, the movement remained small. Over the next three years, the young Muslim community added only 30 to 40 new members. Those who professed Islam were men and women from all clans and all social ranks. Not surprisingly, the message Muhammad spoke had a special appeal to the poor and the young, a fact that provoked more than a little derision from the more powerful members of the tribe.

As the hostility toward Muhammad increased, he received word from Gabriel that he should make the message of Islam more public. Accordingly, he gathered together the heads of the clans and spoke to them from the top of a hill. He began with a rhetorical question: "If I were to tell you that down in this valley armed horsemen are advancing to attack us, would you believe me?" "Certainly," they answered. "You are the Trustworthy One, and you do not tell lies." Having established his credibility, Muhammad then proceeded to speak: "Then believe me when I tell you that I have come to warn you of violent torments. God has called me to admonish you to believe in the oneness of god. I am like the one who sees the enemy approaching and runs to tell his people, Beware! Beware!" The clan leaders were not impressed by Muhammad's lesson. His own uncle, Abu Lahab, was the first to ridicule

Muhammad: "This is why you have gathered us together?" He immediately turned his back and walked away along with the rest of the assembly. The chiefs instantly grasped the significance of Muhammad's message and foresaw how it threatened tribal traditions as well as their own power and livelihood. From that moment, Muhammad began to speak more openly and forcefully.

Initially, it seems, Muhammad understood his mission in very modest terms. He was being called not to create a new religion, to be a new savior, or even to preach a universal message to the world. Rather, he regarded himself as one who has simply come to warn the inhabitants of Makkah of the dangers of deviating from the ideals of a just society. In this respect, he considered himself as just another of the 124,000 prophets that god had sent to the various peoples of humanity, all of whom had preached the oneness of god and his demands for justice and compassion. Eventually, Muhammad came to understand that he had been called to be not simply a *nabi*—an ordinary prophet—but a *rasul*—a messenger, the bearer of a major revelation, the revelation that would be humanity's last. Acknowledging his status as god's messenger would also become part of the *shahadah*, the Muslim profession of faith: "I bear witness that there is no god but God and that Muhammad is His Messenger."

The early revelations stressed the importance taking care of the poor and the orphaned and praise the virtues of simple living and almsgiving. By all accounts, Muhammad himself carefully abided by these values. Even after he became man of great power, he continued to live frugally. His companions urged him to wear fine ceremonial robes befitting, they thought, the messenger of god, but Muhammad continued to wear the plain, coarsely woven cloth of the common folk. Likewise, his home was spartan and often lacking in food to eat because he gave away much of it to the poor who were hungry. Any gifts he received were promptly given to someone else. Even as his understanding of his calling evolved, Muhammad never departed from the basic message of the earliest revelations: a theology grounded in the oneness of god and an ethical vision of a just society based on the principle of human equality.

As the Prophet received new communications from Gabriel, the revelations began to speak increasingly of a Last Day, at which the dead would be resurrected and all souls would judged by al-Lah according to their deeds during life. This new eschatological dimension of Muhammad's message further alienated the Makkans. Resurrection was a novel idea to the Arabs. Traditional Arabian paganism, you will recall, made no allowance for an afterlife. Immortality meant the continued existence of the tribe, not the individual. The proposition that decomposed corpses would somehow arise from their graves struck the Makkans as absurd. The concept of a final judgment, furthermore, meant that *individuals* would be called to account before god; one's communal associations would mean nothing on that day. At the resurrection, the clan or the tribe could provide no protection; the person alone would be held responsible for his or her behavior. Thus, Muhammad's belief in the end time seemed merely an attempt to disrupt old traditions and replace them with an idea that made little sense to his contemporaries. It was to answer this skepticism that one of the early revelations seemed to be intended:

> Does the human being not see that we created him from a tiny drop, then he turns into an ardent enemy? He raises a question to us— while forgetting his initial creation—"Who can resurrect the bones after they had rotted?" Say, "The One who initiated them in the first place will resurrect them. He is fully aware of every creation." He is the One who creates for you, from the green trees, fuel which you burn for light. Is not the One who created the heavens and the earth able to recreate the same? Yes indeed; He is the Creator, the Omniscient. All He needs to do to carry out any command is to say to it, "Be," and it is. Therefore, glory be to the One in whose hand is the sovereignty over all things, and to Him you will be returned.

The god who creates life from a drop of fluid can surely recreate it from the dust it becomes after death.

Despite the rejection and ridicule the Prophet endured from the older and more powerful Makkans, his movement eventually began to enjoy great success. Within five or six years after the first revelation on the Mountain of Light, it almost appeared as if Muhammad would succeed at bringing the

Quraysh to adopt his religious point of view. But apparently, some of the Makkans who had become attracted to the message of Islam misunderstood the stringency of Muhammad's monotheism. They had assumed that they could continue to worship at the shrines of al-Lat, al-Uzza, and Manat—the "Three Daughters of al-Lah"—while recognizing the supremacy of al-Lah and obeying his demands for social justice. When Muhammad made it clear that Islam precluded the worship of these goddesses, many of his recent converts renounced the faith and reverted to their former paganism, which, in fact, they never actually left. It was one thing merely to include al-Lah in everyday religious practice; but it was quite another thing to *reject* the other gods who had been revered by the community for so long. Muhammad's denunciation of the goddesses exacerbated the Makkans' disenchantment with the Prophet and his radical theology, which they considered tantamount to atheism.

At last, the most powerful members of the Quraysh sent representatives to Muhammad's uncle Abu Talib, asking him to relinquish his protection of the Prophet, which would have left Muhammad easy prey for anyone who wished to kill him. Abu Talib was caught in a dilemma. He certainly did not want to invite the wrath of the other clans, but neither did he want to expose his nephew to such peril. When Abu Talib asked Muhammad to desist for both their sakes, Muhammad tearfully replied that he could not do that and would sooner die. Abu Talib then had a change of heart and told Muhammad to speak as his conscience demanded, for the uncle would never abandon his nephew. When Abu Talib refused to withdraw his protection, the clan chiefs tried another tack. They sent another delegation to Muhammad himself and offered him money, political status, and materials goods in exchange for his silence. The Prophet, of course, refused the offer and announced his willingness to accept the consequences of his refusal. This episode in Muhammad's life recalls similar events in the lives of the Buddha and Jesus, each of whom also withstood attempts to lure him away from his spiritual purposes with the enticements of worldly wealth and power.

When Muhammad proved impervious to bribery, the leaders of the clans resorted to insult and ridicule. They said he was possessed by a jinni and called him a homewrecker because he set children against parents, husbands against wives. His fellow Makkans began to ask him to perform miracles and provide them with proof of his claims. Some did this to mock him, others because they were half-serious. Muhammad's response was simple: "I am only a messenger." Threats, bribes, and humiliation all proved ineffective.

While Muhammad enjoyed his uncle's protection, not all members of the Muslim community had the luxury of such security from a powerful clan leader. A great number of Muhammad's followers were down-and-outers, including many slaves. When those opposing the Prophet were unable to deter *him*, they began to persecute his followers. The slaves and the poor were most vulnerable, and they began to suffer greatly. Finally, a husband and wife were tortured and killed for refusing to renounce their faith. Islam had its first martyrs, and Muhammad began to seek a way to protect those who regarded him as god's messenger. The situation was becoming dire.

# Madinah

## Lecture 29

**If Muhammad were to persuade the Makkans to worship al-Lah alone and reject the other gods, then surely the profit and prestige gained from the pilgrimage would suffer immensely. Yet commerce was not the only thing at risk. Muhammad's success could quite possibly bring down the wrath of the other deities.**

The tribe and clan chiefs of Makkah had many reasons to want Muhammad silenced—financial, ethical, and metaphysical. As custodians of the Ka'ba, the Quraysh feared losing the profit and prestige the yearly pilgrimage brought to the city and their tribe. The message of equality and justice for all humans was threatening to the ancient Arabian way of life. And failing to worship all of the gods, they feared, might bring divine wrath upon the people. The Makkan leadership therefore turned to harassing, torturing, and even killing the members of Muhammad's new community of Muslims, the *ummah*.

Muhammad needed to find a way to provide some security for his fledgling community. He sent many followers to take refuge in a Christian kingdom in Abyssinia. After suffering through a boycott of his clan and the death of his wife and uncle, Muhammad experienced the **Night Journey**: Awakened by Gabriel and the Buraq, a Pegasus-like creature, who flew him to Jerusalem, the "Furthest Mosque," he met with Abraham, Moses, Jesus, and other great prophets and prayed with them at the site where the Second Temple had stood. Afterwards, Gabriel escorted him to the heavens, where he was given a vision of paradise and hell and was told that Muslims should pray five times a day, rather than their customary three. Because of this event, Jerusalem is regarded as the third holiest city in Islam, and in 691, the Umayyad caliphs completed a shrine on the Second Temple site, known as the **Dome of the Rock**. Today, the Dome houses the massive boulder from which Muhammad was taken into heaven. The real significance of the story, however, has less to do with Jerusalem and more with the centrality of prayer.

The Prophet reported this experience to his fellow Makkans at the Ka'ba and lost many followers, who thought him mad. Around 621 C.E., however, he converted the two main tribes of the oasis city of Yathrib, which would later be known as Medinah. Muhammad began to encourage other Muslims to move there. When the Makkan leaders became aware that Muslims had been secretly migrating to Madinah, they organized an assassination squad composed of members from each clan. But before they could act, Gabriel told Muhammad to flee to Madinah, following an unconventional and dangerous route to confuse pursuers. This migration—the **Hijrah** as it is known in Islam—was a vitally important strategic and symbolic event in the life of the Prophet and the growing Muslim community. Muhammad would eventually return to Makkah for the pilgrimage, but he lived out his days in Madinah.

After his arrival, Muhammad negotiated alliances with the neighboring tribes, including several Jewish tribes. Muhammad's vision was to create a new community based on religious values rather than kinship, an unprecedented

The Dome of the Rock in Jerusalem. Within the dome is a boulder from which, Muslims believe, Muhammad was taken into heaven.

idea in ancient Arabia. Yet the Prophet never expected the Jews to accept Islam. In his view, they had already received a genuine revelation from Moses and the other prophets, and he considered the Qur'an to be part of the same fabric. He regarded Jews and Christians as "muslims" (with a small *m*), those who submit to the will of al-Lah.

**Muslims now date the start of their calendar to the year of Muhammad's resettlement, which occurred in 1 A.H., *anno hijrah*, or 622 C.E.**

Despite the initial enthusiasm that greeted Muhammad's arrival in Madinah, not everyone remained happy about the presence of the Prophet. Abdallah ibn Ubbay had been preparing to become the king of Madinah and began to foment resistance to the Prophet. Some Jewish allies started to have grave misgivings about Muhammad as well. Muhammad had little interest in social and political leadership. But after the Hijrah, the revelations began addressing practical social and political matters. Muhammad's attention was turning toward consolidating the Muslim community and ensuring its survival. In Makkah, Islam was essentially pacifistic. Now, al-Lah granted permission for the Muslims to engage in combat for a just cause, such as to obtain reparations for lost property and to hold the wicked in check.

Muhammad ordered a series of raids in 623 C.E.; although he later repudiated the act, it demonstrated to Islam's enemies that the *ummah* was not weak. The first real battle between the Quraysh and the Muslims occurred in 624 at Badr. Muhammad proved to be an impressive military leader, and the Quraysh were routed. Muhammad spared the lives of all the prisoners but two who had been especially cruel in the conflict, and he equitably distributed the spoils of battle, both uncommon practices at the time. Muhammad's battle practices followed the guidelines of what ethicists call just war theory. The principal objective in his military operations was to preserve and protect his community. He never fought out of pure aggression or anger. Furthermore, the revelations enjoined the Muslims to spare the lives of women, children, noncombatants, and even crops and animals. Muhammad treated his prisoners humanely and prohibited the Muslims from mutilating or desecrating the corpses of the dead. ■

**Dome of the Rock**: The mosque on Temple Mount, Jerusalem. It was built by the Umayyad caliphs to commemorate Muhammad's Night Journey.

**Hijrah**: The flight of Muhammad and the fledgling Muslim community from Makkah to Madinah in 621 C.E.

**Night Journey**: One of the Prophet Muhammad's spiritual experiences, in which he visited Jerusalem and spoke with al-Lah's previous prophets, including Abraham, Moses, and Jesus. This experience is why Jerusalem is the third holiest city in Islam. It is commemorated in the Dome of the Rock on Temple Mount, Jerusalem.

*ummah*: The Muslim community of the faithful.

## Questions to Consider

1. This lecture describes some of the earliest interactions between Muslims and Jews. From what you have learned, does the faiths' common history seem more a reason for conflict or cooperation?

2. Muhammad struggled with but eventually accepted the idea of a just war. Do you think our other sages would agree with his reasoning?

Lecture 29: Madinah

# Madinah

## Lecture 29—Transcript

The tribe and clan chiefs of Makkah had many reasons to want Muhammad silenced. As custodians of the Ka'ba, the Quraysh had a vested interest in the yearly pilgrimage that brought thousands of Arabs from throughout the peninsula to worship their gods at the sacred shrine. If Muhammad were to persuade the Makkans to worship al-Lah alone and reject the other gods, then surely the profit and prestige gained from the pilgrimage would suffer immensely. Yet, commerce was not the only thing at risk. Muhammad's success could quite possibly bring down the wrath of the other deities. To be sure, Muhammad might be correct in proclaiming that al-Lah was the one and only god; but what if he were wrong? Dare the Makkans take that chance?

When Rome was sacked in 410 C.E. by the Visigoths, many argued that the city's defeat was a punishment from the Roman gods who had been officially abandoned in favor of the god of Christianity. The Makkan leaders were probably unaware of this bit of Roman history, but they were certainly acquainted with the principle involved. Worship of the gods was not merely an individual's affair; the welfare of the entire community depended on the propitiation of the patron deities. Finally, the ethical demands of Muhammad's message were deeply unsettling and threatening to the ancient Arabian way of life. The revelations Muhammad received disrupted the traditional ways of viewing slaves, women, and other marginalized persons and challenged the whole tribal system. Any one of these reasons might have been sufficient for the Makkans to seek to put an end to the prophet's proclamations or even his life. But since he was convinced of the authenticity of his message and was under the protection of his powerful uncle, neither prospect seemed likely. The Makkan leadership therefore turned to harassing, torturing, and even killing the members of Muhammad's new community of Muslims, the *ummah*. Muhammad needed to find a way to provide some security for his fledgling community.

His first effort to protect the Muslims was to send about a hundred of them to Abyssinia—present-day Ethiopia—to seek refuge with the Christian king who reigned there. Muhammad had hoped that the Abyssinian monarch, the Negus, would be receptive to the Muslim exiles since they professed faith in the same god the Christians worshiped and held the Christian messiah in high regard, considering him the greatest messenger next to Muhammad himself. Indeed, the Negus welcomed the Muslims, and even refused to extradite them when the Makkan leaders sent a delegation to bring them back to Arabia. The king had been deeply moved by the beauty of the chanted Qur'an and the Muslims' affirmation of the virgin birth of Jesus. Later, it was said, the Negus himself converted to Islam and maintained close ties with the Prophet. The Muslim exiles remained in Abyssinia for 15 years until they rejoined Muhammad in Arabia under more favorable conditions.

But Muhammad remained in Makkah, and his teachings continued frustrate the civic leaders, so they resorted to new measures. For three years, they imposed a boycott on the Banu Hashim, the Prophet's clan. During this time, other members of the Quraysh tribe were prohibited from having contact with the clan, engaging in trade relations with it, or negotiating marriages for their sons and daughters with the children of the Hashemites. The ban caused great suffering for the clan, but it was finally lifted in 619 C.E. when it became apparent that the sanctions were not having their intended effect. The end of the boycott meant a slight improvement in conditions for the Muslim community generally, but it also marked the start of what Muhammad called his Year of Sorrow. During that year, both Khadijah and Abu Talib died. His wife had been the first to believe in him when he began to receive his revelations, and his uncle had been his steadfast guardian, even though Abu Talib never embraced Islam. Both had furnished Muhammad with immense encouragement during times of self-doubt and danger. He grieved their deaths profoundly.

About this time in his life, Muhammad had an unusual experience later known as the Night Journey. The Qur'an refers to this event only obliquely: "Most glorified is the One who summoned His servant during the night, from the Sacred Mosque to the [Furthest Mosque] whose surroundings we have blessed, in order to show him some of our signs." The details are provided by the *hadith* and the Prophet's early biographers. According to these extra-Qur'anic traditions, late one night, while asleep near the Ka'ba after a vigil of prayer, Muhammad was awaken by Gabriel and taken to a creature called the Buraq, a milk-white horse with wings, similar to Pegasus in Greek mythology, but smaller. Muhammad mounted the Buraq and flew, alongside Gabriel, to Jerusalem, the "Furthest Mosque." There he met with Abraham, Moses, Jesus, and other great prophets and prayed with them at the site where the Second Temple had stood. Afterwards, Gabriel escorted him to the heavens where he was given a vision of paradise and hell and received instructions to enjoin the Muslims to pray five times a day rather than three times a day, as had been their custom to that point. At that time, it was also customary for the Muslims to face Jerusalem when they prayed. A few years later, Muhammad received instructions to face the Ka'ba in Makkah, to distinguish Islam from Judaism.

Nevertheless, Jerusalem remained a sacred place for the Muslims. In 691, the Umayyad Caliphate completed construction of a shrine on the site where Muhammad was believed to have met his predecessors. This shrine, which is known as the Dome of the Rock, still stands in Jerusalem, just above the Western Wall, the most sacred site in Judaism. Within the dome is a massive boulder from which Muhammad was taken into heaven. Muslims believe an imprint of the Prophet's heel is embedded in the stone. In 705 C.E., a mosque was built near the site. It was called al-Aqsa, the "furthest mosque." Jerusalem is regarded as the third holiest city in Islam, next to Makkah and Madinah.

The real significance of the story, however, has less to do with Jerusalem and more with the centrality of prayer. This episode in the Prophet's life, which some Muslims regard as a physical occurrence and others as a vision or a dream, symbolizes the importance of prayer as a spiritual practice for Muslims. So essential was the five times daily prayer that Muhammad was given an exceptional experience to receive the revelation.

Following his journey into the heavens, Muhammad returned with Gabriel to the Temple Mount in Jerusalem and from there back to Makkah. Against the advice of one of his close companions, the Prophet reported his experience to fellow Makkans at the Ka'ba. I'm not sure how Muhammad expected them to respond, but the reaction of the vast majority was to conclude that Muhammad had lost his mind and was demonstrably insane. The story even alienated some Muslims, who subsequently left Islam.

Muhammad was now more vulnerable than ever and began to look beyond Makkah for a source of security for himself and the other Muslims. He sought help from the leaders of the nearby town of Taif, the home of the shrine to one of the daughters of al-Lah. But the chiefs scoffed at his claim to be god's messenger and chased him out of town, hurling both insults and stones. But sometime later, during the annual pilgrimage, Muhammad met with a group of citizens from Yathrib, an oasis city just over 200 miles north of Makkah, and succeeded in converting them to Islam. They returned home and began to preach the faith to others. A year later, probably 621 C.E., they came back to Makkah and reported to the Prophet that the two main tribes of Yathrib had both embraced the faith and ended their ancient hostilities with one another. Furthermore, they offered to provide necessary protection for the Prophet and the women and children among the Makkan Muslims. This new association with the citizens of this city set the groundwork for one of the most important events in Muhammad's life: his migration from Makkah to Yathrib, which later became Madinah, the city of the Prophet. Although it would be a year or two before he himself arrived in Madinah, he immediately began to encourage other Muslims to leave Makkah quietly and take up residence in this more hospitable environment.

In the meantime, Muhammad remarried. He first married Sawdah bint Zam'ah, a widow who had been part of the Muslim community in Abyssinia. About a year later, he became engaged to Aishah, the six year old daughter of his close friend Abu Bakr. According to the early biographers, the wedding ceremony took place when Aishah was nine and Muhammad was around 50. After the wedding, Aishah continued to live with her parents and did not consummate the marriage until she had reached puberty. The *hadith* relate that the marriage was a very happy one for both parties, and, with the possible exception of Khadijah, Aishah was Muhammad's favorite wife. They remained married until the Prophet's death in 632. Throughout his lifetime, Muhammad had 11 or 13 wives—the number varies according to the source. As was the practice in Arabia and other ancient cultures, most of these marriages were arranged to create or solidify political or kinship ties. Occasionally, the Prophet married to assist a woman in need. Many of his wives were older widows or women who had been abandoned by their husbands.

Marriage may have helped Muhammad cope with his grief during this period of his life, but it did little to ameliorate his situation with the Makkan leadership. As they became aware that Muslims had been secretly migrating to Madinah, the clan leaders decided it was time to put Muhammad to death. To avoid a vendetta or having to pay blood money to the Banu Hashim, the chiefs decided to organize an assassination squad composed of members from each of the clans. Before they could carry out the plot, however, Gabriel told Muhammad that he should prepare to leave for Madinah. Having also learned of the conspiracy against his life, Muhammad asked his foster son Ali to sleep in his bed while he and Abu Bakr made plans for the exodus from Makkah. At daybreak the next day, the would-be assassins were about to attack to the Prophet only to discover the ruse at the last minute. A short time later, Muhammad and Abu Bakr left Makkah in the middle of night and began their journey to Madinah, following an unconventional and dangerous route to confuse pursuers.

They arrived in the city of Madinah several weeks later amid the cheers and well-wishes of its inhabitants. The first order of business was to find a residence and begin construction on a mosque. Despite invitations from some of the Madinans to dwell with them, Muhammad declined their offers and allowed his camel to determine the site of his home and the future mosque. The camel roamed freely for a while and finally came to rest on some property owned by two orphans. Muhammad paid them a good price and construction began immediately.

The migration to Madinah—or the *hijrah* as it is known in Islam—was a vitally important strategic and symbolic event in the life of the Prophet and the growing Muslim community. Its significance is reflected in the fact that Muslims now date the start of their calendar to the year of Muhammad's resettlement, which occurred in 1 A.H., *anno hijrah*, or 622 C.E. The hijrah represented a great act of faith. Like Abraham responding to the call of Yahweh to leave his home in Mesopotamia to strike out for the Promised Land, Muhammad's departure from Makkah required a deep sense of trust in al-Lah to venture forth into uncharted territory. On another level, the *hijrah* also connects Muhammad with Confucius, the Buddha, and Jesus, each of whom left his home as part of his own spiritual development. All four sages found it essential to their life's purpose to leave the familiar and open themselves up to the unknown. In Muhammad's case, the departure was both an exodus and an exile, to use as metaphors the two central events of the

Hebrew Bible. As exodus, he and his community were cutting themselves off from the painful circumstances of life in Makkah, just as crossing the Red Sea severed the ancient Israelites' ties to their hardships in Egypt. The *hijrah* was a community taking charge of its own liberation; it was a refusal to comply with an intolerable situation. But as exile, the *hijrah* also symbolized a community forcibly alienated from its home. The Qur'an describes the Muslims being "driven out" of Makkah, as if obliged to leave against their will. That Makkah remained in the hearts of the Muslims was demonstrated in the revelation Muhammad received in 624 C.E., instructing the community to face the Ka'ba whenever they prayed. Muhammad would eventually return to Makkah for the pilgrimage, but he lived out his days in Madinah, his adopted hometown.

After his arrival, Muhammad set about securing his new city as a safe haven for the *ummah*. He negotiated alliances with the neighboring tribes, including several Jewish tribes who were the descendants of the original settlers of Madinah. Muhammad's vision was to create a new community based on religious values rather than kinship. This was a totally unprecedented idea in ancient Arabia. Many of the Arabian pagans found Muhammad's dream appealing, in part because they were so weary of the old tribal hostilities, and so they converted to his monotheism. Initially, the Jewish tribes were also willing to participate in this novel arrangement, and a few even embraced Muhammad's faith. Yet, the Prophet never expected the Jews to accept Islam. In his view, they had already received a genuine revelation from Moses and the other prophets, and he considered the Qur'an to be part of the same fabric. In the Qur'an, Muhammad received these instructions regarding the Jews and Christians:

> Say: "We believe in Allah, and in what has been revealed to us and what was revealed to Abraham, Isma'il, Isaac, Jacob, and the Tribes, and in (the Books) given to Moses, Jesus, and the prophets, from their Lord: We make no distinction between one and another among them, and to Allah do we [submit] our will."

In short, Muhammad regarded the Jews and Christians as "muslims" (with a small "m"), those who submit to the will of the one god. Evidently, Muhammad did not distinguish the Jews and Christians at first, considering them members of the same religion. As he came to understand both groups, he began to recognize the differences between them.

Despite the initial enthusiasm that greeted Muhammad's arrival in Madinah, not everyone remained happy about the presence of the Prophet. Apparently, many Madinans who had converted to Islam were less than sincere about the faith. Over time, their discontent with Muhammad and the migrant Muslims become increasingly evident. Abdallah ibn Ubbay, who was of one of the new converts, had been preparing to become the King of Madinah when Muhammad entered the scene. Now, he was beginning to feel he had been robbed of his crown. Although he remained a nominal Muslim, ibn Ubbay began to foment resistance to the Prophet. The subversive actions of ibn Ubbay and his associates earned them the name "The Hypocrites." Many of the members of the Jewish tribes also joined the growing resistance. Upon reflection, they started to have grave misgivings about Muhammad. They came to believe that his revelations distorted the stories of their Torah, and they came to doubt his claim to be a prophet. In their mind, the age of prophecy was over long ago. Muhammad was bitterly disappointed when the Jews failed to accept him as a messenger of god in the tradition of Abraham and Moses. Not long afterwards, Muhammad received the revelation to face Makkah during prayer.

Based on the earliest revelations in the Qur'an, it is clear that Muhammad had little interest in social and political leadership. He understood himself as a prophet in the biblical vein, calling his contemporaries back to god and a just society. But after the *hijrah*, Muhammad became more overtly concerned with civic leadership. Even the quality of the revelations changed. The earlier revelations in Makkah were relatively brief, focusing on the majesty and mystery of god and his ethical demands. The later Madinan revelations were much longer, addressing practical social and political matters. This distinction, however, is not an absolute one; it simply reflects a shift in emphasis. But it does signal the way Muhammad's attention was turning towards consolidating the Muslim community and ensuring its survival. In Madinah, for the first time, the Qur'an began to speak of the legitimacy of battle:

Permission is granted to those who are being persecuted, since injustice has befallen them, and God is certainly able to support them. They were evicted from their homes unjustly, for no reason other than saying, "Our Lord is God." If it were not for God's supporting of some people against others, monasteries, churches, synagogues, and [mosques]—where the name of God is frequently [recited]—would have been destroyed. Absolutely, God supports those who support Him. God is Powerful, Almighty.

In Makkah, Islam was essentially pacifistic. Now, as this passage indicates, al-Lah granted permission for the Muslims to engage in combat for a just cause. Specifically, this revelation allowed the Muslims who migrated to Madinah to seek compensation for the property they lost when they left Makkah and to take up arms, if necessary, to obtain it. This consent was based on the belief in the need for just persons to hold the wicked in check, lest chaos ensue and even religious institutions be destroyed. In short, the Muslim community had the right to defend itself against injustice.

In 623 C.E., the Prophet sent two groups of emigrants to accost caravans en route to Makkah from Syria. The intent of the raids, which—as we observed in an earlier lecture—were commonplace in ancient Arabia, was to recover for the Muslims some of the value of their homes that were confiscated when they left Makkah. These raids, like most, were not supposed to involve killing since that would incur blood vengeance according to the old tribal codes. The first expeditions were not great successes. Later that year, Muhammad himself led 200 Muslims in a raid on a huge caravan, but it too failed. Finally, the Muslims succeeded in ambushing a Makkan caravan during a month when fighting was strictly forbidden throughout the peninsula. The violation of the sacred truce repulsed many Madinans, and Muhammad later felt compelled to condemn the act, although the raiders were acting on his orders. Although not especially successful, these caravan attacks put the Arabian tribes on notice that the Muslims were willing to put up a fight for their survival and to challenge what they considered an oppressive situation. Muhammad believed that it was important to demonstrate this mind-set, for fear that the new community would leave itself vulnerable to constant aggression. The *ummah* could not afford to let itself appear weak. A confrontation with the Quraysh now seemed inevitable.

The first real battle between the Quraysh and the Muslims occurred in 624. With an army of about 300, the Prophet planned to intercept a caravan at the

Well of Badr, near the Red Sea. The caravan, however, was warned of the plan and sent word back to Makkah for help. More than a thousand Makkans responded to join the fight against the small Muslim army. After witnessing the arrival of reinforcements, Muhammad consulted his close companions and decided to press forward with the plan, despite being outnumbered over three to one. Muhammad proved to be an impressive military leader, and the Muslims fought with such determination that Quraysh were soon routed. When the battle was over, Muhammad spared the lives of all the prisoners but two who had been especially cruel in the conflict, and he equitably distributed the spoils of battle, both uncommon practices at the time. The win was a great moral victory for the Muslims, who viewed their success as a validation of their faith in al-Lah. Henceforth, the Muslim community was regarded throughout Arabia as a force to be reckoned with.

Shortly after the triumph at Badr, one the Jewish tribes at Madinah broke its covenant with the Muslims. Historians are not agreed about what precipitated the violation, but it was clear evidence of a growing disenchantment with Muhammad among the Madinan tribes. Around this time Muhammad received another revelation that he interpreted as addressing this breach. He was told: "When you are betrayed by a group of people, you shall mobilize against them in the same manner. God does not love the betrayers." Muhammad quickly raised an army and defeated the Jews. But as in the battle of Badr, Muhammad spared the prisoners of war and the other members of the tribe. He did, however, banish the entire tribe and kept their belongings, dividing them among the Muslims.

In the Battle of Uhud, on the other hand, things did not turn out so well for the Muslim community. In 625, a Quraysh army of 3000 men and 3000 camels began a march to Madinah to avenge their loss at Badr. Muhammad and his companions decided to meet them in Uhud, about five miles from Madinah, to prevent them from entering the city. Again, the Muslims were heavily outnumbered, but they seemed to be heady with the taste of their previous victories. Early on, it appeared as if the Muslims would win again; but the archers who had been posted in the hills above the battle began to observe that the foot soldiers on the front lines were prematurely collecting the spoils of war. Fearing they would not get a share of the plunder, the archers deserted their posts and the entire battle fell into disarray. Muhammad was knocked off his horse and broke a tooth and sustained other injures, prompting the rumor that he had been killed. Within a short while, the Muslims had lost the battle. In the face of defeat, Muhammad was able to retain composure and did not let his emotions control his actions. According to his biographers, he showed respect to his enemies and, despite his anger, was "neither brutal nor stern" with the archers who caused the loss. A subsequent revelation, however, made it clear that the defeat was the result of the Muslims' greed and disobedience.

Muhammad's battle-practices followed the guidelines of what ethicists call just war theory. The principal objective in his military operations was to preserve and protect his community. He never fought out of pure aggression or anger. The Qur'an was clear about the limits of war:

And fight for the sake of God those who fight you; but do not be brutal or commit aggression, for God does not love brutal aggressors. … But do not fight them in the precincts of the sacred mosque, unless they fight you there. If they fight you, then kill them; such is the reward of scoffers. But if they stop, God is most forgiving, most merciful. And fight them until there is no more strife and there is the religion of God. And if they stop, then let there be no hostility, except against wrongdoers.

The just war was to be fought for self-protection and to put an end to tyranny. A war motivated by greed could not be sanctioned by the Qur'an. Furthermore, the revelations enjoined the Muslims to spare the lives of women, children, non-combatants, and even crops and animals. Muhammad treated his prisoners humanely and prohibited the Muslims from mutilating or desecrating the corpses of the dead.

The migration to Madinah had prompted important changes in the character of Islam and the Prophet's understanding of his mission. Muhammad had become convinced that violence was sometimes necessary when the cause of justice demands it. In the pursuit of justice, al-Lah aids the warrior, but even so, the use of force must always be contained by discipline. In this respect, the development of Islam remained consistent with the values espoused in the first revelations. Madinah and Makkah were not so far removed.

# "There Is No God but al-Lah"
## Lecture 30

"O you who believe! Believe in Allah and His Messenger, and the scripture He sent to His Messenger, and the scripture He sent to those before. Any who deny Allah, His angels, His Books, His Messengers, and the Day of Judgment [has] gone far, far astray." —Sura 4:136

Within a few years of Muhammad's resettlement in Madinah, the salient features of Islam had been defined by revelation and experience. The Qur'an makes clear that God, angels, prophets, revealed books, and a forthcoming day of judgment are the central beliefs of the faith. Muhammad was not introducing a new deity to the Arabs, but he was making a particular assertion about the nature of the ultimate reality. For his time and place, it was a radical statement, and it nearly got him killed.

Muhammad's provocative contention was that the fundamental character of ultimate reality is **tawhid**, or "unity." The very first words of the *shahadah* proclaim: "There is no god but al-Lah" or "There is no god but God"; on the face of it, this seems a straightforward declaration of monotheism. But the claim is not just singleness but singularity: al-Lah is incomparable, utterly unlike anything else in human experience. al-Lah alone is eternal. al-Lah alone has no progenitor. al-Lah relies on no one or nothing else. al-Lah is the only one of his kind. al-Lah alone is indivisible. al-Lah infinitely exceeds human understanding. These statements about the nature of al-Lah help clarify why Islam can tolerate no other gods or goddesses. To suggest that al-Lah is a deity like Hubal or al-Uzza would imply that God can be imagined, envisioned, or understood like these others, and that would diminish the majesty and mystery of the ultimate reality.

To Muhammad, the doctrine of divine oneness was readily apparent: Reason itself dictates that there can be only one supreme being, otherwise the universe would be in complete chaos. The singularity and inscrutability of al-Lah, furthermore, entail certain claims about that ultimate reality that simply cannot be grasped or explained. Al-Lah exists without place, and he alone caused all things to exist. God needs the creation for nothing at all.

Everything that happens—good and evil—occurs because al-Lah wills it; yet al-Lah is never unjust. He never makes mistakes and is fully cognizant of the whole of reality.

Islamic theology distinguishes between the divine essence, which is beyond comprehension, and the divine attributes, which name certain qualities that assist in appropriately orienting the mind toward God. This distinction between a god's essence and his attributes is a common one in the history of world religions.

> **Muhammad was the "seal of the prophets," the final and most important emissary of God, sent not just to a nation but to all humankind.**

A well-known list of al-Lah's unique characteristics is known as the 99 Most Beautiful Names of God. Two of them appear at the start of every sura (except Sura 9) as the **bismillah**: "In the name of God, the all-compassionate, the all-merciful." The other beautiful names complement and supplement these attributes. The bismillah is recited as part of Muslim daily prayers, and it is often spoken as one undertakes a new task. Some Muslims think the bismillah contains the very essence of the Qur'an.

Misappropriating the divine attributes is part of what Islam considers to be the most heinous of sins: *shirk*—that is, connecting with al-Lah something that is less than ultimate or giving to something less than ultimate what belongs to al-Lah alone. *Shirk* is the only sin al-Lah cannot forgive, although only if one dies in this state of unbelief. *Shirk* is idolatry in its broadest sense—not just images of the divine, but whatever finite object becomes the locus of our highest values—money, country, self, religion.

Angels and prophets are the servants and messengers of al-Lah. Angels are beings created of light that can assume any form and travel great distances in an instant. Although sentient, they lack free will. They serve al-Lah in various ways. Angels are also the custodians of paradise and hell and the recorders of a person's good and bad deeds. Satan, or **Iblīs**, is important in Islam, but he is not a fallen angel. Rather, he is a jinni who was created from fire and was fervently devoted to worshiping al-Lah. Possessing free will, Iblīs's great misdeed, according to the Qur'an, was disobeying God's command for all creatures to prostrate themselves before Adam.

Angels and prophets both function as envoys of God, but prophets are human rather than celestial. Muhammad taught that al-Lah had sent prophets to every nation in the world at various points in history. There were slight variations in their proclamations because their words were directed to different audiences, but all taught the oneness of God and submission to divine will. About two dozen prophets are named in the Qur'an, including Adam, Noah, Abraham, Ishmael, Isaac, Joseph, Job, Moses, David, Solomon, John the Baptist, and Jesus. Although not named in the Qur'an, some modern Muslim communities regard Confucius and the Buddha as prophets as well. Muhammad was the "seal of the prophets," the final and most important emissary of God, sent not just to a nation but to all humankind.

Jesus is known in the Qur'an as **Īsa**, the son of Mārīam. He was not only a messenger; he was among the greatest of all human beings. His mission was to bear witness to the oneness of God and the necessity of submitting to the divine will. The Qur'an affirms his Virgin Birth and the miracles, yet—the Qur'an is emphatic about this—Jesus was not, and could not be, the son or incarnation of God.

The Qur'an frequently uses the phrase "People of the Book," which refers to pre-Islamic nations who received revelations from al-Lah in the form of a text—Jews, Christians, and sometimes the Sabians and Zoroastrians. The four pre-Qur'anic revealed books are the Scrolls of Abraham, the Torah, the Psalms, and the Gospel. For Islam, the Qur'an has an ontological status as the word of God. Some revelations allude to a written Qur'an existing in the divine presence even before it was sent down to the Prophet.

Like Jesus, Muhammad anticipated an end to the world as we know it. On the day of requital, the dead will rise, persons will be judged by their deeds, and they will be rewarded or punished accordingly. The time of this eschatological event is known only to al-Lah. But there will be certain signs preceding the Final Days, particularly natural disasters and the rapid erosion of human morality—harbingers of the end times found in eschatological visions throughout the world. The sins that merit condemnation include lying and dishonesty, the denial of the tawhid and God's revelations, refusal to help the poor and hungry, usury, economic exploitation, and social oppression. Yet the mercy of al-Lah is so great that he directs his angels and prophets to rescue those who have done some good, and those who have done just a little good, and even those in whose hearts there is a single atom of goodness. ■

## Important Terms

**bismillah**: The words that begin all but one of the Qur'an's suras: "In the name of God, the all-compassionate, the all-merciful."

**Iblīs**: The Arabic name for Satan; in Islam, a jinni who was cast out of heaven by al-Lah for refusing to bow to Adam.

**Īsa**: The Arabic name for Jesus, who is an important (but not divine) prophet in Islam.

*shirk*: Connecting with al-Lah something that is less than ultimate or giving to something less than ultimate what belongs to al-Lah alone. According to Islam, persisting in *shirk* is the only unpardonable sin.

**tawhid**: Often translated as "unity"; the Muslim doctrine that al-Lah is not simply one but is unique and incomparable.

## Questions to Consider

1.  In Islam, tawhid is the source of the prohibition of images of the Prophet and of al-Lah. Do you agree that religious art or iconography diminishes what it represents in some way? Why or why not?

2.  In your own mind, can you reconcile the tension (in Islam or in any religion) between an all-merciful god and an unpardonable sin? If so, how?

# "There Is No God but al-Lah"
## Lecture 30—Transcript

Within a few years of Muhammad's resettlement in Madinah, the salient features of Islam had been defined by revelation and experience. The Prophet continued to receive messages from Gabriel until his death, ten years after the *hijrah*, but most of the later Madinan suras addressed matters of communal polity as compared with the theological, ethical and spiritual emphases of the revelations received in Makkah and the first years in Madinah. Since the Prophet's worldview had by now attained its essential character and form, this is an appropriate point in our study to discuss his teachings more systematically, using the same categories we've employed for each of the other three sages, namely, metaphysics, anthropology, ethics, and spiritual practices. In today's lecture, we'll focus attention on the metaphysical foundations of Muhammad's teachings, and in subsequent talks we'll explore the remaining areas before returning to discuss the last years of Muhammad's life and his legacy to the world.

A passage from one of the suras revealed in Madinah provides a concise statement of the elements of Muhammad's metaphysical view:

> O you who believe! Believe in Allah and His Messenger, and the scripture [that] He [has] sent to His Messenger and the scripture [that] He sent to those before (him). Any who deny Allah, His angels, His Books, His Messengers, and the Day of Judgment, [has] gone astray, far astray.

Thus, the Qur'an makes clear that God, angels, prophets, revealed books, and a forthcoming day of judgment are vital beliefs in Muhammad's teaching about the nature of ultimate reality. These conceptions will provide the essential points for our study in this lecture.

When he began to proclaim faith in al-Lah, Muhammad was not introducing a new deity to the Arabs. Rather, he was making a particular assertion about the nature of the ultimate reality. For his time and place, that claim was a radical statement, and it nearly got him killed.

Muhammad's provocative contention was that the fundamental character of ultimate reality is unity, oneness, or what is known in Islamic theology as *tawhid*. The very first words of the *Shahadah*, the Muslim profession of faith, proclaim the doctrine of *tawhid*: "There is no god but al-Lah" or "There is no god but God." The doctrine of *tawhid* is the bedrock of Islam. On the face of it, *tawhid* seems a rather simple and straightforward declaration of the principle of monotheism. But much more is involved in this conception than the simple denial of all gods but one. In one of the earliest revelations, Muhammad is told: "Say, "It is God, unique, God, the eternal, not begetting or begotten, not having any equal." This statement reveals that tawhid implies not just singleness but singularity, in the sense that al-Lah is incomparable, utterly unlike anything else in human experience. "There is nothing like God" says Sura 42.

Other beings have limited lifespans; al-Lah alone is eternal. Other beings are born and they reproduce; al-Lah alone has no progenitor and does not procreate; al-Lah relies on no one or nothing else. Other beings are members of species, families of like beings; al-Lah is the only one of his kind. Other bein    gs are composites, made up of parts; al-Lah alone is indivisible. *Tawhid* thus implies God's inscrutability. Because absolutely nothing compares to al-Lah, al-Lah infinitely exceeds human understanding. "No vision can grasp Him," says Sura 6, "but His grasp is over all vision: He is above all comprehension, yet is acquainted with all things." These statements about the nature of al-Lah help clarify why Islam can tolerate no other gods and goddesses. To suggest that al-Lah is a deity like Hubal or al-Uzza would imply that God can be imagined, envisioned, or understood like these others, and that would diminish the majesty and mystery of the ultimate reality. Precisely to avoid this assumption, al-Lah was never represented with images and icons like the members of the Arabian pantheon.

To Muhammad, the doctrine of divine oneness was not only a revealed truth; it was readily apparent to anyone able to use their reasoning powers and read the signs of god found through creation: "God has never begotten a son. Nor was there ever any other god beside Him. Otherwise, each god would have declared independence with his creations, and they would have competed with each other for dominance." In other words, reason itself dictates that there can be only one supreme being, otherwise the universe would be in complete chaos. As Sura 21 says, "If there were a deity besides God in the sky and earth, both would go awry."

The singularity and inscrutability of al-Lah entails certain claims about that ultimate reality that simply cannot be grasped or explained. Al-Lah exists without place and bears no resemblance to his creations. He alone caused all things to exist and brought them into being out of nothing. The whole created order depends on God, but God needs the creation for nothing at all; he is "uniquely independent." Everything that happens—good and evil—occurs because al-Lah wills it; yet, al-Lah is never unjust, not "in the least degree" says the Qur'an. He never makes mistakes and is fully cognizant of the whole of reality:

> And whatever business you take part in, and whatever you read from the Qur'an, and whatever deed you do, We are witnessing you as you are immersed therein. And nothing on earth or in the sky is hidden from your Lord, even to the weight of an atom.

While Muhammad's understanding of al-Lah explicitly affirmed the principle of mystery, it is also true that the Prophet spoke in terms that permitted a partial understanding of God, a concession to the limitations of the human mind. Islamic theology distinguishes between the divine essence, which is beyond comprehension, and the divine attributes, which name certain qualities that assist in appropriately orienting the mind towards God. Without such attributes, the divine reality cannot be spoken of at all. This distinction between God's essence and attributes is a common theological move in the history of world religions. It is a way of both affirming the final mystery of the ultimate reality of the universe and permitting the mind to have some ideas to work with as it attempts to draw closer to that reality.

The Qur'an and the *hadith* both attribute particular qualities to al-Lah but do so in ways that are intended to preclude compromising God's utter unknowability. A well-known list of al-Lah's characteristics is known as the 99 Most Beautiful Names of God. This inventory includes divine attributes that can only be ascribed to al-Lah and no other. Two of the most popularly invoked names are *Ar-Rahman*, the all-compassionate, and *Ar-Rahim*, the all-merciful. Every sura of the Qur'an (except Sura 9) begins with the recitation of these two attributes of al-Lah in a formula known as the *bismillah*: "In the name of God, the all-compassionate, the all-merciful." The *bismillah* is recited several times as part of Muslim daily prayers, and it is often spoken as one undertakes a new task. Some Muslims think the *bismillah* contains the very essence of the Qur'an. It certainly highlights what Muhammad took to be one of the defining qualities of god: complete compassion. The other beautiful names complement and supplement these attributes. Sura 59 offers a listing of about a dozen more of these superlative qualities:

> This is the God, other than which there is no deity: the Sovereign, the Holy, Peace, the Giver of Safety, the Protector, the Almighty, the Omnipotent, the Overwhelming; glory to God, beyond any association they attribute. This is God, the Originator, the Creator, the Shaper, to whom refer the most beautiful names, celebrated by everything in the heavens and on earth, being the Almighty, the Perfectly Wise.

Scattered throughout the Qur'an, *hadith*, and other Islamic literature are many other such beautiful names. All of them, Muslims believe, have only one true referent: al-Lah.

Although these qualities can only be properly ascribed to al-Lah, human beings from the beginning of time have been inclined to misappropriate them, attributing them to realities other than the one to whom they rightly belong. Misappropriating the divine attributes is part of what Islam considers to be the most heinous of sins: *shirk*. The sin of *shirk* is at the root of all transgressions. Literally meaning "association," *shirk* is connecting with al-Lah something that is less than ultimate or giving to that which is less than ultimate something that belongs to al-Lah alone. It is to draw comparisons between God and other realities. Concretely, *shirk* manifests in a variety of forms. To deny the doctrine of *tawhid* by believing in and worshiping deities other than al-Lah is committing *shirk*. To create a physical image or representation of al-Lah is *shirk*. To impute the attributes of al-Lah to anything other than al-Lah is *shirk*. The Qur'an calls *shirk* an "unpardonable sin," indeed, the *only* sin that al-Lah cannot forgive. Even so, *shirk* is unpardonable only if one dies in this state of unbelief. While yet alive, anyone can repent and be forgiven. Indeed, most of the first Muslims were considered idolaters until they embraced Islam.

*Shirk* is idolatry in its broadest sense. The Christian theologian Paul Tillich defined idolatry in very concise terms that seem to capture the spirit of the concept of *shirk*: "Idolatry is the elevation of a preliminary concern to ultimacy," Tillich wrote. "Something essentially conditional is taken as unconditional, something essentially partial is boosted to universality, and something essentially finite is given infinite significance." The great danger of idolatry is not just that it denies the majesty of the divine by drawing it down to the level of the finite and conditional. Perhaps more importantly, it endangers the individual who places his or her faith in an object that is unable to sustain it. Idols will, by their very nature, disappoint us. By "idols" I do not necessary mean "images," although Islam would most certainly include physical representations of the divine under the category of idolatry. Rather, I simply mean whatever serves as our god, the locus of our highest values, that which we trust to provide our lives with meaning and worth. We can make anything our god—money, country, self, religion—whenever we invest it with ultimate significance in our lives. What Muhammad and Tillich would tell us is that the only reality worthy of such loyalty and faith is the inscrutable absolute, what Tillich called our "ground of being" and Muhammad called al-Lah.

Angels and prophets are the servants and messengers of al-Lah. They differ from one another by nature. The angels are beings created of light and can assume any form and travel great distances in an instant. Although they are sentient, angels lack the free will of human beings; they have no choice but to obey God. They serve al-Lah in various ways. The Qur'an and *hadith* mention some of the angels by name and describe their responsibilities. Gabriel, of course, was the angel who revealed the Qur'an to Muhammad, but he was also the one who communicated God's messages to *all* of humanity's prophets. Michael is the angel who distributes rewards to those who live good lives. With a blast of his trumpet, Raphael will announce the coming of the last day. The first sound of the trumpet will destroy everything and at the second, the dead will be resurrected. Islamic tradition also refers to an Angel of Death who is responsible for sundering the individual's body and soul at the end of life. It is said that the soul of a wicked person is ripped painfully from his or her body, while that of a good person is gently removed. Angels are also the custodians of paradise and hell and the recorders of a person's good and bad deeds.

Satan, or *Iblīs*, is important figure in Islam, but he is not considered a fallen angel as suggested by Christian mythology. Iblīs is a jinni who was created from fire and was fervently devoted to worshiping al-Lah. His great misdeed, according to the Qur'an, was disobeying God's command for all creatures to prostrate themselves before Adam, after his creation from a lump of clay. Possessing free will, unlike the angels, Iblis refused bow before Adam, and God cast him out of heaven. At that point, *Iblis* assumed the title Shaitan, or Satan, and was promised punishment for his disobedience at the end of time, the Day of Requital. In response, he swore that he would spend the meantime roaming the world attempting to divert human beings from the straight path.

Angels and prophets both function as envoys of God, but prophets are human rather than celestial. Muhammad taught that al-Lah had sent prophets to every nation in the world at various points in history to preach the same basic message of Islam. There were slight variations in their proclamations because their words were directed to different audiences, but all the prophets taught the oneness of God and the necessity of submitting to the divine will. They were chosen by al-Lah and lived sinless, exemplary lives.

Only about two dozen prophets are named in the Qur'an. All but a few are figures also known from the Bible, although most are not regarded as prophets by Judaism and Christianity. They include Adam, Noah, Abraham, Ishmael, Isaac, Joseph, Job, Moses, David, Solomon, John the Baptist, and Jesus. Although not named in the Qur'an, some modern Muslim communities regard Confucius and the Buddha as two of the prophets dispatched to humanity, although that is by no means a consensus opinion. Muhammad was the "seal of the prophets," the final and most important emissary of God, sent not just to a nation but to all humankind. As we have noted in an earlier talk, some of the prophets are also known as messengers, if their revelations were particularly important or received as a book. The Qur'an specifically names Abraham, Ishmael, Moses, Jesus, and Muhammad as messengers.

Although not all Muslims would count Confucius and the Buddha among the prophets, there is no such dispute about Jesus, who is known in the Qur'an as Īsa, the Son of Mārīam. The Qur'an leaves no doubt that Jesus was not only a messenger; he was among the greatest of all human beings. Like the New Testament, it affirms that he was born of a virgin and further declares that he was the *only* human being ever born this way. The Qur'an acknowledges that Jesus performed many miracles including healing the blind, curing lepers, and raising the dead. It even attributes to Jesus certain miraculous phenomena that the New Testament does not mention, such as the ability to speak as infant and bringing clay birds to life. Yet—and the Qur'an is very emphatic about this—Jesus was not, and could not be, the son or incarnation of god. Sura 4 declares:

> People of the Book! Commit no excesses in your religion. Speak only the truth about God. Christ Jesus the son of Mary was no more than a messenger of God, and his Word, which he bestowed on Mary, and a spirit proceeding from him. So believe in God and his messengers. Do not say "Trinity"! Desist: it will be much better for you, for God is one God. Glory be to him: he is too exalted to have a son.

The Qur'an's admonition obviously rests on the doctrine of *tawhid*. Regarding Jesus as a son of god, as one of the trinity, or as a divine incarnation, in the view of Islam, violates the oneness of God and commits the sin of *shirk*. Muhammad may have thought that identifying Jesus as divine was an error of only *some* Christians, those who went to "excess in their religion"; he may not have been aware that the divinity of Jesus is the *sine qua non* of Christianity. Muhammad also seems to have believed that the Christian trinity comprised God the father, Jesus the son, and Mary the mother, rather than the father, son, and holy spirit, as the ecumenical Christian councils formulated it. In any event, the trinity—however conceived—was a doctrine clearly at odds with Islam.

The Qur'an quotes Jesus as saying that he is only a human being devoted to the worship of al-Lah. His mission was not to die for the sin of humanity but to bear witness to the oneness of God and the necessity of submitting to the divine will. To be sure, Jesus was chosen and blessed by God and given a revelation to deliver to the Christians, the book known in Arabic as the *Injīl*, or the Gospel. The *Injīl,* however, is not quite identical to the New Testament or the four gospels. Most Muslims believe that the original book delivered to Jesus was lost or at least corrupted by his followers, which might explain why Christians went to excess and ascribed divinity to their messenger. The Qur'an also indicates that Jesus served as a forerunner to a future messenger named Ahmed, whom it identifies as the Prophet Muhammad.

The Qur'an frequently uses the phrase "People of the Book" or the "People of Scripture." The expression refers to those pre-Islamic nations who have received revelations from al-Lah in the form of a text. Generally, the People of Scripture are the Jews and Christians, but sometimes included are the Sabians, whose identity is unclear, and the Zoroastrians, members of the ancient religion established in Iran in the 1st or 2nd millennium B.C.E. From among these groups, the Qur'an names four revealed books prior to the revelations to Muhammad: the Scrolls of Abraham, the Torah, the Psalms, and the Gospel.

The Qur'an itself is the quintessential revealed book. We have discussed the Qur'an in some detail already, noting particularly its content and its transmission from Gabriel to Muhammad. But it is necessary to mention the Qur'an as an element in the Prophet's metaphysics. The Qur'an exists not only as a text and as oral scripture. For Islam, the Qur'an has an ontological status as the word of God, the very speech of al-Lah. There are even allusions in some revelations to a written Qur'an existing in the divine presence even before it was sent down to the Prophet.

One of the early controversies among Islamic theologians was whether the Qur'an was eternal or created, a debate that roughly paralleled a similar dispute about Jesus in ancient Christianity. The view that came to dominate theological opinion was that the Qur'an *is* eternal, having existed with al-Lah since before the beginning of time. The Qur'an delivered to the Prophet during the 23 years of revelation was identical to the eternal Qur'an. Muslims believe—and the Qur'an explicitly states—that it is not possible for a human being to produce a book like the Qur'an.

Like Jesus, Muhammad anticipated an end to the world as we know it. Some Qur'anic scholars regard the Day of Requital to be the "dominant message of the Qur'an." On that day, the dead will rise and persons will be judged by their deeds and rewarded or punished accordingly. The time of this eschatological event is known only to al-Lah. Sura 7 says, "It will only come to you suddenly, as a surprise." But, as Jesus also predicted, there will certain signs preceding the Final Days. There will be a disruption of the created order manifesting as natural disasters and the rapid erosion of human morality, both harbingers of the end-time found in eschatological visions throughout the world.

When the last day finally comes, Raphael will give two blasts of his trumpet, the first to destroy all things and the second to signal the resurrection of the dead and the ultimate reckoning. The Qur'an explains that each person, Muslim and non-Muslim, will receive a "book of deeds" that appraises his or her every action and word during life. If the book is placed in the right hand the individual will be permitted into eternal paradise. If the book is placed in the left hand, he or she will be seized, bound, and destined for hell, where they will be received by 19 tormenting angels and exposed to burning fire. The sins that merit condemnation include lying and dishonesty, the denial of the *tawhid* and God's revelations, refusing to help the poor and hungry, usury, economic exploitation, and social oppression. Interestingly, extra-Qur'anic sources indicate that Jesus will play a judging role at the Day of Requital, similar to the function of the Son of Man in the Christian Bible.

After the final judgment, each individual must cross a bridge that leads over and across hell. The righteous will find the bridge a broad path over which they swiftly and freely move, led by Muhammad himself, into paradise. But for the wicked, the bridge becomes so sharp and narrow that they plummet into damnation. Yet the mercy of al-Lah is so great that he directs his angels and prophets to rescue those who have done some good, and those who have done just a little good, and even those in whose hearts there is a single atom of goodness.

Muhammad's metaphysical understanding is a comprehensive vision centered in a transcendent and ultimately mysterious reality that creates humanity and is intimately interested its welfare. Although far beyond the capacity of the human mind to comprehend, this reality endeavors to make itself known by inspiring prophets to go to all the peoples of the earth with the message of god's oneness and compassion. While compassionate, god is also just and demands that human beings treat one another fairly and honestly. Al-Lah's demand for justice is symbolized in the Day of Requital, the moment at which human beings will have account for their lives and ultimately reap the consequences of what they have done. But even to the very end, al-Lah remains all-compassionate, all-merciful.

# The Ethics of Islam
## Lecture 31

**Adam and Eve chose wrongly and had to bear the consequences of their choice. But the Qur'anic story offers some slightly different details from the Bible. ... When al-Lah confronts the pair with their error, they confess, "Our Lord, we have wronged our own selves," then immediately they beg for forgiveness. In Genesis, on the other hand, Adam instantly blames Eve, Eve points the finger at the serpent, and no one says they're sorry.**

From the start of the revelations, Gabriel made it clear that al-Lah had moral expectations of humanity. The ethical precepts of Islam are intrinsically related to its fundamental understanding of the nature and purpose of humanity. This understanding begins with the Qur'an's version of the story of Adam and Eve. The narrative echoes many details and themes of the biblical account but has several significant differences: Paradise was located in heaven, not on earth; when Adam and Eve partook of the forbidden fruit, they and their descendants were exiled until the last day. The eating of the fruit is regarded as a mistake made in a state of forgetfulness brought about by the ploys of Iblis. This forgetfulness is, in Islam, the fundamental human fault.

For Muhammad, the descent of all humanity from the same ancestors entailed two important principles: First, all human beings are prone to the same heedlessness that led to the banishment from Paradise, and second, all human beings are fundamentally equal before God. The only difference of any significance is whether or not one surrenders to al-Lah and acts with justice and humility. This is not a distinction between Muslims and non-Muslims; to surrender to the will of al-Lah did not mean that one had to use that specific name.

What did it mean to submit to the will of al-Lah? Throughout the Qur'an and Hadith, Muhammad enjoins all humans to worship only God, to be good to one's parents, and to refrain from murder and adultery. He makes several statements concerning economic justice and living frugally. Sura 17 makes special mention of the necessity of caring for the poor, the orphaned, and the sojourner; a specific prohibition of killing children was also necessitated by Muhammad's historical context. The clear tenor of Sura 17 is the obligation to care for society's weakest and most vulnerable members.

One area of Islamic ethics that has received special attention in recent years is the role and status of women. The position of women in Islamic cultures throughout history has varied greatly, and the Qur'anic view of women and gender relations is the subject of divergent opinion among both Muslim and non-Muslim scholars. But scholars agree on a few fundamental issues. Muhammad regarded women and men as equal souls before al-Lah. Despite the highly patriarchical structure of pre-Islamic Arabia, Muhammad's teaching was only influenced—not determined—by traditional thinking about gender. Muhammad did believe, however, that men and women served different roles in society and had distinct rights and responsibilities. Whether these different social functions amount to social equality or inequality is a matter of debate.

Muhammad considered marriage a contract in which the woman's consent was essential. In pre-Islamic times, marriage was a virtual trade of property, usually transacted without the woman's permission. The Qur'an mandated that the bride was to receive and keep her dowry, and her personal property remained hers, not her husband's. Muhammad envisioned marriage as a relationship of mutual rights and responsibilities.

Although the Qur'an permits men to take up to four wives, it stipulates that he must be able to treat them all equally and fairly. Islamic **polygyny** has been the subject of much criticism throughout Western history, but the custom had a practical and humane purpose: Women significantly outnumbered men, and without male protection and support, their lives could be miserable. Muhammad recognized, however, that not all marriages were made in heaven, and so stipulated certain conditions under which divorce is possible. The couple must attempt reconciliation by all reasonable means; if reconciliation fails, both partners have the right to end the marriage.

Under Islam, females were given inheritance rights that had been restricted to males during the pre-Islamic period. The Qur'an requires that parents bequeath their property to their daughters as well as their sons, albeit unequally. Men were required to support their parents, wives, children, and sisters, and to pay dowries, while women had no comparable responsibility.

For many in the contemporary Western world, the clothing of Muslim women, particularly the **hijāb**, or veil, symbolizes their religiously sanctioned subjugation by men. But that interpretation is simplistic and, according to many Islamic scholars, misleading. Both women and men are enjoined to dress modestly; Muhammad considered modesty in dress to reflect modesty of the heart. The tradition of veiling, according to many Islamic scholars, is not mandated in the Qur'an. Wearing the veil was a pre-Islamic custom and was practiced by some Jewish and Christian women as well. Veiling was most likely adopted because of its association with the Prophet's wives. Today, many Muslim women defend the veil because they find it a deterrent to unwanted sexual attention from men, and they have resisted efforts in some Western countries to force them to remove it in public.

> It would be an anachronism to suggest that Muhammad was a 7th-century feminist. But it is not inaccurate to say that his teachings greatly improved the situation of women in his time.

It would be an anachronism to suggest that Muhammad was a 7th-century feminist. But it is not inaccurate to say that his teachings greatly improved the situation of women in his time.

No matter how one might judge the subsequent history of the religion of Islam, it is hard to see how the spirit of Muhammad's own teachings, as reflected in the Qur'an and Hadith, point to anything other than an ethical vision based on the fundamental spiritual equality and dignity of all human beings, without exception. ∎

**hijāb**: The veil worn by many Muslim women as a gesture of modesty. Wearing the veil was a pre-Islamic tradition in the Middle East and is not mandated by the Qur'an.

**polygyny**: A marriage of one man to more than one woman; the Qur'an permits men to have up to four wives at one time, but only if he can treat each of them fairly.

## Questions to Consider

1. What do you think of the varying claims made by Muslims and non-Muslims about the hijāb? Consider how your religious and/or cultural background influences your opinion. Does the "other side" have any good points?

2. Concern for society's vulnerable is a major theme in Muslim ethics and the ethics of many other faiths. How do you see this core belief played out in the world today by those of various faiths and those who do not subscribe to any faith tradition?

# The Ethics of Islam
## Lecture 31—Transcript

Muhammad's anticipation of the Day of Requital highlights the central importance of ethical behavior and the standards of justice in his teaching. But even from the start of the revelations, Gabriel made it clear that al-Lah had moral expectations of humanity. During the 23 years he received them, the revelations continued to amplify and refine the ethics of Islam. In our discussion today, we will examine the fundamental principles and ideals of human behavior as Muhammad understood them by means of the messages he received from al-Lah. We begin our study with the Qur'anic view of the human being, that aspect of theology called anthropology. As we shall see, the ethical precepts of Islam are intrinsically related to its fundamental understanding of the nature and purpose of humanity.

In Islam, as in Christianity, the world's first man and woman function as the archetypes for all human beings. An understanding of the Qur'an's perspective on humanity, therefore, begins with the story of Adam and Eve. (Eve is actually not mentioned by name in the Qur'an but she is referred to in other Muslim sources as "Hawa." Mary, the mother of Jesus, interestingly, is the only woman the Qur'an calls by name.) The Qur'anic narrative echoes many details and themes of the biblical account. Adam was created from clay and brought to life when al-Lah breathed his spirit into him. Although the Qur'an does not say so, some *hadith* indicate that Adam was made in the image of god. Adam possessed the knowledge of all things in creation and hence had the ability to name them. The first humans had no power to create like god, but they did have the ability to submit or refuse to submit to god's will. The capacity to know god's will and to decide whether or not to follow it distinguished humans from other animate creatures and made them responsible for their actions.

We all know how the story turned out, of course. Adam and Eve chose wrongly and had to bear the consequences of their choice. But the Qur'anic story offers some slightly different details from the Bible. Paradise, which derives from the ancient Iranian word meaning "garden," existed in heaven, not on earth, according to the Qur'an. When Adam and Eve partook of the forbidden fruit, they were exiled to the earth, where their descendants must now live until the Last Day. On that day, the good among the resurrected will return to the garden whence Adam and Eve were banished. The nature of the first ancestors' sin is also interpreted differently in the Qur'an. The eating of the fruit is regarded as a mistake made in a state of forgetfulness brought about by the ploys of Iblīs, the Satan. When al-Lah confronts the pair with their error, they confess, "Our Lord, we have wronged our own selves"; then immediately they beg for forgiveness. In Genesis, on the other hand, Adam instantly blames Eve, Eve points the finger at the serpent, and no one says they're sorry.

The story of Adam and Eve defines what Muslims see as the fundamental human fault: forgetting al-Lah and his commands. Because of this tendency, al-Lah in his great compassion has provided countless signs in creation and has sent a vast succession of prophets to remind humanity of their fundamental purpose in life: to remember god and submit to his will. Al-Lah intended human beings to give themselves wholeheartedly to their creator so they might flourish. This is the fundamental meaning of the word *Islam*: to relinquish one's own desires for the sake of the highest good. But human beings get distracted by the allurements of the world, particularly its material delights, and we ignore the true center and purpose of existence. It is the same tendency that leads human beings to create idols by putting the things of the world in the place that rightfully belongs to god.

Near the end of his life, Muhammad gathered together members of the Muslim community and delivered his final public address, sometimes known as the Farewell Sermon. In that discourse, which is reported in several collections of *hadith*, Muhammad succinctly restated the understanding of humanity that underlies the entire Qur'an:

All people are from Adam and Eve. An Arab has no superiority over a non-Arab, and a non-Arab has no superiority over an Arab; a white has no superiority over a black nor does a black have any superiority over a white, except by piety and good action.

For Muhammad, the descent of all humanity from the same ancestors entailed two important principles. First, all human beings are prone to same heedlessness that led to the banishment from paradise, and second, all human beings are fundamentally equal before god. Tribal and clan affiliations are of no significance. Ethnicity and skin color mean nothing. The only distinguishing trait of any significance is whether or not one surrenders to al-Lah and acts with justice and humility. This is not, however, a distinction between those *called* "Muslims" and those who are non-Muslims. There were nominal Muslims, such as the Madinan group known as the Hypocrites, who embraced Islam in name but not in practice. By the same token, Jews, Christians, or the members of *any* religion who followed the will of al-Lah were accounted by Muhammad among the righteous and the heirs of paradise. To surrender to the will of al-Lah did not mean that one had to refer to the ultimate reality by that specific name. By revelation, Muhammad is told: "Invoke [al-Lah], or invoke the Benevolent: however you invoke the deity, the most beautiful names are appropriate." This statement permits a certain latitude in the names by which the Absolute One is addressed, but it does not throw open the door to *any and all* names and attributes. The true god may not be called al-Lah in some languages, but the divine qualities of compassion, mercy, and justice must characterize the deity, by whatever name it is known.

And what did it mean to submit to the will of al-Lah? The specific elements of God's will as Muhammad knew them are scattered throughout the Qur'an and *hadith*, but one of the most comprehensive statements appears in Sura 17. Because this passage is fairly extensive, it is an excellent place to gain a good sense of the foundational ethical principles of Islam:

> Your Lord has decreed that you should worship only God, and be good to your parents. Whether one or both of them reaches old age with you, never speak to them harshly, and do not rebuff them, but speak to them in kindly terms. ... And give relatives their due, and the poor and the wayfarer, but do not squander wastefully. For squanderers are the brothers of the devils; ... Do not kill your children out of fear of poverty; We will provide for them, and for you. Indeed, killing them is a great sin. And do not approach adultery, for it is an obscenity and an evil way. And do not take a life that God has made sacred, except for just cause. ... And do not approach the property of the orphan, except with what is better. ...

and fulfill promises, for the promise will be questioned. And give full measure when you measure out, and weigh with an accurate balance. That is fair, and the best determination … listening, looking, and the impulse of the heart will all be questioned. And do not walk on earth insolently, for you cannot circle the earth and you cannot reach the mountains in height.

Much in this passage compares with the moral statements of other traditions, especially the Bible. Injunctions to worship only god, to be good to one's parents, and to refrain from murder and adultery are reminiscent of the Ten Commandments. Some admonitions recall other sages we've studied. Confucius urged his followers to speak gently and humbly to their parents under all circumstances. Both the Buddha and Confucius emphasized the practice of humility, or not "walking on the earth insolently," as the Qur'an has it.

This adumbration also addresses ethical concerns more particular, but not exclusive, to the ancient Arabian context. Several statements concern the fair distribution of resources and issues regarding commerce and property rights. The passage makes special mention of the necessity of caring for the poor, the orphaned, and the sojourner and of living frugally. Indeed, the context of scarcity in which Muhammad lived necessarily made these matters the subject of explicit attention. The prohibition of killing children was also necessitated by Muhammad's historical context. During the Days of Ignorance, female infanticide was a common practice because the male was more highly valued than the female, and girls were considered an economic burden. The Qur'an specifically forbids the murder of infant girls, and in a *hadith*, Muhammad declares the birth of daughters to be a blessing and not, as it was often taken to be, a source of grief. Here, the Qur'an prohibits the killing of any child for fear of impoverishment. The clear tenor of the stipulations in this entire passage is the obligation to care for society's weakest and most vulnerable members. The unnamed evils against which these regulations are directed are self-centeredness and materialism, two deeply disturbing trends that Muhammad had witnessed encroaching on Arab society in his day. Both materialism and self-centeredness, he believed, were rooted in the neglect of al-Lah. Rather than worship the true God, his contemporaries revered the idols of the self and the world.

This list of precepts, of course, does not exhaust the Qur'an's many statements on appropriate human behavior. Nor does the Qur'an address all possible situations demanding an ethical response. Rather, like the Bible and other scriptures, it provides both specific commands and general principles on the basis of which novel ethical situations can be evaluated and appropriate actions determined.

One area of Islamic ethics that has received special attention in recent years is the role and status of women. The Qur'an has much to say about women and their relationships with men. In view of the importance of this issue for both Muhammad and modernity, and to illustrate the dynamics of the Prophet's ethical thought, we will devote the remainder of our talk to considering some aspects of this vital issue.

Let me begin by setting some parameters for this discussion. First, we will be concerned only with the Prophet's understanding of and relationship with women as revealed in the Qur'an and the *hadith*. We are not inquiring into the role and status of women throughout Islamic history nor will we try to determine the extent to which Islam in the post-Prophet era converged with or departed from Muhammad's teachings. The position of women in Islamic cultures throughout history has varied greatly, and it would be a mistake to assume that all aspects of women's lives in these societies derive solely from Islam. That would be like saying the role of Christian women throughout history was determined exclusively by the teachings of Jesus. Second, we must note that the Qur'anic view of women and gender relations is the subject of divergent opinion among both Muslim and non-Muslim scholars. I will indicate where such differences exist to provide a sense of this range of views.

But let us start with a few fundamental issues about which almost all critical scholars are agreed. First, it seems undeniable that Muhammad regarded women and men as equal souls before al-Lah. Sura 4, entitled "Women," proclaims that men and women have been created from one soul. At the Day of Requital, all persons will be judged according to the same standards of conduct and belief. This passage from Sura 33 summarizes Islam's view of the spiritual equality of men and women:

> For the men who willingly surrender to the will of God, and the women who willingly surrender to the will of God; the men who believe and the women who believe, the men who are devout and the women who are devout, the men who are truthful and the women who are truthful, the men who are constant and the women who are constant, the men who are humble and the women who are humble, the men who give charity and the women who give charity, the men who fast and the women who fast, the men who are chaste and the women who are chaste, and the men and women who remember God abundantly, God has arranged forgiveness for them, and a magnificent reward.

Second, many aspects of Muhammad's personal life indicate that his teaching was influenced but not determined by thinking about gender in a traditional way. Despite the highly patriarchical structure of pre-Islamic Arabia, for example, Muhammad accepted a proposal of marriage from a woman far wealthier and more powerful than he, and he treated her as a dear and intimate companion. He remained married to her alone at a time when polygyny was the norm. Even after he attained stature as god's messenger, he was not averse to performing domestic chores, the jobs culturally regarded as "women's work." Finally, virtually all historians of early Islam agree that the reforms Muhammad brought to ancient Arabia immensely improved the situation of women over their status in pre-Islamic society. Muhammad did believe, however, that men and women served different roles in society and, on account of this difference, men and women were given distinct rights and responsibilities. Whether these different social functions amount to social equality or inequality is a matter of debate. To examine the social changes Islam brought about during the life of the Prophet, we will consider three specific areas: marriage and divorce; inheritance rights; and dress.

Muhammad considered marriage a contract in which the woman's consent was essential. The contract was validated when the bride received her dowry, which was often expensive gifts given by the groom. In pre-Islamic times, the dowry was regarded as the bride-price paid to her father, making marriage a virtual trade of property that was usually transacted without the woman's permission. The Qur'an, however, mandated that the bride herself was to receive and keep the dowry as her personal property, even in the event of divorce. The possessions she owned before marriage, furthermore, did not transfer to her husband. According to the Qur'an, the husband's responsibility was to support his wife and family financially, but she was under no obligation to provide for the family out of her properties or from her income after marriage.

Muhammad envisioned marriage as a relationship of mutual rights and responsibilities. In his Farewell Sermon, Muhammad tells the men:

> O Believers, you have certain rights over your women, but remember, they also have certain rights over you. You have taken them as your wives only under al-Lah's trust and with his consent. If they respect your rights, then they have the right to be fed and clothed in kindness. Treat your women well and be kind to them for they are your partners and helpers.

Since most of the Qur'an is directed to Muslim men, the ideals of marital relations focus on the rights and responsibilities of husbands rather than wives. Husbands are instructed to be kind even if they dislike their wives: One sura says: "And associate with them considerately. And even if you dislike them, it may be that God has put much good in something you dislike." In one hadith, the Prophet reportedly told his companions: "the best of you are those who are the best to their wives." The Qur'an placed few restrictions on sexual expression within marriage, but it advises men to leave women alone during menstruation because "it hurts," says sura 2. Although the Qur'an permits men to take up to four wives, it stipulates that he must be able to treat them all equally and fairly. Although Islamic polygyny has been the subject of much criticism throughout western history, the custom had a very practical and even humane purpose. Given the rampant intertribal warfare, women significantly outnumbered the men and without male protection and support, their lives could be miserable indeed. The Qur'an says: "Wed those among you who are unmarried, even the virtuous of your servants and maids.

If they are poor, God will relieve them from the divine bounty." In practice, Muhammad's teaching helped ameliorate the harsh conditions under which women lived by encouraging men to treat them with kindness and provide for those who especially needed it.

Muhammad recognized, however, that not all marriages were made in heaven, and so his teachings stipulated certain conditions under which divorce is possible. Divorce, however, is seen as an absolute last resort in the Qur'an and one that should not be pursued except for the most compelling reasons. In a *hadith*, the Prophet says: "among all the permitted acts, divorce is the most hateful to God." Couples are instructed to pursue all possible remedies whenever their marriages are in danger. When husbands suspect their wives of disloyalty or lewd behavior, for example, the Qur'an advises first to "admonish them, then leave them alone in bed [in other words, deny them their conjugal rights], then [discipline] them. And if they obey you, then seek no means against them." If these approaches fail, the couple should appoint two arbiters, one from his family and one from hers, to try to bring about reconciliation. When all else fails, both partners have the right to end the marriage. Unquestionably, though, it was far easier for the husband to do this than the wife. He simply had to tell her "I divorce you" on three occasions. The wife, on the other hand, must either ask her husband to grant a divorce, in which case the marriage is dissolved by mutual consent, or she may seek a court to nullify the marriage on specific grounds, such as cruelty or neglect of his responsibilities to her. Divorces are undoubtedly unfortunate, but they are not, according to the Qur'an, sinful.

Under Islam, females were given inheritance rights that had been restricted to males during the pre-Islamic period. The Qur'an requires that parents bequeath their property to their daughters as well as their sons. The basic standard for the division of assets, however, was not the same. A daughter was to receive only half as much as a son. Islam justified this difference by noting that the financial obligations of women were much less than that of men. Men were required to support their parents, wives, children, and sisters, and to pay dowries, while women had no comparable responsibility.

For many in the contemporary western world, the clothing of Muslim women, particularly the *hijāb*, or veil, symbolizes their religiously sanctioned subjugation by men. But that interpretation of female dress is rather simplistic and, and according to many Islamic scholars, misleading.

The Qur'an sets out no highly specific rules regarding how women should dress. In a revelation, Muhammad was told: "And tell the believing women to lower their eyes and guard their privates, and not to show their ornaments except the obvious ones, and to draw their coverings over their breasts and not to show their graces except to their husbands" and other members of their family. At the same time, men are also enjoined to lower their eyes and dress modestly. In his teachings, Muhammad considered modesty in dress to reflect modesty of the heart, which he took to be an essential aspect of the faith. Elsewhere, the Qur'an directs Muhammad to "tell your wives, your daughters, and the believing women to put on their outer garments; that is most convenient so they will be recognized and not molested." The intent of this command is to give Muslim women a distinctive appearance to protect themselves from harassment from non-believers. Modest clothing, in other words, was intended to signal a woman's commitment to chastity and fidelity.

The tradition of veiling, according to many Islamic scholars, is not mandated in the Qur'an. Wearing the veil was a pre-Islamic custom and was practiced by some Jewish and Christian women. When the custom first came to Islam, only the Prophet's wives veiled themselves, perhaps to symbolize their special status. Veiling was most likely adopted because its association with the Prophet's wives, who were regarded by the tradition as exemplars of the faith. Today, many Muslim women defend the veil because they find it a deterrent to unwanted sexual attention from men, and they have resisted efforts in some western countries to force them to remove it in public.

It would be an anachronism to suggest that Muhammad was a 7th-century feminist. But it is not inaccurate to say that his teachings greatly improved the situation of women in his time. Prior to the advent of Islam, women had no property or inheritance rights but were considered the property of their fathers or husbands. By instituting rights of property ownership, inheritance, and divorce, Muhammad gave women basic safeguards that they did not have before. Some historians have even maintained that Muslim women in Muhammad's day were able to enjoy certain rights that western women did not receive until relatively recently. This is not to say, however, that the situation of women throughout Islamic history and in the Islamic world today has always been a happy one. The development of every religion through time involves departures from the original inspiration from which it began. Often, the departures are not only serious but even directly opposed to the initial impulse of the tradition. No matter how one might judge the subsequent history of the religion of Islam, it is hard to see how the spirit of Muhammad's own teachings, as reflected in the Qur'an and *hadith*, point to anything other than an ethical vision based on the fundamental spiritual equality and dignity of all human beings, without exception.

# The Greater Jihad
## Lecture 32

"In the name of God, the all-compassionate, the all-merciful. Praise is proper to God, Lord of the Universe, the all-compassionate, the all-merciful, Ruler of the Day of Requital. It is You we serve, to You we turn for help. Show us the straight path, the path of those You have favored, not of those who are objects of anger, nor of those who wander astray."—Sura 1

After the Battle of Badr, Muhammad reportedly said, "We have returned from the lesser jihād to the greater jihād." The word "**jihād**" is often translated as "holy war," but in its basic sense, it simply means "struggle." Muhammad was commenting on the greater difficulty and significance of the internal struggle of the soul versus the external battle with the sword. In the West, much more attention has been given to the lesser than to the greater jihād. In this lecture, we will try to redress that imbalance.

Long before the revelations began, prayer and contemplative retreats were regular observances for Muhammad. The Hadith say Gabriel taught the Prophet the proper forms of prayer, including a set of intricate movements and gestures. Today, the forms and prayers vary somewhat according to context and tradition, but all Muslim rituals contain similar elements, such as making ablutions (to create ritual purity); facing the Ka'ba, standing with open arms, kneeling, and prostration (to embody the act of submission); and specific recitations. Each *raka'ah*, or unit of prayer, for example, begins with an Arabic recitation of the first sura of the Qur'an. Words and gestures, mind and body thus coordinate to create a state of spiritual surrender.

Initially, Muhammad taught that ritual prayer should be practiced twice a day, in the morning and in the evening, the same pattern that Jesus and other Jews observed. Eventually, Gabriel revealed that twice a day was not sufficient. Muhammad learned on his Night Journey to heaven that al-Lah expected prayer five times a day as a regular reminder to the faithful to reorient their lives to him. One may pray alone or with others—although communal prayer was preferred—at specified times of the day that depend on the position of the sun. Muhammad was known to pray in other ways and at other times, holding himself to a higher standard of discipline. He found praying in the quiet of the night especially meaningful because "truly the rising by night is a time when impression is more keen and speech more certain" (Sura 73).

Like daily ritual prayer, fasting during the month of **Ramadān** is compulsory for all Muslims beyond the age of puberty. During this month, Muslims refrain from eating, drinking, sexual activity, and smoking from dawn to sundown. The fast can also be practiced voluntarily at almost any time, except on a few days when it is specifically forbidden. Muhammad fasted, according to tradition, each Monday and Thursday. (It is worth noting that Confucius, the Buddha, and Jesus also fasted at particular times in their lives.)

Fasting takes many forms and serves many purposes. Its principal purpose, I believe, regardless of tradition, is sharpening awareness. Refraining from certain items in our routine experience can make us more conscious of

One of the Five Pillars of Islam, the Hajj is a pilgrimage to Makkah.

ourselves and our world. Fasting also serves to arouse a sense of compassion by enabling the practitioner to feel, even if only for a short while, the pangs of those who hunger and thirst, thereby cultivating greater awareness of those in need. While fasting is only required during Ramadan, Muhammad encouraged his community to practice it more frequently, a minimum of three times each month, but no more than every other day. (Muhammad exempted those who were sick or enduring hardship from the Ramadan fast; he often tempered the letter of the law with the compassionate spirit he believed was characteristic of al-Lah.)

**Today, nearly two million Muslims perform the Hajj each year.**

The *zakāh*, sometimes translated as "generosity," is the practice of charity. Its purpose is twofold: to support the poor and dispossessed of the community and to purify the soul of materialism and greed. Because the *zakāh* is an obligation on every Muslim who is able to pay it, in Islamic countries it is usually levied as a tax.

Pilgrimage to Makkah, or the Hajj, was an ancient practice even in the time of the Prophet; some sources suggest it was little more than a pan-Arabian carnival. But the Ka'ba and the pilgrimage were deeply sacred to Muhammad. His final Hajj, a few months before his death, provided many elements of the ritual still practiced today. All Muslims are required to perform the Hajj at least once in a lifetime, if they can afford it. Today, nearly two million Muslims perform the Hajj each year.

What makes pilgrimage such a powerful and popular spiritual exercise, not just in Islam but in virtually all religions? The five basic stages of any pilgrimage are intention, separation, struggle, transformation, and return. A pilgrimage engages the body and the mind. It is an enactment, not merely the intellectual assent to beliefs and doctrines. It fully involves the senses in ways that other dimensions of religion do not and makes the abstractions of faith more real. To complete a pilgrimage is also to connect oneself to those who have walked the path before—a return to the origins of the faith and the self, but now the place is different because the pilgrim is different, transformed by the experience. ∎

**jihād**: Literally, "struggle." Often misunderstood in the West as "holy war," it refers more properly to humankind's internal struggle with its own spiritual weakness.

*raka'ah*: In Islam, a formal unit of prayer that begins with the first sura of the Qur'an.

**Ramadān**: The Muslim holy month of fasting; the ninth month of the Muslim calendar.

*zakāh*: The Muslim spiritual practice of charity, often levied as a tax in Islamic countries, similar to a tithe in medieval Christianity and some modern Protestant denominations.

## Questions to Consider

1. If your personal spiritual discipline includes prayer, do you prefer to pray alone or communally? Do you prefer formal ritual or spontaneous practice?

2. Have you ever participated in a pilgrimage, whether one formally part of your faith tradition or of a more personal nature (i.e., to a location significant to your ancestors or to a site associated with a historical figure or event)? Was there a transformative aspect to your experience?

# The Greater Jihad
## Lecture 32—Transcript

Upon returning to Madinah from the Battle of Badr, at which the Muslims soundly defeated a Makkan army over three times its size, Muhammad was reported to have said: "We have returned from the lesser jihād to the greater jihād." The Arabic term jihād needs no introduction, of course, but the distinction between the lesser and greater jihād probably requires some clarification. Muslims and non-Muslims alike ordinarily take the word jihād to refer to military action on behalf of Islam. For this reason, the word is often translated as "holy war." In its basic sense, however, jihād simply means "struggle" and can refer to the struggle to bring oneself or one's society into greater alignment with the will of al-Lah. It was in this sense that the Prophet spoke of the "greater" jihād. Muhammad was commenting on the greater difficulty and significance of the internal struggle of the soul as compared to the external battle with the sword. "Though one may conquer thousands upon thousands in battle," said the Buddha, "the one who conquers self is the noblest victor."

In the west, much more attention has been given to the lesser than to the greater jihād. Today, we will try to redress that imbalance by examining the components of the spiritual disciplines of Islam, for those comprise the arsenal of the greater jihād. To appreciate fully the purpose and design of spiritual exercises in Islam, it is essential to bear in mind its understanding of the fundamental flaw in human existence: our propensity to forget about the Absolute One and the obligations incumbent upon us as god's creatures. I have selected for our consideration the four most prominent disciplines in the life of the Prophet: prayer, fasting, generosity, and pilgrimage. These practices, along with the Muslim profession of faith, were eventually incorporated into a cluster of the fundamental elements of the religion known as the Five Pillars of Islam in the Sunni tradition. Each of these practices serves as a vivid and constant reminder of the ideal of the life centered in god.

Long before the angel Gabriel appeared to him on the Mountain of Light, prayer and contemplative retreats were regular observances for the Prophet. We know very little about the exact nature of Muhammad's prayer life prior to Gabriel's arrival. We do know that his retreats into the hills above Makkah were frequent, and tradition tells us that his prayers were exclusively addressed to al-Lah, although some non-Muslim scholars are not wholly convinced that Muhammad had been a *hanif*, or monotheist, his entire life.

The *hadith* indicate that after Gabriel initially spoke to Muhammad, he met the Prophet at the Ka'ba and taught the proper forms of ritual prayer. Perhaps the most impressive aspect of the prayer that Gabriel taught was its intricate physical movements and gestures. For Muhammad, and later for the entire Muslim community, prayer was not only vocal recitations but also carefully choreographed postures that carried deep significance. Today, the specific forms and recitations of the prayers vary somewhat according to context and tradition, but all ritual prayers contain specific elements such as making ablutions, facing the Ka'ba, standing with open arms, kneeling, prostration, and reciting specific passages from the Qur'an and other words of praise and petition.

Prayer always begins with ablution, or the ritual cleansing of the face, mouth, hands, and feet with water. These gestures are intended to create a state of ritual purity and to prepare the devotee's heart for sincere prayer. The postures of standing, kneeling, and prostrating with the bare forehead on the ground are intended to embody the act of submission to god, the very meaning of the word Islam. Ritual prayers are thus not only spoken; they are physically enacted. Each *raka'ah*, or unit of prayer, begins with an Arabic recitation of the first sura of the Qur'an:

> In the name of God, the all-compassionate, the all-merciful. Praise is proper to God, Lord of the Universe, the all-compassionate, the all-merciful, Ruler of the Day of Requital. It is You we serve, to You we turn for help. Show us the straight path, the path of those You have favored, not of those who are objects of anger, nor of those who wander astray.

Words and gestures, mind and body thus coordinate to create a state of spiritual surrender to the god.

Initially, Muhammad taught that ritual prayer should be practiced twice a day, in the morning and in the evening, the same pattern that Jesus and other Jews observed. Eventually, however, Gabriel revealed that twice a day was not sufficient. The Prophet was told: "Pray regularly at the borders of the day and the approaches of the night." But then later, as you will recall from an earlier lecture, Muhammad learned on his Night Journey to heaven that al-Lah expected prayer five times a day. Actually, according to an interesting story, Muhammad was initially told by God to require the Muslims to pray 50 times a day. When Moses learned of this new command back at the Temple Mount in Jerusalem, he told Muhammad to return to heaven and get the number reduced. Fifty times a day was simply too much! Muhammad then got the number cut to ten times a day, but Moses thought that was still too much. Finally, Muhammad returned to heaven, and the number was reduced to five. Moses thought five times was *still* too many, but Muhammad was too embarrassed to ask God to change it, and so he returned to Makkah. Obviously, the frequency of prayer is an important feature in Islam and clearly serves the purpose of reminding the faithful to continually reorient their lives to al-Lah. The Qur'an states: "Recite what has been revealed to you from the Book, and pray regularly; for prayer restrains from that which is evil and repulsive. And remembrance of God is even greater."

Ritual prayers may be made alone at specified times of the day, which vary from day-to-day because they depend on the position of the sun. But Muhammad made it clear that prayer with others was better than individual prayer. He claimed that communal prayer was 25 times superior to praying in private.

In addition to the daily ritual prayers, Muhammad was known to pray in other ways and at other times. He found praying in the quiet of the night especially meaningful. A revelation while he was still in Makkah explained the content and purpose of nightly prayer:

Stand [to pray] by night, but not all night—half of it, or a little less, or a little more; and recite the Qur'an in slow measured rhythmic tones. We shall soon send down to you a weighty Word. Truly the rising by night is a time when impression is more keen and speech more certain. True, there is for you by day prolonged occupation with ordinary duties. But keep in remembrance the name of your Educator and devote yourself to him wholeheartedly.

Before the revelation to pray five times a day, all Muslims were required to pray during the night, sometime between the hours of 1:00 and 4:30. The sura suggests the mind is especially receptive during to god during this period of the day. After the establishment of the five-times daily prayer, Muslims were no longer expected to observe nightly prayer, but Muhammad continued the practice. At one point his wife Aishah suggested he might be overdoing it: "'Don't you take on too much [worship] while God has already forgiven all your past and future sins?' [she asked.] "The Prophet answered: 'How could I but be a thankful servant?'" Muhammad held himself to higher standards of spiritual discipline than he expected of all others.

Like daily ritual prayer, fasting during the month of Ramadan is compulsory for all Muslims beyond the age of puberty. During this month, Muslims refrain from eating, drinking, sexual activity, and smoking from dawn to sundown. But the discipline of the fast is not limited to the holy month; it can be practiced voluntarily at almost any time, except on a few days when it is specifically forbidden.

The Prophet Muhammad fasted, according to tradition, each Monday and Thursday. It is worth noting that Confucius, the Buddha, and Jesus also observed the fast at particular times in their lives. For Confucius, fasting was important during rituals of grief and mourning. The Buddha fasted zealously during his period of extreme asceticism, after which he began to take food in moderation, one meal a day. Fasting was not a *major* part of Jesus' life, but the gospels report that he fasted for 40 days during his vision quest in the wilderness after his baptism.

The practice of fasting takes many forms and serves many purposes. In Islam, as part of the Ramadan celebration, fasting technically means not allowing anything to pass through the lips and abstaining from sex. But fasting can mean, often does mean, more than this. In a *hadith*, Muhammad said: "When any one of you is fasting on a day, he should neither indulge in obscene language nor should he raise his voice; and if anyone insults him or tries to quarrel with him, he should say 'I am fasting.'" Fasting can also mean refraining from lustful or angry thoughts. The principal purpose of the spiritual fast, I believe, is sharpening awareness, and I think this is generally true regardless of tradition. If you have never fasted, and are able to do so, I urge you to go a day without food and observe the effects it has on your awareness of your body, your sense of time and habits, and even your perception of the world around you. One of the favorite assignments I often give students is to practice what I call a "media fast." For merely one day, I ask them to abstain from television, movies, radio, music, the Internet, video games, newspapers, and magazines. Most of them find the assignment very difficult, but eye-opening. The exercise usually teaches them how attached they are to stimulating their mind with inessential information or numbing it with amusements. Fasting from these things shows them how much of life they often miss out on because of the amount of time they spend at the altars of the media. My point is: refraining from certain items in our routine experience can make us more conscious of ourselves and our world. The Qur'an says: "fasting is prescribed to you as it was prescribed to those before you, so that you may be conscious of God." Fasting also serves to arouse a sense of compassion by enabling the practitioner to feel, even if only for a short while, the pangs of those who hunger and thirst, thereby cultivating greater awareness of those in need.

While fasting is only required during Ramadan, Muhammad encouraged his community to practice it more frequently, a minimum of three times each month, but no more than every other day. Like the Buddha, moderation was important to Muhammad. Although Muhammad often fasted, he did not expect other Muslims to do so to the extent that he did, and he exempted those who were sick or enduring hardship from the Ramadan fast. Muhammad often tempered the letter of the law with the compassionate spirit that he believed was characteristic of al-Lah.

I use the word generosity to translate the Arabic term *zakāh*, a word that ordinarily refers to the practice of giving a portion of one's wealth to those in need or to serve the cause of Islam. Although the *zakāh* is ordinarily collected as a tax in Islamic countries today, the word generosity, I think, aptly characterizes the actual intent of the practice as it was instituted by the Qur'an. The word literally signifies purification and is derived from the word that means "to thrive" or "to be wholesome." This derivation suggests that the payment of *zakāh* serves not only as practical way to support Islam's concern for the poor and dispossessed but also the spiritual function of purifying the soul of materialism and greed. The Qur'an tells believers: " ... spend in charity for the benefit of your own souls, for those saved from the covetousness of their own souls are the ones who achieve success."

Because the *zakāh* is an obligation on every Muslim who is able to pay it, it is usually levied as a tax collected by the state. Determining the precise amount of the *zakāh* is a bit complicated. The amount is a percentage of the wealth one has over and above what is necessary for sustenance. The figure of 2.5% is often cited, but that formula applies only to liquid assets and would be different for other kinds of possessions such as livestock or farm produce. But these percentages are only the minima; what is given beyond the minimum is regarded as a pious and meritorious act.

As our final example of the Prophet's spiritual practices we will consider the pilgrimage to Makkah. As we have learned earlier, the yearly pilgrimage, known as the Hajj, was an ancient practice even in the time of the Prophet. Initially intended as a shrine devoted to al-Lah alone, the Muslim traditions contend that the Ka'ba, the centerpiece of the pilgrimage, had degenerated into a house of idols during the days of ignorance. Some sources suggest the pilgrimage during the pre-Islamic era was little more than a pan-Arabian carnival in which the tribes gathered to drink and boast of their own courage, strength, and hospitality while ridiculing the qualities of other tribes. Circumambulating the Ka'ba, these sources say, was a farce. Men and women performed the circuits in the nude while clapping their hands, blowing horns, and whistling. (Whistling, by the way, is associated with sorcery and vulgarity in Islam and is forbidden.) Animals were sacrificed and their blood poured on the walls of the Ka'ba.

Despite these practices, which were later abolished by the Prophet, the Ka'ba and the pilgrimage were deeply sacred to Muhammad. Early in his life he was drawn to the Ka'ba and often went there to pray. He frequently performed the *'umrah*, or lesser pilgrimage, which can be made at any time of the year. Even after he left Makkah to take up residence in Madinah, he fondly remembered the Ka'ba and sought to return to make the greater pilgrimage. Just before the end of his life, he was able to visit the Ka'ba twice, once in the year 7 of the hijrah to perform the *'umrah* and once in year 10 to perform the Hajj. A few months later, he died, as if to suggest that by completing the greater pilgrimage his life's journey had reached its end. His final Hajj provided many elements of the ritual as it has been practiced by Muslims since that time.

Muhammad's final pilgrimage, like the Hajj today, took place over a period of many days and involved several different undertakings. As with ritual prayer, his pilgrimage involved first entering a state of purity to prepare the mind, heart, and body for its encounter with the sacred. Today, before they enter Makkah, pilgrims purify themselves and dress in white, seamless garments, which for men are two simple towels and for women long robes. The uniformity and simplicity of the clothing signifies the equality of persons before God. Differences of race, age, nationality, class, and culture, as we have noted before, are spiritually irrelevant in Islam. These ritual preparations also symbolize entrance into sacred time and space, an extraordinary reality that requires severing ordinary routines and conventions.

As the Prophet proceeded to Makkah, he and his companions recited the phrase that all pilgrims say as they enter the sacred precincts: "At Your service, My God, At Your service." As soon as the Muslims entered Makkah, Muhammad went directly to the Ka'ba and circumambulated it seven times. On each circuit, he stopped to kiss the Black Stone, which he had helped peacefully put in place years earlier when the structure was being renovated. He also stopped to pray at the Station of Abraham, another stone near the Ka'ba that is said to contain an imprint of Abraham's foot, placed there as he was building the shrine with Ishmael. Pilgrims today still attempt to kiss the Black Stone and pray at Abraham's Station, but it is far more difficult now than ever before, given the great numbers of Muslims who perform the Hajj each year—nearly two million annually.

Muhammad remained in Makkah for several days before leaving the city and traveling to the Plain of Arafat just outside the city. It was here that the Prophet delivered his Farewell Sermon. Since that time, pilgrims go to this site and stand in the blazing sun for most of the day, engaged in prayer and self-examination. Standing at Arafat is understood to be a foretaste of the Day of Requital. As Muhammad himself was performing this portion of the Hajj, he received a revelation: "Today I have completed your religion for you, and have fulfilled My favor for you, and approved Islam as a religion for you." By completing the greater pilgrimage and incorporating it as a fundamental element of the faith, Islam as a religion had been perfected. Ever since, all Muslims have been required to perform the Hajj at least once, if they can afford it.

Later, Muhammad traveled to nearby Mina, where he threw seven pebbles at each of three stone pillars, in an act symbolizing resistance to the temptations of Satan. He enacted this ritual many times over the next several days. Then he addressed the Muslims again and urged them to practice the pilgrimage as he showed them and not to revert back to Arabian paganism. Shortly afterward, he sacrificed 63 camels, one for each year of his life, had his head shaved, and returned to Makkah for a final series of revolutions around the shrine. Before leaving Makkah, he partook of water from the well of ZamZam, located near the Ka'ba. According to tradition, this well appeared when Hagar and Ishmael had depleted the water supply given to them by Abraham. In desperation, Hagar runs to and fro as Ishmael prays to God for water. Suddenly, in answer to his prayer, water gushes forth out of the desert, making the sound "zam zam," and it has flowed ever since.

At last, Muhammad returned to Mina, a few miles from Makkah, and stayed there several days before departing for Madinah. He never saw Makkah again.

To grasp the significance of the Hajj and the Ka'ba for Muhammad and to appreciate its importance in Islam, let me say a few words about what makes pilgrimage such a powerful and popular spiritual exercise not just in Islam but in virtually all religions.

To begin, we note that pilgrimage, like Muslim prayer, engages the body as well as the mind. It is an enactment, a performance, and not merely the intellectual assent to beliefs and doctrines. It fully involves the senses in ways that other dimensions of religion, such as theology, do not. The physical actions of the pilgrimage both reflect and shape the interior dynamics of the soul. Movements of the body coordinate with movements of the spirit. This engagement of one's whole being makes the often abstract and intangible aspects of faith more real.

The lesser and greater pilgrimages in Islam, like many pilgrimages in other religions, are ritual reenactments of its primordial history. To go to Makkah, circumambulate the Ka'ba, and kiss the sacred stone is to relive events performed by Adam, Abraham, Hagar, Ishmael, and the Prophet himself. It is also to participate in the long history of Muslims who have been to this place. Symbolically, going to the Ka'ba for Muslims is, as it was literally for Muhammad, a return to one's true home, the center of being and the source of life. The Hajj is thus a way vividly and memorably to bind oneself to a history, a community, and set of shared values. The Feast of Passover functions in a similar way for Jews. Celebrating the Passover reminds the Jews of the events that liberated them from Egypt and encourages remembrance of their dependence on Yahweh. The Hajj and the Passover remind their celebrants of who they are and what the purpose of their lives should be.

The pilgrimage to Makkah, both for Muhammad and for Muslims today, involved discrete stages that facilitated individual and communal transformation. There is a pattern common to many, but by no means all, pilgrimages. To simplify a more complicated scheme, I would identify five basic stages: intention, separation, struggle, transformation, and return. The Hajj and other pilgrimages usually begin with an intention, a decision to travel for a spiritual purpose, such as renewal, healing, or penance. Once one determines to make the pilgrimage, it is necessary to leave the place where one is. This involves a literal and a symbolic separation. At the Hajj, the pilgrim purifies him or herself and puts on new clothes to ritualize the separation from ordinary life. Pilgrimages are not easy. They often involve overcoming obstacles of some sort or engaging in a struggle or contest. Such struggles symbolize the internal, spiritual effort. During the Hajj, standing at the plain of Arafat is a jihād with one's soul as the pilgrim stands before god examining his or her conscience. Throwing pebbles at the stone pillars represents the individual's striving against the devil. And the dangers are not only symbolic. Today, performing the Hajj is more arduous than ever, given the vast numbers of pilgrims who descend on Makkah each year. To overcome obstacles often allows a transformation to occur. In the Hajj, the sense of transformation can be both personal and communal. The Hajj helps bind the Muslim community together in shared activities and reinforces the Islamic belief in the fundamental equality of all human beings. The individual often experiences a personal transformation, a cleansing of the soul, a new understanding or insight. I highly recommend that you read the "Letter from Makkah" in *The Autobiography of Malcolm X*, if you have not already, to gain a sense of the profoundly transformative effects of the Hajj. Finally, the movement of the Hajj is, in a sense, circular. The pilgrim usually goes back to the place from which he or she began. Muhammad returns to Madinah. But now that place is different because the pilgrim is different. Transformed by the experience, the pilgrim is not the same person who left.

Let us draw to a close this discussion of the spiritual practices of the Prophet by reiterating the features most common to them all: repetition and remembrance. Human beings are forgetful creatures. We are so easily distracted by the delights of the world and our daily cares that we often fail to remember who we really are and what things in life are of true and lasting value. Praying daily, fasting yearly, practicing generosity, and performing pilgrimage all serve to prod the memory about those things. The world is big and our minds are small; we never cease needing to be reminded of what is really important.

# The Conquest of Makkah
## Lecture 33

Within two years of the migration to Madinah, Muhammad and the Muslims finally faced the Quraysh in a major conflict at the well of Badr. Against the odds, and with the help of al-Lah, they believed, the Muslims defeated a Makkan army of over 1,000. ... A year later, they squared off against the Muslims at Uhud, just outside of Madinah. This time, due to greed and a lack of discipline, the Muslims were beaten ... [but] had not been utterly destroyed. ... The Makkans returned home victorious but not champions.

Muhammad's farewell pilgrimage a few months before his death in 632 C.E. capped a series of significant episodes that led to the triumph of Islam in Arabia. Within a few years of the migration to Madinah, Muhammad and the Muslims fought several battles against the Quraysh and other tribes, both Arabic and Jewish. Throughout this period, Muhammad was unable to avert a confederation of his enemies, but he was able to contain its size while increasing the strength of his own army. At the Siege of Madinah, the Muslims used trench warfare to outwit an enemy coalition that grossly outnumbered them, and the victorious forces did not show their customary mercy on their prisoners. The Persians and Byzantines took note of this shifting balance of power in the Arabian Peninsula and began to call Muhammad "king of the Arabs."

Muhammad had longed for years to perform the Hajj, but only in 628 C.E., year 6 of the Hijrah, did he feel the situation allowed him to perform the *'umrah*, the lesser pilgrimage. Before he set out, he offered the Makkans a truce but also indicated his preparedness to fight if they did not accept it. The Quraysh were fully aware of the military prowess of the Muslims by now and agreed to the terms of the 10-year Treaty of Hudaybiyyah. Effectively, the Quraysh were acknowledging Muhammad as an equal, and they were impressed by the Muslims' desire to incorporate the ancient pilgrimage into Islam.

In the years following the truce, Muhammad mounted sporadic military expeditions against assorted tribes. He also sent letters to the leaders of the Byzantine and Persian empires and Yemen, inviting them to embrace Islam. They declined. But overall, during this relatively quiet period, Muhammad enjoyed domestic life in Madinah.

The Treaty of Hudaybiyyah did not last for 10 years. In 630, a Quraysh ally attacked a Muslim ally. Muhammad asked the Quraysh to pay blood money and break their association with the ally or consider the treaty invalid. Unwisely, they chose nullification. Muhammad was now committed to the conquest of the Quraysh. Just before 10,000 Muslims besieged Makkah, Abu Sufyan embraced Islam, acknowledging that Makkah's patron deities were powerless before al-Lah. In response, Muhammad promised the Makkans that Abu Sufyan's home would be a safe haven. With just a few skirmishes and minimal bloodshed, Muhammad had conquered the city. Muhammad then made his way to the Ka'ba, opened its doors, removed the images of the gods, and destroyed them. Most of the Makkans adopted Islam, and Muhammad's stature throughout Arabia grew.

> **Muslims have traditionally regarded Muhammad with tremendous affection and admiration.**

During the last year of his life (around 632 C.E./10 A.H.), Muhammad was visited twice, rather than the usual once, by Gabriel for the recitation of the Qur'an. Muhammad interpreted this as a sign that his death was imminent. Accordingly, he made plans to lead the Muslims on the greater pilgrimage to Makkah. During this farewell pilgrimage, Muhammad instructed the Muslims on the proper performance of the Hajj and delivered his final public discourse.

On the return trip to Madinah, Muhammad declared of Ali—his cousin, foster son, and son-in-law—"Whoever has me as his *mawla*, this Ali is also *his mawla*." Shortly after the Prophet's death, a dispute arose as to the meaning of this statement. Those who regarded it as Muhammad's endorsement of Ali as his successor came to be called the **Shi'a**, or "the followers"; those who did not became known as the **Sunni**, or "those who follow the *Sunnah*" (the words and example of Muhammad).

Just a few months after the farewell pilgrimage, Muhammad became ill and suffered severe head pain for several days. He died in Madinah in Aīshah's apartment on or around June 8, 632, at the age of 63. Many Muslims refused to believe that he had actually died. As soon as he received the news, Abu Bakr, one of Muhammad's oldest and closest companions went to the mosque and announced: "O believers, if you worship Muhammad, then know that Muhammad is dead. But if you worship al-Lah, know that al-Lah never dies." The Prophet's tomb now serves as a mosque and a visitation site, especially for pilgrims making the Hajj. It is the second holiest place in Islam, next to the Ka'ba. As directed by revelation, Muhammad's widows never remarried. They became known as the "mothers of the believers." Aīshah survived the Prophet by several decades and helped to collect the Hadith. Hafsah assisted in putting together the first manuscript of the Qur'an.

Muslims have traditionally regarded Muhammad with tremendous affection and admiration. When Muslims say or write the name of Muhammad (or any other prophet in Islam), they usually follow it with the words "Peace be upon him." The Prophet embodies the highest human qualities and serves as the model of true and complete humanity for Muslims. For many non-Muslims, the militarism of Muhammad's last years will no doubt cast a dark shadow on their impression of him. Apologists have used different arguments—for example, Muhammad was following the example of the ancient Israelites. Each of the many arguments makes valid points, but whether these observations amount to justification for bloodshed is still another matter.

Within a few centuries, the religion and culture of Islam had moved beyond Arabia westward through North Africa and into Spain; it had traveled north through Palestine and into Asia Minor and the Balkans, and through Persia eastward into northern India. Eventually, it traveled to China, through Southeast Asia, and into Indonesia, which is today the nation with the largest Muslim population. It is currently the second largest religion next to Christianity and the world's fastest-growing faith. ■

**Shi'a**: Muslims who consider Ali, Muhammad's cousin, his first official successor, rather than Abu Bakr. They constitute 15–20 percent of the present Muslim population.

**Sunni**: Muslims who consider Abu Bakr, not Muhammad's cousin Ali, Muhammad's first official successor. They constitute 80–85 percent of the present Muslim population.

**'umrah**: The "lesser pilgrimage"; a pilgrimage to Makkah that contains fewer ritual elements than the Hajj and may be performed at any time of the year.

## Questions to Consider

1.  Aside from being a spiritual and political/military leader, Muhammad was a devoted and involved family man. How do you think Islamic belief affects Muslim domestic life, and vice versa?

2.  While wars have been fought in the names of all four of our sages, Muhammad was the only one among them to take up arms directly. How do you think this affects non-Muslims' perception of him versus the others? How does it affect your opinion of him?

# The Conquest of Makkah
## Lecture 33—Transcript

Muhammad's Farewell Pilgrimage a few months before his death in 632 C.E. culminated a series of significant episodes in his life that led to the eventual triumph of Islam in Arabia. In our talk today, we will discuss these events, covering the last seven years of his life, from the Muslim defeat at Uhud to his death in Madinah. Then we will briefly outline the developments within Islam in the post-Prophet era. This will conclude our study of the life and teachings of Muhammad, and then we will turn to the comparative portion of the course.

As you will recall, within two years of the migration to Madinah, Muhammad and the Muslims finally faced the Quraysh in a major conflict at the well of Badr. Against the odds, and with the help of al-Lah they believed, the Muslims defeated a Makkan army of over one thousand. Given their humiliating loss, the Makkans felt as if they had no choice but to avenge their defeat. A year later they squared off against the Muslims at Uhud, just outside of Madinah. This time, due to greed and a lack of discipline, the Muslims were beaten, and Muhammad handled the lost with equanimity. But the thrashing at Uhud was not quite the success the Makkans had hoped it would be. The Muslims had not been utterly destroyed as the Quraysh intended. The Makkans returned home victorious but not champions.

Upon their arrival, the Makkans began to plot another attack on Madinah aimed at completely eradicating the Muslim community. The leaders of the Quraysh sought to enlist the aid of nomadic tribes surrounding Madinah. Back in Madinah, Muhammad's strategy was to forestall a major confrontation with the Makkans by breaking up the very alliances the Quraysh were trying to establish. He kept surveillance on the other tribes in region and immediately dispatched armed squads to disrupt any coalitions that were forming against Madinah. Muhammad proved he was extremely serious about protecting the Muslims from hostile alliances. When he discovered that Ka'b ibn Ashraf, the chief of a Jewish tribe in Madinah, had conspired with Makkans against the Muslims, Muhammad ordered Ka'b's assassination and later expelled his tribe from Madinah. Ultimately, however, Muhammad was unable to avert a confederation of his enemies, but he *was* able to contain its size while increasing the strength of his own army.

With the assistance of the Banu Nadir, one of the Jewish tribes banished from Madinah, the Quraysh were able to raise a force of 10,000 men and felt confident about its ability to crush the Muslims. The year was 627 C.E., the fifth year of the *hijrah*. By now, Muhammad's army numbered about 3000 men, much more than before, but far less than the Makkans. The Prophet had been warned that the Confederates were about to lay siege to Madinah and had about a week to prepare for their arrival. Knowing they were vastly outnumbered, the Muslims began think creatively. Something about the knowledge of 10,000 armed troops marching to annihilate you is wonderfully effective in stimulating novel ideas.

Thanks to a Persian convert to Islam, Muhammad learned of a defensive maneuver never before tried in Arabia: to dig a massive trench to protect the most vulnerable part of the city. In six days, every able-bodied Muslim assisted in completing the huge ditch on the northern side of Madinah. The rest of the city was surrounded by mountains and trees, which prevented a cavalry attack. The Confederates were completely unprepared for the surprise tactic. The inability to attack with force, the lack of food, the cold nights, and dissension within the ranks of the coalition, eventually led them to abandon the siege. In 25 days, the Confederates packed up and went home. Their failure to defeat the Muslims resulted in a great loss of prestige for the Quraysh, and their commerce suffered as a result.

During the conflict—which is variously known as the Battle of the Trench, the Siege of Madinah, and the Battle of the Confederates—the Jewish tribe of Qurayza, who lived south of Madinah, had entered talks with the Makkans to join the Confederates in their war against Muhammad. The Qurayza had committed themselves earlier to an alliance with the Muslims, and reneging on that treaty would have left Madinah vulnerable and subject to certain extermination. After the Confederates gave up the siege, the Muslims accused the Qurayza of treachery and attacked them. After 25 days holed up in their fortresses, the Qurayza eventually surrendered. All 700 men, apart from a few who converted to Islam, were executed, while the women and children were taken as slaves. This action was contrary to the clemency Muhammad had shown to his enemies in previous battles. Muslim apologists explain that Muhammad had gained a reputation throughout the peninsula as one who spared his prisoners of war, against the common practice of the time, and this led to his being viewed as weak, making the Muslims even more vulnerable to future attacks. Furthermore, many of the prisoners he spared had returned to their homes to instigate new wars against the Muslims, and this led to his being viewed as incompetent.

Finally, the breach of covenant had been a serious threat to the survival of the Muslim community. Taken together, all these factors persuaded Muhammad to agree to this harsh penalty. One of the female captives became a member of the Prophet's household, either as his servant or his wife; the sources are not clear on this point. The treatment of the Qurayza made it known to all tribes that acts of aggression and treachery against the Muslims would be handled in a similar fashion. The rulers of other nations were also beginning to take notice. The Persians and Byzantines began to call Muhammad the "King of the Arabs."

For years while in Madinah, Muhammad had longed to return to Makkah to perform the Hajj. The conflicts with the Makkans had obviously precluded that. But by 628, year 6 of the hijrah, Muhammad felt confident enough to attempt the '*umrah*, the lesser pilgrimage. He had been emboldened by a vision in which he saw himself with a shaven head, indicating his completion of the pilgrimage.

With 1400 Muslims and herds of sacrificial animals, he set out for the holy city. There is debate among scholars as to whether Muhammad's journey was motivated purely by spiritual purposes. Some have suggested that Muhammad's real intention was to fight the Makkans, but on the way decided against it and hastily converted the expedition into a pilgrimage. Others argue that the Muslims were never sufficiently armed and always intended the pilgrimage to be peaceful. The *hadith* agree with the latter view and quote Muhammad as saying that he wanted to avoid the shedding of blood in the holy city and had come only to perform the pilgrimage. He offered the Makkans a truce but also indicated his preparedness to fight if they did not accept it. The Quraysh were fully aware of the military prowess of the

Muslims by now and agreed to the terms of the treaty. The treaty stipulated that the fighting between the Muslims and the Quraysh would cease for ten years. In addition, Muhammad promised to return to the Quraysh any young man who had joined the Muslims without his father or protector's permission. Finally, the Quraysh agreed to allow the Muslims to come to Makkah in the *following* year, unarmed, to perform the pilgrimage while the Makkans retreated to the hills for three days.

Not all the Muslims were happy with this pact, which was called the Treaty of Hudaybiyyah, named for the area outside of Makkah where it was concluded. Some were upset that the document did not refer to Muhammad as the messenger of god; some simply wanted to fight the Quraysh; others resented the return of some Muslims to their Makkan protectors. But after the treaty was ratified, Muhammad received a revelation telling the Muslims that the agreement should be regarded as a victory for Islam and promising them great benefits from it. Over time, those advantages became apparent. Effectively, the treaty meant that the Quraysh had regarded Muhammad as an equal, and they were impressed by the Muslims' desire to incorporate the ancient pilgrimage into Islam. The benefits would eventually pay off.

In the years following the conclusion of the truce, Muhammad continued with sporadic military expeditions against assorted tribes in the region, particularly those he believed were stirring up hostilities against the community of Muslims. During this time, according to tradition, he also sent letters to the leaders of the Byzantine and Persian empires and Yemen, inviting them to embrace to Islam. They declined. Muhammad and his community were also able to perform the lesser pilgrimage one year after the accord with the Makkans, who honored their promise to allow Muhammad to visit the Ka'ba.

During this relatively quiet period, Muhammad enjoyed domestic life in Madinah. By now, he had married many other women in addition to Sawdah and Aïshah. The exact total number of his wives is not known and may have been as many as 13. Although the Qur'an specifically limited the number of wives to four, Muhammad received a revelation that permitted an exception in his case because of his status as god's messenger. Some of his marriages were happy, like the one with Aīshah; others were not. At one point, Muhammad wanted to divorce Sawdah, but she persuaded him to give up the idea. As I noted earlier, many of these marriages were social or political arrangements, as was the custom at the time, and some were to provide protection to widows of soldiers who had died in battle. One or two may have been motivated by love. Each of his wives had her own small apartment attached to the mosque that served as his residence. The *hadith* say that Muhammad frequently spoke with his wives and even debated with them and asked for their advice. He assisted with the domestic chores such as cooking and sewing and often played with his children.

The Treaty of Hudaybiyyah did not last for ten years, as it had stipulated. In 630, two years after the truce had been signed, the agreement was broken when one of the allies of the Quraysh attacked one of the allies of the Muslims. In fact, the Quraysh had probably abetted their ally in the attack. Muhammad asked the Quraysh to pay blood money, to break their association with the ally, or to consider the treaty with the Muslims invalid. Unwisely, they sent word to Muhammad declaring the Treaty of Hudaybiyyah nullified. Almost immediately, the Makkans regretted their action. Fearing the superior strength of the Muslims, Abu Sufyan, the leader of the Quraysh, went to Madinah to try to restore the agreement. Muhammad refused.

Muhammad was now committed to the conquest of the Quraysh. He mustered an army of more than 10,000 and marched on Makkah. As the Muslims advanced, Abu Sufyan shuttled back and forth between Makkah and the approaching Muslims, trying to avert what seemed to be an inevitable slaughter of the Quraysh. Just before the Muslims were about to besiege the city, Abu Sufyan embraced Islam, acknowledging that the patron deities of Makkah had been powerless before al-Lah. In response, Muhammad promised the Makkans that Abu Sufyan's home would be a safe haven. Anyone taking refuge there would be spared. He extended that promise to anyone who would stay in their own homes and lay down their arms. The Muslims essentially walked into Makkah unopposed. With just a few skirmishes and minimal bloodshed, Muhammad had conquered the city.

Accompanied by his closest companions, Muhammad made his way to the Ka'ba, opened its doors, removed the images of the gods (or had them removed according to some accounts), and destroyed them. One report says he even found pictures of Abraham and Ishmael and demolished them as well. Then he quoted the Qur'an: "The truth has prevailed, and falsehood has vanished; falsehood will inevitably vanish." He addressed the Makkans who had assembled outside the shrine and declared the Ka'ba cleansed and re-dedicated to al-Lah. According to a *hadith*, he issued a general amnesty to all, invoking the example of Joseph, who forgave his brothers who had sold him into slavery to the Egyptians. "Go your way," he told the Makkans, "for you are free." Muhammad did, however, order the execution of ten persons who played especially nefarious roles in the years of conflict. Not all of executions were carried out, for various reasons, and at least one of the condemned adopted Islam, as did most of the Makkans. As a result of the conquest, Muhammad's stature throughout Arabia grew and his military power was widely recognized. Many tribes sent their representatives to declare their submission to the Prophet.

But not all the Arabian tribes were willing to submit to Muhammad's authority. Soon after the conquest of Makkah, a new coalition was amassing, led by the Hawazin tribe, who were the ancient enemies of the Quraysh. The inhabitants of Taif, who had thrown Muhammad out of their town when he still lived in Makkah, joined forces with the Hawazin. Muhammad's army met the coalition and severely defeated it, accumulating many spoils of war.

Later the same year, Muhammad led an immense expedition into northwestern Arabia with the intent of engaging the Byzantines, who had, according to Muslim sources, become increasingly concerned by the growth of Islam and its military might. Upon arriving at Tabuk, the Muslims found no Byzantine army as they expected. Contemporary Muslim sources say the Byzantines had fled upon learning of the approach of Muhammad's army, rumored to number around 30,000. There were no casualties as a result of this venture, but it did garner the Muslims greater prestige and more alliances in this part of the peninsula and probably set the stage for a later Arab-Byzantine conflict. By now, virtually all of Arabia had been unified by Muhammad. Not all of the tribes were persuaded by the superiority of Islam. Many acquiesced to protect themselves from attack or to take a share in the war-spoils. Many of the Bedouin tribes were particularly recalcitrant. They agreed to acknowledge Madinah's rule but tried to maintain their own honor codes and traditions.

After the conquest of Makkah, the Prophet chose to maintain his residence in Madinah. His final year of life was 632 C.E. or 10 A.H. It was during this year that he was visited twice by Gabriel for the purpose of reciting the Qur'an. Since the revelations began, Gabriel appeared to Muhammad once a year to rehearse the messages that had been given to that point. In the year 10, Gabriel came twice. Muhammad interpreted this anomaly as a sign that his death was imminent. Accordingly, he made plans to lead the Muslims on the greater pilgrimage to Makkah, believing that it would be his last. It was also his first genuinely Islamic Hajj, because now the Ka'ba had been solely dedicated to al-Lah. As we noted in the previous lecture, it was during this Farewell Pilgrimage that Muhammad instructed the Muslims on the proper performance of the Hajj and delivered his final public discourse.

On the return trip to Madinah, a seemingly innocuous event occurred that would later have profound ramifications for Islamic history. The caravan stopped near a pond called Khumm, between the two cities. There, Muhammad made a public statement about Ali, his cousin, foster son, and son-in-law. The sources report that Muhammad declared: "Whoever has me as his *mawla*, this Ali is *his mawla*. Oh Allah, befriend whoever befriends him and be the enemy of whoever is his enemy."

*Mawla* is a word that often appears in the Qur'an in reference to God, and it is often translated as "protector." Shortly after the Prophet's death, a dispute arose among some of the Muslims as to the meaning of Muhammad's statement. One faction took it to mean that Muhammad was appointing Ali to be his successor, taking the word *mawla* to mean "master" or "one with authority." The other faction contended that Muhammad was merely defending Ali against unfair criticism and interpreted *mawla* to mean "beloved friend." The dispute eventually entailed a major split within the ranks of the Muslims. Those who regarded the statement as Muhammad's endorsement of Ali to be his successor came to be called the Shi'a, or "the followers," meaning the followers of Ali. Those who did not accept that interpretation became known as the "Sunni," those who follow the *Sunnah*, the words and example of Muhammad.

Just a few months after the farewell pilgrimage, Muhammad became ill and suffered severe head pain for several days. He died in Madinah in Aïshah's apartment on or around June 8, 632 at the age of 63. Many Muslims refused to believe that he had actually died. As soon as he received the news, Abu Bakr, one of Muhammad's oldest and closest companions went to the mosque and announced: "Oh believers, if you worship Muhammad, then know that Muhammad is dead. But if you worship al-Lah, know that al-Lah never dies." Abu Bakr then recited a passage from the Qur'an: "Muhammad was no more than a messenger like the messengers before him. Should he die or get killed, would you turn back on [God]."

The Prophet was buried the next day at the same place where he died. According to Abu Bakr: "Allah does not cause a prophet to die but in the place where he is to be buried." His tomb now serves as a mosque and a visitation site, especially for pilgrims making the Hajj. It is the second holiest place in Islam, next to the Ka'ba.

As directed by revelation, his widows never remarried. After his death, their stature in the community increased, and they became known as the "mothers of the believers." Aïshah survived him by several decades and helped to collect the scattered sayings of and about Muhammad that would comprise the *hadith*. His wife Hafsah assisted in putting together the first manuscript of the Qur'an. Some of the widows even became involved in Arabian politics and took sides when the internal dissension among Muslims increased.

Abu Bakr's words announcing Muhammad's demise effectively eliminated any possibility that Muhammad himself might be deified, although in view of his ardent emphasis on the oneness of god, such a development would likely never occur or long be tolerated. Yet, Muslims have traditionally regarded Muhammad with tremendous affection and admiration. When Muslims say or write the name of Muhammad, or any other prophet in Islam, they usually follow it with the words "Peace be upon him." The Qur'an calls him as "a mercy to the worlds" and says "The messenger of God has set up a good example for those among you who seek God and the Last Day, and constantly think about God." Although he was not divine, Islam asserts that Muhammad was the most perfect of god's creatures. The Prophet thus embodies the highest human qualities and serves as the model of true and complete humanity for Muslims. In particular, Muslims stress his humility and simple life, his equanimity and dignity, his honesty and promise-keeping, his courage and commitment to justice.

For many non-Muslims, the militarism of Muhammad's last years will no doubt cast a dark shadow on some of what they might consider his finer qualities. Apologists have used different arguments to mitigate this concern. Some writers note that Muhammad's military actions—even those that appear to be offensive rather than defensive—were motivated purely by the desire to preserve his community and hence true faith in god. In the ancient Arabian context, raids and the collecting of spoils were necessary to pre-empt attacks by other tribes and clans. Others observe that Muhammad instituted important rules of warfare where there were none before. Finally, some contend that Muhammad's use of the sword was in effect no different from the practices of the ancient Israelites and their prophets, by whom he was inspired. Muhammad and the ancient Israelites believed that God had sanctioned battle with their enemies and even fought on their behalf. Each of these arguments makes valid points, but whether these observations amount to justification for bloodshed is still another matter.

Muhammad's death sparked a crisis in Arabia. The first issue to confront the community was determining his successor. Unlike the Buddha and Jesus, who established *religious* communities, Muhammad governed a political state as well as a religious institution by the time he died. Having only recently unified the peninsula and established a new order of things, Muhammad left Arabia in a precarious position and agreeing upon a *khalif*, or successor to the Prophet, was paramount. Two different views emerged about the how the process unfolded. According to the Sunni view, Muhammad expected the Muslim community to elect a *khalif,* and he clearly favored his close friend, Abu Bakr. Abu Bakr was nominated and chosen by the Prophet's closest companions. The Shi'a view, on the other, contends that Muhammad had in fact appointed Ali at the pond at Khumm, several months before his death. For the Shi'a, Ali was the first *khalif*; for the Sunni, Abu Bakr was the first and Ali was the fourth successor to Muhammad. The dispute was never resolved and remains a point of disagreement between two branches of the religion. Today, the Sunni constitute about 80–85% of the Muslim population and the Shi'a make up between 15–20%.

After uniting the Arabian peninsula, Islam continued to spread throughout the world. Within a few centuries, the religion and culture of Islam had moved beyond Arabia westward through Northern Africa and into Spain; it had traveled north through Palestine and into Asia Minor and the Balkans, and through Persia eastward into northern India. Eventually, it traveled to China, through Southeast Asia and into Indonesia, which is today the nation with the largest Muslim population. It is currently the second largest religion next to Christianity and the world's fastest growing faith.

# Their Lives Compared
## Lecture 34

**Aside from the fabulous birth narratives and the occasional anecdotes about their early lives, we are able to say very little about these four individuals prior to adulthood. ... Whatever the nature of their prescribed education, it is clear that each of them had a thirst for understanding.**

Without losing sight of their rootedness in particular times and places, we will now put those contextual matters in the background so we might give greater attention to the similarities and differences in the lives and teachings of our four sages to determine, as far as possible, what significance these four have for our lives today.

All four sages were born into old, well-established civilizations in the midst of momentous changes. The natures of those changes, however, were not the same. In view of their cultural settings, part of the greatness of each of these teachers must lie in his attunement to the profound issues driving the changes in his society and the clarity of his vision to imagine a way through them. Certainly, that keen awareness was rooted in a heightened sensitivity to the suffering of others.

Each of the four sages could claim a noble heritage but was unable or unwilling to take advantage of his ancestry. More importantly, each tried to redefine nobility as a matter of character, not birth.

The histories of the early lives of our sages are sketchy at best. Each is the subject of stories about how his early life foretold his future greatness or indicated something about his mature outlook on life. What does this really tell us? Probably not a great deal. It is likely that each of these stories was created and transmitted by pious followers who were using fictional devices to convey their beliefs. The stories tell us more about the impressions that Confucius, the Buddha, Jesus, and Muhammad left on their followers than anything of great significance about their historical lives. In terms of marital and family arrangements, Confucius, the Buddha, Jesus, and Muhammad seem to represent the gamut of human possibilities. As with their families of origin, it is difficult to draw compelling conclusions about the role that marriage and children may have played in their spiritual outlooks.

Little is known about these sages' formal education (or lack thereof), but each had a thirst for understanding and a fearless love for the truth that inspired them to endure hardships, such as persecution, exile, harsh asceticism, and even death. All four eventually committed themselves to a life of material simplicity, yet none of them believed there was anything intrinsically wrong with wealth and possessions—rather, they were distractions from the noble life.

All four were committed to spiritual discipline; all thought that becoming a certain kind of person by means of deliberate activities was essential, but each practiced different disciplines. But amid their diverse practices, one form of discipline is common to all four of these sages. Its commonality and centrality in their lives makes it tempting to suggest that perhaps this exercise was the secret of their success: All took time to be quiet, to focus on interior experience, and to allow the mind to settle and become receptive to what the world had to teach them.

**It [is] tempting to suggest that perhaps this exercise was the secret of their success: All took time to be quiet.**

The lives of our four sages remind us of the necessity to stop and pay attention to our lives. Taking time to be quiet and attending to our lives need not result in some intense, enlightening religious experience. Indeed, such intense moments are rare. But it must be a regular practice. It is simply a way to remind ourselves of what is *really* important, because we forget.

Confucius, the Buddha, Jesus, and Muhammad were four lives separated by culture and time, each nurtured in different ways, each brought up with different educations and in different religious traditions, yet connected by a desire to live life to its fullest extent, to understand it at its deepest levels, and to face its truths with courage. ■

1. Has formal education or mentoring played a role in your spiritual or philosophical life? What about the lives of your faith or tradition's leaders?

2. What spiritual or other disciplines, if any, have you found most valuable to your own development?

# Their Lives Compared
## Lecture 34—Transcript

Up to now, we have focused our studies on the lives and teachings of Confucius, the Buddha, Jesus, and Muhammad within their particular historical contexts. This approach has allowed us to appreciate these teachers as individuals influenced by and responding to specific moments and settings within the human experience. It is time now to begin a new stage in our inquiry by considering their lives and teachings from a comparative point-of-view. Without losing sight of their rootedness in particular times and places, we will now put those contextual matters in the background so we might give greater attention to the similarities and differences in the patterns of their lives and teachings. Our ultimate purpose in making this comparative study is to bring us closer to determining what significance these four have for our lives today. We will begin by looking at their life stories, and in the next lecture we will consider the similarities and differences in their teachings.

Early in the course, we noted that Confucius, the Buddha, Jesus, and Muhammad were all born into old, well-established civilizations that were in the midst of momentous changes. The natures of those changes, however, were not the same. China in Confucius' day was struggling with political turmoil as petty kingdoms governed by selfish rulers and self-serving aristocrats began to vie for control of the region. Warfare was rampant, and human life was cheap. These developments necessarily shaped the issues with which Confucius and other Chinese had to struggle: questions about human harmony and appropriate governance.

The political situation in the Buddha's India was far more stable than China at the time of Confucius, but it was undergoing an *intellectual* revolution, a complete shift in worldview. In the centuries just before the Buddha, Indians had adopted the view that life was governed by the principle of karma and that individuals were subject to an invidious cycle of birth, death, and rebirth. The value of the entire phenomenal world had been called into question, and the Buddha responded by discovering and teaching a way to be happy by not denying the impermanence and suffering of existence.

Compared to the cultures of Confucius and Muhammad, the Palestine of Jesus' day seemed closer to the India of the Buddha. At least in the first 30 years of the 1st century C.E. when he lived, Palestine was not subject to the incessant warfare of ancient China and Arabia. But the relative calm in Judea and Galilee could not mask the subterranean tensions that were stretching and ripping the fabric of Jewish society. The stresses on that culture constellated around a number of oppositions: Jew and Roman; rich and poor; collaborators and rebels; clean and unclean; temple and synagogue; Sadducee and Pharisee. These tensions decisively shaped Jesus' outlook on life and informed his vision of a world in which such oppositions no longer existed.

Prior to Muhammad's birth, many ancient Arabs sensed that the old tribal and clan system and its virtues and code of honor were no longer serving the best interests of the Arabian people. As warfare continued to plague the tribes and clans, there was a growing, but mostly unconscious, intuition that something needed to change, yet insight into the nature of that change had not yet broken to the surface. It took someone of Muhammad's perceptive nature to respond to that yearning and listen to the words from deep within to articulate a way to transformation.

In view of the nature of their cultural settings, part of the greatness of each of these teachers must lie in his attunement to the profound issues driving the changes in his society and the clarity of his vision to imagine a way through them. Certainly, that keen awareness was rooted in a heightened sensitivity to the suffering of others. Perhaps some are born with a more compassionate nature than others; perhaps these four came into the world with a greater measure of compassion than most of us. But in any event, they all tell us that concern for others—call it humaneness (Confucius), call it compassion (the Buddha), call it love (Jesus), call it mercy (Muhammad)—is a quality than can be—and must be—developed and matured.

In our first lecture, I mentioned that each of the four sages could claim a noble heritage but was unable or unwilling to take advantage of his ancestry. Confucius was born into a family of nobility who had at one time served the ruling duke of the Kingdom of Song. But the family had fallen on hard times and become impoverished. The only benefit Confucius received from this heritage was his entitlement to an education, of which he took complete advantage. The Buddha was born into the caste of nobility and warriors, although he was probably not a prince as legend describes. He had every advantage his station in life could afford him, yet in the end, he found that having everything was not enough. That heritage and its many benefits were simply not sufficient for Siddhattha Gotama, and he felt compelled to relinquish them. The gospel writers Matthew and Luke trace Jesus' lineage back to Israelite royalty and to some of the luminaries of the Jewish faith. Those genealogies were most likely fabricated, but they serve the very important theological purpose of stating what constitutes genuine power and authentic humanity. The life of Jesus—in its humility and simplicity—was closer to the way of god than was the life of Caesar in all its glory and power. Muhammad, like Confucius, was born into a family that once commanded some prestige but by the time of his birth had fallen on hard times and had tarnished its reputation. His ancestry, therefore, did little to advance his way in the world. But by the end of his life, he was being hailed by some as the King of the Arabs.

While we might say that each of the four was born with a *claim* to noble heritage, what is more important is that they each tried to *redefine* nobility. All four came into cultures that understood nobility to be a status conferred by birth. An individual was *born* an aristocrat or a noble. But Confucius, the Buddha, and Muhammad all said that true nobility was a matter of character—how one acted and treated other human beings—and that real nobility was a possibility for anyone, not merely those born into a certain class, caste, or clan. Jesus did not use the term nobility, but he argued and demonstrated the point in other ways. For Jesus, participating in the kingdom of god had nothing to do with being born into the priestly or ruling class, or being born a "clean" person, or being born a Jew. He illustrated that point by his subversive parables and association with the outcastes. Being a subject in god's kingdom depended on embracing the divine qualities of forgiveness and compassion, not on the status of one's birth.

The histories of the early lives of our sages are sketchy at best. In some cases we have detailed and fascinating reports, but in most instances those accounts border on or enter into the mythic realm. In each case, the stories describe unusual circumstances surrounding his conception, birth, and parentage.

Confucius was born to a very old father and a very young mother who conceived him in the fields. It is not clear if their union was even legitimate. But just as in the stories of the other three, there is the hint of divine intention in Confucius' birth. His parents had prayed for a child at a mountain shrine and regarded Confucius as the answer to their prayers. Like Muhammad, Confucius probably never really knew his father. Shu-liang died when Confucius was three; his mother lived longer, but she too died when he was only 23.

For the Buddha, the stories of his mother's dream on the night of his conception and his birth in the grove of Lumbini point to the extraordinary significance of his coming into the world. Whereas Confucius and Muhammad lost their fathers very early in life, the Buddha lost his mother, Queen Mahamaya, who died one week after giving birth. But he was lovingly raised by his mother's sister and his natural father, who were heartbroken when he decided to leave their home to live the life of a samana. Of the four sages, only the Buddha seems to have had a close relationship with his father.

The gospels intimate that Joseph was not Jesus' real father, and the New Testament has almost nothing to say about their relationship. They *may* have been close, or maybe not; the gospels do not say. We are not even told when Joseph died; it may have been early in Jesus' life. The New Testament does say a fair amount about his mother Mary—as does the Qur'an. Both the Christian and Muslim scriptures indicate that Jesus' birth was accomplished with divine intention and by means of a virginal conception. Yet, we know very little about the nature of Jesus' relationship with his mother. We assume it was close, and there are some stories to support that, but sometimes it is portrayed as strained. In the gospels, Jesus occasionally makes what seems to be a harsh or rude statement to her, such as his retort to her at the wedding in Cana.

Muhammad came into the world as an orphan since his father died before he was even born. The element of divine intention in the story of Muhammad comes in the anecdote where the bright light between his father Abdallah's eyes disappears when the Prophet is conceived. Muhammad essentially had two mothers, his Bedouin foster mother, Halimah, and his natural mother, Aminah. But his relationships with both were short-lived. He stayed with Halimah until he was four, and Aminah died when he was six. For much of his young life, he resided with his uncle Abu Talib and his wife Fatimah, who cared for him like a son.

Each of the four sages is the subject of stories about his early life that foretell his future greatness or indicate something about his mature outlook on life. Confucius was fond of playing at rituals. Astrologers predicted that Siddhattha Gotama would become a great emperor or a great sage. At age 12, Jesus astounded the temple authorities in Jerusalem with his wisdom and wit. When he was four, two men opened Muhammad's chest and cleansed his heart, just as he would later open the Ka'ba and cleanse it of its idols.

What do the comparisons of these stories really tell us about these four individuals or their paths to wisdom? Overall, I would have to say, "Not a great deal." It is likely that each of these stories was created and transmitted by pious followers who were using fictional devices to convey their beliefs in the ultimate significance of their sage or his teachings. The stories tell us more about the impressions that Confucius, the Buddha, Jesus, and Muhammad left on their followers than anything of great significance about their historical lives. We are not even able to draw firm conclusions about how their lives in their families of origins may have contributed to the persons they were to become. One might be tempted, for example, to say that the absence of their natural fathers had a profound effect on Confucius, Muhammad, and perhaps Jesus. It is tempting to suggest that Jesus' relationship with his father—if it *were* disrupted by Joseph's death or perhaps his aloofness—may have driven Jesus to seek the comfort in a "heavenly" father as a form of psychological compensation. But that is to speculate where the Bible is silent.

Furthermore, Confucius and Muhammad, who certainly had absent fathers, did not incorporate a divine father into their views. Muhammad scrupulously avoided even the *hint* that al-Lah had children. Perhaps it is significant that

Confucius, the Buddha, Muhammad, and maybe Jesus each lost a natural parent in their early lives. If so, this similarity might suggest their childhood losses made them particularly empathetic to the suffering of others. Beyond that bit of speculation, I find little in the historical lives of our four teachers to indicate that their extraordinary qualities were somehow determined in their families of origin. But perhaps that fact is meaningful in itself. No matter where we come from or the circumstances of our early lives, genuine humanity always remains within our grasp.

Aside from the fabulous birth narratives and the occasional anecdotes about their early lives, we are able to say very little about these four individuals prior to adulthood. I wish we had more information about these formative years, particularly about their educational experiences. We are reasonably sure that both Confucius and the Buddha had formal schooling, but we are uncertain about Jesus and Muhammad. But whatever the nature of their prescribed education, it is clear that each of them had a thirst for understanding. Confucius loved to read books and clearly derived much of his wisdom from the ancients. In his early life, the Buddha was trained in the Vedas and the skills of warfare, as would have been appropriate for a boy of his caste. Later, he applied the discipline he gained in these pursuits to study himself. The Buddha's quest of wisdom was whetted by the desire for self-understanding. Jesus was a keen observer of society and human relationships. He was deeply sensitive to the ways the prevailing social arrangements of his time disrupted the love and concern for others that god had intended for humanity. Muhammad loved to look at and listen to the world in search of "signs" about the purpose of living. Much like the Buddha and Jesus, he spent copious periods in solitude—waiting, watching, and listening. Each of these four sages had clearly developed a fearless love for the truth that inspired them to endure hardships, such as persecution, exile, harsh asceticism, and even death.

In terms of marital and family arrangements, Confucius, the Buddha, Jesus, and Muhammad seem to represent the gamut of human possibilities. Confucius was married and had two children. But the sources tell us virtually nothing about his wife or children, an odd thing in view of the tremendous importance he placed on family virtues. But if the *Analects* and early biographies are to be taken as a guide, we'd have to conclude that his marriage and family played very little role in his development as a sage. Confucius may have, in fact, divorced his wife, although that is not certain.

The Buddha was married early in life and had a son at age 29. But shortly after the birth of Rahula, he left his family to begin the quest for freedom. After his discovery of the Dhamma, he returned to his parents, wife, and son and shared his teaching with them. His foster-mother became the first nun, and Rahula and Yashodara also joined the sangha. The Buddhist tradition has always regarded Siddhattha's departure from home as a necessary act of compassion so that he might bring back to his family—and to all beings—the path to nibbana.

In all likelihood, Jesus never married or, if he did, became a widower early in life. The New Testament reports that Jesus had close friendships with women and men, but determining the precise nature of those relationships can only be speculative. It is sometimes hard to judge Jesus' attitudes to marriage and family life. The gospels report numerous instances in which he appears to advocate a disruption of the traditional family structure. Mark, for instance, reports a scene in which Jesus ignores his mother and brothers and tells his listeners, "Whoever does the will of God is my brother and sister and mother." It is quite possible that Jesus envisioned the coming of the kingdom of god as supplanting conventional familial relationships.

Muhammad's marital and family life was the most complicated among the four sages. Throughout his life, he had around a dozen wives and many children, although some of his children died young; all but one or two children predeceased him. We have noted before that the motivations for his marriages were diverse: some were political, some humanitarian, some perhaps romantic. We have also observed that some of his marriages were happy and some were not, but that he tried, according to the *hadith*, to treat all of his wives with kindness and told his followers to do the same. It is also clear that Muhammad often consulted his wives—at least some of them—and sought their advice on important matters. Of our four sages, Muhammad seems to be the one who would most deserve the title of "family man."

As with the arrangements of their families of origin, it is difficult to draw compelling conclusions about the role marriage and children may have played in their spiritual outlooks. It would be wrong, I think, to say the marital and familial context was *unimportant* to that outlook, but it does not seem true that a *particular kind* of context was more favorable than another. Developing spiritual maturity, in other words, is possible in different sorts of marriage and family situations, even unhappy ones.

One area at which the lives of our sages do converge is in their adoption of a simple manner of life. All four were eventually committed to a life of having few material possessions. Jesus perhaps articulated a point-of-view with which the others could agree:

Do not store up for yourselves treasures on earth, where moth and rust consume and where thieves break in and steal; but store up for yourselves treasures in heaven, where neither moth nor rust consumes and where thieves do not break in and steal. For where your treasure is, there your heart will be also.

It would not be difficult to find comparable statements in the teachings of Confucius, the Buddha, and Muhammad. Each of the four embraced that principle and lived by it. None of them believed that there was something intrinsically wrong with wealth and possessions. Muhammad, for instance, led raids to recover the property some of the Muslims lost to the Makkans and transmitted revelations concerning the appropriate division of inheritances. Yet all four considered material belongings as a great distraction to living the noble life. Possessions could easily become the object of attachments, to use the language of the Buddha, or idols, to use the vocabulary of Jesus and Muhammad.

Simplicity not only cleared their lives of potential diversions and the source of no little anxiety; it also helped free up the time they required to devote to their spiritual discipline. Like the simple manner in which they lived, all four were committed to practices whose purpose was to bring them closer to their vision of ultimate reality and perfect humanity. None of them thought that the spiritual life was merely a matter of getting their beliefs and doctrines figured out; but they all thought that becoming a certain kind of person by means of deliberate activities was essential. As we've observed, they each practiced different disciplines to facilitate their development. Confucius, you will recall, loved listening to and performing music, reciting poetry, and observing dances. He undertook these activities not for entertainment but for moral edification. The Buddha advocated and practiced exercises to awaken the latent compassion we have for all beings. Jesus loved to eat and elevated the sharing of food to a sacramental level. Muhammad found deep significance in circumambulating the Ka'ba and instituted a carefully planned pilgrimage for all Muslims to undertake. These are all just mundane, ordinary activities—listening to music, sitting and thinking, eating, and walking—but with a particular kind of mindful attention, they became the avenues to human fulfillment.

But amid these diverse practices, one form of discipline is common to all four of these sages. Its commonality and centrality in their lives makes it tempting to suggest that perhaps this exercise was the secret of their success, but I'm reluctant to reduce the richness of their experiences and insights to just one thing. But if I *had* to name one thing, this would be it. Confucius, the Buddha, Jesus, and Muhammad *all took time to be quiet*. Confucius called it abiding in reverence and rectifying the mind; the Buddha called it *bhavāna*, or mental cultivation; Jesus and Muhammad called it praying. In practice, each of these activities was slightly different from one another. Muhammad liked to retreat to a cave or stay up half the night; the Buddha preferred to sit at the base of a tree; Jesus liked the hills and gardens. Confucius sat on a mat in his room. But their disciplines shared common, basic features: they each involved making time to be alone, to focus on interior experience, and to allow the mind to settle and become receptive to what the world had to teach them.

In one of the first lectures on Muhammad, I mentioned Bernard Shaw's play about Joan of Arc, in which she claims to hear voices from god. Later in the play, as Joan is being interrogated for suspicion of heresy, she is asked by King Charles, "Why don't the voices come to me? I am king, not you." Joan tells him:

They do come to you; but you do not hear them. You have not sat in the field in the evening listening for them. When the angelus rings you cross yourself and have done with it; but if you prayed from your heart, and listened to the thrilling of the bells in the air *after* they stop ringing, you would hear the voices as well as I do.

As Joan suggests, there is nothing extraordinary about hearing the voice of god, but one needs to make the effort to listen.

Whether we call what we hear the voice of god or of conscience, the sound of silence or the rhythms of the breath, the lives of our four sages remind us of the necessity to stop and pay attention to *our* lives. Taking time to be quiet and attending to our lives need not result in some intense, enlightening religious experience. Indeed, such intense moments are rare. But it must be a regular practice, just as Muhammad stopped to pray five times a day and the Buddha meditated in the quiet of each night. It is simply a way to remind ourselves of what is *really* important, because we forget.

Confucius, the Buddha, Jesus and Muhammad were four lives separated by culture and time, each nurtured in different ways, each brought up with different educations and in different religious traditions, yet connected by a desire to live life to its fullest extent, to understand it at its deepest levels, and to face its truths with courage.

# Their Teachings Compared
## Lecture 35

Among those who first began to suggest that religions were pretty much the same were the critics of religion, those who thought humanity would be better off without it. Today, many religious folk themselves advocate this perspective, not to put an end to religion, of course, but to see the great divisions and rancor among religions, which have been the source of so much human anguish, diminished and perhaps eliminated.

Comparing religious teachers is not the same thing as comparing religions, which are far more complex realities than the philosophies of individuals. But it is much easier to compare specific teachings than to compare whole religions, and doing so might offer some insight into the problems facing our religiously plural world.

It is in the metaphysical arena that we see some of the greatest differences among Confucius, the Buddha, Jesus, and Muhammad. Not only did they think of the ultimate reality in different ways; they thought differently about the importance of thinking about it. Confucius and the Buddha were reluctant to engage in matters they considered speculative. For Jesus and Muhammad, these topics were central to their perspectives; they were not matters of mere speculation because they had been disclosed in revelation. Yet it is important to note that there were some points at which the metaphysical teachings of all four converge: Each regarded reality as comprising different realms (at a minimum, heaven and earth) and diverse sorts of beings. They each posited an absolute or ultimate reality, and they all agreed that this absolute— whatever it is—is critical to human welfare. But here is how they contrast: To Confucius and the Buddha, the ultimate reality was beyond the gods; for Jesus and Muhammad, however, the one god *was* the ultimate reality.

This raises a question: If Confucius, the Buddha, Jesus, and Muhammad agree that there is some absolute or unconditional reality, are they all talking about the same reality even though they conceptualize and speak of it differently? Some say yes: There is an absolute beyond words, as all four sages (and perhaps all major religions) attest; this ultimate reality is conceived and expressed in different terms and images for cultural and linguistic reasons. Some say no: Father, al-Lah, the unconditioned, and heaven ultimately mean different things; *how* we think of the absolute is significant. Those who see real differences among these metaphysical views might go on to make other claims: Not all of these sages can be correct.

But one need not take that approach. It is possible to say that Confucius, the Buddha, Jesus, and Muhammad were teaching different visions of the ultimate reality leading to different ways of being genuinely human. That does not mean that *any* interpretation is appropriate or *every* style of life is equally suitable. For each of the sages, some ways of living are clearly superior to others.

> **All four sages indicate that satisfaction or happiness lies at the end of the path for those who practice the way of the noble life.**

For the most part, Confucius, Jesus, and Muhammad worked within the frameworks of their cultures' basic understandings of human nature. Only the Buddha offered a comprehensive teaching on the nature of body and self. All four sages believed in the spiritual equality of all persons. Their chief differences were in their understandings of the fundamental problems besetting human beings.

As Axial and post-Axial Age thinkers, all considered the present state of humanity as undesirable. In the Axial Age, religion came to be associated less with sustaining life than with effecting personal transformation. For Confucius, the solution to humanity's problems was education in moral virtue; for the Buddha, it was education in the true nature of reality and themselves. For both Jesus and Muhammad, it was education in the way established for them by God.

The final destinies of humankind envisioned by the four sages are as different as their estimations of the human predicament. Confucius promised no blissful afterlife. The Buddha promised the end to rebirth. Jesus promised eternal life in the Kingdom of God. Muhammad promised a return to Paradise, from which Adam and Eve were exiled. Although imagined in different ways, all four sages indicate that satisfaction or happiness lies at the end of the path for those who practice the way of the noble life. There is an optimistic tenor to each of their teachings.

There is no doubt that all four teachers saw the ethical dimension of life as playing a key role in the meaning and purpose of existence and the ultimate human destiny, an influence of Axial Age thinking. Interestingly, Confucius, the Buddha, Jesus, and Muhammad seem to be closest to one another when we consider their ethical views. All four sages thought that self-centeredness is at the heart of human misery, although they had different solutions (the example of the ancient sages, the comprehension of no-self, and a life centered in God) to the problem. All agreed that the way out of our misery is by the path of kindness, compassion, and humility. ■

## Questions to Consider

1. Have you noticed any similarities among our four sages not mentioned in this lecture? Are there other differences you find worthy of note?

2. Does your own spiritual or philosophical tradition (whether derived from one of these four sages or from elsewhere) give primacy to the problem of selfishness, or does it offer another cause as the root of human misery?

3. Besides those solutions offered by our four sages to the problem of selfishness, what other solutions have you heard suggested? Have any of them been of value to you?

# Their Teachings Compared
## Lecture 35—Transcript

I confess to being a big fan of "The Simpsons." I'm especially amused by the way the series exposes and gently spoofs the foibles of religion. One of the recurring objects of its religious satire is a character named Ned Flanders, the hyper-pious goody-goody Christian who vexes Homer with his saintly ways. Ned's piety even gets on the nerves of Rev. Lovejoy, his minister. At one point, Rev. Lovejoy gets so put out with Ned's sanctity that he invites Ned to convert to another religion: "Have you considered one of the *other* world religions, Ned? They're all pretty much the same." Rev. Lovejoy's belief that the religions of the world are "pretty much the same" voices a modern liberal sentiment held by many today. Interestingly, among those who first began to suggest that religions were "pretty much the same" were the critics of religion, those who thought humanity would be better off without it. Today, many religious folk themselves advocate this perspective, not to put an end to religion, of course, but to see the great divisions and rancor among religions, which has been the source of so much human anguish, diminished and perhaps eliminated.

One of the ways we can begin to assess the validity of this claim is to compare the teachings of our four sages. Comparing religious teachers is not the same thing as comparing religions, which are far more complex realities than the philosophies of individuals. As I emphasized earlier, we cannot simply equate the teachings of Confucius with Confucianism or the teachings of Jesus with Christianity. But it is much easier to compare specific teachings than to compare whole religions and doing so might offer some insight on the problems facing a religiously plural world. So let us turn now to reviewing the perspectives of our sages in relationship to each other. I think it will be apparent that the four teachers did in fact view the world in ways different from one another, and in many cases these differences were substantial. Nonetheless, in some important areas, particularly on matters of spiritual and ethical practice, they are not that far apart. We'll structure our comparative analysis of their teachings with the categories we've used throughout the course: metaphysics, anthropology, and ethics.

It is in the metaphysical arena that we see some of the greatest differences among Confucius, the Buddha, Jesus, and Muhammad. Not only did they think of the ultimate reality in different ways; they thought differently about the importance of thinking about it. We observed in Confucius and the Buddha a marked reluctance to engage in matters they considered speculative. The Buddha regarded certain specific issues such as the origin and limits of the universe and the relationship between body and soul as matters that lead to fruitless and divisive speculation and divert attention from the immediate concerns of attaining the end of suffering. Confucius, as his protégés often noted, did not like to talk much about the gods or human nature. Jesus and Muhammad, on the other hand, spoke freely and openly about some of the subjects that Confucius and the Buddha preferred to exclude from discussion. For Jesus and Muhammad, these topics were central to their perspectives; they were not matters of mere speculation, because they had been disclosed in personal experience and revelation.

Yet, it is important to note that there were some points at which the metaphysical teachings of all four converge. For instance, each regarded reality as comprising different realms and diverse sorts of beings. All four spoke of heaven and earth, although there were some significant differences in the ways they imagined these domains and the relationships between them. The Buddha actually thought there were more than 30 realms of reality, not just heaven and earth. But both he and Confucius understood these domains to be populated with a vast number of spiritual entities, such as gods, ancestors, ghosts, titans, and demons. They also conceived of these realms as permeable; Confucius thought that human beings could become ancestors at death, and the Buddha thought humans could be reborn as demons, and gods could be reborn as humans. Jesus and Muhammad also accepted the idea of beings such as angels, demons, jinn, and the Satan, but these were just the classes of creatures; humans did not *become* angels—and certainly not gods. Yet, angels and the Satan might at times appear in human form. Christians, of course, would later claim that god became human in the form of Jesus, an idea that Muhammad emphatically rejected. I suspect Jesus would have rejected the idea as well had the concept been presented to him in the way it was suggested to Muhammad.

But the notion of diverse levels of reality such as heaven and earth and qualitatively different kinds of beings played different roles in the teachings of each sage. For Confucius and the Buddha, the various realms of the world and beings such as gods and spirits simply described the way reality was structured. These things had no ultimate significance when it came to moral self-cultivation or liberation from *dukkha*, the highest goods of human life, according to Confucius and the Buddha respectively. But for Jesus and Muhammad, god was *essential* to understanding the human's place in the world and achieving salvation at the end of time. Muhammad even made belief in *angels* vital to Islamic belief.

This key difference might be better understood by observing another point on which our sages agree. They each posited an absolute or ultimate reality, and they all agreed that this absolute—whatever it is—is critical to human welfare. But here is how they contrast: Confucius and the Buddha did not identify god or the gods as the ultimate reality; for Jesus and Muhammad, however, god *was* the ultimate reality. To Confucius and the Buddha, the ultimate reality was beyond the gods. For Confucius, it was Heaven, conceived not as a place nor as an anthropomorphized being, but as a principle. For the Buddha, ultimate reality was nibbana, which he sometimes called the absolute and the unconditioned. Confucius and the Buddha conceived of ultimate reality in impersonal terms, when they conceived of it at all. Both spoke of it sparingly, as if speaking of it were to distort it. Jesus and Muhammad, on the other hand, generally thought of the absolute in personal terms with metaphors that suggested human-like qualities: god was lord, creator, king of the universe, protector, teacher, judge, and forgiver. Whether intended or not, these terms have a propensity to conjure a sense of the divine that brings it closer to the human world than words like the absolute and the unconditioned. To be sure, Muhammad took great pains to avoid any comparisons of god with anything humans were or could possibly imagine. In this sense, Muhammad was aware of the same problem Confucius and the Buddha understood: to speak of the ultimate reality is to risk misrepresenting it because the human imagination is simply not up to the task of understanding mystery. Making *shirk* the unpardonable sin was a way to foil the human pretense that we might somehow be able to think adequately about god.

With these similarities and differences before us, let us pose this question inspired by Rev. Lovejoy's comment to Ned Flanders: If Confucius, the Buddha, Jesus, and Muhammad agree that there is some absolute or unconditioned reality, are they all talking about the same reality even though they conceptualize and speak of it differently? Is Confucius' Heaven the same as the Buddha's nibbana? Did Jesus and Muhammad worship the same god, as Muhammad thought they did? Was Jesus' heavenly father the same reality the Buddha intended when he spoke of nibbana? Theologians and philosophers in the modern age have offered conflicting answers to these questions. Some say yes: there is an absolute beyond words as all four sages (and perhaps all major religions) attest. But because of cultural and linguistic differences, this ultimate reality is necessarily conceived and expressed in different terms and images. But those differences are merely incidental, dissimilar ways of packaging the same essential reality. Father, al-Lah, Heaven, the unconditioned—these are just synonyms for the mystery that eludes every effort to articulate it. And some say no: Father, al-Lah, the unconditioned, and Heaven ultimately mean different things. To say the absolute is father is significantly, not just incidentally, different from calling it nibbana. Proponents of this view might point to the way thinking of the ultimate reality as father yields a different way of living in the world than thinking of it as nibbana. Thus *how* we think of the Absolute is significant.

Those who see real differences among these metaphysical views might go on to make other claims. For example, one might say: Indeed, Confucius' view of Heaven is *not* the same as Muhammad's al-Lah, and both cannot be correct. One is the correct view, or more correct than the other, or another view all together is better than either. In short, acknowledging genuine metaphysical differences between these teachings might lead to the quest to find the right or best teaching or to the popular practice of regarding one's own religion as the right one and all others as wrong or less than fully correct.

But one need not take that approach. It is possible to say Confucius, the Buddha, Jesus, and Muhammad were teaching different visions of ultimate reality leading to different ways of being genuinely human. Seeking nibbana and living in the light of the kingdom of god are two ways of leading a noble life. This perspective need not result in a kind of absolute relativism in which one maintains that "they're all pretty much the same." It is conceivable that ultimate reality is such that it can be interpreted in many valid ways, leading to different ways of living an authentically human existence, but that does not mean that *any* interpretation is appropriate or *every* style of life is equally suitable. Some ways are better than others. This is another point on which our sages are in accord. For each of them, some ways of living are clearly superior to others.

In a moment, we will begin to compare their views on the manner of life each thought most congruous with the nature of reality. Before we arrive at that point, however, it will be helpful to remind ourselves of their basic anthropological perspectives, they way each of them thought of human nature and destiny.

For the most part, Confucius, Jesus, and Muhammad did not devote a great deal of time analyzing the basic make-up of human persons or trying to offer a novel viewpoint on the self. All three worked within the frameworks of their cultures' basic understandings of what human beings were. In general terms, each of them considered the human to comprise spiritual and physical components. At death, spirit and body would separate. Confucius thought the spirit would then take up residence in Heaven. Muhammad believed that the last day entailed a resurrection of the body at which time it would be reunited with its spirit. Jesus also believed in a day of resurrection but offered few details to explain his understanding it. Of the four, only the Buddha offered a comprehensive teaching on the nature of body and self. Like Confucius, Jesus, and Muhammad, the Buddha clearly affirmed the impermanence of the body. But he would not accept the idea that those selfsame bodies returned to their spirits at a particular point in time, as suggested in the concept of resurrection. For the Buddha, bodies were in constant flux. The components that make up the body at one time composed other bodies and will in the future be part of still other bodies. Furthermore, for the Buddha, the perceptions, sensations, mental formations, and consciousness—what we might call the spiritual dimension of the person—are also impermanent. The Buddha expressly denied the idea of an immortal or substantial soul or self. On this point, the teaching of the Buddha appears distinctly at odds with the perspectives of Confucius, Jesus, and Muhammad.

But despite these differences, all four sages believe in what we might call the spiritual equality of all persons. Confucius asserted that human beings share a common nature that can be shaped in good or bad ways. The Buddha argued that all persons comprise the five aggregates of being and that differences among people are due the karmic baggage they carry from previous births. But he also contended that all persons, regardless of their station in life, their gender, or their past karmas, are capable of seeing nibbana and ending their suffering on the wheel of existence. Jesus and Muhammad regarded all persons as creatures of the one god and hence fundamentally of equal value. This basic conviction seems to have inspired Jesus' opposition to the social conventions that separated pure and impure, rich and poor, the sinners and the righteous. Muhammad also affirmed the equality of all souls before al-Lah. He did, however, allow for certain social distinctions, particularly between men and women, as did the Buddha and Confucius.

The chief differences in the anthropological views of our teachers come in the ways they interpret what we might call the human predicament, that is, their understanding of the fundamental problems besetting human beings. As axial and post-axial age thinkers, Confucius, the Buddha, Jesus, and Muhammad all considered the present state of humanity as undesirable. Prior to the axial age, that extremely important period between 800 and 200 B.C.E. when the ways human beings thought of themselves and the ultimate reality underwent a revolutionary change, persons were not likely to imagine a fundamental flaw or problem in human nature itself. The purpose of religion before the axial age was to help human beings obtain the essential goods for living life—food, health, children, and protection from enemies—by maintaining cordial or at least respectful relationships with the gods or whatever powers that controlled these things. In the axial age, however, the very function of religion began to change and that transformation is reflected in the teachings of Confucius and the Buddha, who were axial thinkers, and of Jesus and Muhammad, who were heirs of the axial revolution. During and after the axial era, the role of religion came to be associated less with sustaining life by performing rituals to make the crops grow or offering sacrifices to feed the gods and more connected with effecting *personal transformation.* This new function of religion emerged as greater numbers of people came to believe that there was some defect in human beings that needed to be rectified. Religions, at this point, began to provide an explanation of this defect and then proceeded to explain its solution. We see that dynamic at work in the teachings of all four of our sages.

For Confucius, humans were simply unable to live in harmony with one another because they had neglected the ancient ways of virtue as taught by the sages of the golden past. The solution to that problem was to instill moral virtue by means of education, example, and self-cultivation. For the Buddha, beings suffered because of their fundamental ignorance about the true nature of reality and themselves. They wrongly believed in a permanent and substantial self, which led them to crave and become attached to world in constant flux. The proper objective for human beings was to practice the manifold path that fosters insight into the world as it is and eases the desperate attempts to grasp and cling to what is impermanent. For both Jesus and Muhammad, human beings have departed from the way established for them by god. Jesus was especially concerned with the social distinctions imposed on the culture in which he lived. He envisioned a day in which those distinctions were shown to be meaningless and he urged his followers to join him in living as if the kingdom of god were a present reality. Muhammad shared Jesus' concerns about social distinctions and regulations that harmed human well-being, but he viewed these concerns in light of the human tendency to forget god and put other realities in the place where god should be: at the center of all we do and think. The Prophet revealed specific ways for people to remember their god and submit their wills to al-Lah.

The final destinies envisioned by the four sages are as different as their estimations of the human predicament. For Confucius, the goal of human life was perfect goodness, bringing to full manifestation our potential for being humane. Confucius promised no blissful afterlife for the hard work of moral cultivation. Goodness, or genuineness, to use Mencius' term, is its own reward; there is no greater joy. The Buddha promised the end of suffering and liberation from the cycle of birth, death, and rebirth. For Jesus, the reward for living a life centered in god was eternal life, participating in the kingdom established by god, when the values of the current world would be turned on their head. To Muhammad, those who have submitted themselves to al-Lah will enjoy paradise, the place from which Adam and Eve were exiled, and those who have given their allegiance to any other so-called god are destined for hell. Although imagined in different ways, all four sages indicate that satisfaction or happiness lies at the end of the path for those who practice the way of the noble life. There is an optimistic tenor to each of their teachings.

There is no doubt that all four teachers saw the ethical dimension of life as playing a key role in the meaning and purpose of existence and the ultimate human destiny. This characteristic was also a consequence of the religious and philosophical transformations wrought in the axial age. During that period, individual fulfillment became closely associated with the manner in which one treated and regarded other beings. Interestingly, Confucius, the Buddha, Jesus, and Muhammad seem to be closest to one another when we consider their ethical views, particularly when those views are abstracted from their metaphysics and anthropologies.

This fundamental convergence is most apparent when we examine their views on the role of the self in human life. All four sages thought that *self-centeredness is at the heart of human misery*. All four taught about the perils of self-centeredness and all taught ways to diminish the deleterious effects of living selfishly.

Confucius, as we noted earlier, did not engage in much discussion about the nature of the self or the causes of self-centeredness; he simply offered practical advice for living with a greater concern for the well-being of others. He invited his followers to treat others in the manner they would treat themselves:

The humane person, wanting to establish himself, helps others establish themselves, and wanting to be successful, helps others to be successful. Taking one's own feelings as a guide may be called the method of humaneness.

He encouraged humility by example and precept. He told his protégés not to be concerned when others did not praise them: "not to be resentful at others' failure to appreciate one—surely that is to be a true gentleman." Rather than responding to a petty person with judgment, Confucius invites his students to view the moment as an occasion for seeing the imperfections in oneself: "when you see an unworthy person, examine yourself inwardly"

The Buddha not only offered practical advice for living selflessly; he went even further to argue that the self, as that concept is ordinarily understood, is a complete fiction, an illusion, with no basis in reality. When the selfless nature of human existence becomes apparent, persons cannot but help living compassionate lives, taking the suffering of others as seriously as one's own suffering. At the same time, engaging in compassionate practices—refusing to inflict harm and wishing for the well-being of all living beings—enables one to see more clearly the selfless and impermanent nature of reality.

Like Confucius, Muhammad and Jesus did not offer detailed analyses of self-centeredness, but they taught practical wisdom for living life in a more wholesome and liberating way. For Jesus and Muhammad, self-centered living was at the root of the injustices they observed in their societies. The rich and powerful had become so self-absorbed and concerned with their own pleasures that they neglected the well-being of everyone else. Confucius, too, saw this problem in the rulers of ancient China and urged them to return to the old rituals to remind them of their responsibilities to ensure that virtue flourished in their kingdoms. In Jesus' day, even the righteous ones had become self-consumed. In the parable of the Good Samaritan, Jesus criticized the religious authorities and those aspiring to sanctity because they were more concerned about their own holiness than compassionately assisting a fellow human being. In the teachings of Muhammad, we see how self-centeredness need not be a phenomenon solely of the individual. Corporate bodies can act selfishly as well. Muhammad was critical of the way the self-interests of the tribe or clan came to override the basic demands of justice.

Both Muhammad and Jesus contended that the antidote to self-centeredness—whether individual or corporate—lay in re-centering life in god, the absolute, ultimate reality. Indeed, they were so convinced of the priority of god over the self that they were prepared to sacrifice themselves to enable others to grasp to its importance. The Buddha and Confucius saw the situation differently. While they agreed with Jesus and Muhammad that living the self-centered life was fundamentally problematic, they did not envision the solution as putting god in the place of self. The Buddha urged his listeners to recognize the illusory nature of the self and to cling to no beliefs about the self *or* about the nature of ultimate reality. For the Buddha, attachment to ideas about god was just as hazardous as clutching to ideas about the self. Confucius, on the other hand, imagined the solution to self-centeredness to lay in the practices established by the sages of old, activities that would remind the individual that he or she was part of a larger web of relationships.

While Confucius, the Buddha, Jesus, and Muhammad appear to teach very different things about the structure of the world and the nature of human beings, on this simple point about how our lives should be lived, they seem to be of one mind: *the self-centered life is fraught with suffering for individuals, communities, and the world as a whole*. The way out of our misery is by the path of kindness, compassion, and humility. Writing at time much closer to our own, Albert Einstein seems to have captured this fundamental conviction shared by our ancient sages. He writes:

> A human being is a part of the whole called by us "universe," a part limited in time and space. He experiences himself, his thoughts and feeling as something separated from the rest, a kind of optical delusion of his consciousness. This delusion is a kind of prison for us, restricting us to our personal desires and to affection for a few persons nearest to us. Our task must be to free ourselves from this prison by widening our circle of compassion to embrace all living creatures and the whole of nature in its beauty. Nobody is able to achieve this completely, but the striving for such achievement is in itself a part of the liberation and a foundation for inner security.

# Their Enduring Significance
## Lecture 36

**Our four teachers sought to redefine [nobility] in ways that made it accessible to anyone, regardless of heritage or social position. By their very lives, they exemplified ways for human beings to live noble lives and invited the rest of us to aspire to do the same. Their teachings and examples tell us that we are capable of much more than we think.**

For me and many others, Confucius, the Buddha, Jesus, and Muhammad attract our attention not only because they are fascinating historical figures but because their words and examples enrich our lives. Living during times when nobility was understood as a quality of birth, our four teachers redefined it as something accessible to anyone, and their lives were their proof. Yet they are equally clear in telling us the noble life is no easy path. Today, we are more likely to be taught to pursue excellence. Nobility involves excelling, but it also involves discerning which pursuits are worth the effort.

The requirements of the noble life are not difficult to understand, but they are hard to implement. The first requisite is commitment to truth and understanding. Personally, I know I often prefer my pleasant illusions to disturbing realities. What all of our four teachers tell us is that truth is nothing to fear; seeing the world and ourselves as we really are is liberating.

The corollary to a commitment to truth is humility—not self-abasement but honest self-knowledge. The wiser they became, the more the four sages became humble. It's a bit ironic, in a way, that those whom many have judged as humanity's most influential persons have led lives of such simplicity and modesty.

The commitment to truth and humility draws our attention to another virtue shared by these teachers: They were willing to learn, which takes both love for the truth and the awareness of one's limitations. And learning, in turn, requires attentiveness. We have already spoken of the way each teacher set aside time for regular periods of stillness and quietude. I even suggested that this practice comes close to being the single most important factor in the development of their spiritual depths. I fear that our culture has almost completely lost sight of the importance of this discipline. We have become accustomed to seeking ever-new sources of stimulation, and we exercise little control over the things we allow to shape our minds. Our world needs to rediscover the importance of being quiet and paying attention and to make a place for these practices in our daily lives.

**The four sages recognized that the core problem of self-centeredness was manifested in many ways, not simply in the tendency of the individual to act selfishly.**

The noble life as practiced by our sages also entails sensitivity to suffering, both our own and that of others. The great emphasis placed on awareness of suffering by these teachers invites us to examine our lives as individuals and cultures to determine the ways we desensitize ourselves to this fundamental dimension of experience.

Finally, the four sages recognized that the core problem of self-centeredness was manifested in many ways, not simply in the tendency of the individual to act selfishly. Although explained and presented in different ways, for all four sages, the solution to the predicament of self-centeredness lies in transforming our conditioned ways of thinking and acting: Transformation begins in waking up to reality, to gaining clear apprehension.

While on certain aspects of the noble life the four sages appear to come close to one another, in other areas each has something unique to offer. Perhaps Confucius's most interesting belief is his faith in the near-magical power of virtue. Confucius thought that virtuous persons would effortlessly inspire others to act morally. We actually see that phenomenon displayed in the lives of our four teachers. The Buddha's teachings on non-attachment are clear and compelling arguments for the dangers of holding on too tightly to anything—not just material objects but ideas as well. This warning, coupled with his rigorous criteria for approaching claims of truth, seems particularly appropriate for our information-saturated world. Much of Christian belief focuses on the divinity of Jesus; without setting that aside, the view of Jesus presented in these lectures invites us to focus on his humanity for a time, particularly his affirmation of life in the face of death and the courage he showed in practicing his own convictions. Muhammad, like the Buddha, reminds us of our own forgetfulness and demonstrates through his spiritual discipline how to remember to remember. He also invites us to accept the inscrutability of the ultimate reality.

It is customary in Buddhism to conclude such endeavors as this course with a dedication of merits to others. Accordingly, I offer whatever merits that may have been generated by my efforts to the well-being and happiness of my wife and daughter, whose own efforts and sacrifices have made my work possible and who have enriched my life beyond measure; to the good people of The Great Courses, whose hard work and dedication make all of this possible; and to those of you who have accompanied me on this journey. May each and every one of you—and indeed may *all* beings—be well and happy. ∎

## Question to Consider

1. How might you incorporate the wisdom of each of the sages in your own spiritual life and within the parameters of your own faith tradition or ethical philosophy?

# Their Enduring Significance
## Lecture 36—Transcript

When we began this series, I acknowledged that my interest in Confucius, the Buddha, Jesus, and Muhammad is not merely academic but also existential. These teachers attract my attention not only because they are fascinating as historical figures but because they enrich my life, and the lives of countless others, with their words and examples. Now that we have come to the end of our studies of these individuals, and have spent time comparing and contrasting them, let us take a moment to reflect on the enduring significance of their legacies. Much of what I want say in this talk, I freely admit, derives from my personal experiences. I do not pretend to be able to separate my interpretations of these individuals from the rest of my life. My own history as a human being necessarily shapes how I see these four teachers. I'd like to begin with my thoughts about the four collectively and then turn to discuss each of them individually.

Living during times when nobility was understood as a quality of those who were born into a certain social rank, our four teachers sought to redefine that quality in ways that it made accessible to anyone, regardless of heritage or social position. By their very lives, they exemplified ways for human beings to live noble lives and invited the rest of us to aspire to do the same. Their teachings and examples tell us that we are capable of much more than we think. Yet they are equally clear in telling us that the way to the noble life is no easy path. While we are all capable of being noble persons, the demands are heavy and few will actually choose that road. But for those who do, the satisfactions are great and there is no higher calling in life.

I am not sure where we as a culture stand on the concept of nobility. It was not an idea that I heard much while growing up, except with respect to the old world aristocracies, precisely the association that our four sages sought to disrupt. I remember being encouraged to work hard and excel, but I don't recall being encouraged to live nobly.

Still today, we are more likely to hear about the ideal of excellence rather than nobility. Excellence is a fine virtue, of course, but it not the same as nobility. Ordinarily, the virtue of excellence is used in the context of performance. When people or businesses say they are committed to excellence, they are indicating that they wish to do an outstanding job or produce a fine product. Nobility involves doing well, to be sure, but it is doing well at the things that really matter. Nobility involves discerning what things are truly worth the pursuit of excellence.

The requirements of the noble life are not difficult to understand, but they are hard to implement. The first requisite is commitment to truth and understanding. Human beings are so adept at self-deception that this intention is essential, probably much more than we ordinarily think. Committing oneself to truth and understanding is not simply a single step on the noble path but an act that must be renewed continually. I am deeply impressed and inspired by Confucius' practice of rigorous self-examination, his willingness to look within himself and dispassionately observe his own shortcomings. We see the same devotion in the Buddha's quest to see the world "as it is" and not as we want it to be.

What I struggle with in maintaining a commitment to truth is the fear of discovering something painful or unpleasant, something I believe I will be unable to endure. I am fully aware that I often I prefer my pleasant illusions to realities that might interrupt my sense of who I *think* am or who I think I ought to be, or perhaps, to be even more truthful, who I want *others* to think I am. What all of our four teachers tell us is that *truth is nothing to fear*. Seeing the world and ourselves as we really are is liberating; indeed, it is the only path to freedom. The Buddha sent a grieving mother on a quest for a mustard seed from a home that had never experienced death. She returned empty-handed but awakened to the impermanence of life and relieved of the great burden she carried. Jesus stated the point in his characteristically pithy way: "the truth will set you free."

The corollary to a commitment to truth is humility. Humility is not self-abasement; it does not mean thinking poorly of oneself. It simply means honesty in recognizing one's capacities and qualities; humility is merely self-knowledge. It is acknowledging one's limitations in the face of the mighty mystery that confronts us daily. The wiser they became, the more the four sages became humble. The Prophet Muhammad continued to wear the common garb and cook and sew. The Buddha continued on his daily rounds to beg for food. Confucius refused to accept the title of sage and was engaged in self-cultivation to the end of his life. Jesus' humility took him to the cross where he quietly accepted the fate that he believed his mission in life required. It's a bit ironic, in a way, that those whom many have judged as humanity's most influential persons have led lives of such simplicity and modesty.

The commitment to truth and the quality of humility are components of another virtue shared by these teachers: they were willing to learn. It takes both love for the truth and the awareness of one's limitations to be able to learn. The most difficult students to teach, in my experience, are the ones who think they already know.

In Zen Buddhism, one of the first steps on the path to enlightenment is to disabuse the student that he or she understands anything. Only after the novice realizes the limitations and distortions of the conditioned mind is he or she able to see the world afresh, with the pristine openness necessary for learning. Zen master Shunryu Suzuki says, "In the beginner's mind there are many possibilities, but in the expert's there are few."

Each of our sages understood this principle in seeking wisdom. Confucius believed that everyone, regardless of their status in life, had something to teach him. Muhammad constantly consulted his wives and companions for their advice and was willing to be persuaded and corrected by them. The Buddha taught the importance of avoiding attachment to what he called "views," our everyday beliefs and judgments about the way things are. Non-attachment to views means acknowledging the possibility of being mistaken and maintaining an openness to be corrected. Although the later

Christian tradition tended to downplay this aspect of Jesus' life for fear it might compromise claims about his divinity, he too must have been intensely dedicated to learning. I suspect his thirst for understanding led him to seek out John the Baptist as a mentor and led him to the wilderness where he spent 40 days and nights on a quest for clarity about his mission in life. Jesus' wisdom came not because he was omniscient but because he was observant and learned from his experiences.

Humility and the love for truth are augmented by another quality shared by the four sages: attentiveness. We have already spoken of the way each teacher set aside time for regular periods of stillness and quietude. I even suggested that this practice comes close to being the single most important factor in the development of their spiritual depths. So significant was this discipline that they deliberately cultivated lives of great simplicity to devote time and energy to its exercise. In those moments of quiet, they gave attention to their inner life. The Buddha used this time to explore the nature of his own mind and to examine the characteristics of reality. Confucius took time to determine the congruence of his ideal and his behavior. Jesus and Muhammad spent their quiet moments articulating their private thoughts and anxieties and repeating the truths of their traditions. Then they listened in silence.

I fear that our culture has almost completely lost sight of the importance of this discipline. We have become so conditioned to the constant distractions of television, internet, sports, movies, and other amusements and activities that many of us feel empty and even frightened without them. With the advent of these technologies and entertainments, there is little wonder that the average attention span has declined so significantly in the last century, according to many estimates. We have become accustomed to seeking ever-new sources of stimulation, and we exercise little control over the things we allow to shape our minds. The Buddha taught that concentration is a skill that can be developed and refined, but it must be nurtured in the context of silence. Somehow, I believe, our world needs to rediscover the importance of being quiet and paying attention and make a place for it in our daily lives.

As exemplified in the lives of Confucius, the Buddha, Jesus, and Muhammad, the noble life entails sensitivity to suffering, both our own and that of others. A keen awareness of the massive suffering in existence seems abundantly evident in the lives of all four. Confucius seemed especially attuned to those in grief and suffering bereavement. Jesus and Muhammad were particularly moved by the plight of poor, the widowed, the sick, and outcastes. The Buddha made the awareness of suffering the fundamental premise of his Four Noble Truths and he taught ways to help cultivate a greater consciousness of it. He was convinced that the more we recognized and understood the nature and cause of suffering, the more motivated we would be to bring it to an end. The great emphasis placed on awareness of suffering by these teachers invites us to examine our lives as individuals and cultures to determine the ways we desensitize ourselves this fundamental dimension of experience.

We have already spoken at length about the final attribute of nobility as understood by these sages: overcoming self-centeredness. We have remarked how each of them understood the genesis of self-centeredness in different ways and consequently offered different techniques for surmounting it. In large measure, their understanding of this fundamental human predicament was determined by their metaphysical and anthropological perspectives. For the Buddha, self-centeredness was grounded in a misapprehension of the true nature of reality; for Jesus and Muhammad, it was based in the failure to orient our lives towards god and instead place our faith in less-than-ultimate realities that are unworthy of our devotion; for Confucius, self-centeredness arises from the neglect of the way of virtue, the path initially described by the sages of old.

Furthermore, the four sages recognized that self-centeredness was manifested in many ways, not simply in the tendency of the individual to act selfishly. Muhammad saw it in the ways ethnic groups are inclined to pursue their own interests and enhance their own well-being at the expense of others. Confucius and Jesus observed the ways the wealthy and the powerful become so obsessed with their own comforts that they completely ignore the consequences of their actions on the lives in the rest of society. The Buddha even saw self-centeredness in the way human beings neglect the lives of other creatures, thoughtlessly destroying animal life to provide for our pleasures. In short, the propensity to regard the self at the center of reality ramifies throughout our experience in both individual and corporate ways.

Although explained and presented in different ways, the solution to the predicament of self-centeredness lay in transforming our conditioned ways of thinking and acting. For each of the four teachers, transformation begins in waking up to reality, to gaining a clear apprehension of the "optical delusion," as Einstein puts it, that we and those like us are separated from all else.

Having made these general comments about the lessons we can gain from all four sages, let me turn to speak words of appreciation for each one individually. While on certain aspects of the noble life, the four sages appear to come close one another, in other areas each has something unique to offer. Perhaps unique is too strong a term. What I mean simply is that it was through a particular teacher than *I* gained an important insight. That is not to say, necessarily, that the same insight could not be learned from one of the others.

Three things in particular intrigue me about Confucius. Perhaps the most interesting is his belief in the near-magical power of virtue. Confucius thought that virtuous persons, those who practiced the way of moral self-cultivation, would effortlessly inspire others to act morally. We actually see that phenomenon displayed in the lives of our four teachers. Each of them evoked compassion and humaneness in others by their own acts of compassion. Perhaps it was the powerful response to their virtuous lives that led many of their followers to attribute superlative qualities to these sages, even to the point of elevating some them to the divine level. In any event, this Confucian idea reminds us of the importance of keeping before us—as individuals and as cultures—models of virtuous behavior.

I confess that I do not know what happens to us when we die. Perhaps we are reborn; perhaps we wake up in some post-mortem existence; perhaps we dissolve into a state of nothingness. I do not know. In view of my ignorance, I am attracted to Confucius' belief that goodness is its own reward. I have never been really comfortable with the idea that we must act morally because we are commanded to do so or because we wish to be rewarded and avoid punishment. Confucius tells us that goodness is what fulfills our human nature. Perhaps virtuous behavior will pay dividends in some future existence; I do not know. But it reassuring to think there is simple satisfaction in goodness, whether or not that is recognized by a god, rewarded in an afterlife, or even acknowledged by another human being. I urge my students to practice secret acts of goodness and never tell anyone about them.

Finally, I appreciate Confucius' teachings about attention to the mundane details of life and his conviction that our every word, act, and gesture is significant. Everything we do and say reflects our character and in turn shapes it. That attention to detail highlights the importance of living in the here and now with mindful awareness. It is what transforms an ordinary existence into a sacred one. Who knows, this may be the only existence there is. What a shame it would be to squander it.

The Buddha has taught me many things as well, but two now come to mind as more significant than all others. The first is the value of non-attachment. The Buddha's teachings offer a clear and compelling analysis of the dangers of holding on too tightly to anything. Before I studied the Buddha, I was certainly aware of the general principle of how attachment to things could lead to suffering. What transformed my thinking was the Buddha's inclusion of *everything* when he discussed attachments to things. It was easy enough to see that clinging to material possessions or even another person could certainly render us vulnerable to suffering. But the Buddha made it clear that attachment to ideas, beliefs, and values—what I call spiritual attachments— are also prone to cause us suffer. In fact, these spiritual attachments are the most intractable.

Closely connected to the virtue of non-attachment is the Buddha's criterion for truth for accepting anything as true. He urged us to be rigorously critical in accepting any claim or belief or value as valid, including his own teachings. In effect, the Buddha returns to us the responsibility for our own lives. We cannot take the easy way of claiming that our values and beliefs are correct merely because they are handed down by tradition or accepted authorities or respected teachers. The Buddha insists that our practices and convictions are rooted in our own experience of what is wholesome and beneficial to life.

My appreciation of Jesus is complicated by a long history of trying to understand him and his significance for my life. I have distinct recollections of being absolutely perplexed by the man. I remember my deep confusion at age five trying to reconcile two things I was told in Sunday School. First, I was told that I should be good like Jesus or bad things would happen to me, and second, I was told that Jesus was god. That struck me as absolutely unjust: I was expected to live up to the standards set by Jesus, yet he had the great advantage of being god. How on earth could I possibly be expected to be good like Jesus when I was just a kid and he was god? At some point along the way, I settled into the traditional Christian belief that I could *not* live up to the standards of Jesus and therefore had to rely on him to save me. When that happened, Jesus lost his humanity for me and was no longer someone to follow.

Since that time, it has been important for me to see Jesus as a real human being facing some of the same struggles we all face in life: self-doubt, limitations of understanding, the fear of dying. Only after recovering for myself the sense of Jesus' humanity have I been able to learn from him again. What now impresses me about his life and teachings is his courage to affirm life in the face of death and of the forces that threaten to diminish its richness and abundance. I see that affirmation symbolized in the Christian belief in his resurrection but also in the manner in which he lived. He envisioned life in god's kingdom as a joyful celebration devoid of the artificial divisions we impose to separate us from one another. And he lived his life in accord with this conviction, disregarding the complaints and ridicule of those who thought otherwise.

With Muhammad, two things stand out for me. The first is his teaching that near the source of the human predicament is the tendency to forget. Perhaps I appreciate that more today because as I age, I increasingly experience moments of forgetfulness. But of course Muhammad was speaking of something deeper than our occasional lapses of memories. He was speaking of our existential condition, our forgetfulness of the things in life that are of ultimate significance. But Muhammad also taught ways to remember to remember. The practice of praying five times a day was one way. Fasting was another. As individuals, I think we are well advised by Muhammad to seek ways to habituating ourselves to remembrance, regardless of whether that consists of offering prayer to god or simply recalling the things that are most meaningful to us. I can't imagine anything that should stand in the way of a Christian or Jew praying five times a day.

The second aspect of Muhammad's teaching that I find compelling is his insistence that the ultimate reality is inscrutable, utterly beyond our comprehension, completely mysterious. Of course, that conviction is kept in tension with the human need to speak of that reality by means of attributes, but Islam is careful to remind us the absolute is beyond whatever we might attribute to it. The insistence on mystery ultimately reminds us of our limitations and finitude and encourages the sense of humility that is essential to the noble life.

At the mention of finitude and human limitation, I am reminded that it is now time to draw this lecture and this course to a close. As always, when I reach this point in my teaching, I am deeply aware of what I have not been able to articulate whether due to the restrictions of time, the richness of my subject matter, or the paucity of my own knowledge and understanding. At this moment, I am mindful of each of these things.

It is customary in Buddhism to conclude such endeavors as this course with a dedication of merits to others, and it would be most meaningful to me to offer such a dedication. Accordingly, I offer whatever merits that may have been generated by my efforts to the well-being and happiness of my wife and daughter, whose own efforts and sacrifices have made my work possible and who have enriched my life beyond measure; to the good people of The Teaching Company, who whose hard work and dedication makes all of this possible; and to those of you who have accompanied me on this journey. May each and every one of you—and indeed may *all* beings— be well and happy.

# Glossary

**Abba**: An Aramaic word translated as "father"; one of the few Aramaic words that the Greek New Testament preserves in its original form.

**abhidhamma**: The systematic presentation of the Buddha's teachings; part of the Pāli Canon.

**aggregates of being**: The five processes the Buddha considered the only components of human existence: materiality, sensation, perception and apperception, conceptual constructs, and consciousness.

**al-Jāhiliyyah**: Literally, "the days of ignorance"; the Muslim term for the period that began when the Arabs turned away from the religion of Abraham toward polytheism and ended with the founding of Islam.

**al-Lah**: Also spelled Allah; the name of the single god of Islam. According to Muslim tradition, this is the same being as the Judeo-Christian Yahweh/Jehovah.

**al-Qur'an**: The recitation of the Arabic Qur'an text, considered its most meaningful form by the Islamic faithful.

**anatta**: Insubstantiality, the second of the Buddha's three marks of existence; literally, "no self" or "no soul." It does not deny the existence of people but the notion of a core essence that is the self separate from the aggregates of being.

**anicca**: The Pāli word for impermanence in the Buddhist sense—not simply the notion that things change but the idea that change is the only thing that truly exists.

**anthropology**: The philosophical or theological study of the universal nature of humanity, as well as the meaning and purpose (if any) of human existence.

**apophasis**: Saying by way of negation; this is how the Buddha usually described nibbana, which was beyond the power of language to describe.

**arahant**: In Buddhism, an awakened living being.

*ātman*: The Hindu term for the self or soul.

*Avyakata*: The metaphysical matters that the Buddha refused to discuss; the word may be translated as "things that are not revealed" or "things that create unnecessary speech."

**Axial Age**: The era of exceptional religious and philosophical creativity during the 1ˢᵗ millennium B.C.E. that gave rise to the world's major religions.

*bao*: The impulse to respond to kindness with kindness.

*Basileia tōn Ouranōn*: A Greek phrase from the Gospel of Matthew usually translated as "Kingdom of Heaven."

*Basileia tou Theou*: A Greek phrase from the Gospels of Mark and Luke usually translated as "Kingdom of God."

**Beatitudes**: A passage found in similar forms in the Gospels of Matthew (5:3–12) and Luke (6:20–23) wherein Jesus describes how people will live in the Kingdom of Heaven, each line beginning with the phrase "Blessed are. … "

**bismillah**: The words that begin all but one of the Qur'an's suras: "In the name of God, the all-compassionate, the all-merciful."

**Brahman**: The name of the ultimate reality in Hinduism.

**Christology**: The branch of Christian thought that seeks to understand the nature and deeds of Jesus.

*chrīstos*: The Greek translation of the Hebrew term "messiah," meaning "anointed one."

**contemplative prayer**: The Christian practice of prayer in solitude and silence, not unlike the Buddhist practice of meditation.

**crucifixion**: Execution on a cross; in the Roman Empire, this form of punishment was reserved for crimes of sedition and insurrection.

*dao*: The Chinese term for "path" or "way," as in a spiritual discipline.

**Daoism**: An ancient Chinese school of thought that stressed the naturalness of virtue and the value of living simply.

*de*: Virtue; also, moral charisma.

**dharma**: Literally, "truth"; in Hinduism, the duties incumbent on persons according to caste and gender.

*di*: In Chinese religion, earth; the material realm.

**Dome of the Rock**: The mosque on Temple Mount, Jerusalem. It was built by the Umayyad caliphs to commemorate Muhammad's Night Journey.

*dukkha*: Insatiability, the third of the Buddha's three marks of existence. Sometimes translated as "unease," "pain," or "disappointment," it is the opposite of *sukha*, contentment, and is driven by desire.

**eschatological**: Pertaining to the end of days or the ultimate destiny of humankind.

**Essenes**: A Jewish sect active between the 2nd century B.C.E. and 1st century C.E. whose members lived in quasi-monastic communities and were heavily concerned with maintaining ritual purity.

**ethics**: The study of morality and proper human behavior.

**Eucharist**: The Christian sacrament that commemorates the Passover meal Jesus shared with his followers in the Gospels (Matthew 26:17–29; Mark 14:12–25; Luke 22:7–38) shortly before his execution.

**filial piety**: The practice of revering and honoring one's parents both during their lives and after their deaths. To Confucius, filiality was the root of all forms of love.

**First Great Awakening**: Siddhattha Gotama's rejection of his privileged life for a life of seeking nibbana; also called the Great Renunciation.

**five precepts of wholesome action**: In Buddhism, the foundational precepts of moral behavior—namely, refraining from harming sentient beings, from stealing and coveting, from sexual misconduct, from lies and false speech, and from using substances that impair the mind or body.

**Four Noble Truths**: The core doctrine of the Buddha's dhamma—namely, that *dukkha* is a fact of unenlightened existence, suffering comes from attachment, beings can escape from *dukkha*, and cultivating compassion and wisdom leads to freedom from *dukkha*.

**Hadith**: Quotations and vignettes of Muhammad's life written down about a century after his death. Different branches of Islam accept different groups of Hadith as authentic and give different levels of importance to them.

**hanif**: A pre-Islamic Arabian monotheist; according to tradition, the Prophet Muhammad was raised in this faith.

**hijāb**: The veil worn by many Muslim women as a gesture of modesty. Wearing the veil was a pre-Islamic tradition in the Middle East and is not mandated by the Qur'an.

**Hijrah**: The flight of Muhammad and the fledgling Muslim community from Makkah to Madinah in 621 C.E.

**Huáxià**: Literally, "grand florescence" or "illustrious blossoming"; one of ancient Chinese culture's names for itself, implying a sense of cultural superiority.

**Iblīs**: The Arabic name for Satan; in Islam, a jinni who was cast out of heaven by al-Lah for refusing to bow to Adam.

**impending model**: The belief of early Christians (and possibly Jesus himself) that the coming of the Kingdom of God was imminent, within their own generation.

**involvement model**: The belief of later generations of Christians that the coming of the Kingdom of God was not a scheduled event but depended on human action to bring it about.

**Īsa**: The Arabic name for Jesus, who is an important (but not divine) prophet in Islam.

**Jambudvīpa**: An ancient name for India.

**jhana**: A deep meditative state.

**jihād**: Literally, "struggle." Often misunderstood in the West as "holy war," it refers more properly to humankind's internal struggle with its own spiritual weakness.

*jūnzi*: The gentleman; in Confucian thought, this character type is the ideal for a life of political service.

**Ka'ba**: Literally, "the House of God"; the shrine at the center of the Great Mosque of Makkah, the holiest site in the Muslim faith. It dates to pre-Islamic times, when it was used to worship over 300 different gods or godlike beings, including Jesus Christ and the Virgin Mary.

*kahin*: A poet-priest (or priestess) and oracle of pre-Islamic Arabian religion.

**karma**: In Hinduism, action and its consequences, specifically their ethical dimension.

**karuna**: The Pāli word for compassion.

**keen discernment**: The Confucian term for forestalling reflexive actions to obtain a clearer understanding of one's limitations and abilities.

**Kongqiū**: Confucius's given name. "Kong" translates loosely to "gratitude for an answered prayer" and "qiū" translates to "hill."

**K'ung-fu-tzu**: Literally, "Mister K'ung"; the honorific that was Latinized into "Confucius."

**Legalism**: An ancient Chinese school of thought that favored absolutism and the welfare of the state above the welfare of the people.

*li*: The practice of ritual; according to Confucius, this also encompasses etiquette.

*Lunyu*: The Chinese name of Confucius's *Analects*.

**Makkah**: Also spelled Mecca; the birthplace of the Prophet Muhammad and the holiest city in Islam.

**metaphysics**: The study of the fundamental character and qualities of reality, including the origin of the universe and the nature of the divine.

*metta*: Loving-kindness meditation, which involves wishing well on the self, a loved one, a stranger, an enemy, and all beings to train oneself in compassion.

**moksha**: In Hinduism, release from samsāra, equivalent to nibbana in Buddhism.

*murūwah*: Often translated as "manliness"; the Arabic cultural virtue encompassing courage, resilience, a willingness to avenge wrongdoing, and defense of the weak.

**Mushaf**: The printed Qur'an.

**Night Journey**: One of the Prophet Muhammad's spiritual experiences, in which he visited Jerusalem and spoke with al-Lah's previous prophets, including Abraham, Moses, and Jesus. This experience is why Jerusalem is the third holiest city in Islam. It is commemorated in the Dome of the Rock on Temple Mount, Jerusalem.

**Passover**: The Jewish festival commemorating the escape from Egyptian domination. At the time of Jesus, parallels between the Egyptian and Roman domination of the Jews raised Romans' fears of riot and revolt during the festival.

**Period of Warring States**: The last phase of the Zhōu dynasty, during which great social and political unrest led to a flourishing of Chinese philosophy and religion.

**Pharisees**: A Jewish sect that arose in the 2nd century B.C.E. and is the ancestor of modern rabbinic Judaism. Its members believed in the significance of the Oral Torah (later written down as the Mishnah), the primacy of scriptural study over Temple sacrifice, and the doctrine of resurrection of the dead.

**polygyny**: A marriage of one man to more than one woman; the Qur'an permits men to have up to four wives at one time, but only if he can treat each of them fairly.

*Q*: A lost source text used by the authors of the Gospels of Matthew and Luke.

**quiet sitting**: The Confucian term for introspection or meditative practice.

**Qur'an**: The central sacred text of Islam, accepted by all its traditions as the revealed word of al-Lah to Muhammad.

*raka'ah*: In Islam, a formal unit of prayer that begins with the first sura of the Qur'an.

**Ramadān**: The Muslim holy month of fasting; the ninth month of the Muslim calendar.

*rasul*: The Arabic word for "messenger"; in the context of Islam, an important prophet.

*ren*: Humaneness; in Conficianism, the chief virtue of the morally perfect individual.

**Sadducees**: A Jewish sect that arose in the 2nd century B.C.E. that promoted traditional Temple-centered worship and the authority of the priestly class over the scholarly (rabbinic) class.

*samana*: An ancient Hindu ascetic.

**samsāra**: Literally "meandering"; the Hindu term for the transmigration of the soul, suggesting an aimless, meaningless process.

**sangha**: The Buddhist community of monks and nuns.

**Second Great Awakening**: Siddhattha Gotama's enlightenment, the moment he earned the title of Buddha.

*shahadah*: The Muslim profession of faith: "I bear witness that there is no god but God and that Muhammad is His Messenger."

**Shang Di**: The supreme god of the ancient Chinese.

*shen*: The minor deities of ancient Chinese religion.

**Shi'a**: Muslims who consider Ali, Muhammad's cousin, his first official successor, rather than Abu Bakr. They constitute 15–20 percent of the present Muslim population.

*shirk*: Connecting with al-Lah something that is less than ultimate or giving to something less than ultimate what belongs to al-Lah alone. According to Islam, persisting in *shirk* is the only unpardonable sin.

**Sicarii**: A violent anti-Roman Jewish sect of the 1st century C.E. believed to be named for the daggers (*sica*) they carried. Judas Iscariot may have been a member of this group.

**spiritual discipline**: A set of practices designed as a part of the means of attaining full humanity and relating to the ultimate reality.

**stūpa**: An earthen mound containing a relic of the Buddha.

**Sunni**: Muslims who consider Abu Bakr, not Muhammad's cousin Ali, Muhammad's first official successor. They constitute 80–85 percent of the present Muslim population.

**sura**: A verse of the Qur'an.

**sutta**: A discourse of the Buddha; part of the Pāli Canon.

**synoptic Gospels**: The collective name for the Gospels of Matthew, Mark, and Luke.

**tawhid**: Often translated as "unity"; the Muslim doctrine that al-Lah is not simply one but is unique and incomparable.

**three marks of existence**: In Buddhism, the three basic qualities of the material world: impermanence, insubstantiality, and insatiability.

*tiān*: In Chinese religion, heaven; the spiritual realm. It was sometimes conceived of as a force and sometimes as a being.

*tiānming*: Literally, "the mandate of heaven"; the Chinese belief that the right to rule is conferred by the gods on virtuous leaders and removed by the gods from the corrupt, which implies the right of the people to rebel against and depose a leader who is not morally upright.

***ummah***: The Muslim community of the faithful.

**'*umrah***: The "lesser pilgrimage"; a pilgrimage to Makkah that contains fewer ritual elements than the Hajj and may be performed at any time of the year.

**vinaya**: The Buddhist monastic rule; part of the Pāli Canon.

**waywardness**: An inclination to act in self-serving and self-pleasing ways born of one's innate drive of self-preservation.

***zakāh***: The Muslim spiritual practice of charity, often levied as a tax in Islamic countries, similar to a tithe in medieval Christianity and some modern Protestant denominations.

**Zealots**: An aggressively anti-Roman Jewish political sect active between the 1st century B.C.E. and 1st century C.E.

**Zhōngguó**: Literally, "central kingdom"; a name for the ancient Chinese kingdom that grew up in the Yellow River Valley under the Zhōu dynasty.

***Zhuangzi***: The great satirical classic of the Daoist tradition that mocked Confucius but also featured him as a character espousing Daoist views.

# Bibliography

### General and Comparative

Carrithers, Michael, Raymond Dawson, Humphrey Carpenter, and Michael Cook. *Founders of Faith*. New York: Oxford University Press, 1989. This is one of the very few books exclusively devoted to Confucius, the Buddha, Jesus, and Muhammad. The treatment of each sage is written by a different scholar. While each study is excellent in its own right, the text does not attempt to provide any comparative analysis of the four and their teachings.

Hart, Michael H. *The 100: A Ranking of the Most Influential Persons in History*. Rev. ed. New York: Citadel, 2000. The controversial book first published in 1978 that attempted to rate the 100 individuals who had the greatest impact on human history. For an interesting listing of the religious affiliations of Hart's 100, see http://www.adherents.com/adh_influ.html.

Koller, John M. *Asian Philosophies*. 5th ed. Upper Saddle River, N.J.: Prentice Hall, 2006. I use this textbook in my course on Asian philosophy. It is one of the clearest presentations of the basic philosophies of India and China in a single volume. Here you will find not only the classical-era philosophies of Asia but also perspectives such as Islam, Neo-Confucianism, and modern developments in Hinduism and Buddhism. This is a good resource for getting a foundational perspective on the many Asian worldviews. Since this is a secondary source, it should be read in conjunction with the primary texts from each tradition.

Neville, Robert Cummings, ed. *The Human Condition: A Volume in the Comparative Religious Ideas Project*. Albany, NY: State University of New York Press, 2000.

———, ed. *Religious Truth: A Volume in the Comparative Religious Ideas Project*. Albany, NY: State University of New York Press, 2000.

———, ed. *Ultimate Realities: A Volume in the Comparative Religious Ideas Project*. Albany, NY: State University of New York Press, 2000.

I list these three volumes because they are based on a thematic structure similar to the one I have adopted for this course. *Ultimate Realities* juxtaposes Chinese, Hindu, Buddhist, Jewish, Christian, and Islamic perspectives on the nature of the metaphysical absolute. *The Human Condition* does the same for each tradition's anthropological viewpoints, and *Religious Truth* explores the nature of their epistemologies. These volumes do not, however, highlight the teachings of Confucius, the Buddha, Jesus, and Muhammad but rather try to treat the whole historical traditions based on those teachings.

## Confucius

Adler, Joseph A. *Chinese Religious Traditions.* Upper Saddle River, N.J.: Prentice Hall, 2002. This is one of the best short introductions to the history of Chinese religions that I have seen. It is very accessible to the lay reader and scholarly in its research. Charts and photographs nicely augment the exposition.

*The Analects.* Translated by Raymond Dawson. Oxford: Oxford University Press, 1993. A very good English translation of the *Analects*.

*The Analects.* Translated by D. C. Lau. London: Penguin Books, 1979. An excellent translation of the Confucian classic. The introduction is especially good.

*The Analects by Confucius.* The Internet Classics Archive. http://classics.mit.edu/Confucius/analects.html. Another version of the *Analects*, available online.

*The Analects of Confucius*, New ed. Translated by Chichung Huang. New York: Oxford University Press, 1997. There are many English translations of the *Analects*. This is one of my favorites. It is accessible, with helpful notes and explanations.

*The Analects of Confucius: A Philosophical Translation.* Translated by Roger T. Ames and Henry Rosemont Jr. New York: Ballantine, 1998. This is an excellent translation of the *Analects*, and it is a bit more challenging to the lay reader who is relatively unacquainted with ancient Chinese philosophy. The translation is supplemented with good notes and introductory material.

Chin, Annping. *The Authentic Confucius: A Life of Thought and Politics*. New York: Scribner, 2007. This recent biography of Confucius is also one of the best. It uses the earliest historically reliable documents to construct its portrait of the great sage and scrupulously avoids the hagiographical tendencies of other biographical accounts. Although it sometimes gets overly involved in ancillary political details, this book is still the best currently available study for understanding the man Confucius.

Berthrong, John H., and Evelyn Nagai Berthrong. *Confucianism: A Short Introduction*. Oxford: Oneworld, 2000. A very readable overview of Confucianism. The introduction follows an imaginary Confucian family of 17th-century China through a typical day. Very useful for understanding the development of post-Confucius Confucianism.

Brooks, E. Bruce, and A. Taeko Brooks. *The Original Analects: Sayings of Confucius and His Successors*. New York: Columbia University Press, 1998. One of the controversial new works in Confucian studies, which reduces Confucius's contribution to the *Analects* to a part of chapter 4. The rest, these authors argue, was composed over a period of two centuries by followers with very different philosophical outlooks from the sage himself.

"The Chinese Classics." *Internet Sacred Text Archive.* http://www.sacred-texts.com/cfu. This website provides access to many foundational documents of ancient Chinese philosophy, including the *Analects*, the *Mencius*, the *Great Learning*, the *Doctrine of the Mean*, and the Wu Jing, the five Confucian classics. The translations, however, are dated; most are over a century old.

*ConfucianStudies.com.* http://www.confucianstudies.com. This website serves as a clearinghouse for students and scholars of Confucianism and other aspects of Chinese thought and religion. Here you will find links to articles, lists of Confucian scholars, and other resources for the study of the tradition.

Fingarette, Herbert. *Confucius: The Secular as Sacred.* New York: Harper Torchbooks, 1972. Fingarette offers a thoughtful reading of Confucius that attempts to show his relevance for modern life by emphasizing the importance of rituals in daily life. This text is not one with which to begin a study of Confucius, but it is a provocative interpretation for those who have a basic understanding of the Chinese sage.

Fung Yu-Lan. *A History of Chinese Philosophy: Vol. 1, The Period of the Philosophers.* Princeton: Princeton University Press, 1952. This work is a classic. It was first published in the 1930s, but it still ranks as an excellent introduction to philosophical thought in the late Chinese Axial Age. The book is principally written for philosophers and scholars and so assumes some familiarity with the discipline.

Graham, A. C. *Disputers of the Dao: Philosophical Argument in Ancient China.* Chicago: Open Court Publishing, 1989. Graham's work, like Fung's, is also written for scholars. Many nonspecialists may find the book a bit obscure and hard to read, but this is an important analysis of early Chinese philosophy.

Hall David L., and Roger T. Ames. *Thinking Through Confucius.* Albany, NY: State University of New York Press, 1987. This provocative interpretation of Confucius is linguistically detailed, providing a close analysis of key terms in the *Analects* and offering a very different perspective on the sage from that of authors such as Fingarette and Tu Weiming.

Ivanhoe, Philip J. *Confucian Moral Self Cultivation.* 2nd ed. Indianapolis: Hackett Publishing, 2000. A compact book by one of the leading contemporary scholars of classical Chinese philosophy, this text focuses on one of the salient themes of early Confucianism. It also provides useful chapters on both Mencius and Xunzi.

Ivanhoe, Philip J., and Bryan W. Van Norden. *Readings in Classical Chinese Philosophy.* New York: Seven Bridges Press, 2001. This is an excellent anthology containing excerpts from many of the important philosophical works produced during the Chinese Axial Age. Among the works it includes are selections from the *Analects*, the *Mencius*, the *Xunzi*, the *Zhuangzi*, and the complete Ivanhoe translation of the *Daodejing*. The best text of its kind.

Jensen, Lionel. *Manufacturing Confucianism: Chinese Traditions and Universal Civilization*. Durham, N.C.: Duke University Press, 1997. One of the controversial pieces of new scholarship in Confucian studies. As the title implies, Jenson claims that Confucianism was largely the product of later Confucianists and others, rather than the development of the teachings of an historical sage named Confucius.

*Mencius*. Translated by D. C. Lau. London: Penguin Books, 1970. Lau is one of the best contemporary translators of the ancient Chinese texts.

*Mengzi, with Selections from Traditional Commentaries*. Translated by Bryan W. Van Norden. Indianapolis, IN: Hackett Publishing, 2008. Excellent recent translation of the *Mencius*, perhaps the second most influential text in the development of Confucianism next to the *Analects*.

Poo Mu-Chou. *In Search of Personal Welfare: A View of Ancient Chinese Religion*. Albany: State University of New York Press, 1998. Focuses on the "popular" religion of early China and its continuities and discontinuities with "official" religion and philosophy.

Thompson, Laurence G. *Chinese Religion: An Introduction*. Belmont, CA: Dickenson Publishing, 1969. Part of the Religious Life in History Series (which also contains Thomas J. Hopkins's introduction to Hinduism mentioned below), this short text is a good comprehensive overview of religion in China.

Tu Weiming and Mary Evelyn Tucker, eds. *Confucian Spirituality*. Vol. 1. New York: The Crossroad Publishing Company, 2003. I like this book very much. It opened my eyes to the spiritual dimensions of Confucianism and helped me to appreciate Confucian thought and practice in an entirely new way. The text is anthology of essays by leading scholars of Confucian studies.

Van Norden, Bryan W., ed. *Confucius and the Analects: New Essays*. New York: Oxford University Press, 2002. This is a collection essays by wide range of scholars—some sinologists, some philosophers—on Confucius and the principal source of information about him, the *Analects*. This anthology is both accessible to the educated reader and representative of fine scholarship in Confucian studies.

*Xunzi: Basic Writings*. Translated by Burton Watson. New York: Columbia University Press, 2003. A recent reissue of an older translation, this is the most accessible version of the *Xunzi* for the nonspecialist.

## The Buddha

*Access to Insight*. http://www.accesstoinsight.org. This is an excellent website for studying the earliest texts of Buddhism. It contains English translations of texts from the Pali canon, links to the canon itself, study guides, and helpful information about Theravada Buddhism.

Armstrong, Karen, *Buddha*. New York: Penguin Books, 2001. This is very readable introduction to the life and teachings of the Buddha, especially recommended for those interested in a narrative unencumbered by copious notes and academic digressions. Armstrong does a good job of situating the life of the Buddha within the historical and sociological context of northeastern India in the middle of the 1st millennium B.C.E.

Basham, A. L. *The Origin and Development of Classical Hinduism*. New York: Oxford University Press, 1995. This is a clear account of the Axial Age developments that gave rise to Hinduism. Makes a good introduction to the study of Hinduism from an historical perspective and provides a solid background for understanding the intellectual context of the Buddha.

*Basic Teachings of the Buddha*. Translated by Glenn Wallis. New York: The Modern Library, 2007. This is an excellent book for those who want to begin a study the Pali canon. Wallis has chosen and translated 16 suttas that concern foundational features of the Buddha's teaching. The translations are superb, and they are supplemented with lively, sophisticated commentary. Highly recommended.

Bodhi, Bhikkhu. *The Noble Eightfold Path: Way to the End of Suffering.* Seattle: BPS Pariyatti Editions, 1994. http://www.vipassana.com/ resources/8fp0.php. The casual reader may find this presentation of the Buddha's Noble Path a bit dry, but it details about as clearly as possible the spiritual discipline leading to nibbana as it was most probably practiced by early Buddhists.

Brereton, Joel. "The *Upanishads.*" *Approaches to the Asian Classics.* Edited by William Theodore de Bary and Irene Bloom. New York: Columbia University Press, 1990. This essay discusses the major themes of the *Upanishads* and provides a useful introduction to Upanishadic theology and mysticism. Understanding the *Upanishads* is helpful for appreciating the Buddha's religious and philosophical milieu.

Buddha Dharma Education Association. *BuddhaNet Buddhist Education and Information Network.* http://www.buddhanet.net. A comprehensive website with material on all Buddhist traditions throughout the world.

*Buddhist Studies WWW Virtual Library.* http://www.ciolek.com/WWWVL-Buddhism.html. This site links to information about Buddhism topics including the Pure Land, Tibetan, Zen, and Theravada traditions as well as Buddhist art and texts.

Carrithers, Michael. *Buddha: A Very Short Introduction.* Oxford: Oxford University Press, 1996. In just more than 100 pages, Carrithers manages to provide a compelling account of the Buddha's life and teaching. He is especially good at situating the Buddha in the cultural context of the Gangetic basin during India's "second urbanization."

Collins, Stevens. *Selfless Persons: Imagery and Thought in Theravada Buddhism.* Cambridge: Cambridge University Press, 1982. This well-written book is an impressive piece of scholarship. Definitely not an introductory work, it is the best exposition of no-self I have encountered.

Dhamma, Rewata. *The First Discourse of the Buddha.* Boston: Wisdom Publications, 1997. An introductory exposition of basic Buddhist concepts and the Four Noble Truths written by a scholarly Theravadin monk from Burma.

*Dhammapada: A New Translation of the Buddhist Classic with Annotations.* Translated by Gil Fronsdal. Boston: Shambhala, 2005. The *Dhammapada* is a Buddhist favorite. It is a slim collection of short verses taken from various places in the tradition. Fronsdal's is a very good recent translation.

Feuerstein, Georg, Subhash Kak, and David Frawley. *In Search of the Cradle of Civilization: New Light on Ancient India.* Wheaton, IL: Quest Books, 2001. This collaborative work challenges the Aryan "invasion theory" and advances the argument that Indus and Aryan cultures have always been one.

Gethin, Rupert, ed. and trans. *Sayings of the Buddha: New Translations from the Pali Nikayas.* Oxford: Oxford University Press, 2008. I am an admirer of Gethin's scholarship. This anthology is a nice selection of translated texts from the major collections of the Pali canon.

Gunaratana, Henepola. *Mindfulness in Plain English.* Expanded and updated ed. Boston: Wisdom Publications, 2002. If you are interested in the practice of Buddhist meditation, there is no better book with which to start. Highly recommended.

*Harrapa.* http://www.harappa.com. This very well-done website contains hundreds of pictures of artifacts and ruins from the ancient Indus Valley civilization as well as some excellent articles explaining them. There is even an online store for purchasing coffee mugs, T-shirts, and other items featuring Indus Valley images.

Harvey, Peter. *An Introduction to Buddhism: Teachings, History, and Practices.* Cambridge: Cambridge University Press, 1990. This is one of the best comprehensive introductions to Buddhism. It begins with the life and teachings of the Buddha and traces the development of the three major forms of Buddhism, clearly delineating their characteristic features.

Holder, John J., ed. *Early Buddhist Discourses.* Hackett Publishing, 2006. Another fine anthology of translations from the Pali canon.

Hopkins, Thomas J. *The Hindu Religious Tradition.* Belmont, CA: Wadsworth Publishing, 1971. This brief text is one of the clearest presentations of basic Hinduism in English. It is especially good for understanding the Vedic and classical periods in Hinduism. Highly recommended as a short, comprehensive study of Hinduism and the religious context in which the Buddha lived.

*In the Buddha's Words: An Anthology of Discourses from the Pali Canon (Teachings of the Buddha).* Translated by Bhikkhu Bodhi. Boston: Wisdom Publications, 2005. This anthology is a selection of previous published translations of suttas in the Pali canon. Bhikkhu Bodhi, a Theravadin monk, is a fine translator. This collection provides a representative selection of all the sutta collections in the Pali. If you are interested in reading the earliest Buddhist scriptures in English translation, this is a good place to begin.

John of Damascus. *Barlaam and Ioasaph.* World Wide School Library. http://www.worldwideschool.org/library/books/relg/historygeography/ BarlaamandIoasaph/toc.html. This text narrates the story of Josaphat (or Ioasaph), the Indian prince who renounced his right to the throne and converted to Christianity against the wishes of his father. This Christian tale is almost certainly a reworking of the Buddhist story of Prince Siddhattha Gotama.

Kenoyer, Jonathan Mark. *Mohenjo-Daro!* http://www.mohenjodaro.net. This site contains over 100 images from Mohenjo-daro, one of two principal cities of the Indus culture. There is a slide show, an introductory essay, and links to other interesting sites.

Mitchell, Robert Allen. *The Buddha: His Life Retold.* New York: Paragon House, 1989. This is a lively retelling of the Buddha's life drawn from a wide range of sources, including the mythological accounts. For contrast, consult Bhikkhu Ñanamoli's *The Life of the Buddha.*

Ñanamoli, Bhikkhu. *The Life of the Buddha: According to the Pali Canon.* New ed. Seattle: Pariyatti Publishing, 2001. This is the only account of the Buddha's life (that I am aware of) that relies solely on the Pali canon as its source. The text is essentially long passages from the Pali canon connected by narrative comments. For contrast, consult Robert Allen Mitchell's *The Buddha: His Life Retold*.

Ñanamoli, Bhikkhu, and Bhikkhu Bodhi. *The Middle Length Discourses of the Buddha: A Translation of the Majjhima Nikaya (Teachings of the Buddha)*. New ed. Boston: Wisdom Publications, 1995. For someone deeply interested in Buddhism, there is no substitute for reading the suttas themselves. The Middle-Length Discourses is my recommendation as the place to start.

Nelson, Walter Henry. *Buddha, His Life and His Teachings*. New York: Jeremy P. Tarcher/Putnam, 1996. A biography of the Buddha and an introduction to his teachings for the nonspecialist. Very accessible.

Obeyesekere, Gananath. *Imagining Karma: Ethical Transformations in Amerindian, Buddhist, and Greek Rebirth*. Berkeley, CA: University of California Press, 2002. Obeyesekere's work is an impressive volume exploring the conceptualization of rebirth and karma in a variety of cultural contexts. It is useful both for its comparative analysis and its explanation of how rebirth came to be ethicized and connected to the doctrine of karma in the South Asian Axial Age.

O'Flaherty, Wendy D., ed. *Karma and Rebirth in Classical Indian Traditions*. Berkeley, CA: University of California Press, 1980. This work is a collection of essays by leading Indologists on the development of the concepts of transmigration and karma in the classical period.

Radhakrishnan, Sarvepalli, and Charles A. Moore, eds. *A Sourcebook in Indian Philosophy*. Princeton, NJ: Princeton University Press, 1967. A fine selection of important Hindu texts, this work includes primary sources from the six orthodox schools of Hindu philosophy as well as texts from the heterodox traditions.

Rahula, Walpola. *What the Buddha Taught*. New York: Grove Press, 1959. Walpola Rahula was a Sri Lankan monk from the Theravada tradition, the oldest extant Buddhist tradition. His book, first published in 1959, remains one of the best introductions to the Four Noble Truths in English. Highly recommended.

Sharma, Arvind. *Classical Hindu Thought: An Introduction.* New Delhi: Oxford University Press, 2000. Sharma's book is one of the clearest expositions of the fundamental concepts in classical Hinduism available. Each chapter is devoted to a particular idea, such as karma or moksha, which allows the reader to find the subject of his or her interest rapidly. The introduction provides a very helpful overview of Hindu thought, showing the relationship of Niguna Brahman and Saguna Brahman theologies.

*Upaniśads.* Translated by Patrick Olivelle. Oxford: Oxford University Press, 1996. Olivelle's translation is a superb rendering for the modern reader. It is informed by careful scholarship and provides excellent introductory material. This is the best of recent translations.

*The Upanishads.* Translated by Juan Mascaró. Baltimore: Penguin Books, 1965. Although not as accurate or as elegant as later translations, Mascaró's rendering is very accessible and readily available in the Penguin Classics edition. Represents a good selection of the most significant Upanishads.

*Vipassana Fellowship.* http://www.vipassana.com. A very nice website focused on the Buddhist meditation practice called vipassana, or insight. The site contains instructions on how to meditate as well as links to many other useful resources in Theravada Buddhism.

Wheeler, Mortimer. *Civilizations of the Indus Valley and Beyond.* New York: McGraw-Hill, 1972. Wheeler's writings on the Indus Valley provide a wealth of information. This work focuses on the archaeology of the Indus Valley and northern Indian culture up to the Mauryan Empire.

**Jesus**

Barton, Bruce. *The Man Nobody Knows.* Indianapolis: The Bobbs-Merrill Company, 1925. Bruce Barton's interpretation of Jesus was one of the top-selling books in the United States in the 20th century. In his work, Barton portrays Jesus as the consummate salesman and CEO, the veritable "founder of modern business." I mention this work because of its popularity and as an example of the way interpretations of Jesus can easily reflect the interpreter's own preconceptions and unconscious assumptions.

Borg, Marcus. *Jesus: Uncovering the Life, Teachings, and Relevance of a Religious Revolutionary*. New York: HarperCollins, 2006. Marcus Borg is one of the members of the Jesus Seminar and a popular leader of current efforts to gain access to an historical Jesus. This book represents the culmination of his decades of scholarship. It is clearly written and argued, very accessible to the intelligent nonspecialist.

————. *Meeting Jesus Again for the First Time: The Historical Jesus and the Heart of Contemporary Faith*. New York: HarperOne, 1995. One of Borg's shorter works that adumbrates his position that Jesus was a 1st century Jewish "spirit person," or what he calls a "mystic" in later books. *Meeting Jesus*, written specifically for a nonacademic audience, does not attempt to delve into the subtleties of Jesus research but tries to interpret his significance for modern Christians who find traditional claims about Jesus hard to accept.

Borg, Marcus, and John Dominic Crossan. *The Last Week: What the Gospels Really Teach About Jesus's Final Days in Jerusalem*. New York: HarperOne, 2007. Written in response to the popularity of Mel Gibson's film *The Passion of the Christ*, Borg and Crossan attempt to recount with historical accuracy the events leading up to Jesus's crucifixion.

Borg, Marcus, and N.T. Wright. *The Meaning of Jesus: Two Visions*. 2nd ed. New York: HarperOne, 2007. Scholars Borg and Wright take very different positions on the historical Jesus and his significance. For lack of better terminology, they represent, respectively, the liberal and conservative wings of modern Jesus scholarship. This useful book brings together their divergent viewpoints, which enables readers to gain a better understanding of the range of opinions in contemporary research on Jesus.

Bornkamm, Günther. *Jesus of Nazareth*. Minneapolis, MN: Augsburg Fortress Publishers, 1995. This book is a classic in the field, but it is now dated. First published in 1956, Bornkamm's work is particularly useful for its analysis of the role of the kingdom of God and the parables in Jesus's teaching.

Bornkamm, Günther. *Paul*. Minneapolis, MN: Augsburg Fortress Publishers, 1995. Another classic work by Bornkamm, this one focused on Paul, the important early interpreter of Jesus.

Crossan, John Dominic. *The Historical Jesus: The Life of a Mediterranean Jewish Peasant*. New York: HarperOne, 1993. This is a massive tome. It is a scholarly work that draws upon linguistic analysis, anthropology, and cultural history to depict Jesus as a 1$^{st}$-century peasant who challenged what he considered the oppressive structures of his society. This is not light reading.

*Early Christian Writings Historical Jesus Theories*. http://www. earlychristianwritings.com/theories.html. A very helpful website that categorizes various theories about the historical Jesus and provides useful links to the works of the major scholars involved in Jesus research.

Ehrman, Bart D. *Jesus: Apocalyptic Prophet of the New Millennium*. New York: Oxford University Press, 2001. Ehrman argues for a return to the idea, advanced by Albert Schweitzer in *The Quest of the Historical Jesus*, that the historical Jesus was fundamentally motivated by his conviction that the world as we know it was soon to end. Ehrman's position is in tension with that of scholars like Borg and Crossan, who regard Jesus's work as more oriented to this-worldly concerns.

Fredriksen, Paula. *Jesus of Nazareth, King of the Jews: A Jewish Life and the Emergence of Christianity*. New York: Vintage, 2000. Fredriksen provides an interpretation that emphasizes the Jewish character of Jesus's life and teachings.

"From Jesus to Christ." *Frontline*. http://www.pbs.org/wgbh/pages/frontline/shows/religion/. This website is related to the excellent documentary *From Jesus to Christ: The First Christians*. The documentary can be viewed in its entirety here.

Johnson, Luke Timothy. *The Real Jesus: The Misguided Quest for the Historical Jesus and the Truth of the Traditional Gospels*. New York: HarperOne, 1997. Johnson provides a well-argued critique of the positions of scholars such as Borg, Crossan, and Funk and helps illuminate the entire field of current academic research on the historical Jesus.

Kaltner, John. *Ishmael Instructs Isaac: An Introduction to the Quran for Bible Readers*. Collegeville, MN: Michael Glazier Books, 1999. My friend and colleague John Kaltner has written an intriguing study that suggests the Bible and Qur'an can illuminate one another when one carefully examines what each text has to say about the characters common to them both. Kaltner's book includes interesting analyses of the Qur'anic views of Jesus and Mary.

Khalidi, Tarif. *The Muslim Jesus: Sayings and Stories in Islamic Literature*. Cambridge, MA: Harvard University Press, 2003. Many are unaware that Jesus is considered a major prophet in Islam and that the Qur'an has much to say about his life and teachings. Khalidi's book brings together the scattered references to Jesus in the Qur'an and other texts in Islamic history to provide a fine analysis of Muslim perspectives on Jesus, whom Islam knows as Isa.

Kloppenborg, John S. *Q, the Earliest Gospel: An Introduction to the Original Stories and Sayings of Jesus*. Louisville, KY: Westminster John Knox Press, 2008. Kloppenborg's book is one of the best explanations of the so-called two-source hypothesis, which proposes that the gospels of Matthew and Luke drew upon the gospel of Mark and a no longer existing text dubbed "Q" (short for *Quelle*, the German word for "source"). *Q, the Earliest Gospel* is helpful for understanding some of the historical issues facing scholars attempting to construct a portrait of the historical Jesus.

Miles, Jack. *Christ: A Crisis in the Life of God*. New York: Vintage, 2002. This is a very different sort of book about Jesus. Miles is not at all interested in the Jesus available to scholars by modern historiography. His interest resides purely in Jesus as a literary character in the Bible. This book is a sequel to Miles's provocative book *God: A Biography*, in which he treats God as a literary character, just as a scholar might study Hamlet as a literary character in Shakespeare. The results of his approach are fascinating. In *Christ*, Miles asks what it means for God to take human form—not to shed light on issues of faith but as a way of illuminating the character of God as a figure in biblical narrative.

Miller, Robert J., ed. *The Complete Gospels: Annotated Scholars Version.* Revised and expanded ed. New York: HarperOne, 1994. This is a translation of the Gospels, both canonical and noncanonical. I find the renderings more vibrant and compelling than other modern translations. Recommended.

"General Resources." *The New Testament Gateway.* http://www.ntgateway.com/historical-jesus/general-resources. This website is maintained by Mark Goodacre at Duke University. It provides excellent links to resources for understanding the New Testament and the scholarship concerning the historical Jesus.

Pelikan, Jaroslav. *Jesus through the Centuries: His Place in the History of Culture.* New Haven: Yale University Press, 1999. Pelikan's work is not about the historical Jesus but about how the image of Jesus has been interpreted throughout two millennia of Christian history. The book clearly demonstrates that Christian understandings of Jesus have always been intimately connected with the structure and dynamics of the wider culture. Recommended.

Sanders, E. P. *The Historical Figure of Jesus.* New York: Penguin, 1996. This is a very readable text from an eminent scholar of the New Testament. Sanders presents an historical Jesus in his Jewish context as a prophet of the end times who was originally a follower of John the Baptist. Highly recommended.

Schweitzer, Albert. *The Quest of the Historical Jesus.* New York: Macmillan, 1968. Originally published in 1906, this classic book was immensely influential in the history of modern scholarship on Jesus. Schweitzer argued that historians' interpretations of Jesus always reflected their own preconceptions. *The Quest of the Historical Jesus* effectively stopped scholarly inquiry into the historical Jesus for several decades as many New Testament scholars were convinced that the "real" Jesus was essentially inaccessible to moderns. Not an easy read for the nonspecialist.

Vermes, Geza. *Jesus in His Jewish Context.* Minneapolis, MN: Augsburg Fortress, 2003.

———. *Jesus the Jew: A Historian's Reading of the Gospels.* Minneapolis, MN: Augsburg Fortress, 1981.

———. *Religion of Jesus the Jew.* Minneapolis, MN: Augsburg Fortress, 1993.

These three books are intriguing texts, all very useful for understanding the Jewishness of Jesus.

## Muhammad

Ahmed, Leila. *Women and Gender in Islam: Historical Roots of a Modern Debate.* New Haven: Yale University Press, 1993. Although not focused on Muhammad, Ahmed's work provides some important material for understanding early Islamic teachings on gender and sexuality.

*An-Nawawi's Forty Hadith: An Anthology of the Sayings of the Prophet Muhammad.* Translated by Ezzeddin Ibrahim and Denys Johnson-Davies. Cambridge: The Islamic Texts Society, 1997. The Hadith are stories about and sayings of Muhammad that do not appear in the Qur'an. Those considered authentic are highly regarded by Muslims and are considered important in understanding the faith. This is anthology one of the most popular collections for the English-speaking audience.

Armstrong, Karen. *Muhammad: A Biography of the Prophet.* San Francisco: HarperSanFrancisco, 1992. Armstrong's book is a sympathetic treatment of Muhammad that is especially helpful in placing his life in the context of pre-Islamic Arabian religion. Unlike other scholars such as Rodinson, Armstrong is not dismissive of the religious dimension of the Prophet's teaching.

Bennett, Clinton. *In Search of Muhammad.* New York: Continuum International Publishing, 1998. Bennett's is a balanced account of the life of the Prophet and his symbolic significance in Islam. This work is especially useful for elucidating the complex issues involved in creating a portrait of the historical Muhammad.

Emerick, Yahiya. *The Life and Work of Muhammad*. Indianapolis, IN: Alpha, 2002. An accessible and lively biography by a convert to Islam. Recommended for nonscholars who are interested in a brief, well-written narrative about Muhammad's life and teaching.

Esposito, John. *Islam: The Straight Path*. 3rd ed. New York: Oxford University Press, 2004. One of the best introductions to Islam available today. This is a standard text for many college courses.

*Islam and Islamic Studies Resources*. http://www.uga.edu/islam. This website is maintained by Alan Godlas, a professor at the University of Georgia, and is administered through the UGA Virtual Center for Interdisciplinary Studies of the Islamic World. It contains a wealth of sources on Muhammad, the Qur'an, and the entire Islamic tradition. Highly recommended.

*The Life of Muhammad: A Translation of Ibn Ishaq's Sirat Rasul Allah*. Translated by A. Guillaume. Oxford: Oxford University Press, 1955, reissued 2002. A modern translation of Ibn Ishaq's profoundly influential biography of the Prophet written in the 8th century.

Lings, Martin. *Muhammad: His Life Based on the Earliest Sources*. 2nd ed. Rochester, VT: Inner Traditions, 2006. This is a highly regarded (and lengthy) biography of the Prophet by a western convert to Islam. As the subtitle indicates, Lings takes as his sources the earliest reliable documents relating to Muhammad's life. Recommended.

*The Meaning of the Holy Qur'an*. http://islamtomorrow.com/downloads/Quran_YAli.pdf. This is an online edition of the Yusuf Ali translation of the Qur'an, one of the more popular English versions.

*Muhammad: Legacy of a Prophet*. http://www.pbs.org/muhammad. This website is maintained by PBS and contains some good material about Muhammad and Islam related to the film *Muhammad: Legacy of a Prophet*.

*Perform Hajj—A Muslim's Pilgrimage to Mecca*. http://www.performhajj.com. This website is all about the Muslim pilgrimage to Makkah. It is replete with text, photographs, and videos. The links to other sites are also very useful.

Peters, F. E. *Muhammad and the Origins of Islam.* Albany, NY: State University of New York Press, 1994. Another fine biography of the Prophet. Peters's analysis is especially helpful in its discussion of pre-Islamic culture.

Ramadan, Tariq. *In the Footsteps of the Prophet: Lessons from the Life of Muhammad.* Oxford: Oxford University Press, 2007. Ramadan is a Muslim scholar at Oxford University. His biography of Muhammad is especially interesting to both Muslims and non-Muslims who wish to gain insight into how the example of the Prophet's life can inform modern spirituality.

Rodinson, Maxime. *Muhammad: Prophet of Islam.* New York: Pantheon, 1980. Most people tend to really like or really hate this biography of the Prophet. First published in 1961, Rodinson uses Marxist and psychoanalytic presuppositions to provide a thoroughly naturalistic explanation of the life of Muhammad and the rise of Islam.

*The Qur'an: A New Translation.* Translated by Thomas Cleary. Burr Ridge, IL: Starlatch, 2004. This is a fresh and lively translation of the Qur'an. This edition has no critical notes or index, which makes it more like the Qur'an itself. I have frequently used the Cleary translation when quoting from the Qur'an in this course.

*The Qur'an* and *Sunnah and Hadith.* http://www.usc.edu/schools/college/crcc/engagement/resources/texts/muslim/quran/ and http://www.usc.edu/schools/college/crcc/engagement/resources/texts/muslim/hadith/. These two websites maintained by the University of Southern California contain searchable translations of the Qur'an and Hadith.

Sultan, Sohaib N. *Qur'an and Sayings of Prophet Muhammad: Selections Annotated and Explained.* Woodstock, VT: SkyLight Paths, 2007. A compact selection of passages from the Yusuf Ali translation of the Qur'an and from the Hadith, arranged topically with commentary and notes provided by Sultan.

Schimmel, Annemarie. *And Muhammad is His Messenger. The Veneration of the Prophet in Muslim Piety*. Chapel Hill, NC: The University of North Carolina Press, 1985. Annemarie Schimmel was one of the premier Western scholars of Islam, particularly Sufism. This work is not a strictly a biography of Muhammad but a study analyzing the Prophet's example and symbolic importance in the history of Muslim practice.

Watt, W. Montgomery. *Muhammad: Prophet and Statesman*. London: Oxford University Press, 1961. The author's *Muhammad at Mecca* (1953) and *Muhammad at Medina* (1956) are two volumes of what is widely regarded as one of the most scholarly studies of the Prophet's life. Most readers, however, will probably not have the endurance to make through both texts. Fortunately, they have been combined and abridged to create this single, more accessible book.

*The Wisdom of the Prophet: Sayings of Muhammad, Selections from the Hadith*. Translated by Thomas Cleary. Boston: Shambhala, 2001. The Hadith are extra-Qur'anic anecdotes about and sayings by Muhammad. Thomas Cleary, who has also produced a translation of the Qur'an, has selected and translated some of them in this volume. This is a good introduction to the Hadith.

# Credits

EINSTEIN, ALBERT; *THE COLLECTED PAPERS OF ALBERT EINSTEIN*. © 1987-2010 Hebrew University and Princeton University Press. Reprinted by permission of Princeton University Press.

New Revised Standard Version Bible, copyright 1989, Division of Christian Education of the National Council of the Churches of Christ in the United States of America. Used by permission. All rights reserved.

# Notes

# Notes

# Notes

# Notes

# Notes

# Notes

# Notes